Reports of Cases in the Court of Chancery from 1625 to 1660

Center for Law Reporting

General Editor:
W. Hamilton Bryson

Advisory Board:
Paul A. Brand
A. Mark Godfrey
Richard H. Helmholz
Janet S. Loengard
James C. Oldham
C. H. van Rhee
Ian Williams

English Law Reports
of the Early Modern Period

Volume One: *Equity Cases in the Court of Exchequer, 1660–1714*, Edited by W. H. Bryson, 2007. [This volume can be cited as Eq. Cases Exch.]

Volume Two: *Robert Paynell's Exchequer Reports (1627–1631)*, Edited by W. H. Bryson, 2009. [This volume can be cited as Paynell Exch.]

Volume Three: *Robert Paynell's King's Bench Reports (1625–1627)*, Edited by W. H. Bryson, 2010. [This volume can be cited as Paynell K.B.]

Volume Four: *Reports of Cases in the Court of Exchequer in the Time of King George I (1714–1727)*, Edited by W. H. Bryson, 2013. [This volume can be cited as Exch. Cases *temp.* Geo. I.]

Volume Five: *Reports of Cases in the Court of Exchequer in the Time of King Charles II*, Edited by W. H. Bryson, 2017. [This volume can be cited as Exch. Cases *temp.* Char. II.]

Volume Six: *Reports of Cases in the Court of Chancery in the Time of King George I*, Edited by W. H. Bryson, 2019. [This volume can be cited as Chan. Cases *temp.* Geo. I.]

Volume Seven: *Paul Jodrell's Chancery Reports (1737 to 1751)*, Edited by W. H. Bryson, 2020. [This volume can be cited as Jodrell.]

Volume Eight: *Reports of Cases in the Court of Chancery in the Time of Queen Anne*, Edited by W. H. Bryson, 2021. [This volume can be cited as Chan. Cases *temp.* Anne.]

Volume Nine: *Reports of Cases in the Court of Chancery 1660 to 1673*, Edited by W. H. Bryson, 2022. [This volume can be cited as Chan. Cases 1660–1673.]

Volume Ten: *Reports of Cases in the Court of Exchequer from 1685 to 1714*, Edited by W. H. Bryson, 2024. [This volume can be cited as Exch. Cases 1685–1714.]

Medieval and Renaissance
Texts and Studies

Volume 587

———————

Center for Law Reporting

Volume 11

Reports of Cases in the Court of Chancery from 1625 to 1660

Edited by

W. H. Bryson

Tempe, Arizona
2025

Published by ACMRS Press
Tempe, Arizona
© 2025 Arizona Board of Regents for Arizona State University.
All Rights Reserved.

ISBN 978-0-86698-648-9

∞
This book is set in Adobe Caslon Pro.
Printed in the United States of America.

Table of Contents

Preface	ix
Introduction	
I. Fons et Origo	xi
A. Equity Is Conscience	xii
1. Procedure	xv
2. Evidence	xix
3. Contracts	xxii
4. Trusts	xxix
5. Fiduciaries	xxxi
6. Property	xxxii
B. Equity Is Extra-Ordinary	xxxii
C. Equity Acts in Personam	xxxii
D. Summary	xxxiii
II. Whiggery and Chancery	xxxiv
A. Cardinal Wolsey	xxxiv
B. Sir Edward Coke	xxxv
C. John Selden	xliii
D. Lord Eldon	xlvi
E. Summary	xlviii
III. The Indeterminacy of the Chancellor's Foot	xlix
IV. The Common Law and the Equity Thereof	liv
Table of Cases Reported	lvii
Chancery Reports from 1625 to 1660	1
Index of Names	321
Subject Index	327

Preface

These Chancery reports are all that could be found, whether in manuscript or in print, from 1625 to 1660. This is the time from the beginning of the reign of Charles I and of the judicial tenure of Thomas Coventry, Lord Coventry, through the Interregnum, up to the Restoration of the Stuarts in 1660. These cases have been collected from a wide variety of miscellaneous sources.

We thank the Selden Society for permission to reprint some of the material in their volumes 117 and 118. Thanks are also due to the William S. Hein and Co., Inc., for permission to reprint the cases from the Reports of Herne and Duke.

The Court of Chancery

I. Fons et Origo

A chancery is a secretariat. All of the princes of medieval Europe, secular and ecclesiastical, had one. They were necessary in order to manage the production of official, and also private, documents. The English Chancery goes back to Saxon times.

It is an ancient, basic tenet of English law that no writ lies against the king.[1] This part of the law of sovereign immunity is necessary in order to protect the government from disruption from litigation, which might well be in bad faith for the sole purpose of obstruction. In addition, the king's courts cannot decide issues affecting the king because of the ancient rule that no one can be a judge in one's own case. The royal judges are the king's servants, and they adjudicate in his courts in his name. Nor should the king's sheriffs, his agents, act against their principal by serving a writ of process upon him.

There is another tenet of English law that the king wills that no wrong be done in his name. (This rule is sometimes misstated as the king can do no wrong.) The king is the fount and origin of justice.[2] It is his duty to maintain law and order, to administer personally the law, in his courts,[3] and to obey the law. *Rex . . . debet esse . . . sub Deo et sub lege, quia lex facit regem.*[4] The English king is bound by the law of England. Thus, if an agent, officer, or servant of the king commits any common law wrong, he is acting outside the scope of his agency and

---

[1] *Bracton on the Laws and Customs of England* (S. E. Thorne, trans., 1968), vol. 2, p. 33.

[2] "[A]ll men agree that the king is the fountain of justice and mercy, of law and equity...." D. E. C. Yale, ed., *Lord Nottingham's . . . Prolegomena of Chancery and Equity* (1965), p. 191.

[3] The kings of England, in their coronation oath, swore to do 'equal law and justice with discretion and mercy'. *Statutes of the Realm* (*SR*), vol. 1, p. 163, and so in 1689, Stat. 1 Will. & Mar., c. 6 (*SR*, VI, 57), and so up to the present day.

[4] "The king . . . must be . . . under God and under the law, because the law makes the king...." *Bracton on the Laws and Customs of England* (S. E. Thorne, trans., 1968), vol. 2, p. 33; quoted in W. Blackstone, *Commentaries on the Laws of England* (1765), vol. 1, p. 232; J. Chitty, Jr., *Treatise on the Law of the Prerogatives of the Crown* (1820), p. 5.

authority, and the king, who wills that no wrong be done, is not responsible for his errant servant. Thus, if a tort is committed by an agent of the king, the agent is personally liable, but the king is not. The servant may be sued, but he may not be financially able to pay the judgment. If a contract with the king is breached or property is seized in the king's name, no action sounding in contract or property lies against the agent, the agent being merely the king's *alter ego*.

In these latter situations of property and contract, the person aggrieved has a common law right but he does not have a remedy in the common law courts. This is unconscionable. However, the aggrieved person has the remedy to petition the king directly for the king himself to do right and justice according to the common law of England. A person could also petition the King's Council (later called the Privy Council) or Parliament. But a petition that will affect another person's rights should not be decided without hearing the opposing claimant as a matter of basic fairness, which we call due process. The king, the Privy Council, and the Parliament are not judicial institutions by their constitution, and they, therefore, delegated private petitions to the Chancellor, the head of the royal secretariat, to decide them after a hearing of the evidence and arguments on the merits by all concerned parties, the king being represented by the Attorney General. If the king or the king in Council or the king in Parliament can as a matter of the constitution hear petitions, then so also can the king in Chancery. Some examples of delegations of petitions from the Council and Parliament to the Chancery are the Prior of Hatfield's Case (Ch. 1325) and the Abbot of La Roche v. Queen Philippa (Ch. 1347).[5] Alternatively, this can be considered as the legislative creation of an *ad hoc* jurisdiction of the Chancery to hear a particular dispute and make a judicial determination.

The delegation of petitions to be heard to the Chancery became routine in the fourteenth century, and this routine became a judicial jurisdiction in the Chancery. This turned the Chancery *inter alia* into a court of law, the law being the common law of England.

A. Equity Is Conscience
So when are the ordinary remedies of the courts of Common Pleas and King's Bench inadequate, unfair, or inequitable? The answer is when the failure of those courts to act shocks the conscience of right-thinking persons, such as when an agent of the crown violates a private person's rights and no writ at common law lies against the king, the wrongdoer's principal. Here is a wrong without a remedy; this is unfair; it is shocking. The solution is not a demand for justice in the Common Pleas or the King's Bench, but it is a humble petition in the Court

---

[5] *Prior of Hatfield's Case* (Ch. 1325), Chancery Cases Middle Ages, 11, 1 Eagle & Younge 11; *Abbot of La Roche v. Queen Philippa* (Ch. 1347), Chancery Cases Middle Ages, 34, 1 Gwillim 116, 1 Eagle & Younge 15.

of Chancery, where the Chancellor will administer the king's grace and mercy in order to do right according to the common law of England. In substance, the Court of Chancery is a court of the common law as a matter of substance, though, in procedure, the Chancellor has some remedies to give that the older courts did not have.

The Court of Chancery, evolving after the Court of Common Pleas and King's Bench, had more modern remedies that were more sophisticated and efficacious. Perhaps this was possible because, as the English monarchy became more powerful and better organized as time went by, it could better enforce the orders and judgments of its courts, but the established courts could not give new remedies without legislative authority and law reform through legislation was politically difficult — very difficult — in the middle ages. Some of the common law remedies of the early Court of Chancery were the petition of right, *monstrans de droit*, traverse of office, and *scire facias*. These remedies concern property rights.[6]

If the Court of Chancery can act to do justice for a private person against the king where the common law courts would not, then why not grant a remedy for a private person against another private person where the established courts would not? As a matter of *a fortiori* thinking, this was an easy step for the court to take. If the court can act in the cause of justice against the interests of the king, the crown, the government, then it should also act against a subject of the king, a commoner, a private citizen. And so, in the late fourteenth century, the Court of Chancery began to grant remedies to private parties where the established courts of the common law, the Court of Common Pleas and the Court of King's Bench could not or would not grant a complete and adequate remedy to address a common law wrong. Thus, the Latin or common law side of the court was the origin of the equity or English side of the Court of Chancery.[7] Several reports of cases in the medieval Chancery were included in the medieval yearbooks,[8] and numerous pleadings from the equity side of the court after the accession of Richard II have been edited and published.[9]

---

[6] W. S. Holdsworth, 'The History of Remedies against the Crown', *Law Quarterly Review*, vol. 38, pp. 141–164, 280–296 (1922).

[7] *Acherley v. Vernon* (Ch. 1732) (*per* Lord King), Forrester 40; F. W. Maitland, *Equity* (rev. ed. 1936), p. 6; A. D. Hargreaves, 'Equity and the Latin Side of Chancery', *Law Quarterly Review*, vol. 68, pp. 481–499 (1952).

[8] *Reports of Cases in the Court of Chancery in the Middle Ages (1325–1508)*, W. H. Bryson, ed. (2016), includes 138 Chancery case reports.

[9] Note that 147 pleadings in cases on the equity side of the Court of Chancery dating from 1364 to 1471 have been edited by W. P. Baildon, in *Select Cases in Chancery* (1896), Selden Society, volume 10. There are also some examples of medieval Chancery pleadings dating from the reigns of Richard II through Henry VII in J. W. Bayley, ed., *Calendars of the Proceedings in Chancery in the Reign of Queen Elizabeth* (1827, 1830), vol.

One might well ask why the common law courts could not do this themselves? There are two very good reasons.

The first reason was internal to the courts. The courts do not create the law; the law pre-exists the courts. It is the function of the courts to discover the law, state it, and then apply it. The application of the law is then a precedent to be followed in the future. To vary from the precedents of the stated law would be grossly unfair to persons who had made decisions based on the legal precedents declared by the courts of law. Expectations based on the stated law must be enforced. Where the courts have stated the law, whether substantive or procedural, and persons have relied thereupon, the courts are estopped by the most basic principles of fairness to change their minds. By the beginning of the reign of King Richard II, 1377, an enormous body of judicial precedent going back to the reign King Richard I had accumulated.[10] The courts were bound to administer the law as it had been established by case law precedents.

The second reason that courts of common law were bound by their own precedents was that to act otherwise would be to change the law. Changing the law is the function of the legislature, the Parliament. Parliament, or the king in Parliament, was an established legislative body by the fourteenth century. For the courts of common law to change the law would be an unconstitutional usurpation of the legislative function of Parliament. It would also offend against the generally accepted political theory that the Parliament could change the law because the entire community of the nation was there personally or by representation and the king had to consent to its acts. *Quod omnes tangit ab omnibus comprobetur.*[11] Thus once the law was established, the courts of common law could not change it; the courts were bound by it and must apply it to the litigants before it. If this resulted in an injustice in a particular case, the courts of common law were powerless to correct it.

It was often said, 'if men were angels, no government would be necessary.'[12] This saying recognized what we all know, and that is that men are not angels and indeed that there is a tendency in many persons to cheat and defraud their neighbors as far as possible, but certainly as far as the law allows. But, indeed, this is simply unconscionable.

Where the common laws courts could not act against such bad faith, the Court of Chancery did, just as it did when the servants, agents, and officers of the king acted unjustly. This is the jurisdiction of the Court of Chancery later

---

1, pp. i–cxxvi, vol. 2, pp. i–lxxvi; and G. Wrottesley, ed., 'Early Chancery Proceedings, Richard II to Henry VII [1377–1509]', *Collections for a History of Staffordshire*, new series, vol. 7, pp. 240–293 (1904).

[10] To date, 20 volumes of the *Curia Regis Rolls* have been edited and published, covering the years 1189 to 1250.

[11] *Codex Justiniani* 5, 59, 5, 2; *Liber Sextus*, regulae juris, Rule 29.

[12] J. Madison, *The Federalist* (1788), no. 51.

called its equity jurisdiction. The Court of Chancery enforced the equity of the common law, *i.e.* the general intent and policy of the common law in the sense of the expression the equity of a statute, which refers to the intent and general policy of the statute. Indeed, the first Charter of the Colony of Virginia in 1606 referred to the "common laws of England and the equity thereof."[13]

The equity jurisdiction of the Court of Chancery could be invoked where the common law remedies were inadequate in the areas of procedure, evidence, and substance so as to lead to an unconscionable result.

1. Procedure

One procedural inadequacy of the common law is the rule that a cause of action, giving rise to a right to bring an action, does not accrue until damage has been done to the would be plaintiff. Where no cause of action exists, a person cannot bring an action, there being no legal injury. But where a person is threatened with serious and foreseeable future common law injury that cannot be adequately compensated by common law damages, the courts of equity will act to prohibit or avoid it. The person threatened may sue in a court of equity *quia timet*, because he fears an imminent wrong. Examples are the wrongful destruction of an ornamental tree, which would take decades to replace so that monetary compensation would be an inadequate remedy. If the threatened harm was not remediable by common law damages, such as the imminent destruction of property whose ownership was in dispute[14] or waste,[15] then the courts of equity would order the defendant not to do the act threatened.

Another example is the failing debtor, where, if the creditor does not immediately sue upon and collect the debt, the surety will be liable, but his right of subrogation will be uncollectible after the principal debtor has become insolvent. Thus, the surety is given the right to enforce in a court of equity the debt himself.

Where a defendant has instruments or deeds belonging to the plaintiff, the plaintiff fears that the defendant will put bonds in action or transfer deeds to *bona fide* purchasers to the damage of the plaintiff. The courts of common law provided a remedy of detinue of charters only if the plaintiff could name the documents with exactitude and say where they were; moreover, such an action was tried by wager of law, which was to the plaintiff's utter disadvantage. Because

---

[13] *Articles, Instructions, and Orders for Virginia* (10 April 1606), W. W. Hening, *Statutes of Virginia* (1823), vol. 1, p. 68.

[14] E.g. *Bush v. Field* (Ch. 1579 x 1580), Cary 90, 21 E.R. 48; see also *Kidnere v. Harrison* (Ch. 1559 x 1560), Cary 48, 21 E.R. 26.

[15] E.g. *Finch v. Throckmorton* (Ex. 1590), 117 Selden Soc. 136 (preliminary injunction pending an action at common law); *Watson v. Johnson* (118 Selden Soc. 549), No. 298 (preliminary injunction pending an action at common law); *Cole v. Peyson* (Ch. 1636 x 1637), 1 Chancery Reports 106, 21 E.R. 521; *Roberts v. Roberts* (Ex. 1657), Hardres 96, 145 E.R. 399.

of these inadequacies, the equity courts ordered the defendant to deliver up the documents to the plaintiff.[16] Courts of equity could require the cancellation of forged bonds[17] and bonds that have been paid or were presumed paid.[18] The equity court could also enjoin a threatened assault[19] or the payment of money to anyone but the plaintiff[20] or a slander of title.[21] Because the plaintiff feared (*quia timet*) a future harm, the equity court would enjoin its happening so as to prevent the threatened harm. The modern statutes permitting declaratory judgments in the common law courts before a common law right of action has accrued is a statutory expansion of this branch of equity jurisdiction.

Similar to a bill *quia timet* is a bill of peace. The purpose of a bill of peace is to enjoin a multiplicity of common law actions by or against the plaintiff in equity.[22] Multiple litigation was required by the common law rules of procedure in many situations. Where the sheer expense of it will, as a practical matter, defeat a party, the courts of equity will grant relief in the form of an injunction appropriate to the situation. A bill to quiet title[23] is a bill of peace.

A bill of interpleader can be classified as a bill of peace since it combines two common law claims against the same person into a single suit in equity.[24] If

---

[16] *Milner v. Leche* (Ch. 1388), 10 Selden Soc. 8; *Bokelond v. Blount* (Ch. 1394) (semble), 10 Selden Soc. 12; *Wilton v. Kemle* (Ch. 1396 x 1403), 10 Selden Soc. 81; *Bodenham v. Halle* (Ch. 1456), 10 Selden Soc. 137; Note (Ch. 1596), 117 Selden Soc. 212; *Lord Buckhurst v. Fenner* (Ch. 1598), 117 Selden Soc. 155; Note (Ch. 1598), 117 Selden Soc. 221; *Moulton v. Younger* (Ch. 1599), 117 Selden Soc. 270; Note (Ch. 1598 x 1602), 117 Selden Soc. 287; Note (Ch. 1599 x 1604), 117 Selden Soc. 331; *Smith v. Delves* (Ch. 1604), 117 Selden Soc. 338. See also *Calendar of Proceedings in the Chancery*, vol. 1 (1827), pp. xxix, xliv, lxxvi. Where two persons have a right to possession of a document, one cannot sue the other in detinue, but the court of equity will compel discovery: *Worsley v. Which* (Ch. 1469), YB Mich. 9 Edw. IV, f. 41, pl. 26, Chancery Cases Middle Ages 170 (argument of counsel).

[17] *Stampe v. Longworth* (Ex. 1561 x 1572), Public Record Office, E.112/2/36; *Hawter v. Longworth* (Ex. 1561 x 1572), Public Record Office, E.112/36/28; *Barnes v. Longworth* (Ex. 1561 x 1572), Public Record Office, E.112/36/30.

[18] *Carpenter v. Tucker* (Ch. 1634 x 1635), 1 Chancery Reports 78, 21 E.R. 512; *Geofrey v. Thorn* (Ch. 1634 x 1635), 1 Chancery Reports 88, 21 E.R. 515; *Rogers v. Hawkesworth* (Ex. 1664), Hardres 378, 145 E.R. 506.

[19] *Fraunceys v. Clifford* (Ch. 1396 x 1403), 10 Selden Soc. 68.

[20] *Craven v. Salvayn* (Ch. 1415 x 1417), 10 Selden Soc. 110.

[21] *Loterell v. Hayme* (Ch. 1396 x 1403), 10 Selden Soc. 80.

[22] *Pynell v. Underwood* (Ch. after 1396), 10 Selden Soc. 20.

[23] *Denis v. Carew* (Ch. 1618 x 1619), Tothill 63, 21 E.R. 124.

[24] *Verney v. Lee* (Ch. 1535), 117 Selden Soc. 366; *Alnete v. Bettam* (Ch. 1559 x 1560), Cary 46, 21 E.R. 25; *Earl of Carlisle v. Gobe* (Ch. 1660), see below, Case No. 335; *Owen v. White* (Ch. 1667), 2 Freeman 126, 22 E.R. 1102, 3 Chancery Reports 20, 21 E.R. 716; *Anonymous* (Ch. 1685), 1 Vernon 351, 23 E.R. 516, 1 Eq. Cas. Abr. 2, 80, 21 E.R. 828, 893.

two different persons claimed an object or a fund in the hands of a third party, problems could arise in the common law courts. For example, if an expensive diamond necklace had been given to a jeweler to be repaired, the owner had died, and the jeweler had then been sued at common law for the necklace by both the heir and the widow, there would have been a very real danger that the different juries in the two common law cases would both find against the jeweler. To prevent the likelihood of inconsistent jury verdicts and double liability, the courts of equity would allow the defendant jeweler to come into equity and to bring both common law plaintiffs into the case, thus forcing them to litigate in equity their competing common law claims.

Another type of bill of peace is one to abate a nuisance. The common law allowed self help to abate a nuisance, an assize of nuisance, an action of redisseisin, a writ of *quod permittat prosternere*, or an action of trespass on the case.[25] Self help is an inadequate remedy in that it will normally result in a breach of the peace and the injured person will himself be liable for trespass if he acts beyond what is the minimum necessary to remove the nuisance. An action of case will produce damages up to the time of filing the action but will not force an abatement of the nuisance; the injured party will be put to a multiplicity of such actions as new damage will accrue daily in the future. The other common law remedies were types of *praecipe* actions which were extremely slow and procedurally clumsy; moreover, while the sheriff could be ordered to abate a nuisance and charge the cost to the defendant, this was more difficult than simply ordering the defendant to do it himself; furthermore, if the sheriff (and an undisciplined *posse comitatus*) went too far in the abatement, the sheriff, who would be primarily liable, would look to the plaintiff for indemnification.[26] Thus all of the common law remedies are clearly inferior to a personal order to the defendant to himself abate the nuisance and not to commit any nuisance in the future.[27]

A jury-related problem was the common law action of account. When the parties presented an accounting dispute to the court, the jury was required to render a separate verdict on each line in the account; this clumsy procedure was beyond the abilities of a jury of ploughmen, and the courts of equity took over accounting litigation to remedy this deficiency in the common law.

A more serious defect of the common law procedure was that when any party died, the lawsuit died, and the plaintiff had to restart his suit from scratch. Where there were many parties, it was frequently the case, particularly where a whole family was involved as in litigation over a family inheritance, that parties

---

[25] W. Blackstone, *Commentaries* (1768), vol. 3, pp. 5–6, 220–222.

[26] See generally, J. Story, *Commentaries on Equity Jurisprudence* (1836), vol. 2, ss. 925–927.

[27] *Attorney General v. Bond* (Ex. 1587), 117 Selden Soc. 119; *Swayne v. Rogers* (Ch. 1604), Cary 26, 21 E.R. 14 (semble); *Attorney General v. Taylor* (Ex. 1631), 118 Selden Soc. 611 (purpresture was ordered to be demolished or arrented).

would die and new parties be born, so that the case could never be brought to a conclusion. This problem was remedied by the courts of equity, because there a case could be easily revived when there was a change in parties and the litigation would not be frustrated by such accidents.

The fifteenth century in England was a period of political weakness as a result of the drawn-out Wars of the Roses; even during periods of peace, the authority of the crown was weak. England was at the mercy of private armies; the county administrators, the sheriffs, were usually either powerless or beyond the control of the courts. It was a period during which the rich and the powerful of the county could manipulate or intimidate juries and thus pervert the course of justice. Frequently weak and poor litigants had to resort to the court of the Chancellor, the most powerful political figure in the country, to obtain justice against their stronger neighbors.[28] The Chancellor was the king's prime minister in fact, though not in name, and he could do justice and enforce his orders without fear or favor. Thus, many common law disputes were heard in the Court of Chancery in the fifteenth century.

The equity jurisdiction of the chancellor's court grew in the fifteenth century also to cure problems in the administration of justice caused by various defects in the procedures of the old common law courts. One common law rule of evidence was that a party could not testify in court as a witness. Much has been written about the aspect of this rule that a person cannot testify against himself, but we will consider here that a person also could not testify for himself. Thus, where the only witnesses to a transaction or occurrence were the parties thereto, the person injured could not prove his case in a court of common law, because there was no admissible evidence, and since the plaintiff always has the burden of persuasion, the defendant would win by default. Thus, if one were assaulted in a dark alley, one had no practical remedy at common law. To aid the injured party, the courts of equity, where the defendant was required to plead under oath, would allow a person with a common law grievance to sue in equity in order to force the defendant to respond under oath and "discover" (make known) the truth, and then this sworn statement would constitute a binding admission for use in the common law court. In time, the courts of equity, where discovery was needed, began to retain the case and to decide the common law dispute in order to avoid the multiplicity of litigation that would have been involved by sending the plaintiff back to the court of law. This was the origin of the bill of discovery.

One of the most glaring archaic features of the medieval common law was trial by jury. Although the criminal jury was usually up to its task, life was too complicated for the civil jury; civil juries were seldom sufficiently educated or experienced to understand complex issues of financial importance. But regardless of how good the jurors might have been, the jury system required a single

---

[28] *Duchess of Suffolk's Case* (Ch. 1456), Chancery Cases Middle Ages, p. 113.

verdict of liability or not and, if so, what damages. Thus, where there were multiple plaintiffs or defendants, the common law jury was inadequate to sort out issues of, for example, which of the defendants might be liable for what proportion of the damages. In the courts of equity, which arose long after the common law courts had settled upon the use of the jury as the trier of the facts of the case, the judge heard all of the issues of the case and, being an educated and highly competent person, was able to determine complicated issues. In addition, the Chancellor could appoint a delegate, a master or commissioner of the court, to hear evidence and report on it to the court.

Another example of the judicial expansion of equitable remedies is in the area of monetary compensation for breach of contract. If a court of equity determines that specific performance is impossible or inappropriate in a particular case in which it has taken jurisdiction, it can retain jurisdiction and decree a monetary settlement. At first, the court did not decree specific performance, and the parties were dismissed to the courts of common law. But, now, if the bill of complaint alleges a genuine jurisdiction in the court of equity, *i.e.*, if the court could grant specific performance, but the court does not grant the traditional equitable remedy, it may retain jurisdiction in order to prevent a multiplicity of suits, and, thereupon, decree a payment of money.[29]

2. Evidence

The medieval law of evidence created injustice in certain situations. In the action of covenant based on a specialty, a written document under seal, the production in court of the instrument itself was sufficient evidence to entitle the plaintiff to a judgment. The defendant could attack the genuineness of the document itself, but there was no opportunity to raise any excuse or justification for non-performance. Therefore, if one were induced to make the promise of the written contract through fraud and then were sued at common law in an action of covenant, the only way of raising the defense of fraud in the inducement was to resort to a court of equity. The equity court would order the plaintiff at common law to discontinue the action there and recommence in the court of equity, where the defendant could assert the alleged fraud.[30]

---

[29] *Jones v. Tunis*, 99 Va. 220, 37 S.E. 841 (1901) (dictum); *Grubb v. Starkey*, 90 Va. 831, 20 S.E. 784 (1894) (damages awarded in addition to specific performance); *Chinn v. Heale*, 15 Va. (1 Munford) 63 (1810); *Ivan C. Dutterer, Inc. v. Gross*, 14 Va. Cir. 29 (1988); *Rice v. Scott*, 18 Va. Cir. 511 (1969); *Beacon Masonry Co. v. Eugene Simpson, Inc.*, 23 Va. Cir. 270 (1991).

[30] *Craddock v. Dowse* (Ch. 1602), 117 Selden Soc. 322 (fraud, overreaching, and threats); *Herbert v. Lownes* (Ch. 1628), 118 Selden Soc. 578 (fine, trust, and will set aside for fraud); *Gresham v. Gresham* (Ch. 1651), 118 Selden Soc. 727; see also *Calendar of the Proceedings in Chancery* (1827), vol. 1, p. xxix (a person of weak intellect was gotten intoxicated before executing a bond and a conveyance).

In the area of contracts, justice required that each party receive 'consideration', something of value for the performance of his part of the agreement. The common law courts required proof of consideration 'flowing' from the plaintiff to the defendant (the obligor) before a plaintiff (the obligee) could recover on an oral contract. However, if the contract was in writing and under the defendant's seal, the written and sealed instrument was sufficient proof for a common law recovery, even though there was no consideration. A sharp dealer would be able to take advantage of others by always having such an unfair bargain reduced to writing with an eye to future litigation, relying on well-established common law precedent. The common law courts could not change their law, but the court of equity came to require the unconscionable obligee to forgo the unfair gain. The courts of equity required that all contracts be supported by consideration on both sides.[31] Thus, where an action of debt on a specialty was brought but there had been a total lack of consideration in that the bond was given to the plaintiff in return for an assignment of a chose in action that was worthless as a matter of common law, the Court of Chancery ordered the plaintiff at common law to execute a release to the obligor or to deliver the bond to the court for cancellation.[32]

At common law a plea of payment could be proved against a sealed obligation only by a release under seal from the obligee. However, the court of equity would hear parol evidence of the payment[33] or accept a release that was not under seal.[34] This was necessary in order to prevent an unjust double recovery to the obligee who was trying to take advantage of the obligor's negligent failure to recover the bond upon the payment of it.

As a matter of the law of evidence, no person who was a party to a lawsuit was competent to testify as a witness; not only was a defendant forbidden to testify for or against himself, but also the plaintiff could not testify. Thus, if there were no witnesses to the transaction or occurrence in litigation other than the parties themselves, the plaintiff must have lost because he could not sustain his burden of proof. In order to cure this mechanical failure of justice, the courts of equity provided the plaintiff at common law with a bill of discovery. From the

---

[31] *Browne v. Newbole* (Ch. 1597), 117 Selden Soc. 263; *Smith v. Gawdy* (Ch. 1599), 117 Selden Soc. 273; *Pickering v. Keeling* (Ch. 1640 x 1641), 1 Chancery Reports 147, 21 E.R. 533.

[32] *J.R. v. M.P.*, YB Hil. 37 Hen. VI, f. 13, pl. 3 (C.P. 1459), trans. in E. D. Re, *Cases and Materials on Remedies* (2d ed. 1987), pp. 46–48, *sub nom. Reynolde v. Knott*, 51 Selden Soc. 147. A release to avoid the penalty of a bond was ordered in *Zouch v. Lord Zouch* (Ch. 1548), 117 Selden Soc. 368.

[33] *Anonymous* (Ch. temp. Eliz. I), Cary 2, 21 E.R. 1, which distinguished *Anonymous* (Ex. Cham. 1482), YB Pas. 22 Edw. IV, f. 6, pl. 18, 64 Selden Soc. 53, by allowing parol evidence of the parties themselves under oath, rather than any other witnesses (who might be paid to perjure themselves), against the written instrument.

[34] *Hurd v. Dodington* (Ch. 1598), 117 Selden Soc. 266.

beginning of its existence, the court of Chancery had required defendants to appear in court and answer under oath to the plaintiff's bill of complaint. (At first the answer was given orally and afterwards in writing, but always it was to be sworn to.) Thus, the common law plaintiff could sue the defendant in equity and then take the written, sworn answer and read it to the jury in the common law action and thus prove his case. Later the courts of equity also allowed depositions of nonparty witnesses to be taken upon bills of discovery, and these depositions could also be read to common law juries.[35] No final decree could be entered upon a bill of discovery.[36]

Another shortcoming of the common law, which was aided by the courts of equity, was the practical limitation of execution of final judgments to the payment of money or to the transfer of possession of property. It is true that the action of covenant resulted in an order of specific performance, but it was an ineffectual remedy in practice. Perhaps the reason for this was the practical inability of the sheriff (or any other officer of the court), even aided by the *posse comitatus*, to do any more than take by force a person's (defendant's) property, real and/or personal, moveable and/or immoveable, and give it to the plaintiff or sell it and give the proceeds to the plaintiff. In the thirteenth century when the common law was solidifying, the courts of law apparently lacked the machinery or the political or administrative power to force a person to do something himself.

The solution to this problem was the Chancellor's issuing a personal order to the defendant to perform some act or refrain from specified conduct.[37] This order, injunction, was backed up by the threat of imprisonment for so long as the defendant was not in compliance with the injunction. This usually worked.[38] It is a matter of conjecture as to why the chancellor's orders were more effective than the royal justices or why the justices did not issue injunctions. When the common law remedies were being devised and settled, England was less under the actual control of the royal administration than when the equitable remedies came into being. Perhaps the political power and prestige of the office of Chancellor

---

[35] Note (Ch. 1598 x 1602), 117 Selden Soc. 287 (discovery and production of documents); Note (Ch. 1602), 117 Selden Soc. 322 (discovery of secret encumbrances on land); Note (Ch. 1608 x 1620), 117 Selden Soc. 380 (discovery of defendants to a common law action of dower); *Rex v. Christian's Ex'r* (Ex. 1627), 118 Selden Soc. 529 (discovery of decedent's estate); *Hammond v. Shaw* (Ch. 1652), see below, Case No. 310 (discovery of assets of a judgment debtor); *Clarke v. Southcott* (Ch. 1652), see below, Case No. 311 (discovery of debts of a deceased person); *Ingram v. Coply* (Ch. 1653), see below, Case No. 313 (discovery of estates of tenants); Note (C.P. 1655), 118 Selden Soc. 733 (depositions can be read to a common law jury).

[36] *Herbert v. Herbert* (Ch. 1651), see below, Case No. 302.

[37] This is not to argue that the injunction was invented for this purpose. The usual process of injunction, however, was put to this purpose when needed.

[38] For an example of where the defendant went to jail rather than obey an injunction, see the case of *J.R. v. M.P.* (C.P. 1459), cited above.

was greater than that of a royal justice. In any case, the availability of the remedy of injunction attracted various classes of litigation to the courts of equity.

3. Contracts

Most of the situations involving equity jurisdiction and remedies concern issues of contract law. Here, the equity courts do not take away common law contractual obligations, but grant additional remedies for breaches of common law contractual rights. Equity does not destroy the common law but fulfills it; equity accepts the common law and fine-tunes it.

Thus, the common law of damages for breach of a contract will be supplemented by the equitable remedy of specific performance where damages are inadequate to put the obligee into the position of the expectancy of the contract. Some examples are where the object of a contract of sale are unique so that the obligee cannot take the monetary damage of the common law and use them to cover the loss of his or her expectancy. Another example is where the successful plaintiff cannot recover any judgment because of the insolvency of the obligor.

The best example of the superiority of an injunction over an order to pay money is in the area of breach of a contract of sale for a unique item or a specific piece of land. Thus the courts of equity will by means of an injunction specifically enforce contracts to transfer land.[39] No farm is like any other one, and thus the disappointed buyer cannot go and buy another farm to replace the lost bargain, as can the purchaser of a ton of gravel. In agricultural England, the specific enforcement of land sales contracts became so much the normal remedy, that all land is now considered unique as a matter of law, and the remedy of specific performance is always available no matter how indistinguishable one unit of a condominium may be from another. This rule has become the doctrine of equitable conversion, and the equity courts consider the purchaser of land to be the owner before the common law title has been conveyed pursuant to the contract of sale.

Over time, the judiciary has expanded equitable remedies in the area of contract law; there have been no subtractions. As land is unique and cannot be duplicated by a purchase on the open market with the money damages received

---

[39] *Wace v. Brasse* (Ch. after 1398), 10 Selden Soc. 43; *Brook v. Giles* (Ch. 1396 x 1403), 10 Selden Soc. 78; *Badwell v. Clopton* (Ch. 1413 x 1417), 10 Selden Soc. 111; *Cokayn v. Hurst* (Ch. 1456), 10 Selden Soc. 141; *Stewkly v. Lady Lutterel* (Ch. 1576), 117 Selden Soc. 102; *Hutton v. Prince* (Ch. 1582), 117 Selden Soc. 112; *Salisbury v. Salisbury* (Ch. 1585), 117 Selden Soc. 246; *Browne v. North* (Ch. 1594), 117 Selden Soc. 252; *King v. Ridon* (Ch. 1597), 117 Selden Soc. 262; Note (Ch. 1598 x 1602), 117 Selden Soc. 304; *Watson v. Bailiff of Sould* (Ch. 1599 x 1604), 117 Selden Soc. 319; *Jackson's Case* (Ex. 1609), Lane 61, 145 E.R. 299; *Otway v. Heblethwait* (Ch. 1615), 118 Selden Soc. 452; *Wiseman v. Roper* (Ch. 1649), see below, Case No. 275; see also *Calendar of the Proceedings in Chancery* (1827), vol. 1, p. xx, vol. 2, p, xl; *Bond v. Crawford*, 193 Va. 437, 444, 69 S.E.2d 470, 475 (1952); *Hale v. Wilkinson*, 62 Va. (21 Grattan) 75 (1871).

at common law for the breach of the contract and the buyer can get that which he bargained for only by means of specific performance, equity will also specifically enforce the payment of the price for land.[40] Not only land but chattels also may be unique. The courts of equity will grant a specific recovery of personal property which is unique from an objective point of view[41] and of that which has a *pretium affectionis* and is therefore unique only to the plaintiff.[42] The trend expanding the granting of specific performance of contracts relating to chattels was approved in the case of *Thompson v. Commonwealth*.[43] The Court, quoting Professor Williston, stated that "[t]he modern disposition is to be less technical in the application of" this remedy.

There is, in addition, a line of cases approving of specific performance of contracts to convey land which ignores the uniqueness of realty. These were decided on the grounds that the personal services rendered by the promisee as consideration for the conveyance were so unique and individual that no rational value could be placed upon them. Thus, damages would be too speculative and, therefore, inadequate.[44] Note that the emphasis is on the obligation of the plaintiff rather than of the defendant.

According to the common law of contracts, joint obligors are each liable to the obligee for the full amount of the debt. Thus, the obligee may collect the entire sum due from any one of the joint obligors. Typically, the obligee elects to go against only one, usually the wealthiest one, who is most likely to pay. The obligee may sue at common law against one or some or all of them. In addition to this, if the obligee has a judgment against some or all, he may execute the judgment against any one or some or all of them up to the full amount of the debt due. Since this is the substance of the contractual relationships among the obligee and the joint obligors, the common law is satisfied by the full payment to the obligee. If the joint obligors have paid different amounts, this was only what they agreed to, each being liable for the full sum.[45]

This latter situation is clearly unfair as to the joint obligors among each other. The courts of equity, therefore, evolved the maxim that equality is equity.

---

[40] *Pond v. Fisher*, 201 Va. 542, 112 S.E.2d 147 (1960); *Ayres v. Robins*, 71 Va. (30 Grattan) 105 (1878); *Rose v. Nicholas*, Wythe 268 (1794); *Graves v. Boyd*, 1 VCD R45, Randolph Va. 69 (1730); *Hoover v. Buck*, 2 Va. Dec. 106, 21 S.E. 474 (1895).

[41] *Fanney v. Virginia Inv. & Mtg. Corp.*, 200 Va. 642, 652, 107 S.E.2d 414, 421 (1959) (stock of a close corporation); *Summers v. Bean*, 54 Va. (13 Grattan) 404, 412, 413 (1856). *H. P. Reynolds, Inc. v. Rish Equip. Co.*, 9 Va. Cir. 356 (1971) (special equipment).

[42] *Bowyer v. Creigh*, 24 Va. (3 Randolph) 25, 28 (1825) (dictum).

[43] *Thompson v. Commonwealth*, 197 Va. 208, 213, 89 S.E.2d 64, 67, 68 (1955) (electrical machinery otherwise unavailable).

[44] *Clark v. Atkins*, 188 Va. 668, 51 S.E.2d 222 (1949); *Adams v. Snodgrass*, 175 Va. 1, 7 S.E.2d 147 (1940); *Reed v. Reed*, 108 Va. 790, 62 S.E. 792 (1908).

[45] *Wormleighton v. Hunter* (C.P. 1614), Godbolt 243, 78 E.R. 141.

The courts of equity will equalize the payments and obligations of joint obligors among themselves by means of the doctrine of contribution. Moreover, secondary liability to the obligee will result in repayment by means of indemnity or subrogation.[46]

Suits in equity are thus available to enforce a joint obligor's right of contribution, for example, for rents,[47] payments by co-sureties,[48] co-executors and co-trustees,[49] co-parties liable for court costs,[50] for dower rights,[51] and for repairs of bridges, seawalls, drainage ditches, and streets.[52] However, no right of contribution lies against the crown.[53]

Also, a bill in equity can be sued to vindicate a surety's right of indemnity.[54] However, sureties are discharged by any extension of time granted to the principal debtor without their acquiescence;[55] this is because the extension of time changes the original agreement of the surety. A surety will also be discharged where the creditor obstructed the surety's performance.[56]

As to suits to enforce contracts, there are many defenses that are of equitable origin. Dilatory conduct that harms another may result in the refusal of an equi-

---

[46] *Rex v. Ratliff's Ex'r* (Ex. 1609), Lane 39, 145 E.R. 281 (subrogation); Note (Ch. 1631), 118 Selden Soc. 625 (subrogation).

[47] *Anonymous* (Ch. temp. Eliz. I), Cary 2, 21 E.R. 1; *Gardiner v. Lynsell* (Ch. 1585 x 1587), 117 Selden Soc. 270; *Edwards v. Atkinson* (Ch. 1597), 117 Selden Soc. 262; *Morgan v. Anonymous* (Ch. 1603), Cary 23, 21 E.R. 13.

[48] *Whalley v. Mounson* (Ex. 1553 x 1554), 117 Selden Soc.72; *Fleetwood v. Charnock* (Ch. 1629), Tothill 41, 21 E.R. 117; *Morgan v. Seymour* (Ch. 1637 x 1638), 1 Chancery Reports 120, 21 E.R. 525; *contra Lovelace v. Cole* (Ch. c. 1614), 117 Selden Soc. 380.

[49] *Connock v. Rowe* (Ch. 1630), see below, Case No. 84.

[50] See Note (Ch. 1598 x 1602), 117 Selden Soc. 307.

[51] *Tenants of the Countess of Kent's Case* (Ch. c. 1588), 117 Selden Soc. 129; *Watkins v. William* (Req. 1620), 118 Selden Soc. 483.

[52] *Attorney General v. Mewtis* (Ex. 1627), 118 Selden Soc. 530 (bridge); *Williams's Case* (Ex. c. 1635), 118 Selden Soc. 664 (seawall); *Rich v. Barker* (Ex. 1658), Hardres 131, 145 E.R. 416 (tenants of a manor are not liable for contribution for repairs to a public bridge); *Earl of Devonshire v. Gibbons* (Ex. 1660), Hardres 169, 145 E.R. 435 (drainage ditch); *Merial v. Wymondsold* (Ex. 1661), Hardres 205, 145 E.R. 454 (streets paved) (semble).

[53] *Rotherham v. Nutt* (Ex. 1589), 117 Selden Soc. 129; *Anonymous* (Ch. 1597), 117 Selden Soc. 218.

[54] *Kirkham v. Taverner* (Ex. 1554 x 1558), 117 Selden Soc. 81 (a prayer that the principal debtor be forced to pay the creditor); *Hychcok v. Dean of Norwich* (Ex. 1568), Public Record Office, E.112/29/87; *Harris v. Dean of Exeter* (Ex. 1558 x 1572), Public Record Office, E.112/10/7.

[55] *Joulles's Case* (Ch. c. 1614), 117 Selden Soc. 381; *Hare v. Michell* (Ch. 1614 x 1615), Tothill 182, 21 E.R. 162; *Moile v. Roberts* (Ch. 1629 x 1630), Tothill 182, 21 E.R. 162.

[56] *Giles v. Gesling* (Ch. 1631), see below, Case No. 99.

table remedy.[57] A grossly unfair and harsh bargain that 'shocks the conscience' will be set aside by principles of equity even though the common law rules of making the contract were followed.[58]

The courts of equity will grant relief, both affirmative and defensive, against unavoidable accidents[59] and surprise.[60] Moreover, clerical mistakes will be remedied in equity by reformation of written instruments.[61]

Where the plaintiff has himself been guilty of dishonest or inequitable conduct, what later generations will call 'unclean hands', the courts of equity will not be a participant in the injustice and will refuse a remedy and leave the plaintiff to whatever common law remedy may be available. Thus, the court of Chancery refused to enforce contracts whose object was to defraud the crown[62] or the church.[63] The courts refused to enforce trusts made to defraud creditors[64] or other third parties.[65] Concealed titles and estates will not be protected in equity.[66] The court of Chancery refused to enforce a trust the purpose of which was to deceive a lord of a manor into accepting a tenant whom he disliked.[67]

As a general rule, contracts involving personal services will not be specifically decreed.[68] However, the courts have felt free to order specific performance of a contract to do construction work which does not require any unique skill or

---

[57] *Sedgwick v. Evan* (Ch. 1582 x 1583), Choyce Cases 167, 21 E.R. 97; *Randall v. Tyrnney* (Ch. 1612), 118 Selden Soc. 405; *Winchcomb v. Hall* (Ch. 1629 x 1630), 1 Chancery Reports 40, 21 E.R. 501; *Popham v. Desmond* (Ch. 1639 x 1640), 1 Chancery Reports 135, 21 E.R. 530.

[58] *Allen's Case* (c. 1610), 117 Selden Soc. 387.

[59] *Ingram's Case* (Ch. c. 1629), see below, Case No. 50.

[60] *Ramsey v. Goslin* (Ch. 1631), see below, Case No. 97.

[61] *Anonymous* (Ch. 1533 x 1544), Cary 16, 21 E.R. 9; *Ston v. Collar* (Ch. 1596), 117 Selden Soc. 257; *Dyke v. Foxwell* (Ch. 1597), 117 Selden Soc. 260; *Pedley v. Brady* (Ch. 1597), 117 Selden Soc. 262; *Thompson v. Stanhope* (1642), see below, Case No. 269; *Thin v. Thin* (Ch. 1650), 1 Chancery Reports 162, 21 E.R. 538. However, a scrivener's error in a will makes it void: Note (Ch. 1595), 117 Selden Soc. 204.

[62] *Orrell v. Eccleston* (Ch. 1601), 117 Selden Soc. 307.

[63] Note (Ch. 1612), 117 Selden Soc. 376.

[64] *Flatman v. Flatman* (Ch. 1599 x 1604), 117 Selden Soc. 320; Note (Ch. 1613), 117 Selden Soc. 378.

[65] *Pomery v. Ford* (Ch. 1600), 117 Selden Soc. 275.

[66] *Clement v. Sherley* (Ch. 1612), 118 Selden Soc. 403.

[67] *Gale v. Dore* (Ch. 1604), 117 Selden Soc. 329.

[68] *Fanney v. Virginia Inv. & Mtg. Corp.*, 200 Va. 642, 651, 107 S.E.2d 414, 421 (1959) (dictum); *Campbell v. Rust*, 85 Va. 653, 8 S.E. 664 (1889) (to mine and wash iron ore).

judgment and can thus be done by someone other than the obligor himself personally but at the obligor's expense.[69]

Negative covenants will be specifically enforced and buildings will be ordered to be removed or altered to conform to a contract.[70] In the case of *Birchett v. Bolling*,[71] the court affirmed a decree of specific performance of a contract to pay money pursuant to a special partnership. Also a contract for insurance will be specifically enforced against the insurer.[72]

Originally the equity court did not decree this money by way of damages but as "compensation" to the extent of the out of pocket disbursements made by the plaintiff.[73] This idea of compensation was similar to restitution in that it was based on an attempt to restore the *status quo ante*, but it was different from restitution in two ways. First, it was based upon an enforceable contract whereas restitution is based on the theory that there was no contract between the parties (whether no contract ab initio or a rescinded one), second, it was focused upon the attempt to reimburse the plaintiff rather than to take away the unjust enrichment of the defendant. Compensation was similar to damages at law in that it was founded on a contract wrongfully broken by the defendant; it was dissimilar in that it was based on the cost to the plaintiff rather than the value to him of the bargain. Today the courts of equity will order the defendant to pay full legal damages for the breach of a contract.[74]

A further instance of the modern expansion of equity involves one of the negative applications of the requirement of mutuality of remedy. Formerly a memorandum of a contract which was signed by only one party would not be enforced specifically in equity against the party who had signed because the statute of frauds made it unenforceable against the other. Equity required all parties to be treated equally and would not allow to one a remedy not available to the

---

[69] *Chesapeake & O. Ry. v. Williams Slate Co.*, 143 Va. 722, 129 S.E. 499 (1925) (to lay railroad tracks); *Norfolk & W. Ry. v. Supervisors of Carroll County*, 110 Va. 95, 65 S.E. 531 (1909) (to build a highway); *Southern Ry. v. Franklin & C. RR.*, 96 Va. 693, 32 S.E. 485 (1899) (to maintain and operate a railroad); *Grubb v. Starkey*, 90 Va. 831, 20 S.E. 784 (1894) (to lay a water pipe and build a trough).

[70] *Traylor v. Holloway*, 206 Va. 257, 142 S.E.2d 521 (1965); *Spilling v. Hutcheson*, 111 Va. 179, 68 S.E. 250 (1910); *Brooke v. Barton*, 20 Va. (6 Munford) 306 (1819) (to remove fences).

[71] *Birchett v. Bolling*, 19 Va. (5 Munford) 442 (1817).

[72] *American Sur. Co. v. Commonwealth*, 180 Va. 97, 21 S.E.2d 748 (1942); *Interstate Fire Ins. Co. v. McFall*, 114 Va. 207, 76 S.E. 293 (1912); *Wooddy v. Old Dominion Ins. Co.*, 72 Va. (31 Gratt.) 362 (1879).

[73] *Anthony v. Leftwich's Representatives*, 24 Va. (3 Randolph) 238, 265, 266 (1825).

[74] *See Jones v. Tunis*, 99 Va. 220, 37 S.E. 841 (1901) (dictum); *Grubb v. Starkey*, 90 Va. 831, 20 S.E. 784 (1894).

other.[75] In 1897, however, in the case of *Central Land Co. v. Johnston*,[76] this rule was reversed on the theory that by filing his bill the party who had not signed thereby affirmed the contract and it became enforceable against him in equity by the defendant.

There are many situations in which the courts of equity grant substantive relief to debtors, contractual obligors, who were in a disadvantageous bargaining position when they entered into the contract. Fraud in the inducement of a contract will vitiate it in a court of equity. This rule of equity law was later copied by the common law courts. Constructive fraud, where the misrepresentation was unknowing and innocent, but was effectively misleading, will vitiate the contract. Assignments of contractual obligations were first enforced in courts of equity in spite of the absence of privity between the obligor and the assignee. Penal damage contractual provisions were mitigated to compensatory damages. This is the legal theory behind the equitable right of the redemption of mortgages. Then came the remarkable transformation of the mortgagor's equity of redemption from a matter sounding in contract to a matter sounding in property.[77]

In the area of contracts, justice required that each party receive "consideration" — that is, something of value for the performance of his part of the agreement. The common law courts required proof of consideration "flowing" from the plaintiff to the defendant (the obligor) before a plaintiff (the obligee) could recover on an oral contract. However, if the contract was in writing and under the defendant's seal, the written and sealed instrument was sufficient proof for a common law recovery, even though there was no consideration. A sharp dealer would be able to take advantage of others by always having such an unfair bargain reduced to writing with an eye to future litigation, relying on well-established common law precedent. The common law courts could not change their law, but the court of equity came to require the unconscionable obligee to forgo his unfair gain. The courts of equity required that all contracts be supported by consideration on both sides.

---

[75] *Wood v. Dickey*, 90 Va. 160, 17 S.E. 818 (1893); *Shenandoah Valley RR. v. Dunlop*, 86 Va. 346, 349, 10 S.E. 239 (1889) (dictum).

[76] *Central Land Co. v. Johnston*, 95 Va. 223, 28 S.E. 175 (1897); *see also, e.g., Walker v. Henderson*, 151 Va. 913, 931, 145 S.E. 311, 316 (1928) (dictum).

[77] See generally D. E. C. Yale, 'An Essay on Mortgages and Trusts and Allied Topics in Equity', in *Lord Nottingham's Chancery Cases*, 79 Selden Soc. 7–87 (1961).

The courts of equity granted relief from forfeitures[78] and double recoveries.[79] Even though bargained for by an obligor in difficult financial circumstances and thus a poor credit risk, the inequity and inequality of the obligee's bargaining position required relief. Thus, while performance bonds were enforced as liquidated damages, penal bonds in large amounts for the non-payment of a lesser sum of money were relieved against.[80]

Contracts of debt were often secured by penal bonds or mortgages of the debtor's land. The mortgage is a common law conveyance of land to secure a loan; the mortgage contract is written so that, if the loan is repaid in full and on time, the debtor gets his land back, because the mortgage, which contains a condition subsequent, becomes void. However, if it is not repaid in full, the creditor keeps the land and the partial repayment, even if only one payment is not made or if a payment is made only one day late. In many cases, a debtor may be in technical default only, but the common law courts must enforce the contract that was freely entered into by the debtor. To prevent such harsh results, penalties, and forfeitures, the courts of equity allow the debtor to redeem the land by making the payments late (with appropriate additional interest). Thus, the equity courts have created what is called an equity of redemption.[81] (To protect fair-minded creditors, the courts of equity allow a creditor to come into the equity court and prove the hopeless insolvency of his debtor, and the equity judge will foreclose the debtor's equity of redemption; this will give the creditor clear title to the land that is being held as security so that he can sell it and recoup the amount of the defaulted loan.[82]) Although the general common law rule that contracts should

---

[78] *Legges v. Heath* (Ch. temp. Hen. VIII), 117 Selden Soc. 367 (penal bond for the payment of rent); *Anonymous* (Ch. 1595), 117 Selden Soc. 255 (penal bond for the payment of an annuity); *Stokes v. Mason* (Ch. 1610), 117 Selden Soc. 374 (penal bond to pay an arbitral award). However, willful and negligent forfeitures will not be remedied: Note (Ch. 1599 x 1604), 117 Selden Soc. 330. Note also *Attorney General v. Walthew* (Ex. 1646), 118 Selden Soc. 710.

[79] *Legges v. Heath* (Ch. temp. Hen. VIII), 117 Selden Soc. 367; *Dove v. Holmes* (Ch. 1551), 117 Selden Soc. 369; *Derbyshire v. Dampts* (Ch. 1556), 117 Selden Soc. 369; *Pill v. ap David* (Ch. 1581), 117 Selden Soc. 371; *Soare v. Poyncell* (Ch. 1588), 117 Selden Soc. 373; *Ayliffe v. Duke* (Ch. 1655), see below, Case No. 319.

[80] *Johnson v. Cooke* (Ch. 1598), 117 Selden Soc. 224.

[81] *Anonymous* (Ex. temp. Eliz. I), 117 Selden Soc. 169 (enforced by an executor); *Hurd v. Dodington* (Ch. 1598), 117 Selden Soc. 266; *Barker v. Norton* (Ch. 1629), see below, Case No. 98; *Holmixon v. Lemman* (Ch. 1651), see below Case No. 299; *Theobalds v. Nightingale* (Ch. 1651), see below, Case No. 304 (enforced by an executor); *Cowley v. Patron* (Ch. 1656), see below, Case No. 322; see generally R. W. Turner, *Equity of Redemption* (1931), pp. 22–42.

[82] *Edwards v. Woolfe* (1626), Benloe 160, 73 E.R. 1025; *How v. Vigures* (Ch. 1628 x 1629), 1 Chancery Reports 32, 21 E.R. 499; *Earl of Carlisle v. Gobe* (Ch. 1660), see below, Case No. 335.

be kept is well respected by society, everyone's sense of justice will acknowledge that the equity of redemption is a fine-tuning by the courts of equity that results in substantial justice in the individual case where the debtor is acting in good faith but has had a bit of bad luck. The equity of redemption has become a substantive right created of the courts of equity; it is a right that can be bought and sold.

4. *Trusts*

Trusts, formerly called uses, are contractual obligations between settlors and trustees for the benefit of third parties. They were originally a type of contract, usually in reference to land, and were invented after the common law writs had become fixed and unchangeable. A trust is the contractual situation in which the common law ownership of property is given to a person (the trustee) to hold and manage for the benefit of another person (the beneficiary of the trust). There was no common law writ available adequately to enforce a trust because the settlor was in many cases dead when the breach of trust occurred and the beneficiary, not being in privity with the trustee, had no common law remedy. The Chancery clerks and the common law judges could not change the law by inventing a new common law remedy without unconstitutionally usurping the legislative power of Parliament; therefore, the Chancellor enforced them. Written contracts creating uses and trusts may have been actionable at common law by a writ of covenant, but, even so, the successful plaintiff was not given an adequate remedy. The beneficiary of an oral trust did not even have a meaningful action. Thus, the courts of equity were called on to enforce uses and trusts by means of injunctive orders.[83] It was clear to the entire legal profession that justice required the enforcement of trusts and uses. Since the common law courts could (or would) not, everyone agreed that equity should. Thus, over a great length of time, the beneficiary of the trust was held to be the equitable owner of the property in question, and, thus, a contract right was turned into a property right.[84]

---

[83] *Godwyne v. Profyt* (Ch. after 1393), 10 Selden Soc. 48; *Holt v. Debenham* (Ch. 1396 x 1403), 10 Selden Soc. 69; *Chelmewyke v. Hay* (Ch. 1396 x 1403), 10 Selden Soc. 69; *Messynden v. Pierson* (Ch. 1417 x 1424), 10 Selden Soc. 114; *Williamson v. Cook* (Ch. 1417 x 1424), 10 Selden Soc. 115; *Prioress of Thetford v. Wychyngham* (1422 x 1426), 10 Selden Soc. 119; *Annors v. Alford* (Ch. 1422 x 1429), 10 Selden Soc. 129; *Rous v. FitzGeffrey* (Ch. 1441), 10 Selden Soc. 132; *Bale v. Marchall* (Ch. 1456), 10 Selden Soc. 143; *Revelle v. Gower* (Ch. 1471), 10 Selden Soc. 155; *Anonymous* (Ex. Cham. 1459), YB Trin. 37 Hen. VI, f. 35, pl. 23, 51 Selden Soc. 173; *Calendar of Proceedings in the Chancery* (1827), vol. 1, pp. xiii, xxi, xxxv, lxii. For cases from about 1465 to about 1555, see R. Brooke, *La Graunde Abridgement*, `Feffements al uses'.

[84] See generally D. E. C. Yale, 'An Essay on Mortgages and Trusts and Allied Topics in Equity', in *Lord Nottingham's Chancery Cases*, 79 Selden Soc. 87–150 (1961).

Another problem of trusts that was worked out in the early modern period was within the law of forfeiture for treason and felony. By 1600, it was settled law that persons convicted of felony forfeited their goods and chattels to the crown, and their lands and tenements were escheated or forfeited to their feudal lords. In the case of traitors, their lands and chattels were all forfeited to the crown.[85] However, in the more complicated area of trusts and uses where common law ownership of property, both real and personal, is separated from equitable or beneficial ownership, it was not always clear at that time when a person was convicted of a common law crime what was forfeited and by whom. The resolution of the problem was that the beneficial interest of land of inheritance held in trust was not to be forfeited to the crown upon the attainder of the beneficiary, but that of a leasehold so held would be forfeited.[86] '[W]here the tenant of the land is attainted of felony or treason, the use and trust for this land are extinguished; for the king, or the lord to whom the escheat belongs, comes in in the post and paramount [to] the trust and upon a title elder than the use or trust, *viz.* the right of his lordship by escheat for want of a tenant'.[87] Thus beneficial ownership was taken to be the true ownership for the purposes of forfeiture upon a conviction of a crime.[88] On the other hand, there was no problem with the setting aside of fraudulent conveyances that were made to avoid forfeitures to the crown, and they were regularly set aside to protect the crown's rights and the fisc.[89]

The doctrine of prerogative *cy pres* was developed in the seventeenth century in the equity courts. One of the results of the Protestant Reformation in England was a statute that suppressed chantries and the endowments of masses to be said for the soul of a deceased person. Protestant theology did not include the existence of purgatory, and thus masses for the dead in purgatory were considered useless and superstitious, and they were suppressed by statute.[90] What to do with these trusts was a new problem to be solved by the courts of equity. The first solution was that land devised to superstitious uses in trust was forfeited to

---

[85] M. Dalton, *The Country Justice* (1619), pp. 212, 266–268.

[86] *Attorney General v. Abington* (Ex. 1613–1619), 118 Selden Soc. 408; *Goddard v. Goddard* (Ch. 1590), 117 Selden Soc. 189 (dictum); *contra* Note (temp. Eliz. I), 117 Selden Soc. 168; *Attorney General v. Carr* (Ex. 1618), 118 Selden Soc. 475, Exchequer Cases 1604–1648, p. 195 (the interest of a beneficiary of a trust of a lease of a patent to provide wine for the royal household was forfeited to the crown upon his attainder of felony).

[87] *Anonymous*, Jenkins 244, 145 E.R. 172.

[88] However, in *Attorney General v. Wikes* (Ex. 1609), Lane 54, 145 E.R. 294, it seems that where the trustee of a lease of land is attainted of treason but the beneficiary is innocent, the lease is forfeited to the king.

[89] *Attorney General v. Raleigh* (Ex. 1609), 117 Selden Soc. 364, Exchequer Cases 1604–1648, p. 52; *Attorney General v. Bowes* (Ex. 1609), Lane 39, 145 E.R. 281; *Attorney General v. Long* (Ex. 1632), 118 Selden Soc. 635 (a fraudulent trust to avoid a fine payable to the crown).

[90] Stat. 1 Edw. VI, c. 14 (*SR*, IV, 24).

the crown.[91] Then the court of Chancery ruled that grants to illegal religious uses were void *ab initio* and were not forfeited but passed to the heir at law of the grantor.[92] This concept was further developed and refined so that charitable trusts for illegal purposes were to be redirected to legal objectives as closely, *i.e.* *cy pres*, within the intention of the donor as possible.[93]

5. Fiduciaries

In many other situations, the common law of contract damages was a total failure. In situations of feoffees to uses, trustees, executors of wills, and administrators of decedent's estates, money damages are useless. Moreover, the enforcement of such contracts *stricti juris* leads to unconscionable results because the original contracting obligee is most usually dead and the intended beneficiaries have no common law right to sue as they lack privity of contract with the obligor-fiduciaries. In many cases, the trustees have been given control over their beneficiaries' estates and discretion to act on their behalf. Thus, the courts of equity enforce such contracts *ex aequo et bono*, resulting in the law of fiduciary responsibility. Thus, the courts of equity have evolved a law of fiduciary responsibility, which did not exist in medieval England, and administrators of estates, guardians of persons under a disability, and trustees are held to a higher standard of loyalty than are ordinary obligors. Following the Act of Distributions in 1670, the equity courts, by a slow and careful process, turned executors of wills from being residuary beneficiaries into being fiduciaries for the next of kin.[94]

---

[91] *Bell v. James* (Ex. 1554 x 1558), 117 Selden Soc. 80; *Mantell v. Mayor of Wickham* (Ex. 1558), 117 Selden Soc. 86; Note (Ex. 1577), 117 Selden Soc. 102; *Waterchin v. Finch* (Ch. 1580), 117 Selden Soc. 183; *Hotham v. Eynus* (Ex. 1583), 117 Selden Soc. 112 (*de facto* chantry); *Anonymous* (Ex. 1585), 117 Selden Soc. 117; *Regina v. Palmer* (Ex. 1588), Moore K.B. 263, 72 E.R. 569; *Hampden v. Dyott* (Ex. c. 1589), 117 Selden Soc. 133; *Town of Springfield v. Mildmay* (Ch. 1597), 117 Selden Soc. 216; *Town of Diss v. Mildmay* (Ex. 1611), 117 Selden Soc. 393; *Regina v. Hutchins and Belman* (Ex. 1586), 117 Selden Soc. 118 (copyhold land was surrendered to superstitious uses); *Attorney General v. Lord Carrington* (Ex. 1682), Equity Cases Exch. 150.

[92] *Croft v. Evet* (Ch. 1605), 117 Selden Soc. 342; note also *Anonymous* (Ch. 1597), 117 Selden Soc. 153.

[93] *Venables' Case* (Ex. 1608), 117 Selden Soc. 352; *The Case of the Impropriators* (Ex. 1633), 118 Selden Soc. 643; *Attorney General v. Gaynor Jones* (Ex. 1688–1690), Equity Cases Exch. 304; *Attorney General, ex rel. Boucher v. Portington,* (Ex. 1694), Equity Cases Exch. 338; G. H. Jones, *History of the Law of Charity 1532–1827* (1969), pp. 12–15, 76–81.

[94] Stat. 22 & 23 Car. II, c. 10 (*SR*, V, 719–720); *Foster v. Munt* (Ch. 1687–1689), Chancery Cases *tempore* Jac. II, p. 368; *Edwards v. Freeman* (1726–1728), Miscellaneous Chancery Repts. (1714–1730), p. 236, 2 Peere Williams 435, 24 E.R. 803.

6. Property

The common law prohibition on waste forbids tenants of land who have less than fee simple interests from doing permanent damage to the land to the prejudice of future owners. However, there are some serious gaps in the scope of the substantive common law. These unintended omissions have been supplied by the courts of equity, and injunctions forbidding waste lie against various classes of tenants overlooked by the common law prohibitions,[95] persons who have been granted permission to commit waste,[96] and persons who commit waste maliciously.[97]

B. Equity Is Extra-Ordinary

The jurisdiction of the Court of Chancery was needed and was to be exercised only when the already established courts of the common law could not or would not grant a complete and fair remedy. Thus, the jurisdiction of the Court of Chancery is said to be extra-ordinary; it exists only if there is no ordinary remedy available in the other courts or if the ordinary remedy there is incomplete or inadequate to do justice.[98] Equity courts and jurisdiction exist to fulfill and refine the common law, not to supersede or destroy the common law courts.

C. Equity Acts in Personam

How was the Court of Chancery able to accomplish this without changing the law and thus offending Parliament, the legislature, or disregarding the settled common law of the Court of Common Pleas and the Court of King's Bench? The Court of Chancery did not change the common law rights of anyone; it only ordered someone, the defendant, after a judicial hearing of the evidence and legal arguments, personally to do what was just and right, according to the policy and intent of the common law. It was done by a personal order to the litigant enforced only by an imprisonment of the person until some common law act be performed,

---

[95] *Songhurst v. Dixton* (Ch. 1594), 117 Selden Soc. 251 (tenant 'by covenant'); *Rotherham v. Rotherham* (Ch. 1596), 117 Selden Soc. 257 (lessee of holder of mesne life estate); Note (Ch. 1599), Moore K.B. 554, 72 E.R. 754 (life tenant succeeded by a remainder for life); Note (Ch. 1598 x 1602), 117 Selden Soc. 285 (lessee succeeded by a remainder for life); Note (Ch. 1604), Cary 26, 21 E.R. 14 (life tenant succeeded by a remainder for life).

[96] *Morgan v. Perry* (Ch. 1595), 117 Selden Soc. 253; *King v. Blundavile* (Ch. 1629 x 1630), Tothill 83, 21 E.R. 130.

[97] Note (Ch. 1598 x 1602), 117 Selden Soc. 285; *Vane v. Lord Barnard* (Ch. 1708–1716), British Library MS. Hargrave 80, f. 214, 2 Vernon 738, 23 E.R. 1082, Precedents in Chancery 454, 24 E.R. 203, Gilbert Rep. 127, 25 E.R. 89, 1 Salkeld 161, 91 E.R. 150, 1 Eq. Cas. Abr. 399, 21 E.R. 1131, 2 Eq. Cas. Abr. 244, 22 E.R. 208.

[98] *Walwin v. Brown* (Ch. 1460), YB Mich. 39 Hen. VI, f. 26, pl. 36, Chancery Cases Middle Ages, p. 123 (in argument of counsel); *Rede v. Capel* (Ch. 1492), YB Pas. 7 Hen. VII, f. 10, pl. 2, Chancery Cases Middle Ages, p. 261.

such as the execution of a common law conveyance, the payment of money, or the common law transfer of a chattel so that common law justice was accomplished. The Court of Chancery acted only *in personam*, but not *in rem*.[99]

D. Summary

Thus did equity come into existence to supplement and complement the common law. Equity does not compete with the common law but tunes it more finely. The common law is, in theory, a complete system; equity is not a system within itself but rather relates to the common law and aids the common law. Justice came to consist of both common law and equity; English justice would be defective without both. This was recognized as early as the fifteenth century, and so lawyers and judges had to work out in the pleading stage of the litigation whether justice in a particular case was to be served in a court of common law or a court of equity.

Equity does not deny the validity of the common law but rather recognizes it and fulfills it. Equity does not change the common law, but where a person is using the common law to an unjust purpose, the equity judge will order that person not to sue in the common law court or not to enforce a common law judgment. The court of equity does not change the common law or reverse, overrule, or annul any common law judgment, for to do so would be an unconstitutional usurpation of legislative power and an illegal appellate power over the common law courts. But all disinterested persons would agree that the common law courts should not be used in an unjust manner, and thus, the equity court orders that person not to do it. It is against good conscience to do injustice. Equity courts simply force defendants to act according to conscience; consequently, they have frequently been called courts of conscience.

In reading reports of equity cases, both in the Court of Chancery and in the Court of Exchequer, one realizes that most of the debate and discussion concerns the parties' common law rights, and, once they are decided, the equitable remedy appears to be straightforward and uncomplicated.

Thus, the common law and the equity jurisdictions of the Court of Chancery were firmly established and well accepted by the end of the Middle Ages in England, the close of the reign of King Henry VII in 1509. The administration of justice in England required the existence of courts of common law and courts of equity. In the fifteenth century, "over all, common lawyers, judges and counsel alike, were content, as their predecessors had been, to see Chancery as part of the system, not its enemy."[100] And so to the present day among thoughtful jurists.

---

[99] This distinction was taken by Sir Edward Coke himself in *Fourth Institute* (1644), p. 84.

[100] J. A. Guy, *Christopher St. German on Chancery and Statute* (1985), Selden Soc., sup. vol. 6, p. 88, quoting E. W. Ives, *The Common Lawyers in Pre-Reformation England* (1983), pp. 218–219.

II. Whiggery and Chancery

Since the death of Henry VII in 1509, there has been much political misunderstanding and misinformation disseminated as to the origin and nature of the jurisdictions of the Court of Chancery. The Chancellor of England (later Great Britain) was a member of the king's cabinet and, before 1640, the *de facto* prime minister, and thus, when the winds of politics shifted, the Chancellor was the only judge in England to be removed from the bench when his political party falls from political grace and power. Thus, *ex hypothesi*, the Chancellor has been a political supporter of the king until the monarch lost true political power in the early nineteenth century. Because of this political power, the Chancellor, like other politicians, has over the centuries attracted criticism from the political opponents of the ruling monarch. For the purposes of this essay, these opponents will be referred to as Whigs.[101]

A. Cardinal Wolsey

The first chancellor to be criticized by the Whigs was Thomas, Cardinal Wolsey (1473–1530). Wolsey was a man of very modest social background who came to the attention of Henry VIII in the early years of his reign. Wolsey was an intelligent, educated, industrious person who had no family ties to any of the aristocracy and thus no temptation to or reason for disloyalty to King Henry. Here was the man to administer the dull, daily routine of the government while the young king enjoyed himself free from care and responsibility. Therefore, Wolsey was promoted to the highest offices possible in the English church and state, including the chancellorship.

However, the wealth and power went to Wolsey's head, and he became arrogant and overbearing. His political enemies attempted to discredit him by discrediting his court, the Court of Chancery; moreover, the court was to be discredited by attacking the equitable remedies administered therein. The prime target was the common injunction, which was the procedural device used to bring about the effectual removal of a case from a common law court to an equity court. Such injunctions had been the common and accepted practice for over a hundred years before the chancellorship of Wolsey. Apparently, this was the only stick available with which to beat the old man. After Wolsey was removed from office, which was for his failure to secure an annulment of the king's canonically questionable marriage to Catherine of Aragon (1485–1536), the issue of common injunctions evaporated, and it was business as usual among the courts at Westminster.[102]

---

[101] Note H. Butterfield, *The Whig Interpretation of History* (1931).
[102] J. A. Guy, *The Public Career of Sir Thomas More* (1980), pp. 37–93.

Although Wolsey was not trained as a lawyer, there is little or no evidence that he distorted the course of justice in his court or that he introduced any new legal principals or practices other than delegating his judicial duties to vice chancellors. He was rude to counsel, but when he was gone, the rudeness was gone; his successor, Sir Thomas More (1478–1535), was a decent man in all respects.

'Wolsey was prone to occasional lapses, notably of temperament, but his judicial conduct in Star Chamber and Chancery was at best creative, at worst competent. There is insufficient proof to justify the charges made by triumphant enemies after his fall.'[103]

B. Sir Edward Coke

However, a hundred years after the fall of Wolsey, one of most celebrated of all Whigs, Sir Edward Coke (1552–1634), revived the attack. After Coke had achieved the position of Chief Justice of the Court of King's Bench, he began to attack or minimize or subjugate to his court's review every other court in England except the Court of Star Chamber where he sat also.

This was done by postulating that all of the king's duty to administer the common law of England had been delegated by him in the twelfth and thirteenth centuries to the Court of Common Pleas and the Court of King's Bench, with the latter having appellate jurisdiction and thus control over the former. All of the courts that evolved or were created by statute afterwards were 'prerogative' courts. Since the royal prerogative is a part of the common law of England because the king is under the law, the common law courts, especially the Court of King's Bench, define the scope and extent of the royal prerogative. Therefore, the King's Bench defines and controls the jurisdiction and the substantive law of the so called prerogative courts of England. The procedures for exercising this control were the common law writs of prohibition, quo warranto, and habeas corpus.[104] Coke also attempted to intimidate the bar by threatening prosecutions for praemunire. However, Sir Matthew Hale, when Chief Justice of the Court of King's Bench, held that suing in the Court of Chancery was not an act of praemunire.[105]

Before Coke was removed from the bench, he had successfully subordinated the admiralty courts, the ecclesiastical courts, and the Court of Requests. He

---

[103] J. A. Guy, *Christopher St. German on Chancery and Statute* (1985), Selden Soc., sup. vol. 6, p. 69; see generally J. A. Guy, *The Cardinal's Court: The Impact of Thomas Wolsey in Star Chamber* (1977).

[104] C. M. Gray, *Writ of Prohibition: Jurisdiction in Early Modern English Law* (1994); P. D. Halliday, *Habeas Corpus* (2010).

[105] *King v. Standish* (K.B. 1670), 1 Modern 59, 86 E.R. 730, 1 Siderfin 463, 82 E.R. 1218, 1 Levinz 241, 83 E.R. 387, 2 Keble 402, 661, 787, 84 E.R. 251, 415, 497, Gray's Inn MS. 35, f. 679, 73 Selden Soc. 13.

had by the means of *Slade's Case*[106] taken away the monopoly of the Court of Common Pleas as to actions sounding in contract; this was a severe financial blow to the officers of that court. He had even told the king that he, King James, was subject to the common law; it was not necessary to state the obvious conclusion that Coke, as a common law judge, would interpret the law and thus control the king. King James I knew what that meant, and, when Coke saw the king's fury, he recanted this opinion on the spot.[107] Then, Coke's self aggrandizement led him to attack the Court of Chancery along with the others.

Coke attacked the Court of Chancery because he was annoyed by the practice of the equity courts of issuing common injunctions after final judgments at common law.[108] Although there was a problem at the time as to the res judicata effects of final judgments, the case that brought the issue to a boil, *Glanville's Case*[109] was a judgment by confession with release of errors and perfectly demonstrated the need for such injunctions. In this case, a seller had fraudulently sold a gem, misrepresenting a topaz to be a diamond, and received in payment a promissory note with a confession of judgment with release of errors. When the buyer discovered the fraud, he refused to pay the purchase price. The seller then entered the judgment by confession and put it into execution. The judgment was a final common law judgment, but there could not have been a trial at common law where the buyer could have pleaded and proved the fraud. Therefore, the Court of Chancery, after a hearing of the allegations and the evidence, entered an order forbidding the seller to enforce his judgment as obtained by fraud. And this was done because there was no common law remedy available according to the procedures of the common law courts to set aside the fraudulent contract or the confessed judgment. The fraudster disobeyed this order, was held in contempt, and imprisoned for it. However, Sir Edward Coke, the Chief Justice of the King's Bench, granted the fraudster a writ of habeas corpus. These two conflicting orders were taken up by the king in Council, and, after extensive arguments, the Privy Council ruled in favor of the Chancery order. This was the only possible logical and historical result. The original purpose of the Court of Chancery was to grant remedies according to the common law where the older common law courts did not. Clearly, the common law recognizes that fraud in

---

[106] *Slade v. Morley* (1602), 4 Coke Rep. 91, 76 E.R. 1072, also Moore K.B. 433, 667, 72 E.R. 677, 827, Yelverton 20, 80 E.R. 15, note also J. H. Baker, 'New Light on Slade's Case', in *The Legal Profession and the Common Law* (1986), pp. 393–432.

[107] C. D. Bowen, *The Lion and the Throne: The Life and Times of Sir Edward Coke* (1956), pp. 303–306.

[108] For a contemporary collection of 21 of such cases, dating from 1535 to 1610, see 117 Selden Society 366–374.

[109] *Glanville's Case* (K.B. 1615), 1 Rolle Rep. 111, 219, 81 E.R. 365, 444, Croke Jac. 343, 79 E.R. 294, 2 Bulstrode 301, 80 E.R. 1139, Moore K.B. 838, 72 E.R. 939, Hobart 115, 80 E.R. 264, 118 Selden Soc. 440.

the inducement will vitiate a contract. Had the result been the opposite, the Court of Chancery would have been destroyed.

The original purpose of the courts of equity was to provide a just remedy where the courts of common law failed to give one. Thus, where different remedies were available or different results would obtain, the remedy of the courts of equity would, and will, prevail. Thus, for example, if a person is induced through fraud to enter into a contract and that person is then sued in a court of common law in such a procedural manner that the defense of fraud cannot be asserted there, that person can then resort to a court of equity for relief. The court of equity will forbid by means of an injunction the prosecution of the lawsuit in the common law court but allow it in the equity court where the defense of fraud can be asserted and proved. Thus, the suit was removed from the common law court to the equity court at the beginning of the legal proceedings.

However, in the late sixteenth and early seventeenth centuries, defendants were remaining in the common law court and taking their chances with a jury verdict, and then, if the jury ruled for the plaintiff, the defendant would get a common injunction and remove the case to a court of equity and have a new trial. Alternatively, the equity judge could quash the common injunction that had been issued as a matter of course by the clerk, but the defendant would still have delayed the execution of the judgment and caused the judgment creditor additional delay and expense. Not only was this inefficient and wasteful of time and money, but it appeared to give to the courts of equity an appellate review of the common law court's actions. Such an appeal was not a part of the traditional organization of the court system of England. This matter led to the bitter public dispute between Sir Edward Coke, the Chief Justice of the Court of King's Bench, and Thomas Egerton, Lord Ellesmere, the Chancellor of the Court of Chancery. The dispute was temporarily settled in 1616 by King James I himself, who was being advised by Sir Francis Bacon (1561–1626). Bacon was a great rival of Coke, and he soon succeeded Ellesmere as Chancellor.[110]

Even though there was an end to the public dispute in 1616, it took perhaps a century for the issue to be worked out properly. The issue is not a question of an appeal but is one of res judicata. When the dispute between the parties has proceeded to a final judgment, it should not be relitigated, neither in a different court nor in the same court, unless an appellate court reverses that lower court judgment. Thus, if a defendant in a common law court elects to proceed to a final judgment in that court, he should not be allowed to relitigate it anywhere. Thus,

---

[110] J. H. Baker, `The Common Lawyers and the Chancery: 1616' in *The Legal Profession and the Common Law* (1986), pp. 205–229; C. M. Gray, `The Boundaries of the Equitable Function', *American Journal of Legal History*, vol. 20 (1976), pp. 192–226; J. P. Dawson, `Coke and Ellesmere Disinterred: The Attack on the Chancery in 1616', *Illinois Law Review*, vol. 36 (1941), pp. 127–152.

an injunction after a final judgment will be refused at common law or in equity on the grounds of res judicata.

Unfortunately, life is not so simple. In the famous case of Richard Glanville in 1616,[111] the original defendant, who had been the victim of fraud, had neither the opportunity to present a legal defense, nor to appeal, nor to remove the case to an equity court before final judgment because he had been defrauded into confessing a judgment and releasing those rights. This presents the distinction between intrinsic and extrinsic fraud. Intrinsic fraud, as where a person enters into a contract through deceit, is covered by the doctrine of res judicata and cannot be considered in later litigation. On the other hand, extrinsic fraud, as where a defendant is prevented by deceit from going into court to make any defense, is separate from the contract in dispute and is not covered by res judicata. Other examples of extrinsic fraud would be deceit as to the period of the statute of limitations, a judge who had been bribed, and a lawyer who deliberately betrayed his client. Other grounds for an injunction after a final judgment are accident, surprise, and breach of trust, which are well established grounds for equity jurisdiction.

The Chancery case of *Ayliffe v. Duke* (Ch. 1655)[112] is an example of a court of equity granting relief following a final judgment at common law for the same matter. In this case, a series of bonds had been given in favor of various members of two families as part of a marriage contract. Later, due to economic hardships that followed the English Civil War, some of these bonds became unenforceable leaving George and Elizabeth Duke destitute. Mrs. Ayliffe agreed to make a large gift to them, Elizabeth Duke being of her kin. Then George Duke's father forced him to give a bond to his brother, John, so that Mrs. Ayliffe's gift would eventually end up in the hands of John rather than those of the intended donees. When Mrs. Ayliffe heard of this attempted fraud, she refused to go through with the gift. George, thereupon, gave the bond to her, and she cancelled it by tearing it up. Then she gave the money to George and Elizabeth. Four years later after the money had been paid, John Duke sued Mrs. Ayliffe in a court of common law for destroying the bond in which he was the payee. The jury gave a verdict for John, and final judgment was entered by the court. Mrs. Ayliffe then sued in the Court of Chancery for equitable relief against the common law judgment, and the Court of Chancery granted it in order to prevent a double payment and fraud. Since Mrs. Ayliffe was aware of the fraud before the common law action was begun, she should have removed the common law case into the court of equity by means of a routine common injunction before the verdict. Then she could have asserted her equitable defences against John Duke. Perhaps, she could have shown the fraud in evidence in common law. Having failed to do this, the

---

[111] *Glanville's Case* (K.B. 1615), cited above.

[112] *Ayliffe v. Duke* (Ch. 1655), see below, Case No. 319, A. Wijffels, ed., *Case Law in the Making*, vol. 2, pp. 56–61 (1997).

rules of res judicata, as understood today, would have prevented her from suing in equity after the common law judgment, but this would have allowed a great hardship and fraud to be committed against her.

In the case of *Robinson v. Bell* (Ch. 1690),[113] Robinson was sued in a court of common law for money received as the executor of a decedent's estate. He instructed his attorney in the common law court, a court official, to enter a special defense, but a general defense was entered through the mistake of the attorney. In addition, Robinson wrote a letter to Bell, the claimant of the estate and plaintiff at common law saying that he had received the money. Because of these two mistakes, the court of common law ruled for Bell and ordered Robinson to pay her the money. Robinson then sued in a court of equity, and, there, he was relieved from payment of the common law judgment for the reasons of the two mistakes. It is the opinion of this writer that the first mistake, that of the attorney, was a true surprise or accident over which Robinson had no control and was a sufficient ground for equitable relief against the final judgment at common law. He would not have been liable for the second mistake and would not have been ordered to pay money that he had not received from the decedent's estate had he pleaded a special defense. However, admitting receiving money which he had not received appears to have been his own negligence, against which a court of equity would not relieve.

In the case of *Crane v. Hill* (Ex. 1695),[114] Crane was a creditor of Hill and of Hill's insolvent father. When Hill's father died, Crane and Hill came to an agreement as to the debts owed Crane. As a part of this agreement, Hill conveyed to Crane the rectory of the parish church of Hales, which included the right to receive tithes, the rent of the glebe lands, and various other income. Afterwards, Hill acquired a precedent and superior right to the rectory, and he sued Crane in an action at common law and recovered the property. Crane then sued Hill in the equity side of the Court of Exchequer to be relieved against the common law judgment. The equity court granted Crane's petition and required Hill to give up his title and possession. The reason of the equity court was that it was unfair and wrong for Hill to have a double recovery by setting up his new right against his own conveyance of that same right. Hill's common law judgment operated as a fraud upon Crane because of Hill's earlier conveyance to Crane; Crane could not have pleaded this in the common law action of ejectment against him; therefore, relief in equity was granted to him.

---

[113] *Robinson v. Bell* (Ch. 1690), 2 Vernon 146, 23 E.R. 701, 1 Eq. Cas. Abr. 237, 21 E.R. 1015, Public Record Office C.33/274, f. 744v, A. Wijffels, ed., *Case Law in the Making*, vol. 2, pp. 68–73 (1997).

[114] *Crane v. Hill* (Ex. 1695), Equity Cases Exch. 347, Dodd 338, A. Wijffels, ed., *Case Law in the Making*, vol. 2, pp. 73–81 (1997).

In the case of *Ambler v. Wyld* (1794),[115] there was a suit in equity after a final judgment at common law. The plaintiff in equity was asserting that certain papers should not have been considered by the common law jury. The equity judge, George Wythe, ruled that this was not a sufficient ground for equity jurisdiction, but since all parties had consented, he would and did hear the case.

In the case of *Cochran v. Street* (1791, 1792), after a verdict and final judgment at common law, four members of the jury said that they did not agree with the verdict but believed that they were bound by the vote of the majority and were unaware that the verdict must have been unanimous. The defendant at common law thereupon sued in equity in the same county court to have the common law execution stayed. An injunction was granted on the grounds that the false verdict was a surprise on the defendant that was not discovered until after the entry of the final judgment. (Surprise is a good ground for equitable jurisdiction.) This decree in equity was appealed to the High Court of Chancery, and Virginia Chancellor Wythe reversed the County Court and dismissed the bill in equity because the 'surprise' in this case was not sufficient. Upon a further appeal to the Court of Appeals, the High Court of Chancery was reversed, and the suit in equity was reinstated.[116] Edmund Pendleton, President of the Court of Appeals, held that 'as to the unfairness of the trial on the score of surprise, there is no doubt, but that if it were proved, it would afford good ground for granting a new trial. . . .'

In more recent times, the boundaries between common law and equity in reference to injunctions after final judgment at common law have been well defined. "The elements of this [suit for an injunction] in equity are (1) a [common law] judgment which ought not, in equity and good conscience, to be enforced; (2) a good defense to the alleged cause of action on which the judgment is founded; (3) fraud, accident or mistake which prevented the defendant in the judgment from obtaining the benefit of his defense; (4) the absence of fault or negligence on the part of the defendant; and (5) the absence of any adequate remedy at law."[117]

The reference to fraud, however, is to extrinsic fraud only. Extrinsic fraud is fraud that is collateral to the issues before the court. Whether perjury and matters that go to the veracity of the evidence is extrinsic fraud on the court or whether this is intrinsic fraud to be decided by the trier of fact while weighing the evidence is a dispute that has been settled in favor of the latter definition. Otherwise, few judgments would be final because most litigants contest the truth of their opponents' evidence.[118]

---

[115] *Ambler v. Wyld*, Wythe's Reports 235, 2 Va. (2 Wash.) 36 (1794).
[116] *Cochran v. Street*, Wythe's Reports 133, 1 Va. (1 Wash.) 79 (1791, 1792).
[117] *Charles v. Precision Tune, Inc.*, 243 Va. 313, 317–318, 414 S.E.2d 831 (1992).
[118] *Rowe v. Big Sandy Coal Corp.*, 197 Va. 136, 143, 87 S.E.2d 763 (1955); *McClung v. Folks*, 126 Va. 259, 268–272, 101 S.E. 345 (1919).

An example of extrinsic fraud is the case of *O'Neill v. Cole*. In this case, a teenage infant was deceived by her father as to the contents of her uncle's will so that she did not defend her interests in the suit to settle the estate, in which she was a defendant. This was "extrinsic and collateral fraud which precluded her from presenting her true case and rights to the court for adjudication."[119]

Fraud which produces false evidence is intrinsic fraud, but fraud which prevents the consideration of evidence is extrinsic fraud. An example of this distinction is where a condemnor withheld from the court and from the condemnee information showing that the proposed condemnation was for a private purpose so that the condemnee-defendant could not argue against the false allegations of the condemnor.[120]

The following is a good explanation of the proper balance between finality of judgments and relief from final judgments in cases of injustice. "Where a party has had a day [in a court of common law] in which he could make his defense in the proper form before a verdict and judgment against him, equity will not entertain him and grant relief after such verdict and judgment, unless in case of fraud, accident, or surprise, or some adventitious circumstance unmixed with negligence on his part which shall sufficiently account for the omission to seek its intervention before the judgment."[121] "[A] court of equity . . . relieves against judgments at [common] law, not because they were wrong but because of some new matter, which the court of law did not, or could not, pronounce a judgment on, or which, for some just cause, the party could not bring to the consideration of the court of law."[122]

Even after Sir Edward Coke had been removed from the bench and the old Chancellor, Lord Ellesmere, had died, and peaceful co-existence was restored between the two courts, Coke reopened the attack on the Chancery by publishing in full in his *Fourth Institute*,[123] in the section on the Court of Chancery, the indictment drawn up against Wolsey after his disgrace and fall from power.[124] This lengthy indictment was a long list of trivial political and personal offenses, few of which had any relevance whatever to the Court of Chancery or

---

[119] *O'Neill v. Cole*, 194 Va. 50, 57, 72 S.E.2d 382, 385 (1952); *see also Lee v. Baird*, 14 Va. (4 Hening & Munford) 453 (1809), where the defendant at common law was deceived into not making a defense.

[120] *Justice v. Georgia Industrial Realty Co.*, 109 Va. 366, 63 S.E. 1084 (1909).

[121] *Haseltine & Walton v. Brickey*, 57 Va. (16 Grattan) 116, 120 (1860).

[122] *Garland v. Rives*, 25 Va. (4 Randolph) 282, 316 (1826). Other examples of original bills after final judgment at common law are noted in C. Robinson, *Practice in the Courts of Law and Equity in Virginia*, vol. 2 (1835), pp. 212–222, and in R. T. Barton, *Pleading and Practice in the Courts of Chancery*, vol. 1 (1926), pp. 604–611.

[123] This book on the jurisdiction of the various courts of England was written after his dismissal from the bench, though published posthumously in 1644.

[124] E. Coke, *Fourth Institute* (1644), pp. 89–95, copies the full indictment.

to its equity jurisdiction and, especially, not a hundred years later. One of the articles of the bill of attainder was that Wolsey, having syphilis, which was false, breathed on the king. Here was Whig propaganda, Whig history at its worst. It was an attempt to diminish the office of Chancellor and to weaken a monarchical government.[125] To resist an absolutist monarch was in my opinion a good thing to do, but not at the expense of the common law and the equity thereof.

Coke went far beyond attacking the chancellors Egerton and Bacon politically; he attacked the basic principles of equity jurisprudence. In the case of *Bromage v. Genning*,[126] he denied the right of a purchaser of land to an injunction for specific performance on the ground that his only remedy was common law damages. His report of *Cobb v. Moor* (1465),[127] was another attempt to destroy the Chancellor's equity jurisdiction. Had he not been removed from the King's Bench, he might have expanded the use of prosecutions for *praemunire* to deny all access to the Court of Chancery.

Lord Ellesmere was a royalist in his political positions. However, this did not affect his judgments in the Court of Chancery or in his administration of the equity of the common law of England. For Coke to attack the Court of Chancery in order to neutralize his political opponent was of questionable wisdom. It is my opinion that it was fortunate for the future development of the English civil law that King James I, who was being advised by Sir Francis Bacon and others, put a stop to it. In 1681, Lord Nottingham could state 'These extravagant opinions no man will own, no more than the exploded opinion that to sue in Chancery after judgment is a praemunire.'[128]

These political struggles were irrelevant to the quotidian administration of the law in the royal courts, whether common law or equity. Though furious storms lash at the surface of the sea, at the bottom, on the ocean floor, life goes on in its usual, routine ways not much disturbed by what is going on far above. The rule of law must still be applied to settle disputes among private persons. It is unclear to this writer how the equity of the courts of Chancery and Exchequer at this time had anything to do with 'prerogative' governmental rights of the crown or how the Court of Chancery could rightly be called a prerogative court at all.

---

[125] J. H. Baker, 'The Common Lawyers and the Chancery: 1616', *Irish Jurist*, vol. 4, p. 368–392 (1969), rept. in Sir J. Baker, *Collected Papers on English Legal History* (2013), vol. 1, pp. 481–512.

[126] *Bromage v. Genning* (K.B. 1616), 1 Rolle Rep. 368, 81 E.R. 540.

[127] *Cobb v. Moor* (1465), Chancery Cases Middle Ages 130.

[128] *Coulston v. Gardner* (Ch. 1681), 79 Selden Soc. 870, 3 Swanston 279, 36 E.R. 864; D. E. C. Yale, ed., *Lord Nottingham's Manual of Chancery Practice and Prolegomena* (1965), p. 312 'Thus, the question of praemunire stirred by Coke is now in peace and the Chancery out of the statutes'.

C. John Selden

One of the leaders of the next generation of Whigs was John Selden (1584–1654), the famous legal scholar. Charles I was ruling England without consultations with Parliament, and the intention was never again to summon a Parliament into existence. Without legislatively approved new taxes available, the king needed to extend ancient sources of revenue, such as ship money. When the Whigs, now denied their legislative forum, attacked these new measures as illegal, the royal courts were called in to decide the disputes. The royalist party attempted to control the judiciary by placing the common law judges on the short leash of tenure during the pleasure of the king, as the Chancellor had always been.[129] It was against this political background that Selden made his famous jibe comparing the measure of equity to the uncertain length of the chancellor's foot or his conscience. The implication was that the administration of equity was unpredictable and was a matter of the judge's unfettered discretion or whim.

John Selden was quoted as saying:

> Equity is a roguish thing; for [in] law, we have a measure [we can] know what to trust to. Equity is according to the conscience of him that is chancellor, and as that is larger or narrower, so is equity. 'Tis all one as if they should make the standard for the measure we call a foot to be the chancellor's foot; what an uncertain measure this would be.[130]

Selden was too experienced a lawyer to have been serious. It must have been a jest; at worst, it was a distortion in order to discredit the Court of Chancery and the Chancellor, who would have been a royalist. The sitting Lord Chancellor at the time was Lord Coventry (1578–1640), who was a very highly regarded lawyer and judge. It could have been that this jibe was aimed at Bishop John Williams (1582–1650), who was the preceding Chancellor, but who was not trained in the law.

The political, military, and personal defeats of Charles I are well known. As the king, the bishops, and the aristocracy were one by one removed from power, the radicals turned against Oliver Cromwell (1599–1658) and the moderate Puritans, and, in their zeal and ignorance, they attacked the law itself. One of their proposals was to abolish the Court of Chancery. This attack was the low point of equity. This ill-conceived move was referred to a commission set up under Sir Matthew Hale (1609–1676) to study the issue of law reform in

---

[129] A. F. Havighurst, 'The Judiciary and Politics in the Reign of Charles II', *Law Quarterly Review*, vol. 66, p. 62 *et seq.* (1950); A. F. Havighurst, 'James II and the Twelve Men in Scarlet', *Law Quarterly Review*, vol. 69, p. 522 *et seq.* (1953); C. H. McIlwaine, 'The Tenure of English Judges', *American Political Science Review*, vol. 7, p. 217 *et seq.* (1913).

[130] J. Selden, *Table Talk* (F. Pollock, ed., 1927), p. 43.

general, and nothing more was heard of the taking away of the Chancery. This would have been a jurisprudential disaster, and the lawyers in the Long Parliament made sure that the bill met a quiet death in committee. Had it been otherwise, mortgages in default could not have been redeemed, forfeitures and frauds would have gone unchecked, and most of the land of England, which was held in trust, would have ended up in the ownership of a handful of lawyers. During the Interregnum, the Court of Chancery was presided over by a committee of three commissioners, and this assured that it would have no political power. The normal course of equity jurisprudence in the court of Chancery continued unabated during the time of Cromwell.

When the earl of Clarendon was the Lord Chancellor, from 1660 to 1667, he regularly had as judicial assistants judges from the high courts of common law to sit with him in his Court of Chancery, and the Chief Justice of the Court of Common Pleas, Sir Orlando Bridgeman (1608–1674), frequently sat next to him in that capacity. In 1667, Clarendon was replaced in the Court of Chancery by a new Lord Keeper, the highly respected common lawyer and judge, Sir Orlando Bridgeman. And yet Bridgeman also regularly requested the common law judges to assist him in the Court of Chancery. It is interesting to note that one of the best common law judges, when he became an equity judge, felt the need to have assistant judges. This shows that equity and common law were not and are not rivals as to the substantive law.

Since the Middle Ages, the Court of Chancery had been loosely called a court of conscience. Shortly after the removal of Bridgeman, the new Lord Chancellor, Lord Nottingham, put the theory of conscience into its proper perspective when, in *Cook v. Fountain* (1676), he stated that he was not ruling according to the personal conscience of any particular party litigant, himself, or the king but according to the civic conscience of the English legal system. The concept of conscience as administered in the courts of equity is general and institutional; it is to be found in the established practices and precedents of the courts of equity; it applies equally to all persons.

> With such a conscience as is only *naturalis et interna*, this Court [of Chancery] has nothing to do; the conscience by which I [the Lord Chancellor] am to proceed is merely *civilis et politica* and tied to certain measures.[131]

---

[131] *Cook v. Fountain* (Ch. 1676), 73 Selden Soc. 362, 371, 3 Swanston 585, 600, 36 E.R. 984, 990; also D. E. C. Yale, ed., *Lord Nottingham's . . . Prolegomena of Chancery and Equity* (1965), p. 194. Note also the opinion of Sir Francis Bacon: `Uses . . . are guided by conscience, either by the private conscience of the feoffee or the general conscience of the realm, which is Chancery.' J. Spedding, *et al.*, *The Works of Francis Bacon*, `Reading on the Statute of Uses', vol. 7, p. 401 (1872).

Since Lord Nottingham expounded equity doctrine in lucid and rational opinions based on precedent and since his opinions were the first to be systematically composed, he has been called 'the father of equity'.[132]

Referring to the discretion of the equity judge, it was ruled in the eighteenth century as follows, as an example, 'and as it is said in Rook's Case, 5 Rep. 99b,[133] that discretion is a science, not to act arbitrarily according to men's wills and private affections; so the discretion which is executed here is to be governed by the rules of law and equity. . . .'[134] '[I]n equity we must be guided and governed by the rule and reasons of other cases'.[135] The Virginia Supreme Court defined the court's discretion as 'a sound judicial discretion regulated by the established principles of the court'.[136] 'Equity is a complex system of established law and is not merely a reflection of the chancellor's sense of what is just or appropriate.'[137]

The following dialogue from *Fry v. Porter* (Ch. 1670), 1 Modern 300, 307, 86 E.R. 898, 902, is instructive:

> VAUGHAN, Chief Justice: I wonder to hear of citing of precedents in matter of equity, for, if there be equity in a case, that equity is an universal truth, and there can be no precedent in it. So that, in any precedent that can be produced, if it be the same with this case, the reason and equity is the same in itself. And, if the precedent be not the same case with this, it is not to be cited, being not to that purpose.
>
> BRIDGEMAN, Lord Keeper: Certainly, precedents are very necessary and useful to us, for, in them, we may find the reasons of the equity to guide us. And, besides, the authority of those who made them is much to be regarded. We shall suppose they did it upon great consideration and weighing of the matter. And it would be very strange and very ill, if we should disturb and set aside what has been the course for a long series of time and ages.

Throughout the remainder of the seventeenth century and during the eighteenth century, the Court of Chancery was presided over by a series of excellent judges, both as chancellors and as masters of the rolls, most notable Lord Hardwicke (1690–1764).

---

[132] *See generally* D. E. C. Yale, *Lord Nottingham's Chancery Cases* (Selden Soc., vol. 73 for 1954), vol. 1, pp. xxxvii–cxxiv (1957).

[133] *Rooke v. Withers*, 5 Coke Rep. 99, 77 E.R. 209 (1598).

[134] *Cowper v. Earl Cowper* (Ch. 1734), 2 Peere Williams 720, 753, 24 E.R. 930, 942.

[135] *Packington v. Wyche* (Ex. 1709), Equity Cases Exch. 619 at 639.

[136] *Clinchfield Coal Co. v. Powers*, 107 Va. 393, 398, 59 S.E. 370 (1907); *see also City of Richmond v. County of Henrico*, 185 Va. 859, 868, 41 S.E.2d 35 (1947); *Harris v. Harris*, 72 Va. (31 Grattan) 13, 16–17 (1878) (Burks, J., citing Coke and Mansfield).

[137] *Tiller v. Owen*, 243 Va. 176, 179, 413 S.E.2d 51, 53 (1992).

D. Lord Eldon

John Scott, earl of Eldon, (1751–1838) who was the Chancellor during the long and difficult reigns of George III and George IV, the times of a regency and the great Napoleonic wars, was perhaps the most politically conservative and stodgy of all the chancellors of all times. Perhaps this is why he was so viciously attack by the Whigs.

Charles Dickens (1812–1870), a somewhat superficial novelist, pilloried Eldon in the fictitious novel *Bleak House*. This popular book begins with the following description of the Court of Chancery.

> London. Michaelmas term lately over, and the Chancellor sitting in Lincoln's Inn Hall. . . . Fog everywhere. Fog up the river . . . fog down the river. . . . The raw afternoon is rawest, and the dense fog is densest, and the muddy streets are muddiest near . . . Temple Bar. And hard by Temple Bar, in Lincoln's Inn Hall, at the very heart of the fog, sits the Lord High Chancellor in his High Court of Chancery. Never can there come fog too thick, never can there come mud and mire too deep, to assort with the groping and floundering condition which this High Court of Chancery, most pestilent of hoary sinners, holds this day in the sight of heaven and earth.

Whatever slight contacts Dickens may have had with the law in his few months as a solicitor's clerk, he certainly was not a lawyer, and he did not know whether the workings of the Court of Chancery or the doctrines of equity were 'foggy' or not. In any case, the true villain of *Bleak House* was neither the Chancellor nor the solicitors whose fees entirely consumed a very large decedent's estate, but rather it was the very eccentric testator, who made a series of eccentric wills without destroying the earlier ones. In his entirely fictitious novel, Dickens arranges the story so that the testator's several wills are discovered in chronological order so that the necessity to constantly re-open the proceedings increasing the necessary legal fees eventually add up to a sum greater than the value of the estate. This novel is a 'cheap shot'. Unfortunately for the reputation of Lord Eldon, the Court of Chancery, and the principles of equity, the general public has had a hundred and fifty years of mischaracterization and misinformation as to this court and its procedures.

The Whig politicians also had their knives out for Eldon. A commission was appointed to study the delays in the Court of Chancery, which body found intolerable delays and put the blame on Eldon, the other officers of the court, and on the archaic clerical practices of those officers. It is certainly true that the delays in coming to a final judgment in the Court of Chancery at this time were excessive. Eldon replied by putting the blame on the lawyers practicing in his court. It is interesting to note that the lawyers had an acceptable alternative in the Court of Exchequer, but, at this time, the equity practice in the Exchequer was declining, and the practitioners were flocking to the Court of Chancery in spite of the delays.[138]

The Whig politicians were fierce in their attack of Eldon. Walter Bagehot (1826–1877), a glib and impertinent journalist, wrote:

> As for Lord Eldon, it is the most difficult thing in the world to believe that there ever was such a man; it only shows how intense historical evidence is, that no one really doubts it. He believed in everything which it is impossible to believe in — in the danger of Parliamentary Reform, the danger of Catholic Emancipation, the danger of altering the Court of Chancery, the danger of altering the courts of law, the danger of abolishing capital punishment for trivial thefts, the danger of making land-owners pay their debts, the danger of making anything more, the danger of making anything less.[139]

However, Lord Eldon was a very learned and a very good judge. His opinions were carefully reasoned and drafted; many are still cited today. Eldon was judicially conservative, and he felt bound to follow the traditional practices and the established law of the equity courts. Thus, when justice required him to grant a mandatory injunction in the case of *Lane v. Newdigate* (1804)[140] even though no such order had ever been granted before, he felt obliged to disguise it as a prohibitory injunction by phrasing the order as a double negative. Perhaps Eldon's judicial philosophy was caused by Selden's jibe of 150 years before. In *Gee v. Pritchard* (1818), Eldon said 'Nothing would inflict on me greater pain . . . than the recollection that I had done anything to justify the reproach that the equity of this court varies like the Chancellor's foot.'[141] The reproach of the 'chancellor's foot' unfortunately still continues in modern times.[142]

And thus, by the conclusion of Eldon's influential chancellorship, equity had become as rigidly bound by precedent as was the common law. And, indeed, ever since, equitable remedies have been dispensed with the same understanding of precedent and stare decisis as have common law remedies. This will vary according to the judicial philosophy of a particular judge or generation of judges; history shows that the pendulum is always in motion.

---

[138] W. H. Bryson, *The Equity Side of the Exchequer*, pp. 160–166, 168 (1975); H. Horwitz, *Exchequer Equity Records and Proceedings 1649–1841*, pp. 6–7 (2001).

[139] W. Bagehot, 'The First Edinburgh Reviewers' (1855), quoted in C. Woodard, 'Joseph Story and American Equity', *Washington and Lee Law Rev.*, vol. 45, pp. 623, 639–640 (1988).

[140] *Lane v. Newdigate* (Ch. 1804), 10 Vesey 192, 32 E.R. 818.

[141] *Gee v. Pritchard* (1818), 2 Swanston 402 at 414, 36 E.R. 670 at 674.

[142] *E.g. Feuchtenberger v. Williamson*, 137 Va. 578, 585, 120 S.E. 257 (1923); *Marcy v. Graham*, 142 Va. 285, 293, 128 S.E. 550 (1925).

After Lord Eldon's tenure, Parliament added two full-time judges to the Court of Chancery, and the court was able to cope with its work load. In 1873, The Court of Chancery was merged into the new High Court of Justice and, thereby, extinguished.[143]

E. Summary

The conclusion of this section of this essay is that there has arisen over the centuries a false perception of intellectual antagonism between common law and equity. Political disagreements have seriously clouded the legal issues. There is no royalist philosophy in the body of equitable doctrine. The rulings of the judges of the equity courts are not *ex hypothesi* personal, arbitrary, or whimsical. (Of course, some judges are better than others, but the common law courts furnish as many examples of this rule as equity courts.) Modern legal scholars have debunked the origin of equity in the Roman law or the medieval church law, though there was some borrowing from the romano-canonical civil procedure.

The political propaganda of the Whigs as to equity had some serious consequences for the practitioners of the law in eighteenth and nineteenth century America. The English colonies in the south of what is now the United States of America were not troubled by the existence of equity. In Virginia, as one of the guides of Colonial Williamsburg once said, the colonists came with the Crown in one hand and the *Book of Common Prayer* in the other. In Virginia, from the beginning, common law and equity were administered in a single court, though administered separately, as in the English courts of Chancery and Exchequer. In Virginia, from about 1700, most of the disagreements with the crown were compromised successfully until 1776.

However, it was otherwise in the northern colonies which had their origins in religious dissent and anti-royalist or Whig politics. In Massachusetts and Pennsylvania, the Whig mentality led to the establishing of judicial systems that did not include equity courts in any form or the availability of equitable remedies. It is my belief that Whig opinion in colonial America on the subject of trial by jury was also a factor.

The City of London before 1900 because of its wealth had always enjoyed a measure of independence from the king. London, therefore, was one of the centers of Whig opposition to royalist government. The sheriffs of London could and did empanel juries of Whigs when needed, and the Whig juries in effect nullified the king's law in the prosecutions against William Penn (1644–1718) for being a practicing Quaker and John Wilkes (1725–1797) for seditious libel. In New York, a common law jury refused to convict John Peter Zenger (1697–1746) of libeling the governor of New York. (It is interesting to note that Zenger's case arose out of his public opposition in the press to the governor's attempt to

---

[143] The Judicature Act of 1873, 36 & 37 Vict., c. 66.

establish himself as the sole equity judge for the colony of New York.) All three of these men were clearly guilty, but the juries acquitted them for political reason in the disregard of the evidence. All three cases were important landmarks in the development of civil liberties and Whig political theories, but it is to be noted that these were criminal prosecutions, with which the courts of equity have nothing to do.

Trial by jury was not part of equity procedure, but the judge was the sole trier of fact, though his fact finding might be aided by masters in Chancery and special verdicts upon issues out of Chancery. To Whigs with no legal training, the lack of trial by jury in the courts of equity was thought to be royalist and undemocratic. However, the equity of redemption and the specific performance of contracts, for example, have nothing to do with politics. Moreover, neither crimes nor libel, seditious or private, come within the jurisdiction of the courts of equity. It took years of legislation and judicial legerdemain in the early nineteenth century in Massachusetts and Pennsylvania to supply seriously needed equitable remedies.

Of all these misunderstandings, perhaps the most pernicious in the long run was Selden's casual jest at dinner over a bottle of wine (or two) about the indeterminacy of equity jurisprudence.

III. The Indeterminacy of the Chancellor's Foot

'The Realists demonstrated that such principles [*i.e.*, coherent legal principles of general applicability] were always contradictory, that for every principle there existed a potential counter-principle, and that ultimately a methodology that assumed the autonomy, permanence, or objectivity of legal rules was incoherent. Having perfected that critique, Realist scholarships seemed a little at a loss as to what to do next. Some realists rested on what they took to be the inevitably contradictory or subjective nature of legal decision making and embraced nihilism.'[144]

John Selden's jibe of the Chancellor's indeterminate foot echoes even in today's legal mythology,[145] and the Legal Realists extended the myth from equity to the basic common law itself.[146]

That equity is more liable to the accusation of indeterminacy than the common law is the result of the principles of the common law having been established earlier in history than those of equity. Moreover, the very origin of equity

---

[144] G. Edward White, 'The Inevitability of Critical Legal Studies', *Stanford Law Review*, vol. 36, pp. 649 at 651 (1984).

[145] *E.g. Feuchtenberger v. Williamson*, 137 Va. 578, 585, 120 S.E. 257 (1923); *Marcy v. Graham*, 142 Va. 285, 293, 128 S.E. 550 (1925).

[146] White, *supra*.

jurisprudence was the determinacy of the English common law in the middle ages, a determinacy to an unacceptable degree. The remedies of the common law became so settled, fixed, rigid, and determinate that the judges lacked the flexibility adequately to deal with new social problems. Thus, a court of equity was established within the king's Chancery to supplement and complement the common law in the administration of justice.[147] The common law of England, as we know it today, dates from the reign of Henry I (1100–1135) and its records from that of Richard I (1190–1199). The equity side of the Court of Chancery dates from the reign of Richard II (1377–1399), but proper official records of decrees and orders were not begun until 1536. Thus, before about 1400, the development of the law took place in the courts of common law, and, from then until about 1800, it took place in the courts of equity. After 1800 and certainly after the Reform Act of 1832,[148] law reform was done legislatively. In the United States, law reform through legislation began earlier, in 1776, when the English law had to be reconsidered in the light of secession from the British Empire.[149]

The expression law reform is traditional among scholars, but the expression law development, being broader, is preferable for the comments that are to follow. Reform implies error; development implies incompleteness. Most, perhaps all, of equity jurisprudence is a matter of growth to supplement, to complete, and to fine-tune the common law. It is a matter of keeping the law up to date with current economic, social, and political matters. To be out of date is not to be mistaken, false, or evil.

When new situations arise as time marches relentlessly on and as new problems occur, the law relating thereto is indeterminate. And the law remains thus until the bench and bar wrestle the new problems to the ground and make it determinate. The legal profession or the legislature has to address the new problem and determine how the law will address it. Thus, is the law developed, defined, or refined. Some problems are easy, some are difficult, and some may be of such philosophic depth or social complexity that they may never be solved.

But in the courts of equity, as in the courts of common law and in the legislature, many legal problems, great and small, have been solved over the centuries. Much has been firmly and finally laid to rest as clear and established legal doctrine.[150]

---

[147] See *supra*.

[148] The Reform Act of 1832, 2 & 3 Will. IV, c. 45.

[149] See *e.g.* C. T. Cullen, 'Completing the Revisal of the Laws in Post-Revolutionary Virginia.' *Virginia Magazine of History and Biography* (1974), vol. 82, pp. 84–99; K. Preyer, 'Crime, the Criminal Law, and Reform in Post-Revolutionary Virginia,' *Law and History Review* (1983), vol. 1, pp. 53–85, rept. in K. L. Hall, ed., *Crime and Criminal Law* (1987), pp. 653–685.

[150] Factual indeterminacy is a completely different issue that cannot be allowed to deflect our attention from the issue at hand or to muddy the waters. Forgetful and dis-

Why, then, has equity been stigmatized with the myth of the chancellor's indeterminate foot and the common law and legislation not been (except for the cynical nihilism of legal realism)? Legal development by the legislative process is expected to be definitive and not explanatory. Legislation is the declared will of the sovereign and the community. However, the common law appears to be more settled and determinate for several reasons.

First, it is older, and there has thus been more time to settle it.

Second, equity appears unsettled because of the lack of good reports of equity cases before the last third of the seventeenth century and the lack of a sufficient quantity before the last third of the eighteenth century.[151] Also, the official records only go back to 1536.

The importance of written legal precedents cannot be overstated. What is in writing is known to a wider legal audience. It is more definite and fixed than the oral tradition. It is a better basis for discussion and debate, distinction and dissent.

If the law was being developed primarily in the courts of equity from the fifteenth to the nineteenth centuries, why were there so many common law reports and so few equity reports?

The reason often given is that equity is in the discretion of the judge and it is thus not consistent, and thus one case is not reliable as precedent for another. This argument assumes with Selden that equity is the whim of the judge rather than a series of legal principles. If it were the former, equity would not be consistent or predictable, and parties would not have submitted their disputes to such courts. Arbitration would have been used, being quicker and cheaper. Moreover, justice requires like results in like cases. Equity jurisprudence from its inception consisted of agreed-upon principles which were part of an overarching system of justice.

It has also been suggested that equity cases are too fact-specific to be useful precedents. As a general rule, it is true that suits in equity are more likely to be factually complicated than actions at law. This is so because the doctrines of common law were settled at an earlier period of time when life was less complex. Equity arose to address new problems and to sort out situations that were beyond the capabilities of the courts of common law with their fact-finding being done by juries of uneducated laymen. Also points of evidence of facts were argued to and decided by the equity judge in open court rather than to a jury in the country. However complicated the facts of a particular case in equity may be and even though the equity judge may spend much explanation on the facts of the case,

---

honest witnesses do not affect the law itself, only the administration of the law.

[151] By the end of the eighteenth century, the chancellorship of Lord Eldon, equity jurisprudence was as firmly boxed in by precedent as the common law was in the fifteenth century. This was due partially to the large quantity of equity reports in print and partially to Eldon's conservative nature.

the legal principles applicable to those facts are precedents useful to future lawyers and judges and are well worth reporting and studying and citing in future litigation.

Until the late seventeenth century, when the English bar began to specialize, barristers and serjeants practiced in all of the courts, both equity and common law. However, students of the law concentrated their studies on the common law rather than equity. In the seventeenth century and earlier, the common law, and especially the procedure of the common law, being older, was more complicated and difficult to learn. Therefore, it was the tradition, and an ancient tradition at that, for law students to sit in on the courts of common law. The Court of Common Pleas even had a table reserved for them. (It was popularly called 'The Crib.') While in court, the students took notes of the cases they heard and that evening wrote out their notes as reports of cases. These reports are the yearbooks and reports, manuscript and printed, that have survived to the present. Since the students did not sit in on the courts of Chancery and Exchequer, their opinions were not recorded in the same quantity. Also, since the bar of the King's Bench was larger than that of the other courts, there was a greater sales target for the booksellers who, in the period before 1800, chose which law reports to publish.

The lack of law reports retarded the discussion and analysis and development of equity principles. Without reports, there could be no abridgements; without abridgements, the writing of treatises would be difficult. Without a written literature, debate and development is limited to memory of the oral tradition, and this is not as good as can be.

If all law were indeterminate, there would be anarchy, *i.e.*, no law. Yet we know that the rule of law exists in most nations.

If one looks at appellate court cases, there appears to be some amount of indeterminacy even though the judges there are usually very satisfied with their statements of the law; they rarely believe that the cases before them are indeterminate and that they are creating new law.

And at the trial court level, the law is even more settled and clear to all participants and observers, and the problem is to apply the settled law to the facts of the case or to decide what the facts are. Factual indeterminacy is not a reflection on the law or the legal system.

At the bottom of the court system are the state courts for small claims. The vast bulk of the total number of suits are filed in these courts, and in the vast majority of these cases, the defendants fail to appear and the judgment goes for the plaintiff by default. This is so because neither the law nor the facts are indeterminate. The defendant owes a just debt to the plaintiff, and that is that. Thus, in the vast majority of lawsuits, the law is not in any way indeterminate or unpredictable. (The plaintiff creditor is forced to sue in order to avoid the claim's being barred by the statute of limitations.) In fact, the law in most cases of legal dispute, both in court and out of court, is well settled, clear and obvious to all, predictable, and determinate. Thus, most people do what they should and what the law requires.

Contested cases are a small percentage of cases filed. These cases are those where a party is acting in bad faith, either through malice or playing for more time, where the facts are in dispute, and where there is a disagreement over the applicable law.

At the cutting edge, the law is indeterminate, and this is where the practice and study of the law is exciting. This is what legal academics talk about, but it is not what most judges get to do. Only appellate judges who have the ability to limit their cases can dwell exclusively on unsettled points of law and, hopefully, determine and settle them. Also, law teachers can assign their students to learn the settled law on their own outside of class and then spend the class time discussing indeterminate law on the fringes of definition. But the classroom, while intellectually stimulating, is not a good reflection of reality. The perception of the law as indeterminate comes also from the fact that the law is expounded by imperfect jurists, argued by imperfect lawyers, and administered by judges, who being but human are also imperfect. If lawyers, judges, and legal scholars were closer to perfection, the determinacy of the law would be more apparent.

Law is determinate, and, so far as it is indeterminate, it is not law; it may be in the process of becoming settled and thus becoming law. But there is much settled and determinate law, and the observable existence of civilization, especially commerce in daily life, proves it. However, the law cannot become totally determinate until society ceases to grow and to change.

So far as the law is indeterminate it is not law or, at least, not yet law. If a court's holding is reasonably predictable, it is not indeterminate (though the facts may be). If the judge is in error, this is the fault of the judge, not the law; and judges are human and thus imperfect.

If the law of the equity courts is or ever was indeterminate or whimsical, litigants would not have taken their cases there; it would be as unpredictable and unsatisfactory for plaintiffs as for defendants. The popularity of the courts of equity proves that they were not unpredictable or it shows that the courts of common law were truly atrocious (which this writer believes they were not).

We do not know the context of Selden's remark, but he was an astute jurist; he must have been jesting.

To conclude this section, we might compare the law to a tree. The law, like a tree, has a solid, established, and unchanging core, the trunk. Outside is the living, changing, indeterminate part, the bark, that will in due course become fixed as an additional ring to the solid core. Both the law and the tree grow by taking the new and indeterminate parts and settling them into determinate, reliable parts. The indeterminacy of the new problems of human life is a part of the process of settling the law for the use of future generations. But so far as the law is not yet settled and determinate, it is not yet law.

IV. The Common Law and the Equity Thereof

The common law of England, the technical rules and the policy and intent thereof, began with the judges, when presented with a legal dispute, finding and then declaring the law that was applicable to that case at hand. This was and is a precedent for future guidance. Law finding starts off as inductive reasoning from general natural law principles. Whether one finds these principles by using theology or secular humanism does not matter. What matters is that these principles are external ones.[152] Once the law has been found and stated, the application and practice of the law is deductive from the legal precedents. As society, politics, and the economy change, there continues to be a need for the inductive legal process to meet the new situation that has not been previously dealt with judicially. But, where social changes occur that make the declared and settled law to be no longer appropriate, it is the constitutional function of the legislature of the sovereignty to amend it, not the judiciary. Such persons made the law we call the positive law. If the judiciary legislates, the rule of law is destroyed. The courts must be able to enforce the rule of law against the sovereignty in order to protect human rights against the sovereignty. A human right I take to be such a right of every individual that can and should be asserted against everyone else, collectively and individually. If the judiciary is under the control of or part of the sovereignty, it cannot have the independence to enforce the rule of law, but it becomes a part of the rule of men, whether for good or evil.

One hears it argued that, since the judges made the law, they can change it. But the fallacy of this position is that the judges did not make the law; they found and declared the pre-existing law. Having found the law, they cannot change it. To do so would be unfair, as it would upset expectations that may have been reasonably relied upon. Also, to do so would be an unconstitutional usurpation of the legislative power of government. When the judges legislate, they act *ultra vires* and improperly. Whether the positive law, as declared by the judges or the legislature or the prince, is good or bad, virtuous or evil, depends on its congruence with the natural law.

Perhaps the equity of the common law is similar to the ancient philosophical concepts of *aequitas* or *epieikeia*[153] or the Christian ideas of a personal con-

---

[152] To deny the existence of natural law of any sort is to deny the existence of anything super-natural, *i.e.* outside of human experience. This is atheism. It is the denial of rationality, causation, and purpose. It is a belief in irrationality, chaos, and nothingness. But we daily experience order, system, causation, and meaningfulness. Atheism is a belief that requires a leap of faith that this writer cannot make. I believe in something, a something that is external to physical nature, and this something includes natural law.

[153] See generally C. St. German, *Doctor and Student*, edd. T. F. T. Plucknett and J. L. Barton, Selden Soc., vol. 91 (1974); E. Hake, *Epeiekeia: A Discourse of Equity*, ed. D. E. C. Yale (1953).

science.[154] However, it appears to this writer that it arose in the medieval courts of England as a matter of local necessity and developed there by trial and error over the centuries, and this was without any reference to *a priori* jurisprudential or theoretical theories. Certainly, the reports of the cases argued in court make no reference to such theories.

Because the courts of Common Pleas and King's Bench became bound by the established rules of law and could not, would not, and did not grant remedies against the government for legal wrongs done to private persons, the Court of Chancery did. The strict common law rules of procedure were supplemented by petitions. This is the Latin or common law side of the court.

Because the courts of Common Pleas and King's Bench became bound by the established rules of law and could not, would not, and did not reform and improve the substantive and procedural law, most importantly the law in relation to contracts, the Court of Chancery did by petitions. Equity bills of complaint are in the nature of petitions. By getting around the established rules of procedure and evidence, the Court of Chancery was able to reform the substance of the common law of England by building on the foundation and refining it. This is the English or equity side of the court.

Thus, the Court of Chancery is a court of the common law of England, one of the royal courts of the kings of England. In the middle ages, the judges of the Common Pleas and the King's Bench are constantly present in the Court of Chancery as advisors to the chancellors on the law, and cases involving questions of fact are always in common law disputes and sometimes in equity disputes sent to the King's Bench for a trial by a jury. The chancellors regularly sent difficult points of law to the common law community of judges and serjeants assembled in the Exchequer Chamber for debate and advice.[155] There was no separate, specialized Chancery bar before 1660; before then, the lawyers appeared on behalf of their clients in courts of common law and equity as their clients' needs required. And, after 1660, many lawyers practiced in any and all of the courts of England. And thus it is today.

The common law of England, as practiced in the many nations of the world that presently or formerly were associated with the kingdom of England, consists of natural law and positive law. The natural law is the ideal law, which theologians and philosophers study and debate. The positive law is the law that is found and applied by jurists in the courts and made and applied by politicians in the legislatures. Jurists and politicians, being human, do not always come to the correct result in accord with the natural law, sometimes with unfortunate results. But, for the most part, the positive law of England has been worked out over

---

[154] D. R. Klinck, *Conscience, Equity, and the Court of Chancery in Early Modern England* (2010).

[155] For many early examples, see W. H. Bryson, ed., *Reports of Cases in the Court of Chancery Cases in the Middle Ages (1325–1508)* (2016).

the centuries into a constructive and useful legal system. Equity is a part of the systematic positive common law of England. It starts with the common law and perfects it. It is the external natural law that defines the goodness of the local positive law. The role of equity is to improve of the common law of England and to bring it closer to the natural law, the theoretical perfect law, which is the desire of all persons of good will.

After studying the law reports of equity cases, it is my observation that, in substance, equity is a part of the common law of England, that part which corrects and fine-tunes the general principles. This is described by Aristotle in his observations of the administration of the law of his own time.[156] However, the English legal profession was not consciously following Aristotle. It was a natural phenomenon, universally applicable, evolving through many centuries of trial and error. What the students of the English common law call equity is a part of and inherent in the common law, even though it be administered in separate-jurisdiction courts or fused-jurisdiction courts or merged-jurisdiction courts. The courts of equity as well as the courts of common law developed incrementally the substantive law of England.

On the other hand, equity procedure evolved as a separate system from that of the common law courts, the Common Pleas and the King's Bench. Again, this was an evolution that was the result of many centuries of trial and error. Certainly, equity procedure took ideas from the procedures of the English common law courts and the European canon law courts. However, the result is a system unique to the equity courts of England. And thus, the English courts of equity came to administer the equity of the common law of England by means of a procedure that was unique to themselves.

Thus, the division in English jurisprudence between common law and equity is more procedural and jurisdictional, but less substantive.

The royal instructions that accompanied the first charter of the Virginia Company in 1606 stated that disputes in Virginia should be settled by 'the common laws of England and the equity thereof'.[157] The word 'equity' was used there as it was used in the expression of the equity of a statute. The above thoughts are what was intended by this phrase.

And further this deponent saith not.

---

[156] Lord Eldon also was of this conclusion. He said that "equity is invariably that which the law intends" and "equity only `supplies the deficiencies of the law'." M. Johnson and J. Oldham, "Law versus Equity -- as reflected in Lord Eldon's Manuscripts", *Am. Jour. of Legal Hist.*, vol. 58, pp. 208 at 222, 224–225 (2018).

[157] *Hening's Statutes*, vol. 1, p. 68.

Table of Cases Reported

[These references are to case numbers, not page numbers.]

Acland v. Atwell	89
Adler ads. Clovell	295
Alisbury v. Troughton	180
Amby v. Gower	320
Anthill ads. Jolly	146
Aprice ads. Owen	44
Arnold v. Barrington	121
Arundel v. Arundel	174
Arundel v. Trevillian	171
Arundel, Lord ads. Bidlake	181
Ashton, Lady v. Ashton	298
Askwith v. Chamberlain	242
Atkins v. Temple	6
Atwell ads. Acland	89
Austen ads. Hungerford	296
Ayliffe v. Duke	319
Ayloff ads. Stoit	134
Aynsworth v. Pollard	185
Barnstable, Case of	64
Batt v. Hughes	323
Batt ads. Kinseman	279
Barkley v. Southcot	260
Baldwin ads. Naylor	239
Baldwin v. Procter	193
Bales v. Procter	248
Barker v. Norton	58
Barker v. Zouch	80
Barne's Case	160
Barrington ads. Arnold	121
Barrow ads. Jackson	10
Bates v. Micklethwait	170
Baugh ads. Jones	254

Bennett ads. Mayor of London	92
Bentley ads. Bracken	201
Bery v. Burlace	229
Best ads. West Ham Parishioners	331
Bidlake v. Lord Arundel	181
Bishop v. Bishop	247
Bishop ads. Middleton	330
Blackston v. Hemsworth Hospital	207
Blackstone v. Martin	3
Blackwell v. Redman	173
Blodwell ads. Sands	208
Booth v. Booth	49
Booth v. Peckover	243
Bourman v. Wild	245
Bradshaw ads. Meechett	148
Brereton ads. Plunket	5
Bretton v. Bretton	284
Bristol, Mayor of v. Whitson	147
Bracken v. Bentley	201
Bramble v. Havering Paupers	232
Brockett ads. Martin	267
Bromsal ads. Orlibar	309
Brooke, Lord v. Lord Goring	55
Broughton ads. Neville	255
Brownhill ads. Smith	303
Brown ads. Cox	324
Brown v. Thetford	39
Brownlow ads. Town of Market Rasen	179
Buller v. Cheverton	25
Burlace ads. Bery	229
Burman ads. Clench	294
Burton ads. Havers	38
Burwell v. Horner	85
Bury ads. Wood	81
Byard ads. Pratt	282
Byat v. Pickering	169
Cage ads. Regis	190
Caldwell v. Wheat	175
Capel ads. Wiseman	204
Carew ads. Hunt	287
Carlisle, Earl of v. Gobe	335
Carpenter v. Tucker	164
Carr, Lady ads. Hale	218

Cary ads. Thynn	228
Chamberlain ads. Askwith	242
Chamberlaine ads. Nichols	277
Chambers ads. King	293
Champernon v. Champernon	120
Chancey ads. Gorges	234
Charnock ads. Fleetwood	71
Cheverton ads. Buller	25
Chipping Sudbury Case	62
Church ads. Greenhill	189
Church v. Roper	246
Clark ads. Morgan	79
Clarke v. Southcott	311
Clench v. Burman	294
Clerke ads. Anonymous	138
Clobery ads. Rigault	150
Clovell v. Adler	295
Cole ads. Isham	237
Cole v. Peyson	196
Coles v. Emerson	163
Compton ads. Farmer	4
Connock v. Rowe	84
Cooper v. Tragonwel	334
Coply ads. Ingram	313
Copping ads. Grinston	46
Cordell v. Limbry	281
Cornwallis, Viscount v. Savage	37
Cosin v. Young	252
Cotton v. Heath	219
Cowley v. Patron	322
Cox v. Brown	324
Crips ads. May	272
Crook ads. Magdalen College	240
Crouch v. Worcester Citizens	9
Daniell ads. Hulse	59
Darnell ads. Fanshawe	312
Darston ads. Morris	178
Davenport ads. Tanfield	221
Davis v. Higford	41
Davy ads. Feltham	182
Day ads. Pope	183
Dean ads. Leach	257
Dennis v. Nourse	195

Denton v. Denton	305
Derby, Earl of ads. Kinaston	17
Desmond ads. Popham	241
Devaux ads. Hatred	336
Dinham ads. Perryman	264
Dirlton, Countess of ads. Duchess of Hamilton	317
Dorwell v. Dorwell	289
Drapers' Company ads. Hale	285
Drury v. Drury	94
Duke ads. Ayliffe	319
Duncombe ads. Hawton	56
Dymand v. Walton	176
East Grinstead, Case of	139
East Grinstead Paupers v. Howard	128
Edmonds ads. Gwynn	250
Edwards ads. Whitehorn	326
Egerton v. Egerton	136
Eltham Inhabitants ads. Warreyn	155
Emerson ads. Coles	163
Emery ads. Porter	192
Emmanuel College v. Evans	8
Evans ads. Emmanuel College	8
Eyre v. Wortley	28
Eyres v. Eyres	13
Eyres v. Taunton	142
Fachell v. Lassells	86
Fanshawe v. Darnell	312
Farmer v. Compton	4
Feltham v. Davy	182
Fermier v. Maund	211
Ferrers v. Ferrers	43
Fish v. Seaman	35
Flatman ads. Snelling	122
Fleetwood v. Charnock	71
Fletcher ads. Sibson	133
Floyer v. Strackley	129
Ford ads. Hartwell	184
Ford v. Stobridge	249
Fotherby ads. Mauter	158
Game v. Hoe	40
Garrett ads. Miller	300
Gawle v. Lake	72
Geofrey v. Thorn	172

Gesling ads. Giles	99
Gifford v. Gifford	73
Gilbie ads. Tuphorne	77
Giles v. Gesling	99
Gillingham Parishioners ads. Hide	34
Gird v. Togood	253
Glascock ads. Peacock	93
Gobe ads. Earl of Carlisle	335
Goddard v. Goddard	244
Good v. Merton College	21
Goodwin v. Goodwin	329
Gorges v. Chancey	234
Gorges ads. Perriman	23
Goring, Lord ads. Lord Brooke	55
Goslin ads. Ramsey	97
Gower ads. Amby	320
Green ads. Peyton	256
Green ads. Symonds	143
Greenhill v. Church	189
Grenville ads. Earl of Suffolk	10
Gresham v. Gresham	301
Grey ads. Maggeridge	266
Grinston v. Copping	46
Gwynn v. Edmonds	250
Hale v. Carr	218
Hale v. Drapers' Company	285
Hales v. Hales	194
Hall ads. Okeham	2
Hall ads. Winchcomb	78
Hallam v. Hellam	52
Hamilton, Duchess of v. Countess of Dirlton	317
Hammond v. Shaw	310
Hampson v. Lady Sydenham	308
Harding v. Countess of Suffolk	135
Harris ads. St. Nicholas	262
Harrison v. Lucas	236
Harrison v. Slegge	22
Hartwell v. Ford	184
Harvey ads. Merrick	288
Harvey ads. Vendal	137
Hatred v. Devaux	336
Hatton, Lady v. Jay	212
Havering Paupers ads. Bramble	232

Havers v. Burton	38
Hawton v. Duncombe	56
Hayn v. Nelson	199
Heath ads. Cotton	219
Hemsworth Hospital ads. Blackston	207
Henshaw v. Pye	51
Herbert v. Herbert	302
Herbert v. Lownes	32
Herne ads. Ricksers	27
Hicks v. Kilby	30
Hide v. Gillingham Parishioners	34
Higford ads. Davis	41
Hilton ads. Windsor	12
Hinchman ads. Press	259
Hinton ads. Minn	145
Hody v. Lunn	53
Hoe ads. Game	40
Holmixon v. Lemman	299
Hopgood ads. Longman	31
Hopton ads. Smith	270
Horner v. Burwell	85
Horwood v. Rolle	307
Houghton ads. Sherbourn	224
How v. Vigures	45
Howard ads. East Grinstead Paupers	128
Howson v. Martin	20
Hubbart ads. Wroughton	210
Huddlestone v. Huddlestone	124
Huddlestone v. Lamplugh	76
Hughes ads. Batt	323
Huland ads. Woodward	186
Hulse v. Daniell	59
Hungate's Case	19
Hungerford v. Austen	296
Hunt v. Carew	287
Huntington, Lord ads. Moor	90
Hutchings v. Strode	159
Hyde ads. Markall	24
Inglett ads. Rowe	140
Ingram's Case	50
Ingram v. Coply	313
Ireland v. Payne	205
Isham v. Cole	237

Table of Cases Reported lxiii

Jackson v. Barrow	10
Jackson ads. Middleton	74
Jay ads. Lady Hatton	212
Jenney ads. Offley	278
Jennings ads. Pennyman	11
Jernegan v. Palmer	83
Jervis v. Maynard	328
Jolly v. Anthill	146
Jones v. Baugh	254
Jones ads. Thomas	314
Joyce v. Osborne	268
Keck v. Sayers	318
Keeling ads. Pickering	258
Kennedy v. Lady Vanlore	153
Keynell ads. Palmer	213
Kilby ads. Hicks	30
Kinaston v. Earl of Derby	17
King v. Chambers	293
Kington Inhabitants ads. Pember	231
Kinman ads. Morton	286
Kinseman v. Batt	279
Kirby ads. Marsh	161
Lake ads. Gawle	72
Lake v. Lake	162
Lake v. Phillips	152
Lake v. Prigeon	149
Lamplugh ads. Huddlestone	76
Lancaster ads. Popham	191
Langham ads. Lymbree	276
Lasbrook v. Tyler	91
Lassells ads. Fachell	86
Leach v. Dean	257
Leigh v. Winter	222
Lemman ads. Holmixon	299
Levington v. Wotton	125
Lewis v. Owen	206
Limbry ads. Cordell	281
Lippiat v. Neville	251
London Mayor's Case	233
London, Mayor of v. Bennett	92
Longman v. Hopgood	31
Lownes ads. Herbert	32
Lucas ads. Harrison	236

Lucas v. Pennington	69
Lunn ads. Hody	53
Lyddal v. Vanlore	16
Lymbree v. Langham	276
Magdalen College v. Crook	240
Maggeridge v. Grey	266
Markall v. Hyde	24
Market Rasen, Town of v. Brownlow	179
Marsh v. Kirby	161
Marston v. Marston	131
Marston v. Marston	225
Martin ads. Blackstone	3
Martin v. Brockett	267
Martin ads. Howson	20
Matthews v. Thomas	291
Maund ads. Fermier	211
Maundy v. Maundy	226
Mauter v. Fotherby	158
May v. Crips	272
Maynard ads. Jervis	328
Maynard v. Lord Middleton	130
Meechett v. Bradshaw	148
Mere v. Mere	273
Merrick v. Harvey	288
Merton College v. Good	21
Micklethwait ads. Bates	170
Middleton v. Bishop	330
Middleton v. Jackson	74
Middleton, Lord ads. Maynard	130
Miller v. Garrett	300
Mills v. Mills	214
Minn v. Hinton	145
Mitchell ads. Tryon	197
Moor v. Lord Huntington	90
Moor v. Lady Somerset	315
Moor ads. Wright	274
Moore v. Row	48
Morgan v. Clark	79
Morgan v. Seymour	215
Morpeth, Mayor of ads. Henshaw	51
Morris v. Darston	178
Morton v. Kinman	286
Mostian v. Nurse	202

Table of Cases Reported

Moulton ads. Powell	18
Mouse v. Mouse	290
Moyle v. Lord Roberts	70
Nash v. Preston	88
Naylor v. Baldwin	239
Nele's Case	100
Nelson ads. Hayn	199
Nelson v. Nelson	36
Neville v. Broughton	255
Neville ads. Lippiat	251
Newburgh, Lord ads. Rowe	227
Newcastle, Earl of v. Earl of Suffolk	95
Newell v. Ward	188
Nicholls v. Chamberlaine	277
Nightingale ads. Theobalds	304
Norgate v. Pinder	15
North ads. Thomas	265
Northey ads. Smith	283
Norton ads. Barker	58
Norwood v. Norwood	216
Nott v. Smithies	167
Nottingham, Countess of ads. Countess of Peterborough	57
Nottingham, Earl of v. Countess of Nottingham	57
Nottingham, Earl of ads. Countess of Suffolk	102
Nourse ads. Dennis	195
Nurse ads. Mostian	202
Offley v. Jenney	278
Okeham v. Hall	2
Orlibar v. Bromsal	309
Osborne ads. Joyce	268
Owen v. Aprice	44
Owen ads. Lewis	206
Peacock v. Glascock	93
Peacock v. Thewer	220
Peckover ads. Booth	243
Pember v. Kington Inhabitants	231
Pennington ads. Lucas	69
Pennyman v. Jennings	11
Pensterd v. Pavior	230
Perriman v. Gorges	23
Perryman v. Dinham	264
Peter v. Rich	75
Peterborough, Countess of v. Countess of Nottingham	57

Petty v. Styward	127
Peyson ads. Cole	196
Peyton v. Green	256
Pickering ads. Byat	169
Pickering v. Keeling	258
Pinder ads. Norgate	15
Pix ads. Vintner	217
Plomer v. Lady Plomer	151
Plunket v. Brereton	5
Pollard ads. Aynsworth	185
Pool v. Pool	7
Pope v. Day	183
Popham v. Desmond	241
Popham v. Lancaster	191
Porter v. Emery	192
Porter ads. Thomas	271
Powell v. Moulton	18
Pratt v. Byard	282
Press v. Hinchman	259
Preston ads. Nash	88
Prigeon ads. Lake	149
Procter ads. Baldwin	193
Procter ads. Bales	248
Pye ads. Henshaw	51
Palmer ads. Jernegan	83
Palmer v. Keynell	213
Parkhurst ads. Woodford Inhabitants	261
Parr ads. Wynn	316
Patron ads. Cowley	322
Pavior ads. Pensterd	230
Payne ads. Ireland	205
Rallison ads. Welden	325
Ramsey v. Goslin	97
Ramsey ads. Sambroke	203
Redman ads. Blackwell	173
Revet v. Rowe	166
Rex v. Cage	190
Rigault v. Clobery	150
Rich ads. Peter	75
Ricksers v. Herne	27
Rippon v. Thornton	63
Roberts, Lord ads. Moyle	70
Robsart v. Turton	209

Rolle ads. Horwood	307
Roper ads. Church	246
Roper ads. Wiseman	275
Row ads. Moore	48
Rowe ads. Connock	84
Rowe v. Inglett	140
Rowe v. Lord Newburgh	227
Rowe ads. Revet	166
Rugby School Case	14
Rutland, Earl of ads. Willoughby	235
St. John v. Wareham	177
St. Nicholas v. Harris	262
Sambroke v. Ramsey	203
Sands v. Blodwell	208
Savage ads. Viscount Cornwallis	37
Savile, Lady v. Savile	165
Savile, Lord v. Standish	332
Sayers ads. Keck	318
Scott v. Wray	168
Seaman ads. Fish	35
Seymour ads. Morgan	215
Seymour v. Twyford Paupers	156
Shaw ads. Hammond	310
Shea v. Smith	327
Sherborne ads. Townley	144
Sherbourn v. Houghton	224
Sherburn Inhabitants' Case	19
Sibson v. Fletcher	133
Sidley, Lady, Case of	280
Slegge ads. Harrison	22
Smith v. Brownhill	303
Smith v. Hopton	270
Smith v. Northey	283
Smith ads. Shea	327
Smith v. Smith	198
Smith v. Valence	321
Smithies ads. Nott	167
Snelling v. Flatman	122
Somerset, Lady ads. Moor	315
Southby ads. Yate	26
Southcot ads. Barkley	260
Southcot v. Southcot	200
Southcott ads. Clarke	311

Spyer v. Spyer	123
Standish ads. Lord Savile	332
Stanhope ads. Thompson	269
Stobridge ads. Ford	249
Stoit v. Ayloff	134
Strackley ads. Floyer	129
Strode ads. Hutchings	159
Styward ads. Petty	127
Suffolk, Countess of ads. Harding	135
Suffolk, Countess of v. Earl of Nottingham	102
Suffolk, Earl of v. Grenville	101
Suffolk, Earl of ads. Earl of Newcastle	95
Sutton Colefield Case	187
Swain ads. Underwood	292
Swain v. Wall	263
Sydenham, Lady ads. Hampson	308
Symonds v. Green	143
Swame ads. Turberville	103
Tanfield v. Davenport	221
Tanfield ads. Warmstrey	42
Taunton ads. Eyres	142
Temple ads. Atkins	6
Theobalds v. Nightingale	304
Thetford ads. Brown	39
Thewer ads. Peacock	220
Thin v. Thin	297
Thomas v. Jones	314
Thomas ads. Matthews	291
Thomas v. North	265
Thomas v. Porter	271
Thompson v. Stanhope	269
Thorn ads. Geofrey	172
Thornton ads. Rippon	63
Throgmorton v. Wagstaff	132
Thynn v. Cary	228
Togood ads. Gird	253
Townley v. Sherborne	144
Towse v. Trevilian	306
Tragonwell ads. Cooper	334
Trevilian ads. Towse	306
Trivillian ads. Arundel	171
Troughton ads. Alisbury	180
Tryon v. Mitchell	197

Tucker ads. Carpenter	164
Tuphorne v. Gilbie	77
Turberville v. Swame	103
Turton ads. Robsart	209
Twyford Paupers ads. Seymour	156
Tyler ads. Lasbrook	91
Underwood v. Swain	292
Valence ads. Smith	321
Vanlore ads. Lyddal	16
Vanlore, Lady ads. Kennedy	153
Vendal v. Harvey	137
Vigures ads. How	45
Vintner v. Pix	217
Wagstaff ads. Throgmorton	132
Walden, Lord, Case of	110
Wall ads. Swain	263
Walthamstow Paupers' Case	47
Walton ads. Dymand	176
Ward ads. Newell	188
Wareham ads. St. John	177
Warmstrey v. Tanfield	42
Warreyn v. Eltham Inhabitants	155
Weldon v. Rallison	325
Wentworth v. Young	223
West Ham Parishioners v. Best	331
Wheat ads. Caldwell	175
Whitehorn v. Edwards	326
Whitson ads. Mayor of Bristol	147
Wild ads. Bourman	245
Willoughby v. Earl of Rutland	235
Winchcomb v. Hall	78
Winchester, Bishop of v. Wolgar	54
Windsor v. Hilton	12
Wingfield's Case	29
Winter ads. Leigh	222
Wiseman v. Capel	204
Wiseman v. Roper	275
Wiveliscombe, Case of	65
Wolgar ads. Bishop of Winchester	54
Wood v. Bury	81
Woodford Inhabitants v. Parkhurst	261
Woodward v. Huland	186
Worcester Citizens ads. Crouch	9

Worse ads. Wyard	238
Wortley ads. Eyre	28
Wotton ads. Levington	125
Wray ads. Scott	168
Wright v. Moor	274
Wroughton v. Hubbart	210
Wyard v. Worse	238
Wynn v. Parr	316
Yate v. Southby	26
Young ads. Cosin	252
Young ads. Wentworth	223
Zouch ads. Barker	80

Reports of Cases in the Court of Chancery from 1625 to 1660

1

Mitchell v. Anonymous

(Ch. 1625 × 1639)

A royal pardon does not pardon private debts.

British Library MS. Hargrave 30, f. 258

He [Sir John Mitchell] exhibited a bill there [in Chancery] against one.

And the defendant pleaded an outlawry in the said plaintiff after judgment, and demanded judgment whether he must answer.

The plaintiff demurred in law upon the plea, because the plaintiff pretended to have the benefit of the General Pardon.[1]

And the now Lord Keeper, LORD COVENTRY, referred it to Justice Jones for the law, whether the plaintiff will have the benefit of the Pardon before satisfaction to the party.

And Justice JONES certified that he will not have [it], and the said Lord Keeper [LORD COVENTRY] resolved it accordingly.

2

Okeham v. Hall

(Ch. 1625)

Where a defendant in a suit in equity fails to appear, a writ of sequestration lies against him, but he cannot be found in default before an appearance and a failure to answer.

---

[1] Stat. 21 Jac. I, c. 35 (*SR*, IV, 1269–1275).

Nelson 1, 21 E.R. 774

Easter term 1 Car. I [1625]. Lord Coventry.

The defendant stood in contempt for not answering the plaintiff's bill. And, thereupon, a [writ of] sequestration was granted. And the sequestrators were ordered to pay the rents to the plaintiff towards the duty demanded by his bill. And, at the same time that the sequestration was granted, it was likewise decreed that the bill should be taken *pro confesso* unless the defendant showed cause within a certain time limited for that purpose by the court.

But this must be understood, as the practice then was, where the defendant had appeared, for, if he did not appear at all, but stood out all contempts to a sergeant at arms, no decree can be had against him or the bill taken *pro confesso*, for that must be after an appearance and when he stands on contempt for want of an answer.

3

Blackstone v. Martin

(Ch. 1625–1626)

A judgment lien attaches to the land held by the judgment debtor at the time of the execution of the judgment and subsequent purchasers hold subject to it.

In a scire facias in the nature of an audita querela to vacate an execution on his land, the plaintiff-grantee need not allege himself to have been the owner of the land at the time of the execution of the judgment against the grantor.

Paynell K.B. 20

Easter term 1 Car. I.

Between Blackston and Martin, the case was [thus]. A statute was acknowledged, and the conusor sold part of his lands to divers men, and the conusee sued execution upon the purchasers, leaving out some. And he brought *audita querela*, and they were at issue in Chancery whether the conusor will have other lands than those extended the day the recognizance [was] given or ever afterwards and the lands lying in Durham by which the *mittimus* of the issue to be tried was to Durham which was tried and remanded into the King's Bench.

And it was adjudged void and that the record came in without a warrant because, when an issue is joined in the Chancery, the chancellor with his own hands must deliver the record into the King's Bench and, there, it is to be tried and execution [is] to be awarded from there if needed.

Palmer 410, 81 E.R. 1147

Easter term 1 Car.

Audita querela was brought in the Chancery, supposing that he solely was extended upon a statute when the conusor, on the day of the statute, was seised in fee of other lands. And the issue there was taken upon the seisin of the conusor on the day of the recognizance. And the lands of which the seisin was supposed lay in Durham. And it was found for the plaintiff.

Now, it was moved in arrest of judgment because the *venire facias* issued out of the Chancery where it should have been out of the King's Bench because the land is in Durham, because the difference is, when this court [the King's Bench] can can try [it], *venire facias* will be awarded out of the Chancery, returnable here. But, when this court cannot try [it], there, the *venire facias* will issue out of the King's Bench.

And for precedent was cited the Old Book of Entries, *Audita Querela*, 9, f. 99.

And, accordingly, here, at the prayer of Serjeant *Davenport*, a new [writ of] *venire facias* was awarded by all of the justices out of the King's Bench.

Latch 3, 82 E.R. 245

Easter term 1 Car. I.

It was agreed in Blaxton's Case that, when a case comes in Chancery to the issue, inasmuch as the Chancery cannot call a jury to their bar to try it, the Chancellor himself must deliver the issue with his own hands into the King's Bench, and they try the issue there by a jury. And, upon the verdict, they should give judgment, and not return the matter into the Chancery again, because the Chancery is rid of it. And, if the issue be to be tried in Durham or another franchise where they are not compellable at Westminster to try an issue, as in Ireland etc., then the course is that the King's Bench writes to such place to try the issue and return it into the King's Bench, and they, upon this, give judgment, inasmuch as the Chancellor cannot write to any such place to try an issue, because the Chancery has nothing to do with verdicts, which is a common law trial.

And, an account of this, in this case of Blaxton, where the Chancellor wrote to the bishop of Durham to try an issue in an *audita querela*, all was badly done.

Thus, note the power of the King's Bench above the Chancery. And it was ordered by the court that the verdict would be quashed and they proceed to a new trial.

JONES said that, in this case, even though the Chancery had nothing to do with verdicts and, on account of this, the Chancellor could not write in such a case to any to have a trial, yet, he said, if, in the Chancery, an issue be joined that is not tried by a jury, there, the Chancellor himself can write, and not pray in aid the King's Bench, as if, in Chancery, *ne unque accouple en loyal matrimony* be in issue, there, the Chancellor can write to the bishop to certify, and, if the record in Durham etc. be a question, the Chancellor could write to be certified of this record. But he cannot meddle with juries.

And DODDERIDGE said that he had never seen or heard that, before this, the Chancellor had written to any county palatine to try an issue, but the Court of King's Bench well can.

And it was said in this case that the return of the trial out of Chancery cannot be into the Common Bench, though in the New Entries, f. 305,[1] there is one such precedent. But it must be so only returned into the King's Bench.

W. Jones 82, 82 ER. 44

Trinity term, 1 Car.

One Blakeston, Prebendary of Durham, sued an *audita querela* to avoid a [writ of] extent upon his land upon a statute staple. And his surmise was that the conusor was seised in fee at the time of the statute of lands in the County Palatine of Durham which were not extended. *Ideo*, he, being a feoffee of other lands of the conusor and extended, sued this *audita querela* to be discharged of this extent and to make the other land equally contributory to the extent. And they were at issue, that the conusor was not seised of the lands in the County Palatine of Durham, upon which a writ out of the Chancery was sent to the bishop of Durham or his Chancellor for a trial of the issue and, after the trial to send the record into the King's Bench, by which the said issue was tried before the Justices of Assise of York, being the justices to the said bishop for the said County Palatine. And they found for the plaintiff.

And, upon this, the bishop sent the record into the King's Bench. And, in arrest of judgment, it was moved that the record should have been transmitted to the King's Bench before any process was to be sent to the bishop and, after the record was in the King's Bench, they should have written to the County Palatine to try the issue.

And of this opinion was CREWE, DODDERIDGE, and WHITELOCKE.

But JONES doubted whether the record must be first transmitted or not. But he agreed that the record was not well sent into the King's Bench because, as it seemed to him, the proceeding in Chancery will be always *nisi* that it was a trial by verdict, but, because they could not try by verdict, then they will have a *venire facias* returnable in the King's Bench and deliver the record *propriis manibus* to the King's Bench. But, if the proceeding was upon a demurrer in Chancery or upon an issue not triable by jury, as upon a certificate of a bishop or of a record of London of a custom of London, there the Chancery does not send the record into the King's Bench, but the certificate must be returned into the Chancery. And, there, judgment will be given. *Ideo*, they write directly to the County Palatine to try the issue. And when it is tried, as he thought, it must be returned into the Chancery, or, if it was not done thus, then the record should be transmitted be-

---

[1] *Briggs v. Poler* (1562), E. Coke, *A Booke of Entries* (1614), 'False Judgement', pl. 1, f. 305.

fore the process to the bishop. Or, otherwise, if process [be] to the bishop out of the Chancery, the return will be there. And JONES cited 14 Edw. IV, f. 6, where the issue upon a traverse of an office was sent into the [King's] Bench to be tried and, because the tenant to whom the lands [were] put to farm was not warned, it was remanded to the Chancery, and 24 Edw. III, 35, a *scire facias* upon a recognizance and they were at issue upon a release and, upon this, it was sent to the King's Bench, and the plaintiff there was nonsuited, and, this notwithstanding, he brought a new *scire facias* in the King's Bench, and [it was] well.[1]

Another exception was taken because it was directed to the bishop *vel Cancellario suo*. *Vide* for this 1 Edw. IV, 9, that it is good enough.[2]

Vide postea Hilary term 2 *Caroli Regis*.

Paynell K.B. 49

Hilary term 1 Car. I.

Between Blackston and Martin in [a writ of] *scire facias* in the nature of an *audita querela* to avoid an extent of the land in a statute acknowledged by Sir William Blackston because Sir William had other lands at the time of the statute acknowledged, issue was joined upon this. And [it was] found that he had other lands. And now, it was moved in arrest of judgment that the plaintiff in the *scire facias* has not averred himself to be the tenant of the land at the time of the suing of the execution.

And it was said that the *scire facias* here must be as certain as a declaration. As in 32 Hen. VI, 14,[3] in *scire facias* upon a recognizance to appear etc., the condition must be expressed and the certainty of it. Thus [is] Dyer 197;[4] a *scire facias* to revoke letters patent must express the case certainly and the former grant, and it will not be taken here by implication who was the tenant etc. because, he said, it has grave damage that [one] could imply who was a tenant or, otherwise, the land was not extended *ad damnum* of him any more than a declaration will be taken by implication, as Com. 202 and 206, in waste;[5] the plaintiff declared on a grant to himself of a reversion, and it did not appear whether the [waste] was before or after the grant, and, there, it was not good, and yet, there, he concluded that it was to his disheritance, which strongly implied that it was a grant before the waste was [done] etc., but a declaration must contain truth and certainty, as is said in Stradling's case, and so must the *scire facias* which is in the place of it here.

And here, if he was not the tenant at the time of the suing of the execution, even though the land was tortiously charged, yet he will hold it thus as a feoffor

---

[1] *Anonymous* (1474), YB Trin. 14 Edw. IV, f. 6, pl. 8, Chancery Reports Middle Ages 202; YB Mich. 24 Edw. III, f. 35, pl. 35 (1350).
[2] YB Mich. 1 Edw. IV, ff. 9, 10, pl. 18 (1461).
[3] YB Mich. 32 Hen. VI, f. 14, pl. 22 (1453).
[4] *Rex v. Blage* (1561), 2 Dyer 197, 73 E.R. 436.
[5] *Stradling v. Morgan* (1560), 1 Plowden 199, 75 E.R. 305.

holds. And he cited 15 Edw. IV, 24,[1] where the feoffee will not have [a prosecution for] forgery for a forgery in the time of his feoffor, and Penruddock's case, Coke, 5, and F.N.B. 149,[2] that a feoffee will not have admeasurement of dower but he will take in the same plight as the feoffor held.

And it was urged on this side by *Bankes*.

And *Calthorpe* here said that it is alleged that Blackston was seised in fee at the time of the recognizance and it will be intended to continue and, on account of this, if it be not shown, it cannot be intended that the plaintiff was seised at the time of the suing of the execution. And he cited for express authority that the plaintiff should aver himself to be the tenant at the time of the execution, 17 Edw. III, 27, by Seton, and 35, by Thorpe, and 43a, which see,[3] upon which on this side, it was concluded that the *scire facias* was bad and the judgment [was] to be stayed.

On the other side, it was said that the *scire facias* is a writ and the nature of it is to be brief. And on account of this, it will be construed[4] similarly to where a writ was brought to distrain beasts of the plough and it did not aver that he did not have other cattle, but, inasmuch as it is said *contra formam statuti*, it implies as much. And divers precedents were cited where the *scire facias* was as it is here, as Trinity 6 Hen. IV, rot. 505 and 101, in the Common Bench, and Michaelmas 16 & 17 Eliz., [rot.] 1313, and Trinity 34 Eliz., [rot.] 327, and divers others in the Petty Bag.

And of this opinion was the court except DODDERIDGE, who said that he had not advised upon the case and, on account of this, he would not deliver his resolute opinion. But after the other three justices agreed for the plaintiff, he also agreed, and judgment was given for him.

WHITELOCKE said that, here, if he who brings an *audita querela* was not the tenant *tempore* etc., it must have been shown on the other side and not come in on the side of the plaintiff because the *scire facias* is to know what he can say that the extent will not be defeated and, if there be a cause on his part, to show it.

Justice JONES agreed that, if the plaintiff was not the tenant at the time of the suing of the execution, that he could not have this action because he will hold as his feoffor held it. And to this intent, he said that it had been adjudged that, if an inquisition be found of my lands, that my feoffee will not traverse it. But he took a difference because, if an extent be sued for land and, before the *liberate* be sued, a feoffment is made, there, the feoffee will avoid it because he is the party

---

[1] YB Pas. 15 Edw. IV, f. 24, pl. 5 (1475).

[2] *Clark v. Penruddock* (1598), 5 Coke Rep. 100, 77 E.R. 210, also 139 Selden Soc. 902, Croke Eliz. 234, 78 E.R. 490, Jenkins 260, 145 E.R. 185; A. Fitzherbert, *Natura Brevium*.

[3] YB Pas. 17 Edw. III, f. 27, pl. 24 (1343); YB Pas. 17 Edw. III, ff. 34, 35, pl. 46 (1343); YB Trin. 17 Edw. III, f. 43, pl. 32 (1343).

[4] prise per intendment *MS*.

aggrieved for it; otherwise, if he came in after the *liberate*. And he said, if, after the *liberate*, the feoffment be made of part to one and of part to another, that the one will not have contribution against the other, and, also, if a purchaser had a cause for contribution and made a feoffment, his feoffee will not have it. And, in the case at bar, he said that it was in the nature of a Chancery suit and, on account of this, so express certainty is not required in it. And he said that he had enquired of the clerks of the Chancery, who informed him that the constant form of the Chancery was not to aver himself the tenant. By which, he concluded for the plaintiff.

DODDERIDGE, as above.

Chief Justice CREWE: The objections are strong and colorable. And the precedents from ancient times until 35 Eliz. [1592–93] always express that the plaintiff was tenant at the time of the execution. And I have seen many of them upon a command to search for such precedents. But after this time, the constant form is, as this writ in our case is, [in] all the time of King James, by which to overthrow all precedents, I were not now advised, by which etc.

And, thus, judgment was given for the plaintiff.

Benloe 161, 73 E.R. 1026

Hilary term 1 Car.

Marmaduke Blackstone brought a *scire facias* in Chancery returnable there in the nature of *audita querela*. And he showed that Sir William Blackston was seised of a capital messuage with the appurtenances in Blackston in the County of the bishopric of Durham in fee and also the manor of Thorpe and other lands and that the said Sir William Blackston, 3 Jac. [1605–06], acknowledged a statute of £400 to Roger Martin and the said capital messuage was extended only, the other lands being omitted. And he, as terre tenant, prayed relief to avoid execution. And issue was joined whether Sir William Blackston was seised of the manor of Thorpe etc. at the day of the acknowledgment of this statute. And it was found that he was. And divers matters were moved in arrest of judgment. But many of them being trivial, I will not mention [them]. But two precedents were principally pressed, first, whether *scire facias* lies or *audita querela*, second, whether the writ be sufficient, inasmuch as the plaintiff desired to be restored to the same profits and it did not appear when he became the tenant so that it is dubious whether he should have a remedy or not, because, if he came in after the [writ of] extent, he should not have any relief.

And this case was argued at the Reading term in Michaelmas and at Westminster Hilary term 1 Car. by Serjeant *Bridgeman* and *Trotman*, for the plaintiff, and *Davies* and *Bankes*, for the defendant.

And at the last [term], it was adjudged for the plaintiff. And it was resolved *per curiam*, Justice DODDERIDGE, *hesitante*, first that *scire facias* lies or *audita querela*. Pope and Ross's Case, Plo., and Sir William Herbert, Coke 3.[1]

Second, if the plaint came in after the extent, he will not have relief because he must take it as he found it, *vide* Penruddock, Co.; otherwise, if he came in after the extent and before the [writ of] *liberate*.

Third, it will be intended here that he was the tenant before the extent wherefore it is said *ad grave damnum* and *contra legem terrae*.[2] And there is not another form of the writ. And many precedents were shown to this purpose, ancient and modern, in the Petty Bag and elsewhere, as 16 Edw. IV, rot. 505, in *audita querela*, by Roger Moile; and the same term, rot. 101; Boson and Wooley, Michaelmas 16 & 17 El., King's Bench, rot. 1313; Perkins v. Wilde, Trinity 34 El., King's Bench, rot. 637; Charnock and Worsley in *scire facias* and error upon it, 2 Jac.;[3] 33 Eliz., Lovett v. Lacy; same term, Garth and Lacy; Michaelmas 17 Jac., Lockyard and Strourr.

Fourth, that this record must be sent to Durham from the King's Bench or the Common Bench and it must come from the Chancery to the King's Bench of the Common Bench *per mittimus*, and, because it was first sent from the Chancery to Durham, the judgment was arrested after the first verdict. But a second verdict was obtained.

And, in this case, many cases were cited, as 17 Edw. III, 27; 21 Hen. VI, 7; Sir William Harbert, Co., 3; Pope, Plo.; Fitzherbert, *Audita Querela*, 131; 4 Ass., 3, 36; 17 Eliz., Dier 341; Fitzherbert, *Audita Querela*, 105; 21 Hen. VI, 7; 16 Eliz., Dier 132; 11 Hen. VI, 11; 36 Hen. VI, 18; 5 Edw. III, 15; 14 Eliz., Dier; *nullus distringatur etc.*; 11 Hen. IV; *contra legem*; Dier; 2 Edw. IV, 24; Stradling, Plo.; 25 Hen. VIII, Dier.[4]

W. Jones 90, 82 E.R. 47

Hilary term 1 Car.

William Blakeston, clerk, brought a *scire facias* in Chancery in the nature of an *audita querela* against Roger Martyn. And for it, he showed that he was

---

[1] *Ross v. Pope* (1551), 1 Plowden 72, 75 E.R. 114; *Harbert's Case* (1584), 3 Coke Rep. 11, 76 E.R. 647, also 137 Selden Soc. 276, Moore K.B. 169, 72 E.R. 510.

[2] Stat. 25 Edw. I, Magna Carta, c. 29 (*SR*, I, 117).

[3] Perhaps *Charnock v. Worsley* (1588), 1 Leonard 114, 74 E.R. 107, Croke Eliz. 129, 78 E.R. 386.

[4] YB Pas. 17 Edw. III, f. 27, pl. 24 (1343); *B. v. Langwat* (1442), YB Mich. 21 Hen. VI, f. 7, pl. 17; *Harbert's Case* (1584), *ut supra*; *Ross v. Pope* (1551), *ut supra*; *Vernon v. Stanley* (1575), 3 Dyer 341, 73 E.R. 768; *Anonymous* (1574), 3 Dyer 332, 73 E.R. 750; *Anonymous* (1572), 3 Dyer 315, 73 E.R. 714; YB Mich. 2 Edw. IV, f. 24, pl. 22 (1462); *Stradling v. Morgan* (1560), 1 Plowden 199, 75 E.R. 305; Stat. 25 Edw. I, Magna Carta, c. 29 (*SR*, I, 117) (*Nullus . . . disseisiatur . . . [contra] legem*).

seised *unius capitalis messuagii* and divers other lands in Blackston in the County of Durham and that one William Blakestone, knight, and one Jamson acknowledged a recognizance in the nature of a statute staple of £400 to the said Martyn and his wife and that the said Martyn extended the said land and sued a [writ of] *liberate* of it, notwithstanding that Sir William Blakestone was seised in fee at the time of the said recognizance of the said land and also of the other lands in the said county that were omitted in the extent. And, upon this, he prayed relief.

And the said Martyn came in and pleaded that William Blakeston, knight, was not seised of the said lands omitted, upon which, they were at issue.

And, upon this, the record was delivered by the Lord Keeper of the Great Seal to the Court of King's Bench, and they made a mandate to the bishop of Durham to try the same. And the bishop remanded it again and that it was found for the plaintiff. *Vide principium ante termino Paschae primo Caroli.*

And, in arrest of judgment, it was moved by *Bankes* that it must be an *audita querela* and not a *scire facias*.

But it was overruled by the court, and the party could, at his election, have an *audita querela* or a *scire facias, quod vide* 16 Eliz., Dyer, ff. 331, 332, and Reports of Cooke, *pars* 3, in Herbert's Case.[1] And all the precedents in the Chancery are accordingly.

Second, he moved that the *scire facias* is *tenens praemissorum* and it does not say that he was *tenens* at the time of the *liberate*. And, if so, then he cannot have a *scire facias* if another was the tenant at the time of the extent and *liberate*. And it passed his estate to the plaintiff. He cannot have an *audita querela*.

But all of the four justices agreed because it will be intended that he was *tenens* also at the time of the *liberate*. And divers precedents were offered, which proved it to be the common course and form. But they all agreed that, if one be bound in a recognizance and, afterwards, make a feoffment of part of his land and the conusee sues an extent and *liberate* against the conusor of the lands in his hands only and, afterwards, he convey the lands extended to J.S., that J.S. cannot have any remedy for contribution against the first feoffee because his feoffor, *scil.*, the reconusor himself, cannot have contribution, thus nor his feoffee who comes in after the extent and *liberate*.

Second, they held that, if one was seised of two acres in fee and acknowledged a statute and he enfeoff two several persons of the two acres and one acre only is extended and delivered in execution and, afterwards, he enfeoff J.D., that J.D. cannot have an *audita querela* against the other feoffee because it was a chose in action in his feoffor that cannot be transferred to another, as if a lord encroach upon a tenant and, if he make a feoffment over, the feoffee will not have a *ne*

---

[1] *Anonymous* (1574), 3 Dyer 332, 73 E.R. 750; *Harbert's Case* (1584), *ut supra*.

injuste vexes. 7 Ric. II, Fitz., *Admeasurement.*[1] A guardian in fact will not have admeasurement of those things made before his grant.

But [it was held] by CREWE and JONES, if an extent was only and without a *liberate* and, afterwards, before a *liberate*, the feoffment is made and then the *liberate* comes, in both the first cases, he will have an *audita querela* because, by the extent, no wrong was done, nor [was there] any cause of action, but the estate remained in the conusor until the *liberate*. But, if the *liberate* was made, it is otherwise, as is said before, which the other justices did not contradict. But inasmuch as *tenens praemissorum* in a writ is tantamount and by intendment supposes the party to be seised at the time of the *liberate* and extent and if it was otherwise, it will come of the part of the defendant by way of a plea.

Ideo these points were out of the case. And judgment was given for the plaintiff notwithstanding the said exception.

Latch 112, 82 E.R. 300

In a *scire facias* in the nature of an *audita querela*, issue was joined in the Chancery and sent out of the Chancery to the County Palatine of Durham to be tried. And a verdict was given for the plaintiff. And, afterwards, the record came into the King's Bench, and the counsel of the defendant took this exception, first, inasmuch as the issue was not first sent here [the Court of King's Bench] and the judges of this court wrote to the bishop of Durham to try the issue and afterwards to return it here that judgment can be given. And, for this cause, judgment was reversed. And, afterwards, upon an *audita querela*, a trial was had, and a verdict was given again for the plaintiff. And now an exception was taken because the plaintiff showed that he was *tenens unius messuagii* in Durham and that Sir William Blackston was seised of a messuage in D. and of divers other lands and [in] 30 Eliz. acknowledged a statute. And, after this, the conusee had only extended the lands in Durham that the defendant had and not the other land that the conusor had, *ad grave damnum*. And he desired restitution of the mesne profits. The defendant came in and said that Sir William Blackston was not seised of the other lands at the time of the acknowledging of the statute or at any time afterward. And, upon this issue, it was found for the plaintiff. And it was moved in arrest of judgment because it did not appear when the plaintiff became tenant of the land, whether at the time of the extent or afterwards. But it will be intended for the plaintiff that [it was] at the time of the [writ of] *liberate* delivered, because it is *breve ad nomen propter brevitatem* and as it concludes *ad grave damnum*, the law intends that he was the tenant of the land at the time of the *liberate*. Otherwise, it is not *ad damnum*. And, if he had not been a tenant, the defendant must

---

[1] *Courtney v. Gorges* (1383), Trin. 7 Ric. II, Ames Found., vol. 3, p. 62, pl. 7, Fitzherbert, Abr., *Admeasurement*, pl. 4.

have pleaded it and because he had pleaded another thing and this is found with the plaintiff, it is well enough.

And precedents were showed to the court. Trinity 6 Hen. IV, rot. 505, 101; Michaelmas 16 & 17 Eliz., rot. 1313, Common Bench.

On the other part, it was showed that this writ is in lieu of a declaration. And they cited 32 Hen. VI, 14.[1] And in our case, it is not alleged when Sir William parted with possession. But it is alleged that he was seised etc. that will be intended to be until now if the contrary is not showed.

WHITELOCKE: The nature of a *scire facias* is to put all upon the defendant because [there is a] judgment for the plaintiff.

JONES agreed. And he said that suffices that it is *tenens messuagii* because a *scire facias* is only in the nature of a bill in Chancery, and, on account of that, such a certainly is not expected as the common law requires. And all *scire facias*es are in such manner. He said, if it be otherwise, it must come from the other side. And, on account of this, because the constant course [of the court] is thus, he concluded for the plaintiff.

DODDERIDGE was of the same opinion.

CREWE was of the same opinion because the defendant, by his plea, admitted himself a tenant and, further, he pleaded that Sir William was not seised of any other land, by which he lost the advantage of the other. But he cannot have taken advantage of it because this is the common course in a *scire facias* now. And it was in the time of King James, but it was not in the time of Queen Elizabeth, as 33 Eliz., Lovel's Case.

Latch 274, 82 E.R. 383

It was objected that the implication, because it was *ad grave damnum*, it is not sufficient. The implication that the plaintiff was a tenant at the time, no more, that the declaration will be good by implication, as Com. 202, 206, in waste,[2] he declared of the grant of a reversion, and it did not appear whether it was before the waste or afterwards, it is not good, even though he concluded *ad exhaeredationem*, which strongly implies that the grant was before the waste. But the declaration as it is said in Stradling's Case, must contain verity and certainty. And so must a *scire facias*, which is in place of it. And, here, if it was not his land at the time of the execution sued, even though the land was tortiously charged, yet he will hold it so as the feoffor held. 15 Edw. IV, 24;[3] a feoffee will not have a forgery in the time of his feoffor. And Penruddock's Case, 5 Rep.; F.N.B. 149, that the feoffee will not have admeasurement of dower, but will take in the same plight as the feoffor held.

---

[1] YB Mich. 32 Hen. VI, f. 14, pl. 22 (1453).
[2] *Stradling v. Morgan* (1560), *ut supra*.
[3] YB Pas. 15 Edw. IV, f. 24, pl. 5 (1475).

Jones agreed. If the plaintiff was not the tenant at the time of this execution sued, he cannot have this action because he will hold as his feoffor held it. And to this intent, he said that it had been adjudged that, if an inquisition be found, only the lands that my feoffee will not traverse. But if the feoffment be after the [writ of] extent but before [the writ of] *liberate* sued, the feoffee will avoid it because he is the party aggrieved by it. And he said that, if, after the *liberate*, the feoffment be made of part to one and part to another, that the one will not have contribution against the other, and, also, if a purchaser had cause for contribution and made a feoffment, his feoffee will not have it.

Judgment was given for the plaintiff.

3 Bulstrode 305, 81 E.R. 253

In a *scire facias* in the nature of an *audita querela*, the plaintiff shows that, 3 Jac., Sir William Blackston being seised of land in the manor of D. and of other lands and being so seised, 3 Jac., he acknowledged a statute of £400 that he had part of the land subject to the execution and was seised of it, which was taken in execution, there being other lands in the hands and possession of the defendants, subject to the said execution and not extended. Upon this, the *scire facias* here [was] brought in the nature of an *audita querela* for to be relieved against them by way of contribution. This writ [was] directed to the Sheriff of Suffolk, the plaintiff being a feoffee of Sir William Blackstone. And he prays to be restored unto his land and to the profits of the same and to all which he has lost by this extent thus taken out and laid upon his land. The parties were at issue upon the seisin of the plaintiff, and a verdict was found for the plaintiff.

Bankes and *Davies* moved divers exceptions in arrest of judgment, and showed that there was a former *scire facias* in this cause and that, after verdict, judgment was arrested, because the trial was mistaken, for having this writ out of the Chancery and being at issue upon the seisin and this sent down out of the Chancery to the Bishopric of Durham to be tried, they failed in this, and, therefore, after verdict, judgment was arrested, because the same ought to have been first entered in this Court [of King's Bench], the Chancellor to come with the record, and this court to have awarded the trial. Upon this, a new *scire facias* now is brought, and, in this, a trial has been at the last Assises by default. For matter now in arrest of judgment, it was urged that it appears here by the plaintiff's own showing that the statute was acknowledged 3 Jac. and his land extended, that he sued forth a *scire facias* in the nature of an *audita querela*, by which it does not appear that he was tenant of this and of other land at the time of the execution sued. But he shows that he was a feoffee of Sir William Blackston, the conusor, and so prays by this to be relieved, whereas he ought to have showed that he was tenant at the time of the execution, as appears by 22 Edw. III, Fitz., tit. *Execution*, pl. 137.[1] No contribution is to be for the party himself which acknowledged the statute, (as it was urged) not yet for his feoffee, who shall not be in a better case than his feoffor.

And, by 27 Hen. VI, Fitz., *Execution*, pl. 135,[2] the heir is not charged as heir, but principally as terre tenant, and the heir is not to have contribution, as appears by Coke, 3 *pars*, in Sir William Harbert's Case.

To the exceptions taken, an answer was made by *Trotman* and *Bridgeman*, serjeants, for the plaintiff, because he says that he was *tenens*, and it does not appear *quando tenens*, for that if he was not *tenens* at the time of the extent, he can then have no *scire facias*. This is in a writ, *et dicitur breve, quia rem breviter enarrat*, like unto the writ of *monstraverunt* and *quod permittat*, in which it is not needful to show and make expression of all circumstances; no more here in this. But, for to take this exception, the party now comes here too late, for he has appeared to the *scire facias*, and so, by this, he has confessed him to be *tenens*, like unto the case, 17 Eliz., Dyer, f. 341,[3] where the demandant in a formedon is estopped; by reason of his writ against the tenants, he is estopped to say they are not tenants. So, here, by his appearance to the *scire facias*, he is estopped to say he was not *tenens*, by 21 Hen. VII, f. 7, and Fitzherbert, *Natura Brevium*, f. 105, the *audita querela* is in the nature of a complaint in the Chancery.[4] By 16 Eliz. Dyer, f. 332, this is well returned in the Chancery if an *audita querela*, and so if a *scire facias*.[5]

It was further urged that, upon all the parts of the writ taken and laid together, it shall be taken and intended that he was *tenens tempore brevis*. This first begins *ex gravi querela*; this shall be so intended that he was tenant at the time of the writ; otherwise, he had no cause to complain. And writs are so called, because they are penned briefly to contain the substance of the matter. And this is sufficient. 5 Edw. III, f. 150, new print, and f. 197, old print. *Termino* Trinity, Case 23, in an action of trespass, for taking of his cattle and detaining of them, there this rule is put, *scil.* when one word may have a double intendment, *scil.* one according to the law and another against the law, that intendment shall be taken which is according to the law, and this by a reasonable intendment.

It was further urged that, here, in this case, the execution, *fuit minus juste et ad damnum* of the plaintiff *et contra legem terrae*, so that, by this conclusion, he shall be intended to be a tenant at the time of the execution sued.

WHITELOCKE, Justice: The writ is *tenentes narrant*. The point is how this shall be intended. If to be understood that he which is only tenant at the time of the writ and not *pars gravata*; whether we are to intend this to be so. This we are not to do. If he be not prejudiced by this, what remedy is he to have? The reason

---

[1] YB Mich. 22 Edw. III, f. 14, pl. 42, Fitzherbert, Abr., *Execucion*, pl. 134 (1348).
[2] Mich. 27 Hen. VI, Fitzherbert, Abr., *Execucion*, pl. 135 (1448).
[3] *Vernon v. Stanley* (1575), 3 Dyer 341, 73 E.R. 768.
[4] YB Hil. 21 Hen. VII, f. 7, pl. 6 (1506); A. Fitzherbert, *Natura Brevium*.
[5] *Anonymous* (1574), 3 Dyer 332, 73 E.R. 750.

of the *audita querela* [is] because the burden ought to be equally laid, *scil.* all to be charged together, which is not pursued here, but laid upon him alone.

This appears by the records to be his grief, because that, out of this charge, some land is omitted and his land taken. And this is the cause here of his grief and complaint. *Tenens*, this is his title, because the title of the land and all the subsequent part of the record shows and sets forth his grief. The precedents are so, and so the *scire facias* is but a *monitio*. No essoin lies in this, as in other actions. In this, non tenure shall not be pleaded; no protection shall be granted in this; if brought by an executor, he shall not in this be enforced to show *quando, nec ubi judicium fuit*, this being but only a *monitio*, a warning.

And this is the means to have the other cause to show, if he can, why he should not have his judgment and the effect of the same. And so, by this, he puts all the cause upon the other side to defend. He only shows by his writ that he is a person able to have this. He demands nothing at all by it, this being only a monefaction to call in the other party for to answer. And he is not to show in this writ all the whole matter in such precise certainty, as it has been objected.

As to the matter objected of discontinuance, there is no discontinuance at all in the case, for, upon view of the record, this is well aided, and so, in this case, judgment ought to be given for the plaintiff.

JONES, Justice, agreed herein, that the plaintiff ought to have his judgment.

Two exceptions have been taken, which are only material.

As to the continuance, a general continuance, *coram domino rege*, but here it is *dicto* etc. Yet this is good.

As to the issue, the Chancery might make the award not to proceed further there, but to deliver the record in the King's Bench.

As to the two exceptions taken, the precedents are to have a *scire facias* in the Chancery or an *audita querela* in the King's Bench or in the Common Bench, as one of the prothonotaries there, twenty years since in a cause, did inform me. And, then, they showed precedents to the Lord Chancellor to warrant this, F.N.B. and 29 Edw. III, a *scire facias* lies where one conusee is charged and others omitted; the reason of this [is] because the court which has power to grant execution might have granted a *scire facias*.

As to the other point, 7 Ric. II, Fitz., *Admeasurement de Dower*, pl. 4; a guardian in Chivalry, the second shall not have this where the guardian assigns over. It appears that he was *tenens*; he may come to the land since the extent, yet it shall be good upon this reason, that a *scire facias* and an *audita querela* ought not to be so certain as a declaration, being only a writ to be discharged. Where the party says *tenens*, it shall be intended of freehold, at the least. It is also here said *ad damnum*, which cannot be to his damage if he was not *tenens* at the time of the extent. And so, upon the whole matter, as this case is, judgment ought to be given for the plaintiff.

DODDERIDGE, Justice: It is here alleged that he was tenant of the land and that the execution is to his grief and his prayer is to be restored to the profits of the land from the time of the [writ of] *liberate*. Whether this writ be good or not is the question. The second point [is] whether he shall have a *scire facias* or an *audita querela*.

A conusor of a statute shall have a *scire facias*, 4 Hen. VIII, Dyer,[1] and, there, an old book was cited. Here, this is a special *scire facias*, for, by this, he will not only have the possession, but would also be restored unto all the mesne profits at the time of the *liberate*. And it appears not by the record that he was then tenant.

This case cannot be taken by intendment, for his prayer is to be restored to the profits of the land from the time of the *liberate*. And to have this, he ought to make it appear upon the record that he was then tenant; otherwise, he cannot have any benefit thereby, and this he has not here so done. And it shall be a very strange intendment for to intend one to be tenant of the land for any longer time than he himself says that he is tenant.

Intendments, by the law, shall be of probabilities, as for to intend a thing *in mitiorem partem*. But it is very improbable that he which is tenant this day should be intended to be tenant long time before that he himself says he was tenant. He has something to do with the land. He says here that he was tenant at the time of the *scire facias*.

As to the other point, whether he shall have a *scire facias* or an *audita querela*, this *scire facias* here is special, in the nature of an *audita querela*. This *scire facias* is good and sufficient, for, now, the same is returned in Chancery, and is a record of the Chancery, and, therefore, he may well have a *scire facias*, the judgment being there in this case, upon the Statute of 23 Hen. VIII,[2] when the record is there in the Chancery.

As to the return, this is well there in the Chancery, for it ought to be to the same court where he had received it.

And there is no discontinuance here in the case. *In termino* Hilary, he prays an imparlance *coram dicto domino rege* until *termino* Easter; this is true, *et ei conceditur*, so the entry was. This is full, though the king died before the day given; this is no discontinuance, *petit licentiam interloquendi dicto domino regi*.

The sole doubt in the case [is] because he says that he was *tenens* at the time of the *scire facias*, and, by his prayer, he would be restored to the profits, from the time of the *liberate*. And so at this time, for this cause, judgment ought to be given against the plaintiff.

CREWE, Chief Justice: The record is *coram domino rege in Cancellaria*. A Chancery record *est querela*, a complaint.

As to the objection made, because he does not say that he was tenant at the time of the *liberate*, it is good to see the precedents in this how they are. The plaintiff here complains that his land was taken in execution. By this it is to be inferred that he was in possession at the time of the *liberate*. This [is] the ground

---

[1] Note (1512), 1 Dyer 1, 73 E.R. 2.
[2] Stat. 23 Hen. VIII, c. 6, s. 3 (*SR*, III, 373).

of his complaint that the conusor had more land not extended, and his land only [was] extended. Also, he is here *pars gravata*, and it is here laid to be done *contra legem terrae*. If his land was not so taken and extended, he had no cause then to complain, and this is a very strong inference out of the record, that this was his land. And the defendant here admits him to be tenant and that he is the person who has cause to complain. But he says that he has not any such land. It appears here by the verdict that the land was omitted, he ought to have the possession. Otherwise, it could not be taken away from him. 16 Eliz., Dyer; it appears where he is to have a *scire facias* and where an *audita querela*; when the record is here, by 21 Hen. VII, it is here fixed, for the principal point, because he says that he was *tenens* generally.[1]

As to this without any further debate, at this time, it rested upon a *curia advisari vult*. And so, by the rule of the court, this case was adjourned to a further time for the court to be better satisfied herein. But by CREWE, Chief Justice, the plaintiff ought to have his judgment.

Afterwards, *scil. termino Hilarii 1 Caroli Regis*, King's Bench, this matter was moved again, and argued by the counsel on both sides and by all the judges.

WHITELOCKE, Justice: This writ is a *scire facias*, in which the plaintiff shows that he is seised of the messuage and land at the time of the execution. The defendant ought to have showed that he was not *tenens*. He admits him to be *tenens* and that he is the party grieved but takes issue that Blackstone was not seised of the land *tempore executionis*. A *scire facias* differs very much from declarations; all things are not to be so particularized in a *scire facias*. And this does accord with the precedents. Here, the defendant has taken issue upon the seisin at the time of the recognizance acknowledged. The nature of the *scire facias* is to turn all upon the defendant, as appears by 34 Assissar. In this case, forasmuch as the defendant has admitted the plaintiff to be the party aggrieved and a verdict is found for the plaintiff and no material matter showed in arrest of judgment, judgment ought, therefore, to be given for the plaintiff.

JONES, Justice: In this case, the plaintiff ought to have his judgment. As to the precedents which have been showed, they are of no great force and avail in this case. He to whom the conusor passes over his land shall be subject to the execution. If one be seised of two acres of land [and] acknowledges a statute [and], afterwards, he makes two several feoffments unto two men, the land of one of them is extended, he makes a feoffment over, the title of action shall not be transferred over or translated. So it is of admeasurement of dower.

As to the objection made, because it does not appear that he was tenant at the time of the *liberate*, [it is] agreed, if the extent be and, before the *liberate*, he makes a feoffment over, his feoffee shall have an *audita querela*; he has no cause to complain until the *liberate*, and, by this, the wrong does begin.

---

[1] *Anonymous* (1574), 3 Dyer 332, 73 E.R. 750; YB Hil. 21 Hen. VII, f. 7, pl. 6 (1506).

As to the precedents showed, they come not home to this case in question. Here, when he says that he was *tenens praemissorum*, this is but in the nature of a bill in Chancery, for to have a commission, and, in this, such precise certainty in every respect is not requisite to be, as in declarations. It shall be intended that he was tenant until the contrary be showed by the other party. The constant course has been so, and this is not to be altered. And there is very much equity in this case for the plaintiff. And, therefore, he ought to have his judgment.

DODDERIDGE, Justice, agreed now in opinion with them for the plaintiff. The matter rests only upon this word, *scil. tenens*, and does not say *quando*, whether it shall be intended that he was *tenens* at the time of the execution sued, and so a party grieved by the execution. It is sufficient for him to say that he was tenant at the time of the first writ purchased. Then, the execution was sued out, and the same to his grief. I agree that, where a lawful execution is had against the conusor himself, that he shall not have an *audita querela*. Here it appears by the writ that he was tenant at the time of the first writ, and he shall be intended still so to continue tenant if the contrary be not showed (as here it is not). And so, he, being the party grieved, had just cause of complaint. And, having a verdict found for him upon the matter put in issue and nothing material moved in arrest of judgment, therefore, in this case, judgment ought to be given for the plaintiff.

CREWE, Chief Justice: It is here said that he was *tenens messuagii* and of the capital messuage of Blackstone and that Martin procured one of them to be extended *minus juste et contra legem terrae*. Blackstone, upon this, brings this *gravis querela*.

The objection which has been made is of great force. If I cannot deliver myself of this by example and precedent, the objection being because he does not show *quando tenens*, whether, at the time of the execution, if extended in the hands of the feoffor, his feoffee shall not have an *audita querela*. It does not appear here when the *liberate* was sued out.

It is objected that he was not tenant at the time. But by all here together, and it does well and sufficiently appear, Blackstone here has brought this action. And it does not appear that he was tenant at the time of the *liberate*, as it has been objected. But this does well appear to be so, for he says that this was to his prejudice *et minus juste*, and prays to have the profits of his land to him delivered from the time of the *liberate*. The defendant, to this, might have answered and said that he was not then tenant. He has not so done, but the contrary, for he has admitted him to be tenant and that the land was taken from him in execution. All this is by him admitted, and this makes for the plaintiff. And, because that the defendant himself has admitted of this, I will not now make this a question, whether he was tenant at the time of the *liberate* or not. As to the precedents, I have seen divers of them, and I have also examined the course and usage. And I do find the constant course to be so, as here it is in this case. One precedent showed, which was 33 Eliz., Morley against Lovet, there it was showed how he was tenant and that he was tenant at the time of the *liberate*, and all this was there showed in certain;

41 Eliz., Dutred against Toppe, in an *audita querela* against an assignee, shows the seisin *et adhuc seisitus existens*. But, in modern times, *scil.* in the time of King James, all the precedents run according to the precedent of this case now here in question before us. And so, upon the whole matter, judgment in this case ought to be given for the plaintiff.

And so, according to this resolution of the whole court, by the rule of the court, judgment was given and so entered for the plaintiff.

[Reg. Lib. Trinity 1 Car. I, f. 773.]

4

Farmer v. Compton

(Ch. 1625–1626)

A court of equity can take jurisdiction over a suit for advice and guidance filed by a trustee.

A marriage settlement is enforceable where the parties were married beforehand and the other parties to the settlement afterwards consented to the marriage.

1 Chancery Reports 1, 21 E.R. 490

The plaintiff and defendant came to a treaty for a marriage between Sir John Farmer, the plaintiff, Sir Richard Farmer's son, and Dame Cecily, daughter of the said defendant Sir Henry Compton, with whom he was to have £4000. And it was agreed that £800 *per annum* should be settled on her for a jointure and that the plaintiff should deduct £200 *per annum* thereout during his life. Direction was given to draw writings accordingly, but, before the assurances were perfected, the said Sir John, the son, married her without the knowledge of the said fathers. And the plaintiff and defendant, being ignorant thereof, made the assurances, and the defendant Sir Henry Compton agreed they should marry. But, in the said assurances, the deduction of £200 *per annum*, as is aforesaid, was omitted in the drawing of the said deeds. And, after the marriage was confessed by the said Sir John to one Benskin, who acquainted Sir Henry therewith, and £1150 of the £4000 was paid to the plaintiff, which portion of £4000 was originally to be raised out of the said lands according to a conveyance thereof made by the countess of Dorset, the same Dame Cecily's grandmother, to the said Benskin and others to the intent that they should, out of the profits thereof, pay to the same Dame Cecily her said portion of £4000 at her age of twenty-one years or when, with the consent of her father, she should be married, which should first happen, and, if she should die before such age or marriage, then £1000 of the said portion should be paid to her sister Anne, who had the like portion given unto her by the said countess, and the other £3000 to be distributed amongst other the younger children of the said Sir Henry Compton. And, for that the said

Sir John Farmer died before any of the £2850, being the remainder of the £4000 portion given by the said countess to the said Dame Cecily, as aforesaid, was paid and the said Dame Cecily being married, as aforesaid, and the defendant Benskin being trusted by the said countess, as is aforementioned, he doubts that, if he should proceed to pay the said remaining £2850 and increase thereof according to the agreement aforesaid, whether he might not again be called in question for the same by the said Lady Farmer and the younger children if the said Dame Cecily should die before twenty-one years of age, and he prays the judgment and decree of the court for his indemnity.

And, *per curiam*, as touching the payment of the residue of the £4000 according to the conveyance made by the countess to Benskin and others in trust as aforesaid for raising of the said portion and how the said Benskin shall be discharged thereof and of the money already paid, this court ordered a case to be made out of the deed.

And a case, being made and agreed unto, was by the Lord Keeper [LORD COVENTRY] sent to the judges at Serjeants' Inn in Fleet Street.

And all of the said judges were of opinion that the said marriage between the said Sir John Farmer and his Lady, having taken effect in the manner before declared, ought in equity and justice to be esteemed a marriage had with the consent of the said Sir Henry Compton, her father, of which opinion His Lordship [LORD COVENTRY] is also in respect there was an express consent of the said Henry, both before and after the said marriage consummated, and no disagreement or alteration of his good liking in the meantime.

And this court decreed the residue of the money to the plaintiff and the said Benskin and his heirs etc. discharged of the said £4000, notwithstanding that the said marriage was had without the assent of the said Sir Henry Compton, as aforesaid, or any other pretense or matter whatsoever.

[Reg. Lib. 1 Car. I, f. 1088.]

5

Plunket v. Brereton

(Ch. 1625–1626)

A conveyance of a rent is enforceable in equity even though here is no right to enforce the rent by distress.

1 Chancery Reports 4, 21 E.R. 491

Sir Randall Brereton, seised in fee of the manor of Creswell and Blunhill, made a lease of the manor of Creswell to Dr. Compton for divers years to come, rendering £40 *per annum* to Sir Randall, his heirs, and assignees, after which Sir Randall, in consideration of a marriage between Richard Brereton, his brother and heir, and the plaintiff Mary, daughter of Sir Walter Heveningham, and of £2000 portion paid by Sir Walter, agreed that the said Mary should have in augmentation of her jointure the £40 *per annum* reserved on the manor of Creswell and £10 *per annum* reserved on Blunhill. And, thereupon, Sir Randall conveyed the said manors to the feoffees and their heirs to the use of himself for life, and, after, to the use of the said Richard, his brother, and the male heirs of his body, and, after, to the use of the defendant Sir Thomas Brereton, yet, nevertheless, that the said Mary, wife of the said Richard, might have the said rents of £40 *per annum* and £10 *per annum* for her life for supply of her jointure, which conveyance being settled, Sir Randall died.

And Sir Richard, his brother, entered and made a lease of Blunhill with a covenant to free it from the said £10 *per annum*, and he died without male issue. And, so, the inheritance in tail of all the lands came to the defendant, Sir Thomas Brereton, who refuses to let the said plaintiff Mary have the said rents of £40 and £10 *per annum*, he claiming the same as due to himself.

This court, having maturely considered of the said conveyance and of some cases in law presented by both sides, declared they were clear of opinion that the said rents of £40 and of £10 *per annum* in equity are due and ought to be paid to the plaintiff Mary during her life, howbeit the said plaintiff in point of law cannot distrain for the same unless the said leases are out and determined. And [the court] decreed the same to be paid, according to the intent of the said conveyance made to her thereof, as aforesaid.

6

Atkins v. Temple

(Ch. 1625–1626)

A court of equity can restrain waste in the form of the plowing up of ancient meadow and pasture land.

1 Chancery Reports 13, 21 E.R. 493

The bill is to restrain the defendant from plowing up ancient meadow and pasture grounds, being the plaintiff's inheritance, which premises, according to the grant of them, were to be used only as meadow and pasture, and not otherwise, and which ground was rich and fertile, little or nothing inferior to good meadow ground for goodness of soil or yearly value to be let, and has not been plowed in the memory of man.

This court, in respect of generality of the case, directed precedents to be produced. The precedents being produced, His Lordship [LORD COVENTRY], assisted with judges, declared that he did find by divers precedents, part in the time of the Lord Ellesmere and others since, that the plowing of ancient pasture has been restrained by decrees of this court and declared, that, in those cases so decreed, it did not appear that the pasture restrained from plowing were either so ancient or so rich and fertile as in this case. And His Lordship [LORD COVENTRY] did further declare that, whereas plowing of meadow by the law is waste, he conceives that the plowing of ancient pasture is of equal value with meadow, as no less prejudicial either to the landlord or to the commonwealth, than the plowing of meadow, and, therefore, fit to be restrained in equity, the judges being of the same opinion. And he decreed the defendant to forbear plowing as aforesaid.

[Reg. Lib. 1 Car. I, f. 1064.]

7

Pool v. Pool

(Ch. 1625–1626)

Where lands are conveyed to an heir, the heir must perform his deceased ancestor's contractual obligations.

1 Chancery Reports 18, 21 E.R. 494

The plaintiff, being ordered to perform his father's covenants, refused, insisting that he is not chargeable with his father's covenants as heir, the lands being conveyed to him, nor as executor, having no assets.

This court ordered that the plaintiff shall seal the said covenant according to the said articles of his father and, thereby, covenant to free the premises from leases and encumbrances or stand committed to the Fleet [Prison].

[Reg. Lib. 1 Car. I, f. 4.]

8

Emmanuel College, Cambridge v. Evans

(Ch. 1625–1626)

A late payment of a debt is a sufficient payment in equity to defeat a condition subsequent.

In this case, the right of a remainderman was upheld against the claim of a subsequent purchaser from the original grantor.

1 Chancery Reports 18, 21 E.R. 494

The earl of Huntingdon, seised in fee of the manor of North Cabury with an advowson appendant, and, for payment of debts by way of mortgage, 25 Eliz. [1582–83], made a lease for 500 years of the said manor with appurtenances, not mentioning the advowson, by express name with a clause of redemption. And, for the advancement of learning and religion, of his free disposition in 28 Eliz.

[1585–86] by deed, he granted the said advowson to Sir Francis Hastings and others and their heirs to the use of the said earl for life, remainder to the master, fellows, etc. of the said College and their successors forever. And, shortly after, in the same year, he paid his said debts. And, for valuable considerations, the said earl sold the said manor to the said Sir Francis Hastings, yet the advowson was not mentioned in the said deed of sale, but was mentioned in the fine.

Which this court observed and conceived thereupon that it was purposely omitted in the deed, for, otherwise, the covenant of the said earl had been broken. But it was put into the fine on purpose to convey the advowson to the said Sir Francis Hastings during the life of the said earl only.

And this court conceived the said advowson being leased not by special name, but as appendant to the manor, and that only by way of counter-security, and the money thereby secured but £100, and, at the time of granting the said advowson to the said College, the said earl took no notice of the said lease of 500 years, as a thing of validity, for that it had been absurd in the said grant to reserve to himself an estate for life after 500 years, that the said lease was assigned by the said earl to Matthew Evans, the defendant's uncle, in trust for the said Sir Francis Hastings for securing his purchase. And this court conceived the said lease being but a security and that money paid, the said lease had been void, as well against the said College, as against any other. And, though the money was not paid at the day, but afterwards, the said lease ought to be void in equity, as well as, on a legal payment, it had been void in law against them.

The defendant insisted that Sir Francis Hastings, after his purchase of the said manor and advowson, did present thereunto one Sibthorp, who was instituted and inducted and enjoyed the same, as under the title of the said Sir Francis.

This court therein declared the said Sibthorp was presented in the lifetime of the said earl by the said Sir Francis, according to the intention of his purchase, and, he being then in possession of the said manor whereunto the said advowson was appendant as *cestui que trust*, the same was no usurpation. But the said Sir Francis, after the death of the earl, selling the said manor with the appurtenances to Matthew Evans, under whom the defendant claims, there was no mention made of the conveyance or fine of the said advowson, and the defendant also insisting that he claims as heir to a second purchaser, both being for valuable considerations, this court conceives that neither the said Sir Francis, nor the said Matthew Evans, were any clear purchasers of the said advowson, but the said lease was intended only to be kept on foot to defend the said manor from encumbrances, and not to carry away the said advowson any longer than the said earl's life, nor to prejudice the earl's grant to the said College. And this court observed that the said Matthew Evans himself, who was a learned man in the laws and one of the Barons in the Exchequer, would not upon his second purchase have left the said advowson out of the deed and fine if he had thought he had purchased the said advowson.

So, this court is of opinion that neither the said Sir Francis's nor the said Baron Evans's purchases ought to be admitted in equity to take away the benefit of the gift to the said College, but that the plaintiffs have good right in equity to the said advowson and that a charity of this nature ought to be relieved as soon as a purchaser against such a lease.

[The court] decreed the plaintiffs to enjoy accordingly.

[Reg. Lib. 1 Car. I, L. A, f. 980.]

9

Crouch v. Worcester Citizens

(Ch. 1626)

Leases of lands belonging to charities that are disadvantageous to the charity will be declared to be void.

Herne & Duke 52

Thomas Wild gave lands to the bailiff, aldermen, and citizens of Worcester to erect a school, which they did accordingly. [John] Crouch obtained a lease of some part of the school land from the governors of the school. One Closer got another lease of other lands, and others got other leases of other lands. And by inquisition, the said leases were found and that the lessees had acquired much above the rents reserved and that the said leases were made at under values and for too long terms. And the commissioners decreed all those leases void and to be delivered up.

And the then Lord Keeper [Lord Coventry] confirmed the decree.

10

Jackson v. Barrow

(Ch. 1626)

An assignee of a creditor who has levied on a leasehold can force the tenant to pay him the rent due and to make discovery of the terms of the lease and the amount of the rent due.

Nelson 2, 21 E.R. 774

Easter 2 Car. I [1626]. Lord Coventry.

The plaintiff, being an assignee of an extent, exhibited his bill against the defendant, who was tenant of the lands, to enforce him to attorn tenant to him and to pay the arrears of rent which were in his hands and to deliver unto him a true note in writing of the date of the deed and for what term of years he had it in lease and under what rent reserved, but not any of the covenants or conditions contained therein.

As to the arrears of rent, the court desired to see precedents before the decree was made.

And, thereupon, a precedent was produced in point between Shute and Mallery, 5 Jac. I.[1]

And, in the principal case, a decree was made accordingly.

11

Pennyman v. Jennings
(Ch. 1626)

Lands can be devised to churchwardens for a charitable use.

Herne & Duke 56

Lands were given to churchwardens of a parish to a charitable use. Although the devise be void in law, it was decreed good in Chancery by the words 'limited and appointed' within the Statute.[2]

[Other reports of this case: Tothill 34, 21 E.R. 115.]

Public Record Office C.33/149, f. 872v

26 June 1626. William Pennyman, Esq., *et al.*, plaintiffs; John Jennings, knight, and Thomas Lawson, defendants.

Forasmuch as this court was this present day informed by Mr. Serjeant *Richardson*, being of the plaintiffs' counsel, that Alice Hawes, being long since seised of the messuage and land in the bill mentioned, about the beginning of the reign of King Henry VIII made a feoffment thereof to the use of her will and, by her will dated 19 December 6 Hen. VIII [1514], did appoint that the feoffees of the premises should stand seised thereof to the end the revenues should remain to the church wardens of the Parish of St. Peter's in St. Albans to the use of the church and poor of the said parish and appointed that the feoffees should make a new feoffment to other persons at the denomination of the church wardens, and, after her death the feoffees accordingly made a new feoffment, ever since which time, which was about 19 Hen. VIII [1527–28], the church wardens have taken the profits of the premises and have yearly made their account to the parishioners and have from time to time by the permission of the feoffees made leases thereof which lands, being within the parish of Sandridge, the manor of Sandridge upon the dissolution of the Abbey of St. Albans came to the King Henry VIII,

---

[1] *Mallory's Case* (Ch. 1607), 117 Selden Soc. 348.

[2] Stat. 43 Eliz. I, c. 4, s. 1 (*SR*, IV, 968–969).

who, about the latter end of his reign, granted the same to Sir Robert Rowlet, knight, who about 7 Eliz. [1564–65] by confederacy with five or six of the parishioners of St. Peter's procured them to take a lease from him of the premises, but the same was done without the consent of the other parishioners or of the church wardens, and now, by color thereof, the said Sir John Jennings, as heir of Sir Ralph Rowley and by color of some pretended escheat, does make title to the said premises whereof, if any such escheat was, it was in the abbot's time or at least before the grant made by King Henry VIII to Sir Ralph, and has sealed a lease upon the ground thereby intending to question the title of the said church, whereupon in respect of the [. . .] of their possession, it is thought meet and so ordered by this court that an injunction be awarded as well for establishing the parties' possession as against the said defendants, their counsellors and attorneys and solicitors, for stay of their further proceedings at the common law in the said *ejectione firmae* until the matter shall be here heard and determined or otherwise ordered by this court.

Public Record Office C.33/150, f. 969v

28 June 1626. William Pennyman, Esq., *et al.*, plaintiffs; John Jennings, knight, and Thomas Lawson, defendants.

Whereas, by an order of the 26th of this month, it was ordered for the reasons therein contained that an injunction should be awarded as well for the establishing of the plaintiffs' possession as against the defendants, their counsellors, attorneys, and solicitors for stay of their farther proceedings at the common law until the matter should be here heard and determined or otherwise ordered by this court, forasmuch as this court was this present day informed by Mr. Serjeant *Crawley*, being of the defendants' counsel, that the plaintiffs have held and enjoyed the lands by the space of sixty years last past until such time as their lease determined, which ended at Michaelmas last and continually paid the rent, being 18s. 8d., for the same to the defendants and now the said defendant having made his entry, the plaintiffs do set on foot a new title and pretend that the inheritance is in them by reason of the last will and testament of one Alice Hawes, who indeed was a married woman as well at the time of the making of the said will as at the time of her death if any such will were made, as the defendants' counsel now alleges, it is therefore ordered that Mr. Pennyman do attend Sir Robert Rich with the said will and evidences touching the said lands which may satisfy the master that the inheritance is in the plaintiff or any others to the use of the church or the poor and the defendant is then also to produce the said lease before any injunction be passed in this court, but if they can give the said master satisfaction that the inheritance is in them or any other as aforesaid, then the said injunction is to pass according to the former order, which in the meantime is stayed.

[Other copies of this order: Public Record Office C.33/149, f. 862v.]

Public Record Office C.33/150, f. 1032v

13 July 1626. William Pennyman, Esq., *et al.*, [plaintiffs]; John Jennings, knight, *et al.*, defendants.

Upon the opening of the matter this present day unto the Right Honorable the Lord Keeper by Mr. Serjeant *Richardson*, being of the plaintiffs' counsel, and upon the reading as well of an order of the 26th of June last as also of an order of the 28th of the same month and also of a report made by Sir Robert Rich, knight, one etc. to whom it was by the said order of the 28th of June referred to see the evidence of both parts and to certify to this court in whom the inheritance of the premises in question was, his Lordship concerning this cause fit for the hearing and determination of this court, being concerning a pious and charitable use does therefore order notwithstanding anything now said to the contrary by Mr. Davies, being of the defendants' counsel, that an injunction be awarded according to the said order of the 26th of June last and, to the end this cause may receive a speedy hearing in this court, it is ordered by his Lordship by assent of the counsel on both parts that the said plaintiffs shall forthwith reply and the defendants to rejoin *gratis* to the end a commission may be awarded to examine witnesses this vacation and that publication may be had the next term according to the rules of the court and the cause to proceed to hearing accordingly with all convenient speed.

[Other copies of this order: Public Record Office C.33/149, f. 929.]

Public Record Office C.33/150, f. 1054

21 July 1626. William Pennyman, Esq., Thomas Adams, *et al.*, plaintiffs; John Jennings, knight, *et al.*, defendants.

Whereas, by several former orders of this court, the possession of the lands and premises in question were established with the plaintiffs by the injunction of this court until the hearing of the cause of this court unto which the said parties are to proceed with all convenient speed, now, upon the defendants' petition this day exhibited unto the Right Honorable the Lord Keeper, it is ordered for the reasons therein contained that the said plaintiffs, their agents, servants, farmers, and workmen and all claiming from, by, or under them shall forebear to fell or cut down any timber trees growing upon the said premises and shall not commit any waste thereupon whilst the suit between them is depending in this court for which purpose the said defendants may likewise take an injunction if they please.

[Other copies of this order: Public Record Office C.33/149, f. 956.]

12

Windsor v. Hilton

(Ch. 1626)

A bill of review does not lie to a bill of review. Therefore, a bill of review does not lie to a decree affirming or reversing an order made by charity commissioners, but the party must petition for a review in the House of Lords.

Herne & Duke 53

In the case between Thomas Windsor, plaintiff, and Robert Hilton and others of the Town of Farnham [Surrey], defendants, upon a reference to the judges out of the Chancery, it was resolved by the judges of the King's Bench that, if upon an appeal in Chancery or Duchy, the decree and orders of the commissioners for charitable uses be confirmed, the party aggrieved can have no bill of review, because the appeal is in the nature of a bill of review, and no bill of review lies after a decree is confirmed upon a bill of review, for then it may be infinite vexation. But in such a case, the party aggrieved may prefer his petition in Parliament and there have his complaint examined.

And the Lords in Parliament may confirm, alter, or annul the decree, which is to be final, as it was resolved by the judges and the king's counsel, assistants in the House of Peers, 20 *Caroli*, 1643, between the Poor of East Ham in Essex, plaintiffs, and the Lady Kemp and others, defendants,[1] where Dandy, one of the almsmen of the almshouse in East Ham of the foundation of Giles Breame, Esquire, complained by petition before the Lords in Parliament to have a decree made by the Lord Coventry annulled, who by his decree altered the decree of the commissioners, and the said defendants excepted that the said decree could not be annulled without [a] bill in Parliament, for the reason aforesaid. And upon reference to the said judges and counsel, they certified as aforesaid, and then the Lords proceeded to examine the said Lord Keeper's decree and confirmed it.

Croke Car. 40, 79 E.R. 639

Upon a reference out of Chancery between Thomas Windsor and the inhabitants of Farnham to Sir Randolph Crewe, Chief Justice, Sir John Walter, Chief Baron, Sir William Jones, and to myself [Sir George Croke], the sole question being whether a decree made by commissioners upon the [Statute] 43 Eliz., c. 4, of Charitable Uses,[2] and exceptions put in against it in Chancery and there examined, heard, and confirmed in part and altered in part, may now be re-examined upon a bill of review, as other bills of review upon decrees in Chancery. And it was resolved by all of us that this bill of review is not allowable, but the decree in

---

[1] *Poor of East Ham v. Lady Kempe* (1644), *Lords' Journal*, vol. 6, pp. 335, 519, 666.
[2] Stat. 43 Eliz. I, c. 4 (*SR*, IV, 968–970).

Chancery is conclusive and not to be further examined, because it takes its authority by the Act of Parliament and the Act does mention but one examination, and it is not to be resembled to the case where a decree is made by the chancellor by his ordinary authority.

And Jones said that so it is upon a decree made upon the Statute of 37 Hen. VIII, c. [*blank*],[1] by the major part and confirmed by the chancellor, which is not re-examinable, and so those opinions were certified in Chancery.

Public Record Office C.33/152, f. 395v

24 October 1626. Thomas Windsor, Esq., plaintiff; John Hilton, Robert Austen, *et al.*, inhabitants of Farnham in the County of Surrey, defendants.

Whereas by an order of the 26th of April last, it was ordered that before any review should be had of the decree made against the plaintiff on the behalf of certain poor [persons] of Farnham, the lord Chief Justice of the King's Bench, the Lord Chief Baron, Mr. Justice Jones, and Mr. Justice Croke were desired to consider of the said decree and of the Statute made in 43 Eliz. and certify their opinions whether the said decree, being settled upon exceptions preferred, shall by the intent of that Statute be after[wards] questioned and reviewed and the plaintiff was to bring unto this court all the money in arrear and due by virtue of the same decree and in the meantime upon bringing in of all the arrearages all contempts were suspended and the said judges upon deliberate hearing of counsel learned on both sides and due consideration of the said Statute do certify that they are of opinion that the proceedings before the Lord Keeper by virtue of that Statute be in the nature of a review of the orders and decrees made by the commissioners which orders had been final but that the Statute gives an appeal to the Lord Keeper and when upon complaint made by the party aggrieved, the matter has received a due examination and is settled upon a full hearing as this case has been by examination of witnesses upon the exceptions [ad]ministered thereupon the said lord chief justice and judges did conceive that it was the meaning of the said Statute in such case to settle the charitable uses in peace not to be questioned or reviewed afterwards by bill of review or otherwise. Upon the opening of the matter this present day unto this court by Mr. *Davies*, being of the defendants' counsel, and upon the reading of the said certificate, it is ordered that no bill of review shall in this case be granted and, if there be any such bill already had, the same is hereby clearly dismissed out of this court, and the said charitable use settled in peace according to the former decree in the court and the defendants are to take the money out of this court which is brought in by the plaintiff and the plaintiff is to pay the arrearages of the pension behind. And the defendants are at liberty to prosecute the contempts upon the decree made on their behalf against

---

[1] Stat. 37 Hen. VIII, c. 4 (*SR*, III, 988–993).

the said Windsors in that behalf. And this court wishes that this opinion of the judges be likewise entered in the Petty Bag.

[Other copies of this order: Public Record Office C.33/151, f. 381.]

13

Eyres v. Eyres

(Ch. 1626)

In this case, the codicil in issue did not expressly revoke legacies given in the original will.

Croke Car. 51, 79 E.R. 648

Robert and William Eyres against the executrix of Christopher Eyres.

In a suit in Chancery, this case was made and referred to the Master of the Rolls [Caesar], Dodderidge, Jones, and myself [Croke], justices, and to Sir John Ward and Doctor Lee, masters of the Chancery and civilians.

Christopher Eyres, the testator, 15 Jac. I, made his will in writing, and he thereby devised legacies to charitable uses and to the plaintiffs, Robert and William Eyres, his brothers, to the one £200 and to the other £1000, and divers other legacies to his other kindred. And he made his wife executrix, saving that he appointed his said two brothers to be conjoined with her as executors in trust for his wife, for the performance of his will. Afterwards, 22 Jac. I, being sick and sending for Mr. Davenport, parson of the parish, and for Mr. Stone, a reader of the Temple, they came and demanded of him what friend he thought best to be his executor to take care of his funeral and see his will performed and whether he trusted any person more than his wife. He answered that his wife was the fittest person, and, therefore, should be his sole executrix. Being then moved by Mr. Stone to give legacies to his father, brethren, and kindred, he answered he would not give or leave them anything, but he bequeathed to Lionel Atwood, his godson, 20s. or 30s. And, being thereupon requested by his wife to give him a greater legacy, he answered her 'Thou knowest not what thou doest; do not wrong thyself; thirty shillings is money in a poor body's purse'. And, for others, he left them to his wife's discretion or disposition. And the testator did speak these words, or the like in effect, *'animo testandi et ultimam voluntatem declarandi'*. All this was set down in a codicil, and the first will and that codicil were proved *in communi forma*.

Whether this codicil were a revocation of the first will for the legacies given to his two brothers, now plaintiffs, was the question.

After divers arguments, as well by the civilians as the common lawyers, it was resolved by them all and so certified under their hands that they conceived it was not a revocation of the said legacies. But they did not certify their reasons. The principal reasons of their said resolution were because there was an absolute and formal will made in his health and there being no speech made by him of his former will nor of the legacies thereby devised to his father, brothers, and kindred, nor that he seemed to remember his former will, that an answer to a doubtful question shall not take away the legacies devised before, for *non constat* what his intent was in using those words, for it may be his meaning was not to give more than he had given before or that he would not give more at that time by that will and *non constat* that he heard all the words when he was moved to give to his father, brethren, and kindred and he answering, 'I will not give them anything', *non constat* what he intended by those words and, therefore, upon such doubtful speeches to nullify a will advisedly made without clear or perspicuous revocation or words which tantamount shall not be permitted.

Also, the civilians affirmed that there is an express canon, there cannot be a revocation of legacies amongst children without precise mentioning the first will and legacies given thereby to the children. And they said the law is taken to be so when he has not any children and devises legacies to his brothers. And there does not appear any cause of misdemeanor to provoke him to revoke his will, nor do his words import any such intention.

So, upon these opinions, the Lord Keeper [LORD COVENTRY], being assisted with the Master of the Rolls [CAESAR] and the said three justices, decreed the said legacies to the brothers, the said codicil not having made any revocation of them.

14

Case of Rugby School

(Ch. 1626–1627)

Violations of the Statute of Charitable Uses are to be tried in the county where the corpus of the trust is located rather that the county where the beneficiary is located.

Herne & Duke 59

One, seised in fee of houses in Gray's Inn Lane, London, gave these houses to certain persons in trust to build a school at Rugby in the County of Warwick, and, upon breach of the trust, a commission was taken out in Warwickshire to enquire of this gift. And by a jury there, the gift and breach of trust was found, and a decree [was] made by the commissioners in that county to settle the lands according to the donor's will.

And, upon an appeal, the decree was reversed, for the inquisition and decree was not made nor found by jurors and commissioners of the county where the lands given to such uses do lie. The words of the Statute[1] be 'to enquire by the oaths of twelve men or more of the county of such gifts, limitations, and

---

[1] Stat. 43 Eliz. I, c. 4, s. 1 (*SR*, IV, 968–969).

appointments and of the breaches of trust of such lands and goods' etc., which is intended to be by jury and commissioners of that county where the lands do lie.

15

Norgate v. Pinder

(Ch. 1626–1627)

An arbitral award will be vacated for fraud in the choosing of the umpire.

British Library MS. Hargrave 174, f. 72v, pl. 3

The bill was to be relieved against fraud and circumvention in the defendant's procuring Gardiner to be an umpire between the plaintiff and Pinder. And the fraud appearing thereupon, the award and [the] bond for performance [were] decreed[1] to be brought into court to be cancelled, and no advantage [was] to be taken of them.

[Other copies of this report: British Library MS. Hargrave 99, f. 109, pl. 139.]

Nelson 6, 21 E.R. 775

Easter 3 Car. I [1627]. LORD COVENTRY.

An award was obtained by fraud, by which the arbitrators did award that one of the parties to the submission should seal and deliver a bond to the other after general releases first given, all which was done pursuant to the award.

And, upon a bill to be relieved, it was decreed that the bond to stand to the award and the arbitration itself and the releases and the other bond executed by the parties should be brought into court and cancelled.

[Order of 7 November 1626: Public Record Office C.33/151, f. 466, C.33/152, f. 407v.]

16

Lyddal v. Vanlore

(Ch. 1626–1627)

In this case, the marriage settlement in issue was valid and enforceable.

---

[1] agreed: British Library MS. Hargrave 99, f. 109.

1 Chancery Reports 9, 21 E.R. 492

The case is *viz.* that Sir Richard Lyddal, by and under several grants and assignments made unto him, was before any assurance made thereof by him to Sir Peter Vanlore[1] possessed of all the premises, for several terms of years unexpired, the old rent, of all, which comes to £20 6s. 6d. yearly. The said Sir Richard Lyddal, by deed 1 January 7 Jac. [1610], in consideration of a marriage between him and Dame Judith, and for a jointure for the said Judith, did assign such of the terms as he had at the time of the said assignment, making unto James Askew, Samuel Hare, and William Holiday, upon this trust expressed in the said deed, *viz.* that they, their executors, and assigns should permit the said Sir Richard Lyddal, during his life and the said Dame Judith after his death, during her life, and the male heirs of their bodies after their several deceases, to take all the rents, issues, and profits of the said premises, during the several terms therein to come, if the said Sir Richard Lyddal and Dame Judith or any male issue of their bodies should so long live and, if they should be all dead, then that such daughters as the said Sir Richard and Dame Judith should have between them should equally during all the said terms take the profits thereof and, in default of such daughters, then the executors of the said Sir Richard to take the profits during the terms with a covenant therein contained on Sir Richard's part to procure the reversion and inheritance of parcel of the premises, *viz.* of the mill and water of Sonning, both which were of the yearly rent of £6 6s. 8d., to be conveyed to the said Sir Richard and Dame Judith and the heirs of the said Sir Richard of the body of the said Dame Judith, the remainder to the right heirs of the said Sir Richard of the body of the said Dame Judith, the remainder to the right heirs of the said Sir Richard, and, further, upon purchase of the inheritance of any other of the premises assigned as aforesaid, to procure the like conveyance to be made thereof.

And the said mills and water were 20 June, 8 Jac. [1610] accordingly conveyed, after which the said Sir Richard conveyed as well all the said leases and inheritance, as also one other lease for years, of part of the premises which the said Sir Richard did purchase after the said assignment of the said Sir Peter Vanlore for the consideration in the order of reference mentioned.

This case was referred to the judges, who, having advisedly considered thereof, do find that the trust here is not fixed or settled upon any person certain after the decease of the said Sir Richard and Dame Judith, but, generally, upon the heirs male of their bodies, and, after[wards], upon their daughters, they, then, at the making of the said assignment, having no issue at all and as yet no daughter. And, if a conveyance were of land of inheritance in such form, the words 'heirs male' would be words of limitation, and not words of purchase. And, if they should be words of purchase, yet it would be in the power of the tenant for life to

---

[1] V. Larminie, 'Vanlore, Sir Peter (c. 1547–1627)', *Oxford Dictionary of National Biography*, vol. 56, pp. 122–123.

destroy such a remainder. And, being in a case for a term of years, if such term had been limited to the said Sir Richard and his Lady and the male heirs of their bodies by way of estate and interest, and not by way of trust, such limitation to the male heirs had been utterly void, and the said term for years should have gone to the executor, and not to the male heir. And Sir Richard had then had power to dispose of his term at his pleasure, so as it may be doubtful whether the said Sir Richard and Dame Judith have not the like power in equity to dispose of the trust in this case. And the judges do further observe that there is no other consideration mentioned in the said deed to make this assignment, but only to make provision for Dame Judith during her life. Neither is there any person *in esse* now, nor, at any time hereafter during the lives of the said Sir Richard and Dame Judith, can be *in esse*, that can complain of any prejudice done them by the granting or selling over of the said terms, though the executor of the surviving trustee should join with Sir Richard and Dame Judith in the sale thereof. Nor can any of their children, though they were all of full age, make any assurance thereof, for, until the death of the said Sir Richard and Dame Judith, it cannot be known who shall be the male heir of their bodies and that it appears that the lease of the said mills and water being £6 6s. 8d. *per annum* of the said yearly old rent of £20 6s. 6d., there is not above twenty years to come and, in another lease, but thirty-two years to come and, in another, but twenty-four years to come, and another but forty-five years to come; so as it is not unlikely but that the said Sir Richard and the said Dame Judith or one of them may survive the said terms, which would prevent all questions touching the same. Wherefore, if the agreement between the parties for the purchase of the premises should not now take effect, we conceive that it would tend to the extreme damage and prejudice, if not to the utter undoing of the said Sir Richard and Dame Judith and of all their children, for, then, the said Sir Richard and Dame Judith would not only want means of present relief and maintenance for themselves, but education for their children. For all which reasons we are of opinion, that this case falls not within the general case of trusts, and, further, that, in this special case, accompanied with these several circumstances, the said Dame Judith being willing thereto to join with her husband in a fine, it is just and fit that the said agreement should be decreed.

The judges' certificate was confirmed.

[Reg. Lib. 2 Car. I, L. B, ff. 452, 720.]

17

Kinaston v. Earl of Derby

(Ch. 1626–1627)

A court of equity can establish the authenticity of copies of court records.

1 Chancery Reports 15, 21 E.R. 493

This court, with the assistance of the judges, ordered copies of depositions and other records to be recorded and used and to be authentic.

[Reg. Lib. 2 Car. I, f. 1441.]

18

Powell v. Moulton

(Ch. 1626–1627)

In this case, the devise in issue was enforced, but, if the decedent's estate was insufficient to pay his debts, the devisees were to pay them out of the profits of the lands devised.

1 Chancery Reports 15, 21 E.R. 494

Robert Moulton, father of the plaintiffs, Amy, Merriel, Margaret, Mellicent, and Mary, being possessed of the manor of Churchamborne by virtue of several leases and having but one son named William Moulton, the said Robert Moulton and one Savage, who had an estate therein in trust, by deed 6 June, 13 Jac. [1615], granted several leases to William, the son, but upon trust and agreement that the said William should grant the same to friends in trust to the uses agreed. And, though after[wards], *viz*. 7 Ju. 13 Jac. [1615], William assigned the said leases to the defendants Croker and Palmer to commence immediately after his decease for the residue of the said term in the said leases to the use of the defendant and male issue of William and, for default of such issue, to the use of his female issue, equally to be divided between them and, for default of such issue, to the use of the said Merriel, Mellicent, Margaret, Mary, and Amy, by equal parts to be divided, and to the issue of their bodies and, for default of such issues, to the use of the several executors and assigns of the said Merriel, Mellicent, Margaret, Mary, and Amy, for their several parts and portions, with covenants for quiet enjoyment of the said leases, according to the meaning of the said deed and a covenant for farther assurance within two years with a proviso and condition that, if William died within twenty years after the date thereof without issue, that it should be lawful for him to charge or otherwise, by will, to devise £300 out of the profits for the payment of his debts or otherwise before his five sisters should take the benefit thereof. William being since dead without issue, he made the defendant Amy, his wife, executrix, who claims the said leases as executrix, and insists the agreement to be void in law, and William's debts at his death to be £700, and that, without the leases, she has no assets.

This court, on reading the deeds and William's will, was fully satisfied that it was the intent of Robert Moulton, the plaintiffs' father, and of William that, for want of issue of William, the leases should go to the use of the said Merriel, Mellicent, Margaret, Mary, and Amy, by equal parts, and to their issues, and, for default of such issue, to the several executors and administrators of the said Merriel, Mellicent, Margaret, Mary, and Amy and the said assignment by William was in pursuance thereof. And William affirms the said assignment, having thereby bequeathed the defendant Amy £300, which was reserved by a proviso in the assignment. And though the assignment be questionable in law in respect of the commencement for quiet enjoyment according to the intent and the covenant for farther assurance and though the defendant Amy insists there are debts owing by William whereto she is liable, this court, on the plaintiffs' offer, do decree the said assignment shall take place and the plaintiffs shall enjoy the said leases during their continuance, according to the meaning of the assignment, and that, if there be debts exceeding the personal estate and monies which is or shall come to the defendant's hands, the plaintiffs shall pay the same out of the profits of the premises and discharge the defendant Amy of the same.

19

Case of Hungate, *ex parte* Sherburn Inhabitants

(Ch. 1627)

A chose in action may be transferred for the creation of a public charity, such as a school.

Herne & Duke 60

A debt owing by statute, bond, judgment, or recognizance, which in law is a thing in action, was given for the creation of a school. And this was decreed to be a good appointment within the Statute[1] to maintain a charitable use.

Tothill 29, 21 E.R. 114

A debt, which is a charitable use in action, was given for the erection of a school. And this was a good appointment within this law.

20

Howson v. Martin

(Ch. 1627)

A bill of review lies to rectify a fraud committed against the court in which one party was prevented from presenting his argument.

British Library MS. Add. 25246, f. 71v

Doctor Howson's case, then bishop of Oxford but now bishop of Durham, and Doctor Martin's, judge of the prerogative and admiralty court.

---

[1] Stat. 43 Eliz. I, c. 4 (*SR*, IV, 968–970).

Sir Thomas Erskine, earl of Kellie, obtained a lease of a manor, parcel of the possessions of the bishopric of Oxford, the which lease was voidable by [the] statute law.[1] And Sir Henry Martin, judge of the admiralty and prerogative court, purchased that lease. And Doctor Howson, the succeeding bishop, made a new lease of the premises to the use of his wife and children warrantable by the statute law and entered and sealed a lease. And upon an ouster, he brought his action at law. And Sir Henry Martin exhibits his bill in Chancery before the bishop of Lincoln [Williams], then Lord Keeper, and had an injunction. And upon a motion for the plaintiff, it was ordered by the said Lord Keeper that a case should be made and referred to Justice Chamberlaine and Baron Bromley to report the law therein. And by surreptitiousness[2] the plaintiff obtained the report of the judges for him, and so thereupon the said Lord Keeper immediately made his decree accordingly for Sir Henry Martin.

The bishop of Oxford upon the remove and discharge of the bishop of Lincoln [Williams], Lord Keeper, exhibits his bill of review in 3 Car. [1627–28] before Sir Thomas Coventry, the succeeding Lord Keeper, to avoid the former decree.

First, for that the former decree was made upon a false case in law only made by Sir Henry Martin and his counsel.

Secondly, for that the counsel of the bishop of Oxford did not see the former case.

Thirdly, for that both the judges the next day after their report made, perceiving how they were abused by Sir Henry Martin, countermanded their report and certified the abuse, because their report was not filed when the countermand came, and yet notwithstanding the decree was made upon the false case and foundation as aforesaid.

This Lord Keeper [LORD COVENTRY], therefore, upon the causes and reasons aforesaid notwithstanding the former decree, has referred the cause to a trial at common law and has reserved the equity thereof to that court.

[Other copies of this report: Northants. R.O. MS. F.H.33, f. 4v.]

21

Good v. Warden of Merton College

(Ch. 1627)

A bill will not lie to quiet title obtained by the fraud of the plaintiff's predecessor in title.

In this case, the plaintiff consented to refer the case and accept an out of court compromise.

---

[1] Stat. 13 Eliz. I, c. 10, s. 2 (*SR*, IV, 544–545).
[2] surreption *MS*.

British Library MS. Add. 25246, f. 73

Doctor Brent's Case, warden of Merton College, in the Chancery.

The earl of Leicester, [in] the 16th [year] of Eliz. [1573–74], intending to procure a lease for one thousand years of a manor in Surrey with the advowson appendant, parcel of the lands of the said Merton College, of the said warden and fellows of the yearly value of £500 under the yearly rent of £40, did procure his secretary Sir John Attye,[1] a fellow of that house seven years before, to make a canvass for him by the votes and voices of the fellows, but, being afraid of the canvass and to animate his party, he put on his gown at the screen and gave his voice, because his name was not crossed out of the book of fellows in that college, and his voice made the greater number. But the good old Doctor Brelisse,[2] then warden, would not seal the lease of one thousand years by reason of the fraud and practice of Doctor Attye as aforesaid. And, thereupon, he was sent for by a pursuivant to come to the court, and both by land and water he was threatened that if he did not seal the lease, that they would kill him or drown him. And thereupon the said warden with tears promised the Queen Elizabeth to seal the lease. And he did seal it accordingly.

The earl of Leicester gave that lease to Attye, and he sold it to the lord Lumley, who sold it to Mr. Good for £2080, and he enjoyed the manor with the advowson forty years, for that Sir Henry Savile, the warden, would not sue for it to oppose Attye who made him warden. But Doctor Brent, after[wards] warden, entered and sealed a lease to try the title at the common law. And [Good sued] to avoid the lease, for that he was a stranger to the fraud aforesaid and to the practice and had paid a valuable consideration for it and has bestowed £1000 in building. Note that the said lease was made between the statutes of thirteenth of Eliz. and eighteenth[3] and so it differs from Magdalen College Case printed in the Lord Coke's *Reports*.[4]

Upon full proof of all which said premises, as well on the part of the plaintiff as the defendant, before the Lord Keeper COVENTRY, Judge DODDERIDGE, and Judge HUTTON, and upon two full hearings of the said cause, the Lord Keeper was resolved to dismiss Mr. Good's bill, except he would refer the end thereof to him and to the said two judges before such a day and did give his consent therein under his hand and seal, the which the plaintiff did accordingly.

The decree, therefore, was that the plaintiff should surrender his lease for one thousand years and take a new lease for four score years of the said manor un-

---

[1] Sir Arthur Atye (d. 1604), J. Foster, *Alumni Oxonienses*, ser. 1, vol. 1, p. 44 (1891).
[2] Thomas Bickley (d. 1596), J. Foster, *Alumni Oxonienses*, ser. 1, vol. 1, p. 121 (1891).
[3] Stat. 13 Eliz. I, cc. 10, 20 (*SR*, IV, 544–545, 556); Stat. 18 Eliz. I, cc. 6 and 11 (*SR*, IV, 616–617, 622–623).
[4] *Warren v. Smith* (1615), 11 Coke Rep. 66, 77 E.R. 1235, also 1 Rolle Rep. 151, 81 E.R. 394, 2 Bulstrode 146, 80 E.R. 1021, Croke Jac. 364, 79 E.R. 312.

der the yearly rent of £80 *per annum* excepting the advowson which was decreed to the college. And the plaintiff took a new lease accordingly for four score years. But before the surrender, the plaintiff caused the incumbent aged eighty years to resign to a young man by him presented to the Church and he is inducted.

And upon this fraud, the warden brings an [action of] *quare impedit* to remove that clerk who is encroached therein contrary to the decree. And the Lord Keeper does give way thereunto.

[Other copies of this report: Northants. R.O. MS. F.H.33, f. 6.]

[Order of 28 March 1628: Public Record Office C.33/153, f. 616v.]

22

Harrison v. Slegge and Sherwood

(Ch. c. 1627)

The grant of a municipal office that was obtained by fraud and against a lawful custom will not be protected in a court of equity.

British Library MS. Add. 25246, f. 74v

The case in Chancery between the mayor of Cambridge and the aldermen and commonalty for the granting of the office of the town clerk in reversion.

The mayor of Cambridge in the plague time in 2 Car. [1626–27] grants a patent of the office of the town clerk under the common seal in reversion with the consent only of four of the aldermen to A.B.

The town clerk dies, and the said A.B. is in possession, and the aldermen and commonalty go to a new election according to their custom. And they grant the said office by the greater number of voices to C.D. and not to A.B. And A.B., being disturbed in his possession, puts in his bill in Chancery for an injunction to confirm his possession. And the defendant C.D. pleads the custom and the election of him by the greater number of the aldermen and commonalty.

The Lord Keeper COVENTRY sent for the two chief justices to assist him at the hearing of the said cause. And they all agreed that a grant of an office in reversion under the seal of the corporation was good, as it is in Dyer in Savage's Case (8 Eliz. [1565–66]), and in 8 Assises, and in 22 Edw. IV, in the Abbott's Case of a grant of an office.[1] But in this case, seeing that the custom and prescription is to pass it by free election of the greater number of voices and that the former grant was not by voices but by the act of the mayor with his friends alone in a clandestine manner to confound the election and the custom therein, the

---

[1] *Sir John Savage's Case* (1567), 3 Dyer 259a, 73 E.R. 574; perhaps YB 8 Edw. III, Lib. Ass., f. 14, pl. 7 (1334), or YB 30 Edw. III, Lib. Ass., f. 172, pl. 4 (1356); perhaps YB Mich. 22 Edw. IV, f. 37, pl. 20 (1482).

LORD COVENTRY therefore and the said two judges did all of them agree against the said patent as savoring of fraud in the mayor to destroy a lawful custom. And so the decree was for C.D. according to the custom and prescription to grant it by voices.

C. H. Cooper, *Annals of Cambridge* (1845), vol. 3, pp. 220–221

On the 12th of February, LORD COVENTRY, Lord Keeper, made a decree in a cause relating to the town clerkship of Cambridge between North Harrison, plaintiff, and Roger Slegge and John Sherewood, defendants. His Lordship having advised with the judges, they were of opinion that the plaintiff ought to enjoy the office of town clerk until the defendant Slegge should evict him by due process of common law, and His Lordship ordered and decreed accordingly. At a common day held on the 23rd of February, Slegge, in obedience to this decree, delivered up the books of the Corporation to Harrison, who was thereupon sworn into the office of town clerk.

[Order of 12 February 1630: Public Record Office C.33/157, f. 409v.]

23

Perriman v. Gorges

(Ch. 1627–1628)

A contract to convey copyhold land will be specifically enforced, even though the land was subsequently sold to a purchaser for value.

Nelson 3, 21 E.R. 774

3 Car. I [1627–28]. LORD COVENTRY.

The father, in consideration of money borrowed of the plaintiff, did promise to surrender certain copyhold lands to him for and during the term of two lives in reversion to commence after an estate for life then in being. And he sent a note under his hand to the steward of the court for that purpose. But, before the plaintiff was admitted, the father died. The defendant, being his heir-at-law, was desired to make the surrender that the plaintiff might be admitted, which he promised to do, and took a further sum of money of the plaintiff for that purpose. But, before the same was done, he sold the reversion of the said copyhold estate for a valuable consideration.

And yet the plaintiff was relieved, for the defendant was decreed to surrender according to the agreement of the father in his lifetime.

24

Markall v. Hyde

(Ch. 1627)

In this case, an issue out of Chancery was ordered to try a right to an advowson.

Nelson 4, 21 E.R. 775

Easter 3 Car. I [1627]. Lord Coventry.

One Green, being seised of a manor to which the advowson of the rectory was appendant, did in consideration of £50 grant the next avoidance of the church to one Stockman, his son-in-law. And, afterwards, by deed enrolled, he sold the said advowson to one Pool and his heirs for the sum of £100, and covenanted that it was free from encumbrances except the grant of the next avoidance as aforesaid.

Afterwards, Pool granted the advowson to the plaintiff Markall and his heirs. But the defendant Hyde had before that time purchased of Green the aforesaid manor to which this advowson was appendant, but the advowson was not mentioned in the purchase deed, only the manor *cum pertinentiis*. There was a schedule annexed to the deed to this effect, *viz.* one grant of the advowson dated etc. (naming a date long before the date of the deed to Pool) excepted, and, in the fine levied by Green to Hyde, the advowson was specially named.

The defendant, by his answer, set forth that he had contracted with Green both for the manor and the advowson. And it was proved that he did know both of the grant of the next avoidance to Stockman and of the grant of the advowson to Pool. And now the grant of the next avoidance being by several mesne assignments come to the defendant Steward and the church being void by the death of the incumbent and Steward intending to be presented, the defendant Hyde affirmed that the right of presentation was in him by the purchase of the manor and the advowson. And Steward, unwilling to contend the right, was persuaded not to insist on his own title, but to accept of a presentation from the defendant Hyde, which was done accordingly. And, afterwards, Steward was instituted and inducted, and so the church became full of him.

Pool, not knowing but that Steward, the incumbent, was presented by virtue of the grant of the next avoidance, as aforesaid, did sell the fee simple of the said advowson to the plaintiff Markall and his heirs, who exhibited his bill against the defendants to be relieved against the usurpation of Hyde and to prevent any title that might be made thereby when the church should become void of Steward.

And it was decreed that no benefit should he had by this usurpation so as to defeat the plaintiff's title, neither should it be given in evidence against him at a trial at law but that the plaintiff standing upon the validity of his grant of the advowson and the defendant Hyde insisting upon the strength of his conveyance of the manor and also of the advowson, the right should be tried at law as if no such usurpation had been without prejudice to the title on either side. And a trial was ordered accordingly.

25

Buller v. Cheverton

(Ch. 1627)

A re-settlement of a marriage settlement made with the consent of all of the parties thereto will be specifically enforced by a court of equity.

1 Rolle, Abr., *Chancerie*, pl. R, 15, p. 377

Trinity [term] 3 Car. between Sir Richard Buller and Cheverton v. Cheverton and Polwheel, decreed in Chancery by Justice JONES.

If there be an agreement upon a marriage between A. and E. that a jointure will be made by a grant of a rent to B., the father of A., the wife, his executors and assigns for the life of the wife and that, for default of payment, B., the father, will have an estate for certain years in the land out of which it issues if A., the wife, so long live and, afterwards, the rent is granted accordingly and, for divers subsequent years, this grant is confirmed and the wife of C., the father of E., the husband, joins in a fine with C., her husband, for the better settlement of it and, then both of the husbands grant a lease for years in trust for the wife of C. to the intent that she will pay the said £80 rent to A., the wife, and that she herself will have £40 *per annum* and that, if the rent be not paid, the lease will be void, afterwards, B., the father of A., died without making any assignee of the rent, by which the rent is extinct in law, yet it will be made good against the wife of C., and the lessees in trust for the wife of C., because she gave her consent to it by the fine and the trust is to be guided in a court of equity.

26

Yate v. Southby

(Ch. 1627–1628)

Later proceedings in other courts cannot be a ground for a bill of review to reverse a final decree in equity.

1 Chancery Reports 25, 21 E.R. 496

A bill of review was brought to reverse a decree for tithes made by the Lord Ellesmere in respect the plaintiff has had a verdict at law and sentence in the ecclesiastical court since the decree.

This court would not reverse the decree notwithstanding anything urged against it.

[Other copies of this report: 1 Rayner 12, 1 Gwillim 431, 1 Eagle & Younge 361.]

[Reg. Lib. 3 Car. I, f. 1159.]

27

Ricksers v. Herne

(Ch. 1627–1628)

In this case, the money in issue was held not to be within the original contract.

1 Chancery Reports 26, 21 E.R. 497

An unmarried woman makes an agreement with others to distribute the residue of the estate of one Katherine Debel amongst them. And after[wards] she marries the defendant. The question is whether the defendant is bound by this agreement of his wife as to any of the residue which came to his wife after marriage.

This court is of opinion that what came in between seven and eight years after the marriage by the death of the said Katherine was not within the compass of the agreement, but was to go to the benefit of the husband.

[Reg. Lib. 3 Car. I, f. 883.]

28

Eyre v. Wortley

(Ch. 1627–1628)

Interest is payable on an unpaid judgment.

1 Chancery Reports 57, 21 E.R. 506

Twenty marks percent damages were allowed until the performance of the decree.

[Reg. Lib. 3 Car. I, f. 314.]

29

Wingfield's Case

(Ch. 1628)

In this case, a gift for the good of a church was upheld even though the gift was in general terms.

Herne & Duke 62

Money was given for the good of the Church of Dulk. And this was resolved to be a good gift, notwithstanding these general words.

Tothill 30, 21 E.R. 114

Money was given for the good of the Church of Dale. And this was ruled good upon these general words.

30
Hicks v. Kilby
(Ch. 1628)

A charitable trust cannot be directed to any purpose other than that intended by the donor.

Lincoln's Inn MS. Hill 125, f. 20, pl. 1

Sir Baptist Hicks etc. v. Kilby, 9 January 3 Car.
    A charitable use [was given] for a school and poor of D. The profits of the lands were employed to make the town a corporation and to build a bridge. [They] were disallowed because not within the institution of the charitable foundation.

31
Longman v. Hopgood
(Ch. 1628)

Where there is insufficient evidence to compel specific performance of a contract to convey land, a court of equity will grant damages for the breach of the contract.

Herts. R.O. MS. Verulam XII.A.50, f. 76v, pl. 1

8 February 3 Car. [1628].
    The bill was to be relieved against Hopgood touching his promise to convey certain lands unto the plaintiff upon his marriage with any one of the daughters of the said Hopgood, which lands the said Hopgood, contrary to [his] promise, had conveyed to the defendant Bishop upon his marriage with Alice, another of the daughters.
    Although the proofs were not sufficient to ground a decree to take away the lands from Bishop, yet the court did decree that Bishop should pay the plaintiff the sum of £80.

[Order of 8 February 1628: Public Record Office C.33/153, f. 633, C.33/154, f. 589.]

32

Herbert v. Lownes

(Ch. 1628)

A fine, trust, and will can be set aside and declared void in equity for fraud.

Where a defendant refuses to obey the decree of an equity court, lands in question can be taken upon a writ of sequestration and possession given to the plaintiff.

British Library MS. Add. 25246, f. 75v

The case in Chancery concerning Mr. Bland, the usurer, and Mr. Lownes, his scrivener.

Mr. Lownes was[1] the scrivener for Mr. Bland, who had lands in fee simple of the value of £500 *per annum* and £5000 in money, and he had three daughters and heirs, whom he had bestowed in marriage to Sir Walter Herbert etc. And the usurer, being aged and impotent and deprived of understanding, was persuaded by Lownes, who had married his daughter's daughter, to remove into the country from London to Lownes's house to take the air and to be free from unnecessary company, the which he did upon the persuasion of the said Lownes and by his combination therein with the usurer's man not to acquaint the kindred aforesaid where their father and grandfather was, although he was sent for [by] them.

And thereupon Mr. Bland was persuaded by the said Lownes through the opportunity and combination aforesaid. And by reason of his age and weakness, he was willing to levy a fine and to declare the uses of his lands by indenture to the said Lownes and his heirs upon a reservation or limitation of some yearly allowance out of his own lands to himself during his natural life and for payment of small legacies to his daughters and their children. Lownes, to confirm his grace and favor with the said Mr. Bland and to color his fraud and to insinuate his integrity, procured the Lord Treasurer Ley[2] to dine with him at his house in the country a little before the fine was appointed to be levied. And so Mr. Bland was made merry beyond his usage. And the Lord Treasurer departed after dinner knowing nothing, but [he] was only brought as a veil to color Lownes's villanies and to exalt his greatness. But then appeared Serjeant Digges and Mr. Minshell, who was privy to all the premises, and [they] came to take the fine and to see the indentures of uses sealed and delivered and the will published. And he, the sergeant, did take the fine of Mr. Bland and had £50 of Lownes. And the deed was delivered and the use of the fine declared to be to Lownes and his heirs, although the said Digges and Minshell did know and was party and privy to all the fraud

---

[1] being *MS.*

[2] W. Prest, 'Ley, James, first earl of Marlborough (1550–1629)', *Oxford Dictionary of National Biography*, vol. 33, pp. 686–688.

and complotment aforesaid and though the indenture and will were never read unto him but laid down upon a table and he said yea, yea.

The three sisters, daughters and heirs to the said Mr. Bland, and their husbands presently after his death sued Lownes by bill in Chancery to avoid the fine and indenture of uses aforesaid and the will.

And upon proof of all the special matters as aforesaid, in 4 Car. [1628–29], the Lord Keeper COVENTRY, with the assistance of two judges, did by decree make void the said fine and indenture of uses and the said will and did decree the said lands for the heirs as aforesaid, for that the said fine and indenture and will were fraudulently and by practice procured from the usurer without any consideration of money and unduly when the said Mr. Bland was not of perfect memory or understanding and upon proof that ten days before he made three wills and all for the benefit of his daughters and their children.

Lownes complained in Parliament against the decree, which was erroneous as he said. And Lownes did sit [out] divers commissions of rebellion in Chancery and could not be taken. And a sequestration was granted for the said lands and others for divers contempts. And after[wards] he, being taken, was committed close prisoner in the Fleet for words against the Lord Keeper. And the heirs enjoyed all the lands and goods by that decree, and the possession [was] delivered [to] them by a serjeant at arms.

1 Chancery Reports 22, 21 E.R. 495

This suit is touching some conveyances made by Peter Bland, deceased, whereby he conveyed to the defendants Laurence Lowns, James Mills, and Jolliff Lowns several lands to them and their heirs and also touching a will made by the said Bland 1 Car. [1625–26] against which the plaintiff prays relief.

In the year 1615, the said Bland made his will, whereby he divided all his estate amongst his three children and their issues. And, in the year 1617, the defendant Laurence Lowns, being a scrivener, was entrusted with the management of Bland's estate. And, in the year 1621, the said Bland settled his estate on his brother, John Bland, and the defendant Laurence Lowns, and their heirs in trust to sell and dispose of the money according to his will, and, in default of such appointment, to be distributed amongst his children and grandchildren, as the said trustees should think fit, with a proviso to revoke the same, paying to the said trustees £200 apiece. And, in 1622, the said Bland made a second will, and thereof made the defendant Laurence Lowns, John Bland, and one Baldwin executors, and he put the said will in a box under three keys. And each executor had a key, which said will is not extant, but supposed to be for the good of his children and grandchildren, as the said Bland had declared, but the said will was concealed or burnt by the said Lowndes. And the said Bland, afterwards, in the year 1624, being very weak, was by the said Lowns drawn to make two other wills. And the said estate being reassured to the said Bland, he was procured to convey the same again to the aforesaid defendants and their heirs. And other writings were made declaring the considerations of the said deeds. And, afterwards, 1 Car. [1625–26], the said defendant Lowns, when the said Bland grew weak, got him to make a new will and other deeds and to levy a fine and do other acts much to his and his children's prejudice.

The defendant excepts to the plaintiff's bill because it was exhibited by the children and grandchildren to question the said will and conveyances in the said Bland's lifetime.

The Lord Keeper [Lord Coventry] did now declare that, although he could not, upon this bill, decree any particular sums of money, either to the plaintiff or any other of the said Bland's kindred, yet the bill was sufficient to ground a decree to reform any circumvention, fraud, and practice wrought upon the said Bland in his weakness, and to remove any deeds so fraudulently obtained, and that the estate of the said Bland might come to those who of right it does belong to by law.

[There were] several debates of the counsel on both sides whether the said Bland were of sound and disposing mind.

This court declared that, although it has been often taken that a testator answering ordinary and familiar questions, was not a sufficient proof of a disposing memory, because to a disposing memory it is necessary there be an understanding judgment fit to direct an estate, yet this court would not pronounce that the said Bland was not of a disposing memory at the making of the said will and conveyances. But this court was fully satisfied, and did pronounce, that the said Bland was a very weak man, and apt to be circumvented. And, therefore, although the said deeds and will were not void in law, as not being made by a man of non-sane memory, yet so much thereof as was drawn from him by practice and circumvention ought to be made void in equity.

This court declared upon all the circumstances now appearing that they would not make void the latter will and conveyances because a man somewhat imperfect, yet disposing his estate, with the advice of his friends and good counsel and amongst his friends and kindred, it is hard to avoid it by saying he was not of a disposing memory, whereof this court is and shall be very tender. But this court and all the Masters then assisting were clear of opinion that the benefit redounding to the defendant Lowns by the said deeds drawn from Bland in his weakness by circumvention, being a paralytic man, without consideration and the intention of Bland, was always to advance his children and grandchildren until this fraud. This court decreed that the said Lowns and the other trustees, their heirs, and assigns shall not have any benefit from henceforth by the said conveyances, but shall convey the said lands to the Six Clerks to be by them conveyed to whom of right they shall belong and the defendant Lowns shall not meddle in the performing of the will without his co-executors.

1 Lee 255, 161 E.R. 95,
Misc. Delegates Repts. 212

Mr. Bland made his will in favor of his children. When he grew weak, Lowndes, a scrivener, persuaded him to make a will and deeds in favor of him. [There was] much evidence that the testator was weak.

The court decreed that he was not absolutely insane, yet, since there was fraud and management, the deeds should be set aside, and ordered that Lowndes should not execute the will without his co-executor.

[Orders of 7 February, 4 and 14 March, 30 April, 6 May, 2, 4, 9, and 18 July, 7, 16, and 23 October, 11 and 14 November, 3, 9, 11, and 19 December 1628 and 9 and 16 January 1629: Public Record Office C.33/153, ff. 594v, 665v, 718v, 1045v, 1070, 1076v, 1136v, 1171, 1223v, C.33/154, ff. 555, 652v, 672v, 971v, 1023, 1036, 1067v, C.33/155, ff. 53v, 76, 149, 198, 277, 343, 367, 395v, 408, C.33/156, ff. 53, 72, 190v, 267, 307v, 326, 363v.]

33

Anonymous

(Ch. c. 1628)

A servant or a son of a Master of the Chancery is not privileged to be sued in the Court of Chancery.

British Library MS. Add. 25246, f. 78

Sir John Mitchell, as a master of the Chancery, grants a writ of privilege to A.B., an inhabitant in the County of Middlesex, who was called before the justices there to maintain a bastard according to their order upon the Statute.[1] And he pleads the privilege aforesaid to the justices, as a servant to the said master of the Chancery, to be exempted from the said order.

The justices, upon the view of the said writ of privilege, return the cause of their summons aforesaid to the Lord Keeper COVENTRY, and also sent to him the said writ of privilege and humbly demanded his opinion upon the special matter aforesaid.

The said Lord Keeper [LORD COVENTRY], upon a public motion at the bar, thereupon disallows the writ of privilege and orders the said A.B. to perform the order of the justices.

And by another motion before the said Lord Keeper [LORD COVENTRY], it was moved at the bar to deliver the son and heir of the said Sir John Mitchell out of prison for debt for that he had a writ of privilege out of the Chancery from his father at the time of the said arrest. The Lord Keeper [LORD COVENTRY] in open court disallowed that privilege, for that the son was not any usual clerk of the

---

[1] Stat. 18 Eliz. I, c. 3, s. 1 (*SR*, IV, 610).

court nor a menial servant, and so the arrest was allowed and the imprisonment was justified upon the report of Judge Croke to whom the Lord Keeper [LORD COVENTRY] referred the consideration of the law in that writ of privilege.

34

Hide v. Gillingham Parishioners
(Ch. 1628)

A rent seck granted out of certain land is payable in full, with any arrearages, by whoever holds the land.

Seisin of a rent seck can be given before the rent is due and payable.

Where a rent given to a charitable use is misemployed, the current owner of the land is not liable for the payments before he became owner.

Where a rent given to a charitable use is concealed and not paid, the current owner of the land is liable for the arrearages in the payment.

A purchaser of land that is subject to the payment of a rent is not liable for a penalty for non-payment that is personal to someone else.

A trustee of a charitable trust who attempts to destroy the trust can be removed as trustee.

A rent seck that is given to a charitable trust cannot be converted into a rent charge by charity commissioners.

Herne & Duke 60

Trinity, 4 Car. [1628], Barnard Hide's case against the parishioners of Gillingham, Dartford, and Sutton in Kent.

Katherine Banne grants by deed a rent seck out of 208 acres of land for relief of the poor in those parishes and limits this to commence after her death and gives seisin of this in her life. The rent is behind for thirty-six years. Hide purchases the land, having notice of the charitable use. And, in the grant, there was a *nomine poenae* of 50s. if the rent be not paid by her heirs within fourteen days after it was due by the grant. And it was found that Hide had held the land seven years. Upon a commission for charitable uses, the commissioners decree that Hide shall pay all the arrearages for thirty-six years and also the arrearages of the *nomine poenae* for seven years, being the time he had enjoyed the land, and decree that the grantor shall distrain for the rent for ever after. And the commissioners' decree being returned in Chancery, the Lord Keeper [LORD COVENTRY] referred it to the judges, who resolved these points:

First, that Hide should pay all the arrearages for thirty-six years, for that the land is chargeable with the rent in whose hands soever it comes.

Secondly, that the seisin given by the grantor in her life is good, although the rent did not commence or was *in esse* at the time of the seisin given.

Thirdly, if land or rent be given to a charitable use and misemployed, a purchaser which has notice of the gift shall not be further charged than during his own time; but where the rent is concealed, a purchaser shall answer for all the time of the concealment, for the land is a debtor, *et transit cum onere*.

Fourthly, if a rent be granted out of land to a charitable use and one buys the land for a valuable consideration of money, having no notice of the charitable use and rent, yet the rent remains, because it is collateral to the land and another thing; and the notice required by the Statute[1] is to be given, as well of the land as of the charitable use.

Fifthly, [it was] resolved that the purchaser shall not pay the arrearages of the *nomine poenae*, because it was a personal charge upon the heir, who ought to have paid the rent, and it does not charge the land.

Sixthly, when the heir or others charged to pay a charitable use do break the trust, the commissioners may transfer the trust unto others, as to the churchwardens or other parishioners of the parish, where the charitable use is to be distributed.

Lastly, it was resolved that, if a rent seck be granted to a charitable use, the commissioners by their decree cannot make this a rent charge by adding a clause of distress, unless it be, for that this alters the nature of the rent in the creation of it and is against the mind of the donor.

35

Fish v. Seaman

(Ch. 1628)

A debt not sued on for a very long period of time will be deemed to have been paid off.

Lord Nottingham, *Prolegomena*, p. 350

2 July, 4 Car. I.

Lands were devised to Margaret paying 20 marks *per annum* to Alice, her mother, during her life. The land is sold. The mother lives twelve years, after which the son, the heir at law, enters for a condition broken, supposing the 20 marks were not duly paid *et utcunque* that there is not any surrender of the copyhold to warrant this conditional devise.

It was resolved by COVENTRY, Keeper, assisted by HUTTON and YELVERTON:

First, that the plaintiff shall be relieved against the breach of the condition, because she was a purchaser from them who had long quietly enjoyed and because, after long cohabitation of the mother and daughter, payment is to be presumed or some other satisfaction for it in diet and maintaining the aged mother, she having no other subsistence, and because it were hard to put a purchaser to

---

[1] Stat. 43 Eliz. I, c. 4, s. 6 (*SR*, IV, 969).

prove exact payment, as this case is, and because the defendant is in no way prejudiced by the non-payment;

Second, that a commission should issue to inquire what spoils the defendant had done and what profits he had received since his entry;

Third, the defendant was left to law to try the defect of a surrender, but he was not to give the breach of condition in evidence;

Fourth, the defendant was to continue in possession until the corn sown is reaped.

36

Nelson v. Nelson

(Ch. 1628–1629)

An agent can be compelled in equity specifically to perform the agency agreement.

Nelson 7, 21 E.R. 775

4 Car. I [1628–29]. LORD COVENTRY.

The defendant being tenant of the manor of H. was employed by the plaintiff to purchase the same for him, which he, the said defendant, agreed to do. But contrary to the said agreement, he purchased the same in his own name, but was afterwards persuaded to let the plaintiff into the purchase, which was done by a deed mutually executed between them. But, in that deed, there were several omissions of many things comprised in the purchase deed.

And, thereupon, the plaintiff exhibited his bill for relief against the said omissions

And, accordingly, it was decreed.

37

Viscount Cornwallis v. Savage

(Ch. 1628–1629)

In this case, the various grants in issue of annuities were enforceable by a court of equity.

1 Chancery Reports 6, 21 E.R. 491

Viscount Cornwallis v. Savage and Cornwallis.

This case is to be relieved for several annuities. The case is *viz.* that one Henry Breton, gent., being possessed of a lease of 99 years of the lands in question made in the time of King Edward VI by the then bishop of Salisbury, did assign the residue of the said term to George Breton, his son, and Anne, the wife of the said George, who, by their deed, the 19 Eliz. [1576–77] assigned the said lease to one Thomas Cornwallis and Lady Katherine, his wife, one of the daughters of the then earl of Southampton. And, afterwards, the said Thomas Cornwallis dying and the Lady Katherine surviving, she, by deed, 6 Jac. [1608–9], granted to the plaintiff, William Cornwallis, and to the plaintiff's then wife, two several annuities of £15 *per annum* to be issuing out of the premises during the residue of the said 99 years then to come if the said plaintiff, William Cornwallis, and Mary, his then wife, or any issue of their bodies should so long live to have and to hold the one annuity of £15 *per annum* from Lady Day [25 March] or Michaelmas [29 September], which first happens after the death of the said Lady Katherine. And the Lady Katherine, by her will, in May 1623, gave to the plaintiff, Dennis Breton, and Mabel, his wife, £10 *per annum* to be issuing out of the premises during the years to come if the said Breton and Mabel, his wife, should so long live. And also, by the said will, she gave to the plaintiff, William Breton, son of the said Dennis, 20 nobles *per annum* to be issuing out of the premises during the years to come if he so long lived. And the said Lady Katherine, by deed, in 1 Car. [1624–25], granted an annuity of £10 *per annum* to Elizabeth Breton out of the said premises during the said term to hold after the death of the said Lady Katherine. And the said Lady intending to establish the said lease upon one Thomas Cornwallis, her husband's near kinsman, by deed, 8 December 22 Jac. [1624], assigned the said lease for twenty years to begin after her decease, and caused the said Thomas Cornwallis to covenant that he should, after her decease, allow to the plaintiffs all annuities by her granted or to be granted. And, after[wards], the said Lady died in 2 Car. [1626–27], and the said Thomas Cornwallis survived. And he, by several deeds, confirmed the said annuities to the said plaintiffs, but, by his deed, 2 Car. [1625–26], he assigned his interest in the premises to the defendant Viscount Savage in trust for payment of his debts and other trusts. And he died about January last.

The defendant, Viscount Savage, insists that the grants of some of the said annuities are void in law, by reason of the said uncertainties of the *habendum* and that the covenant of the said Thomas Cornwallis, assignee of the said Lady Katherine, extends only to grants by her made and to be made, and not to the bequests by her will, and that the said Thomas Cornwallis had assigned his interest in the said lease to the defendant, Viscount Savage, before he did confirm the said annuities, so as the same were void in law.

Yet this court, notwithstanding, upon the whole case, did declare that the said several grants and bequests of the said several annuities are good in equity to bind the said Thomas Cornwallis, the assignee of the said Lady, and all claiming under him, and decreed that the defendant, Viscount Savage, should pay the plaintiffs their said annuities and arrears, according to the said grants and bequests to them made during the said lease.

[Reg. Lib. 4 Car. I, L. A, f. 995.]

38

Havers v. Burton

(Ch. 1628–1629)

In a case of hardship involving a London widow's devise from her deceased husband, a court of equity can order an out of court compromise to be made.

1 Chancery Reports 26, 21 E.R. 497

Robert Havers, the plaintiff's husband, deceased, having £1000 left to him by his father, being a citizen and freeman of London, and the said plaintiff's husband, being an orphan under age, and his portion being in the Chamber of London, the said Robert Havers married the plaintiff, who brought unto him a good portion. And, afterwards and before the said Robert Havers came of age, he died, but, by will, he gave the plaintiff the £1000.

The defendant insists that the said Robert's portion by the custom of London survived to his brothers and sisters and that £500 of the £1000 in the Chamber of London was a legacy given to the said Robert to be paid at twenty-one or, if he died before then, to go to his brothers and sisters, and so he could not dispose of it.

This court, nevertheless conceiving it a hard case against the plaintiff, who brought a portion, ordered it to be referred to the Master of the Rolls [CAESAR] and two serjeants-at-law to settle the difference, who did order the said brothers and sisters to pay the plaintiff £240.

[Reg. Lib. 4 Car. I, L. A, ff. 47, 714.]

39

Brown v. Thetford

(Ch. 1628–1629)

The question in this case was whether a court of equity can take jurisdiction over a modus decimandi.

1 Chancery Reports 27, 21 E.R. 497

The bill is to maintain the prescription of a *modus decimandi*, to which bill the defendant demurred, and says it is proper for the common law or ecclesiastical court.

This court allowed the demurrer, and dismissed the bill.

But note the time etc., such bills having been often allowed both before and since.

[Other copies of this report: 1 Rayner 12, 1 Gwillim 431, 1 Eagle & Younge 369.]

[Reg. Lib. 4 Car. I, L. A, f. 62.]

40

Game v. Hoe

(Ch. 1628–1629)

Where chattels are given to a person with a trust that the donee permit the donor to use them for his life, such chattels belong to the administrator of the donee.

1 Chancery Reports 27, 21 E.R. 497

Richard Hoe, by deed, gave to Elizabeth, his daughter, all his plate, jewels, household stuff, and his other personal estate whatsoever and all the jewels, wearing apparel, and ornaments of Alice, his wife, upon trust that the said Elizabeth, her executors, etc. should permit the said Richard during his life and the said Alice during her life to have the use of the said plate, jewels, and personal estate.

Touching the disposition of which personal estate, this court made no question, the said Alice being dead, but the same do appertain and belong to the said plaintiff as administrator to the said Elizabeth, his wife, according to the said deed of grant. And [the court] decreed the same accordingly.

[Reg. Lib. 4 Car. I, L. A, f. 65.]

41

Davis v. Higford

(Ch. 1628–1629)

A bond that lacks a date of payment is valid and enforceable.
In this case, compound interest was not allowed.

1 Chancery Reports 28, 21 E.R. 497

The question is touching the validity of a statute in respect the same wanted a day of payment, which was debated in the Court of Common Pleas.[1] And, upon several arguments, both at the bar and bench there, it was adjudged good in law.

And this court would not allow interest for the sum of £60, being interest money, and the defendants [was] to allow the plaintiffs interest for such monies as has been made out of the lands extended.

[Reg. Lib. 4 Car. I, f. 204.]

---

[1] *Hickford v. Machin* (1624), Winch 82, 124 E.R. 69.

42

Warmstrey v. Tanfield

(Ch. 1628–1629)

A grant of a future possibility is not good at common law, yet a possibility of a trust in equity can be assigned.

1 Chancery Reports 29, 21 E.R. 498

The plaintiff's title appeared to be that one William Freeman, being possessed of the third part of the parsonage for the whole term to come, granted all his interest therein to one Alborough in trust for the use of the said William Freeman and Alice, his wife, during their lives, and, after[wards] to the use of such male issue of their two bodies as the said William should by will appoint. And, after[wards], the said will appointed the premises after the death of the said Alice unto Richard Freeman, son of the said William and Alice. And the said interest in law of the said Alborough came by a mesne conveyance unto John and Robert Palmer. And the said Richard Freeman, during the life of the said Alice, who not long after died, assigned the premises unto the plaintiff, and also released to the plaintiff. And the said Palmers assured their interest in law in the said premises to the plaintiff.

The defendant insists for title that the said Richard Freeman, about two years after his assignment aforesaid to the plaintiff, made a lease of the premises to Walter Thomas and John Makerith, who passed their estate to one Evans and Hawkins in trust for the defendant, the Lady Tanfield, and had possession given her.

This court, with the judges, taking consideration of the said assignments, grants, and release, were of opinion and declared that, howbeit, a grant of a future possibility is not good in law, yet a possibility of a trust in equity might be assigned, and the said Richard Freeman's assignment of his said trust unto the plaintiff is also confirmed by the assignment of the said Palmer, who had the interest in law. And the said plaintiff's assignment is also precedent to the deed made to the said Thomas, by which the said defendant, the Lady Tanfield, claims the said lease.

1 Equity Cases Abr. 46, 21 E.R. 863

A., possessed of a term, settles it in trust to the use of himself and his wife for life, remainder to the use of such issue of the husband and wife as he should by will appoint. He, by will, settles it on B., his son, who, in the lifetime of his mother, assigns and releases it to C., to whom the trustees likewise assign their interest.

And it was held by the court with the advice of the judges that, though a grant of a future possibility is not good in law, yet a possibility of a trust in equity may be good and that it was the rather so in this case because the trustees joined in it.

[Reg. Lib. 4 Car. I, L. A, f. 151.]

43

Ferrers v. Ferrers

(Ch. 1628–1630)

The question in this case was whether a widow can sue on a contract made with her deceased husband that he would do nothing to defeat her dower rights.

1 Chancery Reports 30, 21 E.R. 498

This suit is touching a portion of £4000, the plaintiff claiming the same as heir to William Ferrers. The case is that a marriage being intended between the said William Ferrers and Jane Vanlore, daughter of Sir Peter Vanlore,[1] the said Sir Peter agreed to give with his daughter to the said William £4000 to be laid out in a purchase of land to be settled on the said William and Jane and the heirs of their two bodies, the remainder to the right heirs of the said William. And Sir Peter gave a bond of £8000 for the payment of the said £4000 within three months after demand and to pay £400 *per annum* in the interim. And by a deed of the same date with the bond made between William Ferrers, father of the said William, of the first part, the said William of the second part, and Sir Peter of the third part, it was agreed that the said Sir Peter should detain the said £4000 until such purchase as aforesaid. But, before the said purchase was made, Jane died, having issue a son, who soon after died. And the said William, the younger, surviving and accounting the £4000 and interest as part of his personal estate, declared it should go to his executors to pay his debts and legacies and that the said William, the younger, had received £400, part of the £4000 of the said Sir Peter. And the said William, the younger, died leaving the defendant his executor.

This court, with the judges, declared and are of opinion that, if the land had been purchased, yet the said Jane and her son being both dead, the said William, the younger, might have conveyed away the same from the heir at law, notwithstanding the agreement. And, by the said bond of £4000, being to be paid to the said William Ferrers, his executors, or administrators, the same in law and equity belongs to the defendant. And [the court] decreed the money to the defendant as the law had appointed it with interest.

---

[1] V. Larminie, 'Vanlore, Sir Peter (c. 1547–1627)', *Oxford Dictionary of National Biography*, vol. 56, pp. 122–123.

Lincoln's Inn MS. Maynard 75, f. 44v

Ferrers, a citizen of London, upon the marriage with his wife, covenanted that he would not do any act by which she would be hindered of her dower, both at common law or of her part of his goods according to the custom [of London], and that if he purchase any land, he would purchase it in his own name alone so that she could have dower.

Afterwards he purchased lands in the name of himself and his son, whom he had by another wife, and also he demised great legacies, and he entered in the name of his son to the use of his son £800 in the East Indian Adventure. And he died.

The wife, for this cause, preferred her bill in the Chancery against his heir and executor.

The wife being present at the deeds [?] etc. to her husband and the son and not contradicting it was not insisted on as a considerable circumstance.

It was prayed by *Glanvill* that dower be decreed to her in equity according to the covenant.

But the Lord Keeper [LORD COVENTRY] said he had no precedent for it, because here it was not due at [common] law.

Because [there was a] good remedy at [common] law, therefore he dismissed the bill here because the jury will give damages.

Glanvill moved that, here, the friends of the wife should have their covenant against the executor who is to answer for the widow's part and, thus, by this recovery of the part of the widow upon the minor. Thus, he prayed that the Lord Keeper would have the consideration of it.

The Lord Keeper [LORD COVENTRY] [said] it should be the minor because if the friends should receive [it] in the lifetime of the husband, it would not be her part the less, thus now.

It was agreed that the widow's part should not be impaired by any legacies of the husband which he gave, but it will be by the debts.

[Other copies of this report: Lincoln's Inn MS. Hill 125, f. 4v.]

[Order of 11 November 1630: Public Record Office C.33/159, f. 173v; Reg. Lib. 4 Car. I, L. B, f. 948.]

44

Owen v. Aprice

(Ch. 1628–1629)

A person can sue in an English court of common law for lost mesne profits, notwithstanding a decree for the same in the Court of the Marches of Wales.

1 Chancery Reports 32, 21 E.R. 499

This court left the plaintiff to take her remedy at law for the recovery of the mesne profits, notwithstanding a decree for the same in the [Court of the] Marches.

[Reg. Lib. 4 Car. I, L. B, f. 1247.]

45

How v. Vigures

(Ch. 1628–1629)

A bill of foreclosure lies against the heirs of a mortgagor, but not against the heirs of a devisor of the mortgaged land.

1 Chancery Reports 32, 21 E.R. 499

William Grills, being in his lifetime seised of fee and right in a reversion of lands depending upon the life of one Katherine Hicks, mother of the said Grills, being the jointure of the said Katherine, the said Grills, by deed 25 November 18 Jac. [1620], mortgaged the said lands to William Atwel and William Gallion and their heirs, which mortgage became forfeited. And, afterwards, the said Gallion, by deed, 1 March 22 Jac. [1625], released all his right, title, and interest in the said lands unto the said Atwel and his heirs forever. And afterwards, Atwel, by will, devised the same premises to the plaintiff and his heirs forever. And the plaintiff, being a merchant and his livelihood consisting in the returns of money, and the consideration in the said deed of mortgage being £340, disbursed in 18 Jac. [1620–21] as aforesaid, upon a dry reversion, the plaintiff, by his bill, seeks that the defendants, who are heirs at law unto William Grills, the mortgagor, may repay the said £340 with damages or else the lands be decreed to the plaintiff to the end he may sell the same.

This court declared that no decree could be made against the heir of the devisor, but only against the mortgagor and his heirs, and decreed the heirs at law of the mortgagor to pay the plaintiff the £340 with damages or, in default [thereof], the premises mortgaged are decreed to the plaintiff to be sold for the satisfaction of his debt. This was *nisi causa*, and none was showed.

[Reg. Lib. 4 Car. I, L. A, f. 307.]

46

Grinston v. Copping

(Ch. 1629)

An action of dower will be enjoined where the widow had accepted a contracted for legacy in lieu of dower.

British Library MS. Harley 1576, f. 233v, pl. 1

The husband devises goods and lands to the wife [with a] proviso [that] she shall not claim dower, and [he] dies. The wife accept[ed] the legacy and after[wards] brings [a writ of] dower. [There was a] decree against her dower, yet no act of the husband without her acceptance could bar her.

[Order of 12 February 1629: Public Record Office C.33/156, f. 556.]

47

Walthamstow Paupers v. S.

(Ch. 1629)

Exceptions to reports of commissioners will be overruled where the procedural errors complained of did not result in ultimate illegality.

Notice given to a party's counsellor, solicitor, or attorney is fair and valid notice to the party.

A surviving co-executor who never acted with regards to the decedent's estate will not be liable out of his own assets for any waste of the estate.

Interest is payable on money wrongfully detained from a charitable use.

Herne & Duke 62

Between the poor of Walthamstow in Essex and upon a devise of money by one Colby to relieve the poor there, these points were resolved:

First, S. took exception upon his appeal in Chancery that he had no notice of the time and place of the execution of the commission from the commissioners, whereby he lost the benefit of his challenge to some of the jurors that were inhabitants in Walthamstow, as being parties interested.

And upon proof, it appeared that the number of eighteen were sworn upon the jury, whereof three of them were substantial men of Walthamstow and none of the poor there to take benefit by the gift. And the Lord Keeper [LORD COVENTRY] disallowed the exception for that it appeared [that] fifteen others were of the jury against whom no exception is taken and a verdict of twelve or more is good, although others of the jury above the number of twelve dissent. Also, the three inhabitants were not parties interested in the gift and may be jurymen, they being none of the poor of the said parish.

Secondly, if one be authorized by a party subject to the decree of the commissioners for a charitable use, as a counsellor, solicitor, or attorney, to solicit and defend his suits and notice is given to his attorney, counsellor, or solicitor by the commissioners of the time and place for execution of the commission against the person so entertaining him, telling and advising him to acquaint the party interested therewith, and gives him timely notice to acquaint him accordingly, and, at the time and place of meeting, neither the party interested nor any other comes to make defense and challenge, if the commissioners proceed to inquire and make a decree, it is good, and the notice to his clients is sufficient. And, in the case of S., it was proved that he was an aged man and not able to follow his own business, dwelling in a remote county, and that he had a son, a counsellor at law, who attended his father's business in other things, unto whom the commissioners gave notice of the time and place for executing the commission, and that he might have given his father timely notice of it, and it was taken as a neglect [on] purpose to avoid the commission; also it was proved that the father had personal notice of the time and place appointed by the commissioners to make the decree, and his son came to attend it but did not take any exception to the jurors; and the Lord Keeper said that notice was sufficient, although he had no notice of the inquiry.

Thirdly, if one devise money to a charitable use for relief of the poor and make two executors and die and they prove the will and jointly intermeddle with the receipt of money and one trust the other with the money given to perform the charitable use and to pay it accordingly and he waste it and die insolvent, the surviving executor shall be charged to pay the money for the charitable use, if the testator left assets to pay it, for that they jointly meddled in the execution of the will; but, if the executor that died had only proved the will in the name of both executors and the surviving executor never meddled in the execution of the will but left all to the other and he had wasted the estate and died insolvent, the surviving executor shall not be charged with the charitable use out of his own estate, for that the other executor had a joint authority with him from the testator, and he would not prevent his intermeddling, and the survivor had no other means to prevent his charge than by his refusal.

Lastly, if money be given to a charitable use by will and the executors detain it in their hands many years without employing it according to the will, having assets, the commissioners may decree the money with damages for detaining it, to be employed in the charitable use, according to their discretion, not exceeding £8 *per centum* for a year for the damages.

48

Moore v. Row

(Ch. 1629)

A barrister cannot sue for his professional fees.

British Library MS. Add. 25246, f. 80v

Mr. [George] Moore exhibits his bill in Chancery against an attorney for counselor's fees upon agreement between them to be paid at the end of every term, as namely for a motion at the bar so much, for his hand to any pleading so much, *et sic de caeteris*. And the plaintiff avers by his bill that the agreement aforesaid was in private and that the defendant in such a term did owe him for fees £11 and so that the debt due to him amounts to £11 by virtue of the said agreement. And the plaintiff avers likewise that at several times upon account by virtue of the said agreement there was paid to the plaintiff by the defendant the several sums of £10 and £12. And so he prays relief in that court.

The attorney demurs in law to the complainant's bill for that a lawyer ought to have his fees in hand by the common law and usage thereof and cannot sue for fees at the common law but that the defendant may wage his law thereunto, that he owes him nothing, and therefore pleads that the pretended agreement was against law, for an attorney of record may lay forth fees for his client and recover them after[wards] at common law and by the statute law, and no client can wage his law to an attorney's declaration for fees or charges disbursed, but that a lawyer cannot sue for fees for the causes aforesaid.

And the Lord Keeper COVENTRY, upon a motion, allowed the demurrer and dismissed the bill for fees and said that it was *pro bono exemplo jurisperitorum*. For he said that he never knew that that client that paid not his fee in hand would ever come again to his lawyer or that a lawyer of any worth would send after or for such a client. Secondly, he said *ridendo* that a lawyer ought to take his fees by retail and not in gross. Thirdly, *asseverando*, he maintained all that was alleged before and as aforesaid.

1 Chancery Reports 38, 21 E.R. 501

The plaintiff, being a counselor at law, brought his bill for fees due to him from the defendant, being a solicitor and [who] was to account with him at the end of every term. The defendant demurs. This court allowed the demurrer *nisi causa*.

The demurrer was affirmed, and the bill was dismissed.

[Reg. Lib. 5 Car. I, f. 168.]

[Order of 23 January 1630: Public Record Office C.33/158, f. 285.]

49

Booth v. Booth

(Ch. 1629)

In this case, the bill in equity for an accounting from executors was dismissed upon a demurrer for various reasons of law and fact.

British Library MS. Add. 25246, f. 81v

Mr. Claydon, as guardian and overseer for an infant, puts in his bill in Chancery against Samuel Booth and Thomas Chamberlaine and Rebecca his wife, executors etc.

John Booth, an infant, plaintiff in Chancery in 5 Car. [1629–30] by Mr. Claydon, clerk of the rolls, his guardian and the overseer of his father's will, against Samuel Booth, clerk, and Rebecca Chamberlaine, the late wife of John Booth, the father, crier of the Chancery, and mother-in-law to the infant, as executors in trust to and for the use of the said John Booth, the infant, and against Thomas Chamberlaine, the husband, defendants, supposing that Booth the father died worth £3000 in money, plate, utensils, debts, leases etc. and that he did by his will in writing devise to his said son, the complainant, £1000, and to Rebecca his wife £300, and £300 more to other persons, and that he did demise the residue of his estate to the said infant. And the said Mr. Claydon by his bill avers misemployment of the said estate and goods and suggests that the executors have procured a false appraisal and delivered an untrue inventory of the said goods and estate, and alleges the taking and converting of the money, debts, and bonds into their own names to defraud the infant and pretends that they have given no sufficient security in the prerogative court for so great an estate, but only their own bonds, the which he alleges to be no good security and prays that the use of the portion money due to the infant plaintiff by the will as aforesaid, being £2000 and above, may be yearly superadded to increase the infant's portion and that they should not have so much yearly allowed to them to their own use only for the education and maintenance of an infant of seven years of age but only £20 *per annum* until the infant were of fourteen years of age and then £40 *per annum* after until he did accomplish his age of twenty-one years, when he ought to have his said portion. And so Mr. Claydon, on the behalf of the said infant, prays relief in the premises and that they may make an account as executors in that court and give good security in that court and to answer the premises etc.

And the defendants demur in law:

First, for that Booth, the infant, neither in person in this court nor by writing under his hand and seal prayed to have John Claydon [as] his guardian.

Secondly, for that this suit is commenced without the privity, consent, or desire of the infant.

Thirdly, for that John Claydon is no executor but an overseer and desired by the testator to assist the defendants in the executing of the said will only.

Fourthly, for that the defendants are named executors and have proved the will and are bound in great bonds in the prerogative court; and that the said will hitherto has not been in any part infringed or violated and that if they fail therein, they are there properly to be sued and not in this court; and that they are sure to be sued there, and so to be sued in two courts for one and the same cause, which is against all reason and equity.

Fifthly, for that the said defendants are not only executors in trust for the said John Booth, the infant, but also for the poor kindred of the testator, if the said infant should die within the age of twenty-one years, to divide and distribute his portion amongst the poor kindred of the said Booth, the father.

Sixthly, for that the government of the said John Booth, the infant, was granted unto the defendants by the words of the will; and therefore that they are to have the profit of his portion according to the will until it be paid; and that this court cannot appoint any other guardian contrary to the words of the will and intent of the testator.

Seventhly, for that the defendants are not charged by the will to pay the portion of £1000 to John Booth until the said infant should come to twenty-one years of age.

Eighthly, for that if there be any misemployment, releasing, or giving up of any bond etc., the defendants are liable to the forfeiture of the bond of £2000 and to the breach of their articles which they formerly made and delivered to the said John Claydon, complainant, on the behalf of the said infant, John Booth.

Ninthly and lastly, for that all the said monies put forth are by and with the consent, nomination, and appointment of the said Claydon and all the securities and bonds are put into a chest in the Chapel of the Rolls, and that the defendants, the executors cannot come unto them without the consent of Mr. Claydon, the usurped complainant, who has a key thereof.

Upon all which said causes and reasons, Mr. Justice CROKE did allow the demurrer, and the bill was dismissed.

50

Ingram's Case

(Ch. c. 1629)

Where a person imprisoned for debt is allowed out of prison upon an improper writ of habeas corpus, the jailer is not liable to the judgment creditor where the debtor's return to prison was prevented by the accident of his death.

British Library MS. Add. 25246, f. 84

The case of the *habeas corpus* in Chancery directed to Mr. Ingram, warden of the Fleet [Prison].

One Steward, a Scotsman in execution in the Fleet, upon suggestion that his friends at the court at Newmarket would pay the debt, procured his majesty's writ of *habeas corpus* from the King's Bench in 20 Jac. [1622–23] returnable the next term. And Mr. Ingram, warden of the Fleet, thereupon suffered him to depart into the country with his keeper. And at that time, it was a common course for all the courts to grant *habeas corpus* for prisoners in execution returnable the next term although it was against the law, and that all jailers did obey the writs as it was agreed by all the judges at Reading Term[1] in the year 1 Car. [1625–26] that it was against the law in case of execution.

The prisoner was sick at the day of the return and did not render his body according to the writ to the prison and died presently after. And the creditor brought his writ of escape *quod permisit ire ad largum* against Ingram, the warden. And thereupon, Mr. Ingram exhibits his bill in Chancery to be relieved and discharged in equity against the creditor, for that he did suffer the prisoner to go at large in obedience of the king's writ, as it was then usual for all other jailers to do, for that the law was not then published to the contrary; and that it was the act of God that the prisoner died before his coming to the jail and in his coming thither and not any voluntary or willful escape in him or act by him. And at the hearing of the cause at Reading Term 1 Car. [1625–26], the Lord Keeper Coventry assembled Judge Hutton of the Common Pleas and Judge Jones of the King's Bench to assist him. And he relieved the warden in equity against the alleged and pretended escape.

First, for that it was a usual course by all the courts to grant such writs and the warden was not to dispute the law with the judges but to obey the writ, but contrarily as the Lord Keeper then said in all escapes in that nature after the law published to the contrary, for then he protested that he would relieve no jailer in equity in the like case upon any accident whatsoever.

Secondly, for that it was the act of God to visit him with sickness and after with death before the said Mr. Steward, the prisoner, could return to prison and that there was no other apparent negligence, act, or default in the said warden.

Judge Jones got angry and said that Doctor Steward, prisoner in the Fleet by virtue of a decree in Chancery, did daily practice at the [Doctors'] Commons by virtue of a *habeas corpus* from the [Court of] Common Place, although there was no cause of necessity to grant him such a writ, and that the Doctors' Commons was direct contrary[2] and not on[3] the way from the Fleet to the Court of Common Pleas.

51

Henshaw v. Pye, Mayor of Morpeth

(Ch. 1629)

Charity commissioners have jurisdiction under the Statute of Charitable Uses to examine breaches of trust by visitors of charities.

---

[1] Because of an outbreak of the plague in London, the courts adjourned up the Thames to Reading in Berkshire.

[2] *I.e.* in the opposite direction from.

[3] in *MS*.

It is a breach of trust for trustees not to use the entire income from the trust to the charitable purposes thereof, even though the income has increased since the original establishment of the trust.

Where a trust is established for a valid charitable use and also for an invalid purpose, such as a superstitious use, the trust will not fail.

Herne & Duke 64

King Edward VI gives land to the Mayor and commonalty of Morpeth [Northumberland] of the value of £20 *per annum* to maintain a schoolmaster there and appointed them visitors of the schoolmaster and scholars, that they behave themselves according to his orders. This land increases to £100 *per annum* and the corporation did only bestow on the schoolmaster the £20 *per annum* according the value at the time of the first gift. A commission is granted to reform this breach of trust. And the corporation, upon summons, refused to appear before the commissioners, for that they are appointed visitors and the proviso of the Statute[1] exempts in such cases the power of the commissioners. The commissioners certify this to the Lord Keeper and that the visitors were the persons trusted and did break the trust.

And Serjeant *Thomas Crewe* moving the Lord Keeper upon this certificate the 22nd of May, 5 Car. [1629], the Lord Keeper [LORD COVENTRY] declared his opinion to be that the commissioners might proceed in the execution of their commission for the visitors, being trustees and parties breaking the trusts, are not within the intent of the proviso; and, if it should be otherwise construed, this breach of trust would escape unpunished, unless [sued] in Chancery or in parliament, which would be a tedious and chargeable suit for poor persons.

And the Lord Keeper said that the not bestowing of the increased value of the land given was a breach of trust in the corporation if no other use be expressed in the letters patent.

Also it was then said, if land be given to maintain a charitable use for relief of [the] poor and also that the schoolmaster or [the] poor shall pray for the donor's soul, that the charitable use shall be said the principal intent of the donor and the praying for his soul but an accessory, and therefore the charitable use shall support and preserve the land.

Public Record Office C.33/156, f. 838v

22 May 1629. Brian Henshawe, clerk, plaintiff; Thomas Pye *et al.*, defendants.

Whereas, by an order of the 18th of this instant May, it was ordered that unless the said plaintiff should by the beginning of this next term show to this court good cause to the contrary, then the matter is from thenceforth clearly and absolutely dismissed out of this court, now the opening of the matter this day unto

---

[1] Stat. 43 Eliz. I, c. 4, s. 3 (*SR*, IV, 969).

the Lord Keeper by Mr. Serjeant *Crewe* and Mr. Davies, being of the plaintiff's counsel, it was informed that the Bailiffs and Burgesses of the Town of Morpeth have unlawfully and contrary to the founder's meaning labored to displace the schoolmaster and do detain from him his salary by the space of six years now at Lammas [1 August] next without just cause and that they have misemployed and turned to their private uses much of the lands, possessions, and revenues belonging unto the said school and conceal the lands and keep it in their own hands or in their undertenants and pay little or no rent for it and have made many leases thereof and taken great fines to their own use and have made waste and spoil of an orchard and dovecote and other edifices belonging to the said school and for one lease in Nether Wootton, for which the tenants lately have paid or now do pay £30 *per annum*, they do allow the schoolmaster thereout but £5 *per annum* or little more and have also hindered the schoolmaster in executing of his place by laying violent hands upon him in the school by causeless attachments and by many other vexations; besides the defendants have not made a perfect answer but speak only to the employment of the rents and nothing to the lands itself in their several occupations. And to the misemployment of the school house which was anciently allotted to the master, his Lordship being therefore unwilling that the feoffees or the school master should be put to unnecessary charge in maintenance or defense of a suit in this court to waste the school revenue, it being alleged by Mr. *Bankes* and others, being of the defendants' counsel, that the misemployment is denied by the defendants and his Lordship being of opinion, upon consideration of the Statute of 43 Eliz. made to redress the misemployment of lands given to charitable uses, that although the gift be to the Bailiffs and Burgesses of the Town of Morpeth, who are pretended to be a corporation and to be appointed governors or visitors of the said school for which the lands are given, that nevertheless a commission may be awarded within the intent of that Statute to enquire of the misemployment by the said pretended corporation of the lands given to the said school and that the proviso in the Statute does extend where the corporation are the governors and visitors and are not feoffees or where they are feoffees and others are specially named to be governors or visitors and not where the corporation are feoffees and governors and do misemploy the profits and rents of the said school and that so it has been several times resolved in this court, it is therefore thought fit and so ordered by his Lordship that notwithstanding anything said to the contrary by the defendants' counsel, that a commission shall issue according to the said Statute of 43 Eliz. directed to the lord bishop of the diocese and his chancellor and to other indifferent and fit commissioners to enquire and proceed according to the said Statute both concerning the said school and school master and the said commissioners shall and may proceed notwithstanding any plea or title pleaded in bar thereof by color of the proviso of the said Statute that the same shall not extend to any city or town corporate where there is a special governor or governors appointed to govern or direct such lands neither to any college, hospital, or free school which have special visitors, governors, or overseers appointed by the founders.

And it is further ordered that until the return of the said commission and other order made to the contrary, the said bill depending between the said parties shall continue as now it is without any further proceedings therein and without prejudice to either party.

[Other copies of this order: Public Record Office C.33/155, f. 1344.]

52

Hallam v. Hellam
(Ch. 1629)

A devise of land for charitable purposes can be made to a corporation.

Herne & Duke 67

A devise was made of lands to the Company of Leather Sellers in London to maintain a charitable use there. Upon a decree by commissioners to settle the lands upon the Company, an appeal was [taken] and exception [was] taken for that the Company of Leather Sellers was a corporation and the Statute of Wills[1] excepts devises of land to a corporation. But the decree was confirmed, there being many precedents in it.

Public Record Office C.33/156, f. 1025

16 June 1629. Mary Hallam, plaintiff; Warden and Fellows of Leather Sellers [of] London, Robert Freeman, *et al.* [defendants].

Upon the hearing of the matter this present day in the presence of the counsel learned on both sides, the court being assisted by Mr. Justice Hutton and Mr. Justice Yelverton for and touching the will of Jasper Hallam, deceased, for the advancement and maintenance of the said plaintiff and for settling of the land devised to her by her father and also for some provision to be made for the said defendant Richard Hallam as also for the establishing of the charitable uses therein mentioned, forasmuch as, upon the reading of the said will, it appeared that some questions and doubts will arise thereupon and for that by the said will if any scruple shall arise the construction and expounding thereof is referred to the resolution and judgment of any two of the justices of the Common Pleas according to their opinion and judgment with such further power to them given as by the said will appears, it is therefore this present day ordered by assent of all the said parties, being now present in court, that the said two judges, who are desired by this court, shall some time this term at their best pleasure look into

---

[1] Stat. 34 & 35 Hen. VIII, c. 5 (*SR*, III, 901–904).

the said will and settle the lands devised in the said will as they shall think fit unto whose resolution and judgment all parties did refer and submit themselves and such their opinion, resolution, and judgment to put in writing under their hands and what the judges shall do therein, this court will then decree the same.

[Other copies of this order: Public Record Office C.33/155, f. 1074.]

Public Record Office C.33/156, f. 1113v

8 July 1629. Mary Hallam, plaintiff; Warden and Fellows of Leather Sellers, London, Robert Freeman, Matthew Jampes, Thomas Andrews, John Mayoe, Thomas Abraham, Daniel Hodson, Robert Key, Ranulph Patson, Daniel Vincent, Thomas Skymer, Henry Meeler, and Margaret Hellam and Richard Hellam, defendants.

Upon opening of the matter this present day before the right honorable the Lord Keeper by Mr. *Stone*, being of the plaintiff's counsel, and upon the reading of a certificate made in the cause by Mr. Justice Hutton and Mr. Justice Yelverton according to an order of the 16th of June last taken upon the hearing of the cause, it is thought meet and so ordered by His Lordship that the said certificate and all the matters therein contained be ratified and confirmed by the decree and authority of this court to be performed by the said parties to all intents and purposes according to the tenor and true meaning thereof.

[Other copies of this order: Public Record Office C.33/155, f. 1175.]

53

Hody v. Lunn

(Ch. 1629)

A widow's right of dower cannot be defeated by an unexecuted conveyance, even though the doweress agreed to the conveyance before her husband's death and then refused to complete the conveyance afterwards. However, the husband's estate is liable to refund the purchase price paid by the buyer.

1 Rolle, Abr., *Chancerie*, pl. Q, 2, p. 375

Michaelmas [term] 5 Car.

If a husband, seised in tail of land, for a valuable consideration, bargain and sell it to another in fee and covenant that he and his wife will levy a fine for the better assurance to the bargainee and it is agreed that £30, part of the consideration, will be paid to the husband upon acknowledgment of the fine by the husband and wife and, afterward, the husband and wife acknowledge a fine before a judge in the circuit in the vacation and, afterwards, the said £30 is paid and it is received by the wife, the husband being ill in his bed, and, afterwards, the husband dies before the term and, upon this, the wife stays the passing of the fine and, afterwards, she brings a writ of dower, the bargainee will not have any remedy in equity against the [action of] dower because it is against a maxim in law that a married woman will [not] be bound without a fine.

[This was] resolved by the Master of the Rolls [CAESAR], Justice JONES, and the Masters in Chancery. And the plaintiff was dismissed accordingly as to the [action of] dower. And they then said that it was so resolved before in Master Dewes' Case, one of the Six Clerks. But the court agreed that, if the wife had any personal estate as executrix or administratrix to her husband, she will be liable for it.

And, upon this, a commission was granted to enquire of assets.

1 Equity Cases Abr. 62, 21 E.R. 876

If a man, seised in tail, for valuable consideration, bargains and sells to another in fee, and covenants that he and his wife will levy a fine for better assurance and it is agreed that £30, part of the consideration money, shall be paid unto the wife upon the cognizance of the fine by the husband and wife and, after[wards] the husband and wife acknowledge a fine before a judge in the circuit in the vacation and the said £30 is paid to the wife, the husband being sick abed, and the husband dies before the term [of court], and, thereupon, the wife stops passing the fine, and after[wards] brings a writ of dower, the bargainee shall have no remedy in equity against the dower, because it is against a maxim in law, that a married woman should be bound without a fine.

54

Bishop of Winchester v. Wolgar

(Ch. 1629–1634)

A court of equity can restrain the cutting down of timber trees by a tenant of a manor except for cutting down timber trees for necessary repairs, even though the lease is without impeachment of waste.

3 Swanston 492, 36 E.R. 954

Die Jovis, 25 Junii, termino Trinitatis, anno regni Caroli regis quinto, 1629. Richardus, Episcopus Wintoniensis, querente; Williamus Wolgar, A. Anville, defendentes.

Forasmuch as this Court was this present day informed by Mr. *Browne*, being of the plaintiff's counsel, that the plaintiff being seised in his demesne as of fee in the right of his church of and in the manor of Havant in the County of Southampton, whereof the defendant claims an estate without impeachment of waste under a demise made unto Sir Richard Cotton, knight, in the time of King Edward VI without any consideration appearing in the lease except the rent reserved, by reason whereof the defendant, being assignee of the said tenement, does commit great waste and spoil and threatens to cut down the woods and timber trees growing upon the said manor, wherewith it is replenished, from the doing whereof, the several lessors of the said manor have been restrained by an order made by His Majesty's Privy Council, regard being had of the common weal and the commodiousness of the said timber for the maintenance of the shipping, in consideration whereof and for that the said waste, if the Lord Bishop himself should commit any excessive waste or spoil of woods, the same ought to be prohibited and restrained by the law, it is thereupon ordered that the defendant be enjoined from felling any more trees until he can give good satisfaction to the Court for doing thereof, and an injunction to that purpose is awarded against him and his workmen inhabiting the same.

[Reg. Lib. 1628 A, f. 1140.]

3 November, 5 Car. 1629.

Whereas, by an order of the 25th of June last, for the reason's therein set forth, it was ordered that the defendant should be enjoined from felling any more trees until he could give good satisfaction to this Court for the doing thereof and an injunction was to that purpose awarded against him and his workmen, inhibiting the same, upon opening of the matter this present day unto this Court by Mr. Serjeant *Bramston*, being of the defendant's counsel, and upon reading of the said order, as also of a letter from the Lords of the Council directed to the High Sheriff of the County of Southampton, it was alleged that the lease by and under which the defendant claims was made in the time of King Edward VI, and confirmed by the Dean and Chapter, and is dispunishable of waste, and the defendant claims as a purchaser for great and valuable consideration, it is, therefore, thought fit and so ordered by this Court that, if Mr. *Browne*, being of counsel with the plaintiff and who moved the former order, having notice thereof, shall not on Saturday next show to this Court good cause to the contrary, then His Lordship [LORD COVENTRY] does dissolve the said injunction without further motion.

[Reg. Lib. 1629 A, f. 75.]

8 December, 5 Car. 1629.

Upon opening of the matter this present day unto the Right Honorable the Lord Keeper [LORD COVENTRY] by Mr. Serjeant *Davenport*, being of the plaintiff's counsel, and upon the showing forth of an order of the 3d of November last, by which the plaintiff was to show cause on Saturday then next following, or else the injunction should be dissolved and of other orders whereby further time was given to the plaintiff to show his cause, it was moved in regard as was alleged the said defendant has already felled 150 of the timber trees and the matter is very difficult upon point of law whether the defendant upon the clause in the lease without impeachment of waste may cut down trees and make spoil at his pleasure in this case, it is ordered that the two Lord Chief Justices shall be attended, who are entreated together with Mr. Justice Hutton and Mr. Justice Whitelocke to take the matter into their consideration, and certify their opinion what they think fit to be done in such case, and then His Lordship [LORD COVENTRY] will give further order and, in the meantime, the aforesaid injunction is to continue and stand in force.

[Reg. Lib. 1629 A, f. 215.]

7 June 1630.

Upon opening of the matter this present day unto this Court by Mr. *Brampston*, being of the defendant's counsel, and upon reading of a former order of the 7th of December last and showing forth of an affidavit by which it appears that the houses belonging to the manor in question are most of them down and that part which is standing is much decayed and not habitable and, unless a speedy course be taken for the reparations, they will all fall down, and, therefore, it was prayed that the defendant may be at liberty to fell and cut down such timber trees as will necessarily serve to repair and build up the said houses and for necessary boots, now this Court, in the presence of Mr. *Mason*, being of the plaintiff's counsel, does order accordingly, unless the plaintiff shall upon Saturday next show unto this court good cause to the contrary.

[Reg. Lib. 1629 A, f. 675.]

14 June 1629.

The order, after reciting the last, proceeds thus. Upon motion this present day made by Mr. *Mason*, being of the plaintiff's counsel, it is ordered that the said defendant shall fell and cut down such timber only for his boots and reparations as shall be assigned him by the plaintiff's officer or officers and not otherwise, which, if the defendant shall otherwise do, then the said defendant shall be deemed to have broken the injunction of this Court.

[Reg. Lib. 1629 A,. f. 675.]

Die Martis 2 Decembris termino Michaelis anno regni 10 Car. 1634. Walterus, Episcopus Wintoniensis, querente; Williamus Wolgar, et A. Anville, defendentes.

Whereas, by an order of the 25th of June *anno 5 Caroli Regis* made in a suit then depending in this Court, between the Right Reverend Father in God Richard, then the Bishop of Winton, plaintiff, and the said Wolgar, defendant, upon the information of the said then plaintiff's counsel, that, he the said plaintiff, being seised in fee in the right of his church of and in the manor of Havant, in the County of Southampton, whereof the defendant claims an estate without impeachment of waste under a demise made unto one Sir Richard Cotton, knight, in the time of King Edward VI without any consideration appearing in the lease except the rent reserved, by reason whereof the said defendant, being assignee of the said term, did commit great waste and spoil, and threatened to cut down the woods and timber trees growing upon the said manor, wherewith it was replenished, from the doing whereof the several lessees of the said manor had been restrained by an order made by His Majesty's Privy Council, regard being had of the commonwealth and the commodiousness of the said timber for maintenance of shipping, in consideration whereof and for that the said waste, if the Lord Bishop himself should commit any excessive waste or spoil of woods, the same ought to be prohibited and restrained by the law, it was thereupon then ordered that the said defendant should be enjoined from felling any more trees until he could give good satisfaction to this Court for doing thereof, and an injunction was then awarded against him and his workmen from inhibiting the same after which injunction sued forth and sundry other orders made in the said former cause by an order of the 17th of June, seventh *Caroli Regis*, it was ordered that the said defendant should fell and cut down such timber only for his necessary boots and reparations, as should be assigned him by the then plaintiff's officer or officers and not otherwise and, if the said defendant should otherwise do, then he should be deemed to have broken the said injunction, now, forasmuch as the Right Honorable the Lord Keeper [LORD COVENTRY] was this day informed by Mr. *Carter*, being of the said now complainant's counsel, that the said former suit being abated by the translation of the said late Bishop of Winton, to the Archbishopric of York, and the now plaintiff being since lawfully constituted Bishop of Winton the defendant as well in the vacancy of the same see as since, has felled and carried away a great number of timber trees and other trees lately growing upon the said manor etc. without any assignment, part of which trees are still lying upon the demised premises, and that the plaintiff for stay of the same waste and preservation of the inheritance of the said church, has exhibited his bill of revivor against the defendant for reviving the said former suit and proceedings thereupon, as by a certificate from the plaintiff's attorney appears, it was therefore humbly prayed by the plaintiff's said counsel that the said injunction might be revived and renewed for prohibiting the said defendant, his assignees, servants, and workmen from felling or cutting any more timber or other trees in or upon the said manor and demised premises or to carry away or dispose of any of the said timber or other trees already felled, except the timber only for his necessary boots and reparations, as shall be assigned him by the now plaintiff's officer or offices according to the said order of the fourteenth of June, which request His Lordship [LORD COVENTRY] conceived reasonable, and does order that an injunction be awarded accordingly.

[Reg. Lib. 1634 A, f. 241.]

9 February 10 Car., 1634.

Whereas, by an order of the second of December last, for the reasons therein contained, an injunction was awarded for prohibiting the said defendant, his servants, workmen, and assigns from felling or cutting any more timber or other trees in or upon the manor and premises in question or to carry away or dispose of any of the timber or trees felled, except such timber only for his necessary boots and reparations as should be assigned him by the now plaintiff's officer or officers, upon opening of the matter this present day unto this Court by Mr. Serjeant *Brampston*, being of the defendant's counsel, it was alleged that the said manor, being parcel of the possessions of the bishopric of Winton, was heretofore demised to Sir Richard Cotton, knight, for ninety-nine years without impeachment of waste, which lease, being by mesne assignment, come to the defendant, who, by reason that the said manor house and the out houses belonging thereunto are ruinous and fallen to decay, has caused some timber to be felled on the premises, which he intended only to employ in reparations upon the premises, which, if the plaintiff's officers shall not assign unto him by reason of this restraint, the said houses must needs become ruinous, it is, therefore, ordered that, if the said plaintiff, his solicitor having notice hereof, shall not at the first or second general seal after this term, show unto His Lordship good cause to the contrary, then the said defendant, notwithstanding the said injunction, should have liberty to take such of the timber already felled as shall be necessary to be employed upon the premises only for reparations and not to any other use, and the plaintiff is to proceed with effect to bring the cause to hearing.

[Reg. Lib. 1634 A, f. 410.]

55

Lord Brooke v. Lord Goring

(Ch. 1629–1630)

A court of equity will enforce a trust against a trustee who attempted fraudulently to defeat the object of the trust.

A patent granted upon false information is void notwithstanding any clause of non obstante therein.

British Library MS. Add. 25246, f. 86v

Sir Fulke Greville, baron Brooke,[1] in 20 Jac. [1622–23], having the patent of the chief prothonotary within all the circuits of Wales for [the] entering up of judgments before the judges in all Wales for his life, he takes another patent in reversion in the name of Varney, his sister's son, in trust to the use of him and his assigns.

The said lord Brooke, by indenture between him and the said Varney sealed and delivered by each party the one to the other, did covenant, limit, and declare

---

[1] J. Gouws, 'Greville, Fulke (1554–1628)', *Oxford Dictionary of National Biography*, vol. 23, pp. 786–790.

that the said office, after his death, and all the profits thereof should be [given] to the new lord Brooke, nephew and heir male to the said old lord Brooke, and that the said Varney should have £200 *per annum* during his life out of the said office after the death of his uncle.

Varney, in 2 Car. [1626–27] and a little before the death of his uncle, having the said patent in his possession during the life of his uncle, by and with the privity and consent of the lord Goring to procure a new patent thereof to him the lord Goring, did surrender the former patent made to him to King Charles. And he granted a new patent in reversion to the lord Goring for and in consideration of service etc., who after the death of the old lord Brooke, by virtue of the grant aforesaid, took the profits of that office.

And the young lord Brooke brings his bill in Chancery against Varney and the lord Goring upon the trust aforesaid and upon the agreement aforesaid by indenture and upon the practice and combination aforesaid.

The lord Goring denies and disclaims any notice of the trust or of the covenants and agreements by the indenture or of the practice with Varney, but [he] confesses the surrender of the patent and his notice thereof and the new patent made to him.

Varney denies that he did ever read the indenture of covenants or that he ever heard it read to him, but he confesses the indenture and the sealing and delivery thereof. And [he] says that he sealed it by the command and obedience of his uncle when it was brought to him and that his uncle did bid him keep the said patent. But [he] confesses that the said patent was procured only by the old lord Brooke without his knowledge, means, or privity.

And so, as I have credibly heard, the office is decreed in Chancery for the plaintiff, the young lord Brooke, according to the trust and indenture aforesaid.

Croke Car. 197, 79 E.R. 773

Upon the Lord Keeper's request, all the justices and barons were assembled for their resolution in the case between Lord Brooks and Lord Goring, which was thus.

Queen Elizabeth, in the nineteenth year of her reign, granted to Fulke Grevill, Esq., the office of the Clerk of the Council of the Marches of Wales for his life. And, by another patent, 25 Eliz., she granted to him the office of Secretary there for his life. And, in 1 Jac. I, without recital of these patents, the said king grants the said offices to Sir Fulk Grevill, then knight, for his life. After[wards], in 9 Jac. I, the king, reciting the said patent of 1 Jac. I, grants those offices to Adam Newton for his life, when, after the death, surrender, or forfeiture of the said Sir Fulk Grevill, they should become void. And after[wards], in 14 Jac. I, by another patent, reciting the patents of 1 and 9 Jac. I and omitting the grants of 19 and 25 Eliz., the said king granted the said offices to John Venor and John Mallet, '*habendum* for their lives, *cum post mortem* of the said Fulk Grevill or Adam Newton, surrender, forfeiture, or other determination, *vel alio quocunque modo* the said offices should be void or should come to the king's hand to dispose with a *non obstante*, a *male nominando*, or a *male recitando praedicta officia, et non obstante male recitando, male nominando, vel non recitando, aliquod donum vel concessionem praeantea factum de officiis praedictis*.

And whether the patent of 14 Jac. I be good or not was the question.

It was argued several days, *viz*. by *Hedley*, Serjeant, against the patent 14 Jac. I, and by *Noy*, for the patent; and, at another day, by *Bankes*, against the patent, and by *Finch*, Serjeant, for the patent.

And it was agreed by all the justices and barons that the patent of 1 Jac. I was merely void, for, first, it was agreed by the counsel of each side that the patents of 19 and 25 Eliz. were good and nothing was objected against them; then Sir Fulke Grevill, being the patentee and alive and he accepting a new patent in 1 Jac. I without reciting the former patents and not any *non obstante*s [being] therein, it is clearly void, as it was agreed in Harris v. Wing's,[1] that, if a lessee for years of the queen take a new lease for years of the same thing without recital of the former lease, it is merely a void lease, and no surrender of the former lease. And it is stronger in this case, for the grant of an office cannot be surrendered by the taking of a second grant, for there is not any revocation thereof.

Secondly, it was agreed by all the justices and barons that the patent of 9 Jac. I, reciting the patent of 1 Jac. I as a good grant, which is void and no *non obstante* [being] therein, this grant is merely void.

Thirdly, the principal question was whether the clauses of *non obstante* in the patent of 14 Jac. I makes it good, for, otherwise, without a *non obstante*, it was agreed by them all that it was void, because it recites the two patents which are void and omits the recital of the two patents which are good and makes the *habendum* after the death or determination of the said patentees which are void, so the king is deceived in his grant and misinformed, and whether the *non obstante* does help it was the principal question.

HYDE, Chief Justice, held clearly, as to that point, that the *non obstante* helps it and makes it a good patent, because the king relinquishes the advantage of non-recital or false recital and intends to grant it by whatsoever means the same shall become void.

JONES seemed to doubt thereof, and would not deliver any opinion herein.

But RICHARDSON, Chief Justice of the Common Pleas, HUTTON, HARVEY, and DAVENPORT, justices of the Common Pleas, DENHAM, TREVOR, and VERNON, barons of the Exchequer, WHITELOCKE and myself [CROKE], justices of the King's Bench, conceived that this patent of 14 Jac. I is merely void by reason of those mis-recitals, which are not properly mis-recitals or false recitals, but rather false informations or suggestions whereby the king was deceived, for, by intendment, the king conceived those grants were good which are void, and granted

---

[1] *Harris v. Wing* (1590), 3 Leonard 242, 74 E.R. 660, Croke Eliz. 231, 78 E.R. 487, Moore K.B. 415, 72 E.R. 665, 2 Rolle Rep. 70, 81 E.R. 666.

those offices after the determination of the said grants, *vel alio quocunque modo etc*. So the king is deceived, and the *non obstante* shall not aid such false informations and false suggestions. 6 Co. 55, Chandois Case; 3 Eliz., Dyer 197, Blague's Case.[1] But there was not any certificate made of these judges' opinions, because the parties compounded.

British Library MS. Hargrave 111, f. 58v

Trinity 6 Car. [1630].

In a case pending in the Chancery between Robert, lord Brooke, plaintiff, and George, lord Goring and John Verney, defendants, upon the hearing of the matter before SIR THOMAS COVENTRY, Lord Keeper of the Great Seal, the case was thus. The Queen Elizabeth, by her letters patent bearing date 9 February *anno* 19 [1577], granted to Fulke Grevill, Esquire, the office of one of the clerks of the council in Wales and the Marches of it when it will be void also the office of Clerk of the Signet there when it will be void for his life. Afterwards, 20 April 25 [1583], the said queen granted to the said Fulke Grevill the office of secretary there when it will be void for his life. *Anno* 34 Eliz., all those offices being void by the death of the prior patentees, the said Fulke Grevill was admitted and exercised the said offices until 1 Jac., in which year, around the 24th day of July in the same year [1603], the king, without a recital of any of the patents of 19 or 25 Eliz., granted the said offices to the said Fulke Grevill for life in as ample manner as Charles Fox and others *aut idem Fulco Grevill seu eorum aliquis vel aliqui vel aliquis alius sive aliqui alii officia predicta ante hac habens seu exercens habentes seu exercentes unquam habuerunt seu gavisi fuerunt habuit seu gavisus fuit aut aliquo modo habere et gaudere debuerunt ratione seu praetextu officii praedicti* without any *non obstante* in the said patent. Afterwards, 8 July *anno* 9 Jac. [1611], the king, reciting so much only, the patent of 1 Jac., granted these offices to Adam Newton, Esq., for his life *habendum immediate post mortem praedicti Fulconis Grevill vel immediate cum et quam primum praedicta officia per forisfacturem vel sursumredditionem praedicti Fulconis Grevill vel aliter vacaveruit aut donationem, concessionem, vel dispositionem nostros heredes vel successores nostras pertinebunt vel pertinere debuissent si haec praesens concessio minime facta esset* without any *non obstante* in the said patent. 2 December *anno* 14 Jac. [1616], the king, reciting the several patents of 1 and 9 Jac., granted these offices to John Verney and John Mallet *habendum* for their lives when they will be void by the death, surrender, or forfeiture of Fulk Grevill and Adam Newton *vel immediate cum et quam primum praedictum officia per mortem, forisfacturem, vel sursumreddionem aut per aliquam alium determinationem quacumque aut aliquo modo quocumque vacaverit aut ad manus donationem, concessionem, vel dispositionem nostras heredes vel successores nostras pertinebunt vel*

---

[1] *Duke of Chandos's Case* (1606), 6 Coke Rep. 55, 77 E.R. 336; *Rex v. Blage* (1561), 2 Dyer 197, 73 E.R. 436.

pertinere sive devenere debuissent vel debebunt si haec concessio minime facta fuisset non obstante male nominando vel male recitando vel non recitando praedicta officia et cetera praemissa aut aliquam inde parcellam et non obstante male recitando, male nominando, aut non recitando aliquod donis sive concessionum praeantea facta de officiis praedictis vel eorum aliquo vel aliquibus etc. And whether the patent made in 14 Jac. was good or not was the only question.

The resolution of this was reserved to the consideration of all the justices of England and the barons of the Exchequer before assembled at Serjeants' Inn in Fleet Street.

The case was well debated by *Bankes* of Gray's Inn for the defendants to this effect. I agree that by anything that appears to you, My Lords, in this case, the patents of 19 and 25 Eliz. are good and not disputable. But I conceive the patents of 1 and 9 Jac. void. And thus, in the end of my argument, the patent in 14 Jac. would inure to be void also. And it is for these reasons: first, because it is grounded upon a false recital; second, because the letters patent limit the beginning of them upon the expiration of the estates granted in 1 and 9 [Jac.], which are no estates in law; third, and such defects are not aided by the *non obstante*.

First, in the patent of 1 Jac., I will consider that it would be the law, if it had been made to a stranger (because, in our case, it is a grant to the same patentee of 19 and 25) and, if it had been granted to a stranger and without any *non obstante* or recital of the former patents of 19 and 25 Eliz. (as in our case), it had been void. If the king grant an office to me for a term of life and, afterwards granted the same office to B. for life without a recital of my grant, I being in possession, the second patent is void. 11 Edw. IV, 1b; 6 Hen. VII, 14a; 11 Hen. VII, 12b. And this is the reason of the case in Dyer, fol. 77, pl. 38. The king leased Richmond fee with all deodands that fall within to C. for years; afterwards, he granted all deodands generally to the Almoner. The term of C. expired. The king made a new lease to C. for years. And it was held that the grant to the Almoner was void, because it had not recited the lease to C. and with this accords the reason in 32 Edw. III, title *Avowry*, 112, of a court leet. But this rule admits of two exceptions, because, if a prior makes a lease for life of a manor, which manor comes to the king by the Statute of Dissolutions and the king makes a lease of the manor without a recital, the reversion passes because the king will not recite the grant of a common person. Dyer, fol. 233, pl. 10.[1] Thus, if D. give the manor of A. to B. in tail and the reversion coming to the king by an attainder of treason, the king grants the *manerium* of A. in fee, the reversion passes without a recital of the estate tail, because by a common person. The Lord Shandos's Case, r. 6, fol. 16a.

---

[1] YB Trin. 11 Edw. IV, f. 1, pl. 1 (1471); YB Hil. 6 Hen. VII, ff. 13, 14, pl. 2 (1491); YB Hil. 11 Hen. VII, f. 12, pl. 3 (1496); *Harrington v. Pole* (1552), 1 Dyer 77, 73 E.R. 166; YB Hil. 32 Edw. III, Fitzherbert, Abr., *Avowrie*, pl. 112 (1358); *Ap Rice v. Rogers* (1564), 2 Dyer 233, 73 E.R. 514, also Benloe 24, 123 E.R. 19.

Second, in case that be of an estate ended, no recital is necessary, as if the king, tenant in tail, made a lease for years or life and died, the heirs can make another grant without a recital because it was ended by his death. In 38 Hen. VIII, Br., *Discontinuance*, 35, *Taile*, 39, *Patents*, 101; Alton Woods Case, r. 4, fol. 44b.[1]

But, in our case, they are grants of divers offices by the queen in 19 and 25 Eliz. which are good patents, and they have a continuance. And, on account of this, they must be recited.

But it has been objected that inasmuch as the patent in 1 Jac. is made to the same patentee in respect that here it is in a surrender of those of 19 and 25 [Eliz.] or at least a discharge of the execution of the offices and thus the patent in 1 Jac. amounts to a new grant, for these reasons, the patents of 19 and 25 [Eliz.] need not be recited.

I answer that it is clear by our books that, when the king would grant an office, he must be truly informed, as well of the estate of which he is seised as of the estate that he would grant, or otherwise the grant is void. And this is the reason of the case where the king has a wardship of land or a lease of land for years and, by his letters patent, he grants the land for life or in fee, this grant is void. 7 Hen. IV, 42b; 21 Edw. III, 17; Alton Woods Case, r. 1, fo. 44b; because he was not fully informed of his own estate. If the king license his tenant in tail to alien to two and their heirs, this license is void because the king was not truly informed that he has the reversion in himself. 21 Ass., pl. 15.[2] Thus, if the king, seised of the manor of Terrington and of a market and fairs within the said manor, incorporates the vills of Terrington and does not grant to them *feriam* or *nundinium suum*, but creates a new fair, the grant is void, because he not apprised of his own estate. r. 1, fo. 49a, Alton Woods Case. Thus, in our case, when the king by his letters patent in 1 Jac. granted these offices for life to commence presently, the king was not informed nor appraised that any estate was out of him, and thus [it was] void.

Second, if this patent will inure as a surrender of the precedent patents and a grant *de novo*, it will inure to two intents, where one is concealed from the king, which the law will not permit. Englefield's Case. r. 7, fo. 14a, the king, seised of an estate *pur auter vie* with a power of revocation, the king made a lease for forty years, the lease is good and the power is not tolled because the demise of the king will not extend to a demise of the land and also to a suspension of the condition of which he had not any information. 35 Edw. III, Fitz., *Grants*, 103. The king [had] a license to *amortisare terras et tenementa* to the value of £5; there *terras te-*

---

[1] 38 Hen. VIII, Brooke, Abr., *Discontinuans de possession*, pl. 35, *Taile*, pl. 39, *Patentes*, pl. 101 (1546); *Attorney General v. Bushopp* (1600), 1 Coke Rep. 26, 76 E.R. 64, also 140 Selden Soc. 1061, Jenkins 251, 145 E.R. 178, 2 Anderson 154, 123 E.R. 596, *sub nom. Welshe's Case*, Moore K.B. 413, 72 E.R. 664.

[2] *Ferrers v. Cotton* (1406), YB Pas. 7 Hen. IV, ff. 41, 42, pl. 8; *Attorney General v. Bushopp* (1600), *ut supra*; *De Haule's Case* (1347), YB 21 Edw. III, Lib. Ass., pl. 17, p. 80.

nus in capite could not be aliened in mortmain by force of the said license. If the king give land to an alien or a villein, this is not a denization to the one nor an enfranchisement to the other, as *qua supra*, 2 Hen. VII, 13a.[1]

Thus, the patent of 1 Jac. cannot inure to two intents, first to make it a new grant and also a surrender, the first patents being enrolled.

I agree with the Case of St. Saviour's, in the 10th r., fol. 66,[2] where there was no *vacat* of the enrollment and, notwithstanding, the second lease [was] good because, there, the first lease was not concealed from the king, but [it was] recited in the second patent with the express intention of the king, so that there the second patent could be a surrender of the first and no new lease, but not in our case where the intent is not revealed.

I also agree that, if there be two intents and both revealed, that the grant will inure to both, especially where one depends necessarily upon the other, as the principal case. In Grendon's Case, Com., fol. 501, 502, where a patent inures as a grant of the advowson to a dean and chapter and also to dispense with the Statute of Mortmain,[3] because, there, both intents depend naturally, the one upon the other, and the intent to amortize is not foreign. If the king license one to give £10 of rent to such a vill, this license primarily amounts to incorporate the vill, and thus the grant of the rent, because the one intent cannot stand without the other. 2 Hen. VII, 13.[4] But the intent of the surrender of the first patent is not revealed in our case, but it is foreign, for which to this the patent of 1 Jac. will not inure. Trinity 32 Eliz. and adjudged Easter 34 [Eliz.] between Harris and Wynne, upon a special verdict in the King's Bench; the case was thus. The King Henry VIII demised the site and hospital of St. John's at Aylesworth for years and, afterwards, granted the reversion to the bishop of Bath and Wells and his successors, and he died. The King Edward VI repurchased the reversion, and, afterward, demised the said site and hospital to Aylesworth for years without any *non obstante* or recital of the first lease, and this lease [was] upon record. The question was whether it should be recited. It was opposed that not, but that the second lease was good for two reasons, first, because the first lease was ended and surrendered by the acceptance of the second. Second, after the second lease was made, there it was a reversion of the inheritance out of the crown and thus the first lease, as made by a common person, which need not be recited. But it was

---

[1] *Regina v. Englefield* (1591), 7 Coke Rep. 11, 77 E.R. 428, also Moore K.B. 303, 72 E.R. 595, 4 Leonard 135, 169, 74 E.R. 779, 800, Popham 18, 79 E.R. 1139, 1 Anderson 293, 123 E.R. 480; YB Mich. 33 Edw. III, Fitzherbert, Abr., *Graunt*, pl. 103 (1359); YB Hil. 2 Hen. VII, f. 13, pl. 16 (1487).

[2] *Attorney General v. Churchwardens of St. Saviour* (Ex. 1613), 10 Coke Rep. 66, 77 E.R. 1025, Lane 21, 145 E.R. 266, Exch. Repts. 1604–1684, 116.

[3] *Grendon v. Bishop of Lincoln* (1576), 2 Plowden 493, 75 E.R. 734, also Benloe 293, 123 E.R. 206; Stat. 7 Edw. I (*SR*, I, 51); Stat. 18 Edw. I, c. 3 (*SR*, I, 106).

[4] YB Hil. 2 Hen. VII, f. 13, pl. 16 (1487).

held that the second lease was void for the default of a recital because Aylesworth had notice of the first lease and he could have informed the king of the first lease. Also, the second lease will not inure to a surrender because it was a foreign intent. Which case is more strong than this here because this was of land where there was a reversion in the king. But here it is to have an office of which there cannot be any reversion but only a future power to dispose. 3 Hen. VII, Olburie's Case; 1 Hen. VII, 29; 6 Hen. VII, 14; 8 Hen. VII, 12; r. 8, fol. 55.[1] My third reason [is] here is a good grant of two offices by 19 and of the third office by the patent of 25 [Eliz.], both which are in force, it was not the intention of the party to surrender them nor of the king to accept them. Thus, the law will not make a construction that the franktenement will be divested out by him without the intent of the party or of the king. Kempe, in Dy. 195b, [it was] given in evidence a surrender by Lord Darcy of an office before Hare, Master of the Rolls, which was not recorded, the patent cancelled, nor a *vacat* entered in the lifetime of Hare, and it was held no surrender.[2] *A fortiori* in our case, because there was an intention of this surrender. But, here, there is not any record of it nor any intention of the party or of the king that the first patents would be surrendered, on account of which, the letters patent, not reciting them in 19 and 25 [Eliz.] nor containing any *non obstante*, are voided.

Second, I conceive the patent of 9 Jac. also void, first, for the non-reciting of the patents of 19 and 25 [Eliz.], which are good grants, and, second, for the recital of that of 1 Jac., which is void. The first reason holds well for the reasons which are the patent of 1 [Jac.] void, having also (as that of 1 [Jac.]) no *non obstante* to aid it; the second reason I thus enforce [is], if the patent be good notwithstanding the reciting of a void patent, it will inure as a grant of the reversion or in possession, not in reversion, because the king cannot grant the reversion of an office reserving to himself a particular estate any more than he could grant the reversion of an advowson after the death of J.S. when he was seised of it in the present, because there was no reversion. 38 Hen. VI, fol. 38a, Prisot.[3] Nor could these offices pass in possession because Adam Newton is not to have them until *post mortem, forisfacturem*, or the surrender of Fulke Grevill, the patentee, in 1 Jac., which cannot be, because the patent of 9 [Jac.] is also void.

Third, then follows that of 14 Jac. to be considered, by which the king granted the said offices to John Verney and John Malet *habendum* for their lives *post mortem* Fulke Grevill and Adam Newton etc. which patent I conceive to be also

---

[1] *Crofts v. Lord Beauchamp* (1486), YB Trin. 1 Hen. VII, f. 28, pl. 6; YB Hil. 6 Hen. VII, f. 13, pl. 2 (1491); YB Pas. 8 Hen. VII, f. 12, pl. 5 (1493), also Chancery Repts. Middle Ages 278; *Earl of Rutland v. Earl of Shrewsbury* (1608), 8 Coke Rep. 55, 77 E.R. 555, also 1 Bulstrode 4, 80 E.R. 710, 2 Brownlow & Goldesborough 229, 123 E.R. 913, Jenkins 283, 145 E.R. 205.

[2] *Kempe v. Makewilliams* (1561), 2 Dyer 194, 73 E.R. 429.

[3] *Rex v. Abbess of Syon* (1460), YB Trin. 38 Hen. VI, ff. 33, 38, pl. 2.

void, first, because of the void recital of the patents of 1 and 9 [Jac.] because it recites that Sir Fulke Grevill and Adam Newton were seised for their lives of these offices by force of the patents of 1 and 9 Jac., which are false recitals, and, on account of this, void, because where in a recital of a matter of record which is false, this recital vitiates the patent even though it is not material. [It is] otherwise of a matter in fact not material or part of the consideration, as appears by the Case of Sir Hugh Cholmeley, rep. 2, fol. 54.[1] One Christopher Holford was tenant in tail, remainder in tail to George Holford; George, by a deed indented and enrolled, bargained and sold his remainder to J. Warren for the life of Christopher, the remainder to the king. The king, reciting that the grant made by the said George was by fraud and covin, granted the remainder to Christopher. In this case, though the remainder was not granted upon a fraud so that the recital was false, yet it did not vitiate the patent because whether this was upon fraud or not was not a material thing, because it was a matter *in pais*, not of record, not material nor valuable. And, on account of that, it will not impeach the grant. And this is the reason. If the king, rehearsing the good service that I have done to him beyond the seas in his wars, grant to me lands notwithstanding that I did not ever do to him service, yet the grant is good because the service recited is a matter in fact not material. Com., fol. 455a. But, in our case, the patents of 1 and 9 Jac. are matters of record that, being false and recited, vitiate the grant. And this is the reason that these letters patent taking effect [. . .] the date must be recited or pleaded truly touching the day, year, and place. And it is similar to the recital of an act of Parliament that, even though it be surplusage, yet, if the party recite this, and falsely, in respect of the day or year, it will aggrieve him. Com., fol. 59b; Dyer, fol. 203a. Queen Mary, reciting in her patent a grant of the custody of the castle of Carlisle by Henry VIII to Lord Darcy made in the 33rd year of his reign where, in truth, the patent was made in *anno* 32nd, and the recital was held such that it will impeach the grant. Dyer, fol. 194, pl. 35.[2]

So that my first reason why I conceive this patent made in 14 Jac. to be void is in regard of the false recital that, even though it be not any part of the consideration, yet being a matter of record, it will impeach the patent.

My second reason is because he, reciting the patents of 1 and 9 Jac., granted these offices to John Verney and John Mallet *habendum* for their lives *post mortem, forisfacturem, vel sursumredditionem* of the patentees, Fulk Grevill and Adam Newton, which recital without doubt vitiates the patent, because, if the king, by his letters patent, would recite a void office and reserve the commencement to the end of the void estate, this grant is void in the substance of it.

---

[1] *Cholmley v. Hanmer* (1597), 2 Coke Rep. 50, 54, 76 E.R. 527, 537, also 139 Selden Soc. 758, Moore K.B. 342, 72 E.R. 617.

[2] *Wroth v. Attorney General* (Ex. 1573), 2 Plowden 452, 75 E.R. 678; *Wimbish v. Tailbois* (1550), 1 Plowden 38, 75 E.R. 63; *Walgrave's Case* (1561), 2 Dyer 203, 231, 73 E.R. 448, 511, also Jenkins 223, 145 E.R. 154; *Kempe v. Makewilliams* (1561), *ut supra*.

Robert Blage, the King's Remembrancer, by a patent for his life, was made a baron of the Exchequer *quandiu se bene gesserit*, afterwards, the king granted the same office of Remembrancer to Blage, his son, *pro termino vitae suae habendum immediate cum primum et proximum post mortem dicti Roberti Blage sursumreddendem vel dimissionem vel seu aliquo modo quocunque et quandocunque vacare contingerit. Et pro eo quod iste litterae patentes facerunt insufficientes eo quod dicti Roberti Blage nullum habuit legalem statum tempore confectionis eorundem nec aliquo tempore postquam idem Robert Blage fuit constitutus tertius Baron*, the last letters patent were revoked. Dyer, fol. 196, pl. 45. And, upon this reason, was Auditor Curle's Case adjudged, r. 11, fol. 4; and Bozon's Case, r. 4, fol. 55b, where the words of the license are, if the lease in possession be doubtful, either good or not, which the king's lease recited and the grant of the reversion and afterward it is determined by a judgment in law that the lease was void, the grant will be also void.[1]

Against this, the book of 38 Hen. VI, 37, Danby's opinion, has been objected, which is also abridged by Brooke, but, otherwise, that the license at large could warrant. Br., *Patents*, 96, where it is said that, if the king in his grant of a reversion misrecited that first lease in the date of it, *vel huiusmodi*, this is not material, because [it is] sufficient in pleading to say that the king, reciting how he leased to A.B. for life, had granted to A.C. the reversion.[2] But, admit that this case is law, yet it cannot rule our case, because it cannot be applied to the patent of 1 Jac., because, in this, there is not any recital, nor to that in 9 Jac., because there was an omission to recite the good patents of 19 and 25 [Eliz.] and it had recited the void patent of 1 Jac. nor could it be applied to this last patent of 14 [Jac.] because it was not recited of a void estate and limited the commencement of the said patent after the commencement of it; so that the opinion of Danby concludes nothing in the case in question.

Fourth, the last point in debate is the *non obstante*, which, not being in the patents of 1 and 9 Jac., is added to that of 14 [Jac.], whether it will aid the defects of the patent, I conceive not, because, where the letters patent are void in themselves in the body of the grant and the *habendum*, there, no *non obstante* could make them good, as appears by Holt and Rolfe's Case, reported by Serjeant Bendloes,[3] which was thus. The abbot of Westminster, in 21 Hen. VIII [1529], made a lease to Sir Thomas Moore for forty-four years, who, afterwards, was attainted of misprision of treason, and the term, by this, was forfeited to the king. 31 Hen. VIII [1539], the abbot surrendered to the king, who died. Edward

---

[1] *Hunt v. Coffin* (1561), 2 Dyer 197, 73 E.R. 435; *Auditor Curle's Case* (1610), 11 Coke Rep. 2, 77 E.R. 1147; *Bozoun's Case* (1584), 4 Coke Rep. 34, 76 E.R. 970, also *sub nom. Futter v. Boorome*, Godbolt 35, 78 E.R. 22, 1 Eagle & Younge 86.

[2] *Rex v. Abbess of Syon* (1460), YB Trin. 38 Hen. VI, ff. 33, 37, pl. 2, 2 Brooke, Abr., *Patentes*, pl. 96.

[3] *Holt v. Roper (Moore's Case)* (1560), Benloe 38, 73 E.R. 958, Benloe 84, 123 E.R. 65, also 1 Anderson 6, 123 E.R. 324, 3 Leonard 5, 74 E.R. 504.

VI made a lease to Rolfe for twenty-one years to commence after the end of the term granted to Sir Thomas Moore. And it was resolved, first, that the lease was void, because the lease made to Sir Thomas Moore was ended by the surrender, to which the second lease having reference for a commencement was void in substance. But then, it was objected that the Statute of 1 Edw. VI, of confirmations,[1] had made it good inasmuch as the said Act aided all non-recitals and misrecitals and, here, it was only a misrecital. But it was, secondly, resolved that this lease was not aided by the said act, because it was void in the substance and body of it, to which leases this Statute did not extend. And it was a void lease in substance inasmuch as it was limited to begin after the end of a lease ended before the making of the second. Now, if an act of Parliament cannot aid a lease void in substance, *a fortiori* neither the *non obstante* in our case, which cannot more do [it] than an act of Parliament.

I find that a *non obstante* will not aid a patent void by the common law, any more than a custom warranting the contrary, nor will it dispense with an act of Parliament that gives a private interest. And, on account of this, a protection will not be allowed in an [action of] *quare impedit* even though he had a *non obstante*. 39 Hen. VI, fo. 39, Fitz., *Protection*, 15. And the reason is because this patent is against the common law, nor will it dispense with an act of Parliament which gives a private interest. The statutes of 11 Edw. III and 32 Hen. VIII make the Prince [of Wales] Duke of Cornwall and also to the said dukedom certain manors in Cornwall. Queen Elizabeth granted the manor annexed to the duchy by 32 Hen. VIII to Sergeant Hele and others in fee, *non obstante* the said Act of 32 Hen. VIII. And it was held that this *non obstante* did not toll the force of the said Act of Parliament, because it will not prejudice the prince who now is of his right in the said dukedom. The Prince's Case, in 8 r., fol. 21b. The Chief Justice of the Common Bench had the power by custom to dispose of any office within the court; if the king now would by his letters patent grant any office that is vacant within the same court with a *non obstante* the said custom, yet this patent is void even though the *non obstante* be there, because it is not aided by it, being against the custom, the law of the place. 20 Hen. VI, 8b, strongly.[2]

The patent of 14 Jac. in our case is void in the body of the grant, first, in regard of a void recital, the second, in respect that it limits the commencement of the grant after the death, surrender, or forfeiture of a patentee void before the making of it and the *non obstante* will not aid it. Thus are also the patents of 1 and 9 Jac. (as he argued), the one for the defect of the recital of the patents of 19 and 25 Eliz.; the other for the recital of the void patent of 1 [Jac.], being matter of record, and the a non-recital of those of 19 and 25 [Eliz.], being effectual.

---

[1] Stat. 1 Edw. VI, c. 8 (*SR*, IV, 13–14).

[2] YB Hil. 39 Hen. VI, f. 38, pl. 3, Fitzherbert, Abr., *Protection*, pl. 15 (1461); *The Prince's Case* (1606), 8 Coke Rep. 1, 77 E.R. 481; *Pilkinton v. A.* (1441), YB Mich. 20 Hen. VI, f. 8, pl. 17.

Serjeant *Finch*, recorder of London, argued for the lord Brooke to this effect. It has been agreed that the patents of 19 and 25 [Eliz.] are good but that the other three are not so. It has been urged, first, that the defect in one of the recitals of the good patents of 19 and 25 [Eliz.] vitiates. I confess that regularly the recital of precedent patents is necessary in the subsequent grants, be it of land or offices or, otherwise, the second patent will be void, inasmuch as the king is apparently deceived because he granted this in possession what he did not have, unless in reversion. And thus are the books of 11 Edw. IV, 1b; 6 Hen. VII, 14a; 8 Hen. VII, 12b; 39 Hen. VI, 48b; 3 Hen. VII, *casu ultimo*; Fitz., *Grant*, 35.[1] But this is when the second patent is made to a stranger, because, if it be made to the first patentee (as in our case), I do not know any rule in our law to impeach it.

But it has been objected that, even though it be made to the same person, yet a recital is necessary to inform the king. In the case of Harris and Wynne, it was resolved that, if the patent had been made to a stranger without a recital, yet it had been good, first, in regard the reversion was once out of the crown and the lease could on account of this be ended by a surrender without matter of record and it is similar to a lease of a common person; second, the subject is not bound to make his search any further than the last title from the crown. And it is well known of what regard in law the search of the subject is. And, on account of this, if a warranty of attorney be not entered in the roll of warranties of attorneys or if the party be essoined and the essoin be entered in the plea roll, it is erroneous, because the plea roll is not the proper place for the essoin to be entered and it is not intended that the adverse party will search there for it. Dyer, fol. 33, pl. 18.[2] But the grant being to the party himself, who cannot of his knowledge inform the queen the first being made to himself, for this cause, he himself has done a prejudice to the queen, and, on account of this, it will of avoid his patent.

But the case there differs greatly from our case, because, there, the second patent be it for years, as has been said, or in fee, as my report is, yet a greater estate was by it granted to the same party which he did not have before and, on account of this, by intendment, a prejudice could be to the king by non-information. But, in our case, the same estate is granted by the second patent as was by the first, not a greater estate. And, on account of this, by no intendment in law, the king could be prejudiced, because the intent was only to have one patent for the three offices where, before, they were granted by divers. And, on account of this, our patent, made to the same party for the same estate, need not recite the first, but the first is surrendered by way of a surrender. And it is without an act of surrender notwithstanding what has been said against me, because an act in law

---

[1] YB Trin. 11 Edw. IV, f. 1, pl. 1 (1471); YB Hil. 6 Hen. VII, f. 13, pl. 2 (1491); YB Pas. 8 Hen. VII, f. 12, pl. 5 (1493); YB Hil. 39 Hen. VI, f. 48, pl. 11 (1461); YB Mich. 3 Hen. VII, f. 1, pl. 31 (1487); YB Hil. 3 Hen. VII, f. 15, pl. 30, Fitzherbrt, Abr., *Graunt*, pl. 35 (1488).

[2] *Anonymous* (1537), 1 Dyer 33, 73 E.R. 74.

would do it, as if a justice of the Common Bench had a patent and was sworn a justice of the King's Bench. Dyer, fol. 158.[1] And the Case of Blage, King's Remembrancer in the Exchequer, and he was made a baron of it; it was a surrender in law of the first [patent]. Dyer, fol. 197b, pl. 47. If a man make a lease for years to begin *in futuro*, this interest cannot be surrendered actually; yet if he accept another lease, the first interest is extinguished and surrendered in law. The wardens of the Church of St. Saviour could not be a corporation aggregate to make an express surrender without a writing; yet, if they took any new lease, by this acceptance, it is an act in law, *scil.* their first lease is surrendered without a deed. r. 1, fo. 67b.

So that I conceive that the patent of 1 [Jac.] is not void, but effective and a surrender of the precedent [patents] of 19 and 25 [Eliz.]

If it be void, then, it is not any surrender, which was expressly resolved in the said Case of Wynne and Harris. And it is not similar to the Case of Fulmerstone and Steward, in the Commentaries, fol. 102;[2] there, a void lease was a surrender of the first, true it is, because the second lease was once good, even though it be made void by a subsequent act of Parliament. But, in our case, if the patent of 1 [Jac.] be void, it would be void *ab initio* and thus no surrender. Also, by the patent of 1 [Jac.], the king granted to Fulke Grevill the said offices in as ample a manner as Charles Fox and others *aut idem Fulko Grevill seu eorum aliquis vel aliqui sive aliquis alius vel aliqui alii officia praedicta ante hac habens seu exercens seu habentes seu exercentes unquam habuerunt seu gavisi fuerunt*. So that the king could as to the said grant or, at least, to one who had the possession of the said offices who, at the said time, was Fulke Grevill. And, on account of this, it could be well within the intent of the king, especially where no greater estate is granted, but only to put all the offices into one patent. And the king was not deceived and at no prejudice. There is not any necessity of a recital.

But it has been objected that then the patent of the king will inure to two intents, which cannot be, to enforce, for which he cited the case of a grant of land to a villein or to an alien. This grant amounts to a grant of land and an enfranchisement or endenization. I agree, but, in our case, the intent is not double, but singly that My Lord will have them for his life by one patent which he had before by divers [patents].

And, thus, for the patent of 1 [Jac.] as of 9 [Jac.] following, it is to be considered, as I conceive, to be good, though the first be admitted to be void, because I suppose that the recitals of them of 19 and 25 [Eliz.] is not material for two reasons. First, it is agreed that the suggestion, recital, or misrecital of a thing immaterial does not vitiate the patent. Now, the patent of Adam Newton recites that Fulke Grevill had the offices for his life by a patent, which is true. But he did not

---

[1] *Dyer's Case* (1558), 2 Dyer 158, 73 E.R. 344, also Jenkins 214, 145 E.R. 146.

[2] *Harris v. Wing* (1590), *ut supra*; *Fulmerston v. Steward* (1554), 1 Plowden 102, 75 E.R. 160, also 1 Dyer 102, 73 E.R. 225.

have them by the patent of 1 [Jac.], as was surmised, but by those of 19 and 25 [Eliz.]. Yet this false recital of the date will not prejudice the patent if there be words sufficient in it to pass the thing granted, either in possession or reversion, according to the intent of the grant. And, in our case, without doubt, the words are sufficient if the false recital will not harm, which it should not, as appears by 38 Hen. VI, 37, the Abbot of Syon's [Case], where the king misreciting the first lease in the date, yet the second patent was good, because the date in pleading is not material inasmuch as it suffices if the king took notice of his tenant, his estate, and of the thing granted. Br., *Patent*, pl. 96.[1]

In our case, the king was fully informed of the name of his tenant, Fulke Grevill, of his estate for life, and of the thing that he had in grant, the three offices, which three things are truly recited. And, for the date, the recital is immaterial. If the king make a lease for thirty years and, afterwards, grant the reversion, reciting that he had made a lease for twenty years, this recital is void, because, there, the king was not truly informed of the estate of his tenant. But, on the other hand, if the king make a lease for twenty years the first day of August to begin at Michaelmas [29 September] next ensuing, if, afterwards, the king, reciting that he had made a lease for twenty years to begin at Michaelmas by a patent bearing date of the second day of August, grants the reversion, this grant is good, because the term is not misrecited, nor the thing granted, nor the person to whom, but only the date, which is not material. Which case I frame upon that of Dyer, fol. 116, pl. 70,[2] which case, even though it be in a case of a common person, yet the reason of it proves our case. And it was thus. A man made a lease for twenty-one years by an indenture bearing date the thirtieth day of August to begin at Michaelmas following and, afterwards, an indenture reciting the former lease to be made by him the sixth of August, *habendum* from the Feast of St. Michael for twenty-one years, demised the land for twenty-one years more to another. Afterwards, the second lease being in question, in pleading, it was said that the first lease bearing date the 30th day of August, as the truth was, without this that the lessor *dimisit modo et forma* to the second lessee *prout superius allegavit*. And [it was] adjudged that *modo et forma* was not material, but the matter *se demisit* [was]. Thus, in our case, the mistake is only in the circumstance of the date which does not vitiate. But here, it is a false recital. I say that it is not material that every suggestion be true. If the king mistakes his title, as if he had a title to present [to a church] in regard that he was the true patron and he presents *ratione lapsus*, such presentation is void, because, there, the king

---

[1] *Rex v. Abbess of Syon* (1460), YB Trin. 38 Hen. VI, f. 33, pl. 2, 2 Brooke, Abr., *Patentes*, pl. 96.

[2] *Mount v. Hodgkin* (1554), 2 Dyer 116, 73 E.R. 255, also Benloe 38, 123 E.R. 30, 1 Anderson 3, 123 E.R. 322.

is deceived. Greene's Case, r. 6, fol. 29b.[1] Or, if he recite that he came to it by an attainder of J.S. and he is in of another title, but, if he recite that he came to the land by the attainder of J.S. where, in truth, he came to it by the attainder of J.D., perhaps, in this case, the grant would be good. Or, if the king license me to alien in mortmain the manor of Dale held of J.S. where it is held of himself, I cannot alien it, but, if it be held of J.D., I may well [do it], because it is not material to the king whether it is held of J.S. or J.D., because it is not requisite that the suggestion be always true if no prejudice come to the king. If the king, rehearsing the good service that I have done to him beyond the sea in his wars, grant to me land, still it is not material whether I have done to him any service or not, because it is not a prejudice nor advantageous to the king. 26 Hen. VIII, 1; Com., fol. 455a. The king granted to an abbot *eo quod* it was *libero capella regis* that he will not be a collector when a tithe will be granted *per clerum Angliae*; afterward, a tithe was granted and he was assigned a collector, in discharge of which he pleaded this grant and he did not aver that it was *capella libero regis*. And it was held that, notwithstanding, the grant was good. 21 Edw. IV, 61a; Fitz., *Grant*, 29; Br., *Patents*, 1; Com., fol. 455; Alton Woods, r. 1, fol. 43a. In the Case of Hugh Cholmeley, it was not necessary to aver that the bargain and sale of the remainder to the queen by George Harford was upon fraud and covin; r. 1, fol. 54b; because it was the intent of the queen to grant it, and it was not material whether it came to the crown by fraud or not.[2]

Thus, in our case, if the day of the date is not material, neither is the year of the king, the thing granted, the estate, and the name of the tenant, nor a mistake, by which I conceive that the patent of 9 [Jac.] is good.

But, admitting that [it is] not, yet that of 14 Jac. is good, if the patent of 1 [Jac.] be void, then the patent of 14 [Jac.] for the non-recital of those of 19 and 25 [Eliz.] is void. And, if the patent of 9 Jac., then is the king greatly deceived, because he conceived that the offices were granted for the two lives of Fulke Grevill and Adam Newton where the grant to Adam Newton was void. But, in this patent of 14 [Jac.], we have a *non obstante*, which is not in the patent of 1 nor 9 [Jac.], which *non obstante* (I say) aids the non-recital of the grants of 19 and 25 [Eliz.], to enforce which my opinion, I speak not of the recitals in general.

---

[1] *Green v. Baker* (1602), 6 Coke Rep. 29, 77 E.R. 295, also Yelverton 7, 80 E.R. 6, Croke Eliz. 679, 78 E.R. 916.

[2] YB Pas. 26 Hen. VIII, f. 1, pl. 4 (1534); *Wroth v. Attorney General* (Ex. 1573), *ut supra*; YB Mich. 21 Edw. IV, f. 60, pl. 32 (1481); *Abbot of Waltham's Case* (1481), YB Mich. 21 Edw. IV, f. 44, pl. 6, Fitzherbert, Abr., *Graunt*, pl. 29; YB Pas. 26 Hen. VIII, f. 1, pl. 4, 2 Brooke, Abr., *Patents*, pl. 1 (1534); *Attorney General v. Bushopp* (1600), *ut supra*; *Chomley v. Hanmer* (Ex. 1597), *ut supra*; *Hunt v. Gateley* (1581–1593), 1 Coke Rep. 54, 76 E.R. 121, also Popham 5, 79 E.R. 1129, Jenkins 250, 145 E.R. 177, 4 Leonard 150, 74 E.R. 788, Moore K.B. 154, 72 E.R. 501, 1 Anderson 282, 123 E.R. 473, Gouldsborough 5, 75 E.R. 958, 137 Selden Soc. 246, 138 Selden Soc 485.

I agree that, regularly, a recital is necessary in all of the grants of the king. And this is for two reasons mentioned in Alton Woods Case, first, for the safety of the king so that he be not deceived or prejudiced in his estate; second, for the honor of the king that he not make double grants of one and the same thing. I observe that this maxim takes place not only in lands that the king has *in jure coronae* but in lands that he holds in another right, because, if the king would make a lease of duchy land and, afterwards, grants the reversion, the recital would be necessary, as was held in 24 Eliz., in the Duchy Chamber, in the case of one Gray, where, because the lease made to him of duchy land did not recite a precedent lease made to one Haseborough, it was adjudged void. A recital is also necessary even though the thing granted by this grant is extinguished, as if the king be the founder of an abbey and has granted the corody to J.S. for life and then he grants it to the same abbot and his successors and that they will be acquitted of it, without a recital of the precedent grant to J.S., it was held void, even though, if the grant had been good, it had inured by [way] of extinguishment. 8 Hen. VII, 12, Fitz., *Grant*, 42.[1]

In our case, the king did not also have the reversion, as it was said on the other side, but only a future disposing power; yet a recital is necessary. 11 Edw. IV, 1; 6 Hen. VII, 14a; 8 Hen. VII, 12b. If the king grant the manor of D. to A. for life with a view of the frankpledge if the king grant to another without a reciting of the former grant, the patent is void. 32 Edw. III, Fitz., *Avowry*, 112. If the king grant an office to J.S. and, afterwards, grant the same office to another, [it is a] void patent if it does not have any recital of the former. But it is to be intended that, in no construction, both grants could stand together; in a good intendment, a recital is not necessary, as it was adjudged in the Case of Webb, for the Tennis Court at Whitehall in an assize brought by him 6 Jac., because, there, it was adjudged that the second patentee had the soil and occupation of the house in the absence of the king, the first patentee [had] the use of the office when the king was there using it. But, if both, they could not be together without confusion, there without a recital, the second grant will be void.[2]

Throckmorton's Case, in the Exchequer, 32 Eliz., and, afterwards, affirmed in a writ of error. In which Case of Throckmorton, it was secondly resolved that, notwithstanding that the second patent was void as to the recital, yet, having a *non obstante*, it was aided by it. Michaelmas 35 & 36 Eliz., in the term at St. Alban's, the Marquess of Exeter's Case, it was referred out of the Chancery to the

---

[1] YB Pas. 8 Hen. VII, f. 12, pl. 5, Fitzherbert, Abr., *Graunt*, pl. 42 (1493).

[2] YB Trin. 11 Edw. IV, f. 1, pl. 1 (1471); YB Hil. 6 Hen. VII, ff. 13, 14, pl. 2 (1491); YB Pas. 8 Hen. VII, f. 12, pl. 5 (1493); Hil. 32 Edw. III, Fitzherbert, Abr., *Avowrie*, pl. 112 (1358); *Webb v. Knyvet* (1608), 8 Coke Rep. 45, 77 E.R. 541.

consideration of the two chief justices, the chief baron, the attorney general, and the queen's solicitor [general]. And it was thus.[1]

The marquess of Exeter, being tenant in tail of the gift of King Henry VIII, was attainted of treason and executed in 31 Hen. VIII [1539], having issue, Edward Courtney; King Henry VIII died, and then Edward VI. Queen Mary, before an office found, granted the land to Edward Courtney and his heirs, which grant was afterwards confirmed by the Statute of 4 & 5 Ph. & Mar., 1. They resolved that, at common law, this patent was void, as well *quoad* the grant of the possession as of the reversion, because it could not pass the possession because, even though the lands entailed were given to the king and forfeited by the attainder of treason by 26 Hen. VIII, cap. 13, yet the actual possession of them was not in the king without an office found. Com., fol. 486; Dyer 31b; Br., *Offices*, 17; Com., fol. 483b; Br., *Charters of pardon*, 52; r. 1, fo. 42a; Alton Woods; Dowtye's Case, r. 3, fo. 10a.[2] But, until such an office found, the tail descends to the issue of the Marquess Edward Courtney, but to the king comes only a right, *scil.* a possibility to have the land in possession by force of the said Act upon the finding of the office, which right or possibility the king cannot grant over, because the grant *quoad* the possession was void, because it will inure as a grant of the reversion. It could not, because the estate tail was not recited which in right was forfeited to the queen and it will be actually vested in her upon the office found. And thus, at common law, this grant was void. But it was resolved that, by the Statute of 4 & 5 Phil. & Mar., cap. 1, this patent was aided, which Act confirmed all grants notwithstanding any misrecital, misnaming, or non-recital of any of the same honors etc. or any lack of finding offices or inquisitions of and in the premises whereby titles of the queen's highness therein ought to have been found before the making of the same letters patent or other writing of any misrecital or non-recital of leases thereof before made as well of record as not of record etc., which patent was not aided by the clause of non-recital or misrecital, because there is not any mention made in the said clause of confirmation the non-recital of the estate, but only of the land, of the true value of it, or of the place, or of the name of the grantee, so that the non-recital of the estate tail is not aided by this clause, but by the clause of lack of finding offices or inquisitions of and in the premises etc., because, if this office had been found, then the king had been in possession, because the right was in him before, by which the defect of this office is aided; the

---

[1] *Finch v. Throckmorton* (Ex. 1591), Moore K.B. 291, 72 E.R. 587, Croke Eliz. 221, 78 E.R. 477, 138 Selden Soc. 598.

[2] *Courtney's Case* (1593), O. Bridgman 452, 124 E.R. 685; Stat. 4 & 5 Phil. & Mar., c. 1, s. 2 (*SR*, IV, 314–315); Stat. 26 Hen. VIII, c. 13 (*SR*, III, 508–509); *Nichols v. Nichols* (1575), 2 Plowden 477, 75 E.R. 711, also Benloe 245, 123 E.R. 173; YB Mich. 22 Edw. IV, f. 23, pl. 3, 2 Brooke, Abr., *Office del Court*, pl. 17 (1482); 29 Hen. VIII, 1 Brooke, Abr., *Chartres de pardon*, pl. 52 (1537); *Attorney General v. Dowtie* (Ex. 1584), 3 Coke Rep. 9, 76 E.R. 643, also 137 Selden Soc. 259, 1 Leonard 21, 74 E.R. 19.

patent is good. But the estate tail, by the common law, must be recited so that it be the grant of the land in the right of the crown or otherwise in the king or of the Leet Office or things which by it are extinct or forfeited. Yet all these must be recited, yet, now, this recital is not so necessary, but sometimes, in the case of the king, his grant could be good without a recital.

In the case of Harris and Wynne, it was adjudged necessary, because it was made to the patentee, but, if it had been made to a stranger in regard that the reversion was once *habendum* of the crown, it was held that it was not necessary, especially when the last title of the king was within the making of the lease. If a lease be made, reserving a rent to be paid at the Exchequer or *alibi*, after a tender is made of it to the bailiff of the king in the country, upon this an office is found that the lease is ended by the non-payment of the rent, afterwards, the king grants the land to another, in this case, a recital is not material, even though the lease be in being, because it is recited upon the record to be ended. 26 Ass., pl. 55, where it is held that, if the king grant certain land to the queen for life and, afterwards, he grant it to the prince in fee without a recital of the precedent grant, still the reversion passes. And the reason of the difference is that every subject must search, but, when the king gives it to his son, the law presumes that the intention of the king is that the prince will have the land, be it in reversion or possession. And it is greatly for the honor of the king of this general learning of recitals I will make use, even though, in divers cases, a recital is necessary, yet many cases they have, in which the recital is surplusage, so that it is not often the essential part of the grant. If, then, the king would grant this term notwithstanding any non-recital, without doubt, this grant is void, the recitals not essentially necessary.

In Throckmorton's Case, above cited, the *non obstante* aids the patent. In Bozoun's Case, r. 4, fo. 36, it was resolved that when the grant of the king is good *ex vi termini*, but the law would not suffer him to be deceived, in this case, the *non obstante* aids the patent. But in the principal [case], there, the *non obstante* could not help the grant because it was void *ex vi termini*. *Adhuc* for authorities following the reasons of my opinion, first, the *non obstante* is tantamounting as if the king had said, be the land in reversion or possession, or in lease or out of lease, yet I intend that the grantee will have it, so that the king could not be said to be deceived in his grant, to avoid which deceit is the principal cause of the recital and *sublata causa* which could hinder the efficacy of the grant.

I grant the case of the protection in a *quare impedit* cited in 38 Hen. VI, 39; Bozoun's Case; that a *non obstante* will not aid such a protection, because such a grant is against the body of the law. But, if the common law or statute law provides for the safety of the king, yet the king can dispense with it. Divers statutes have been made for the non-pardoning of murder, 14 Edw. III, ca. 14; 27 Edw. III, ca. 2; 13 Ric. II, ca. 8, which acts contain large words to annul charters made against the form of them, yet, by a *non obstante*, the force of the said statutes is taken away. Stanford, fol. 101. For the safety of his land at common law, if the king had granted the manor of Dale of the value of £10 where, in truth, it was worth only £5 *per annum*, yet this grant was good, as it was held by Popham, 2 Jac., in the King's Bench, in the Case of Chambers. By the Statute of 1 Hen. IV, ca. 6, in [petitions], that those who ask of the king lands or tenements, offices, etc. make express mention of the value of them, yet, if the king would grant any land or office with a *non obstante* of the non-expressing of the value, this grant is good, because, by this *non obstante*, he has dispensed with the Statute.[1]

The statutes of 28 Edw. III, cap. 3, [and] 42 Edw. III, ca. 9, will that no one will be a sheriff beyond one year. The king granted the shrievalty of the County of S. to A. for life with all the profits to it appertaining etc. *non obstante* the said acts of 28 and 42 [Edw. III], and it was held good. 2 Hen. VII, 6; 3 Hen. VII, 12, Br., *Patents*, 109. The reason is there given by Ratcliffe, because the king, by his prerogative can dispense with the statutes by the clause of *non obstante*. By the Statute of *Praerogativa Regis*,[2] it is ordained that, if the king grant a manor with the appurtenances, that an advowson appendant will not pass without express words, yet, if the king would grant a manor *cum pertinentiis non obstante*, [by] the Statute of *Praerogativa Regis*, this grant is good enough to pass the advowson so that, if the king would pass in this case the reversion without a recital of the first lease and this with a *non obstante*, it is good by way of a dispensation. But, if the patent of 9 [Jac.] be void, then it is not any non-recital, but a misrecital of the precedent grants in the date, which is not material, nor a thing of substance.

But it has been objected that the king is much deceived, because, if the patent of 9 [Jac.] be admitted to be void, then, it appears by the grant of 14 [Jac.] that the king thinks that the offices were out of him for two lives so that he had a greater power and disposition than he supposed he had. And they enforce this with the Case of Sir Thomas More, which case I agree [with], because, there, there was a lease made of a reversion after the expiration of the lease made to him, where, in truth, his lease was ended, which second lease, if it had been in the case of a common person, it had commenced presently. But, in the case of the king, it could not, because the king was deceived inasmuch as he passed the possession in lieu of the reversion and it was not aided by the statutes of confirmations, because it was limited to commence in reversion when the second lease was limited to commence after the lease ended, and *non aliter*, The Lord Shandois' Case; Auditor Curle's Case; Blage's Case; and that of 8 Hen. VII, 1, confirm the Case of Sir Thomas More, where the second lease is of a reversion *post mortem* etc. or the end of the first.

But our case has a special limitation, *habendum* for their lives when they will be void by the death, surrender, or forfeiture of Fulk Grevill and Adam Newton

---

[1] W. Staunford, *Plees del Coron* (1557), f. 101; *Mason v. Chambers* (1604), Croke Jac. 34, 79 E.R. 27, Yelverton 42, 47, 80 E.R. 31, 34; Stat. 1 Hen. IV, c. 6 (*SR*, II, 113).

[2] Stat. 28 Edw. III, c. 7 (*SR*, I, 346); Stat. 42 Edw. III, c. 9 (*SR*, I, 389); YB Mich. 2 Hen. VII, f. 6, pl. 20 (1486); YB Mich. 3 Hen. VII, f. 12, pl. 7 (1487), 2 Brooke, Abr., *Patents*, 109; *Prerogativa Regis* (*SR*, I, 226).

vel immediate cum et quam primum praedicta officia per mortem, forisfacturem, vel sursumredditionem aut per aliquam aliam determinationem quamcunque aut aliquo modo quocunque vacaverit aut ad manus donationem, concessionem, vel dispositionem nostras, heredes, vel successores nostras pertinebunt vel pertinere vel devenire debuissent seu debebunt si hac concessio minime facta fuisset, so that this grant is not limited to begin *post mortem* or the end of the grant of 9 [Jac.]. But it is a grant for their lives when the offices will be void or come to the hands of the king. If this grant had not been, and, at the time, if this patent had not been made, all of these offices had been in the hands of the king and in his power to give them, the first patents being void by your own admittance. If the king made a lease for life to J.S. and, afterwards, reciting the said lease, grants that the land remain to another, it is a good grant to pass the reversion, because it is a good grant in the case of a common person, and thus, it is also in the case of the king. He is not deceived. 38 Hen. VI, 37b, Danby, Br., *Patents*, 96.[1]

In our case, the grant had been good in the case of a common person; thus, it will be also in the case of the king, [who is] not deceived, on account of which etc.

[It was] compounded [out of court].

[Other copies of this report: British Library MS. Hargrave 24, f. 55, pl. 58.]

Harvard Law School MS. 106, f. 399, pl. 5

Upon a bill exhibited in Chancery by Robert, lord Brooke, against the lord Goring and John Verney of the Middle Temple, Esquire, the case fell out to be thus. Queen Elizabeth, by her letters patent bearing date the 9th day of February in the 19th year of the queen [1577], granted unto Fulke Grevill the office of Clerk of the Council in Wales and also the office of Clerk of the Signet there when the same should happen to be void, for the term of his life. After that, 20 April 25 Eliz. [1583], the queen granted the office of Secretary to the same Fulke Grevill when the same should become void. 33 Eliz. [1590 × 1591], these offices being void, Fulke Grevill was thereunto admitted, and did execute them. In 35 Eliz. [1592 × 1593], he was made one of the Council of the Marches. 24 July 1 Jac. [1603], the king without any recital, either of the patent of 19 Eliz. or 35 Eliz. granted these offices to Fulke Grevill by the name of Fulke Grevill, Esquire (whereas the very same day, he was make Knight of the Bath and the king's hand for the patent was not obtained until 25 July as that was made to appear) for his life in *tam amplis modo et forma prout Carolus fore aut alii aut idem Julio aut eorum aliquis vel aliqui vel aliquis alius suis aliqui alii officia praedictae ante hac habens et exercens habentes et exercentes unquam habuerunt sive gavisi fuerunt habuit sive gavisus fuit aut aliquo modo habere et gaudere debuerunt aut debuit ratione officii praedicti* without any *non obstante* in the patent. And, upon this patent, he was never either

---

[1] *Rex v. Abbess of Syon* (1460), YB Trin. 38 Hen. VI, ff. 33, 37, pl. 2, 2 Brooke, Abr., *Patentes*, f. 96.

admitted or sworn. And, for the procuring of this patent, he gave to Sir David Fowles £1000. 28 July 14 Jac. [1616], the king, reciting only the grant of 1 Jac., grants the said offices to Sir Adam Newton for the term of his life when the same should become void, and that without any *non obstante* in the patent.

2 December 14 Jac. [1616], the king, reciting the several grants of 1 Jac. and 9 Jac., grants the said offices to John Verney and John Mallett, *habendum* for their lives when they should become void by the death, surrender, or forfeiture of Fulke Grevill and Adam Newton *vel alioquorumque modo ad manus donationem, concessionem, vel dispositionen nostras pertinebunt seu pertinere debuerunt si haec concessio facta non faisset*. And, in this patent, there is a *non obstante male nominando vel male recitando vel non recitando praedicta officia vel aliquod donum sive concessionem praeantea factam de officiis praedictis sive de eorum aliquo vel aliquibus*.

2 December 14 Jac. [1616], John Varney and John Mallet, by an indenture under their hands and seals, declared that this office was taken in trust in their names for Fulke, lord Brooke, to be disposed at his will and pleasure, and they joined in a declaration of the trust for Fulke, lord Brooke, for his life and, afterwards, for William Grevill during his life. And there were also covenants for the surrendering up of these letters patent upon the request of the lord Brooke and in no other sort to surrender or forfeit the said office. And there was a certainty therein expressed what John Verney should have for executing the said office and also what he should have in case he did not execute the said office.

John Mallet died 30 December 1628; Fulke, lord Brooke, dies 11 May 5 Car. [1629]. John Verney surrendered by a deed enrolled in the King's Bench both these offices, and, after that, *viz.* 12 May 5 Car. [1629], the king grants to George, lord Goring, who had a general knowledge by hearsay, but no particular knowledge of John Verney nor of any other of any trust in John Verney for the said offices after the death of Sir Adam Newton. And, in the patent, there was a *non obstante*.

Now, the Lord Keeper, SIR THOMAS COVENTRY, for the determining of this clause, called to his assistance SIR NICHOLAS HYDE, lord chief justice of the King's Bench, SIR RICHARD HUTTON, ancient judge of the Common Pleas, and SIR WILLIAM JONES, ancient judge of the King's Bench. And the debate of this cause lasted two days.

And, upon the debate of this case, the Lord Keeper [COVENTRY] did declare his opinion to be, and no man denied it, that a trust may well be fixed to an office, for, although an office be a thing of trust as to the king that grants it, yet may it be in trust for another well enough and that trustee shall be compelled in Chancery to execute the trust, as in the case of a bargainee, who has an estate by the Statute of 27 Hen. VIII,[1] may very well have it upon a trust. And this is warranted by many precedents in this court, as, for example, the case between

---

[1] Stat. 27 Hen. VIII, c. 16 (*SR*, III, 549); note also Stat. 27 Hen. VIII, c. 10 (*SR*, III, 539–542).

Peacock and Sir George Renell for the office of the Marshalsea, in the King's Bench;[1] the Case of the Duke of Buckingham and Sir George Paul, in Michaelmas 5 Car., in this court for the office of Preignotary of the King's Bench, at which cause, Hyde and Hutton were both present; and the Case of Olbury for the Registership of the High Commission when Jones was present. These offices being taken in the names of others in trust were decreed according to the trust. And this case was the more strong for that John Verney had bound himself by covenants in the indenture.

Second, it was resolved that these covenants between the lord Brooke and John Verney were not within the Statute of 5 & 6 Edw. VI, cap. 16, for that it is an indenture that disposes only the profits of the office according to the trust.[2]

Third, it was resolved that the making of the lord Brooke one of the Council of the Marches was in no sort a determination of the office, for he is only made one of the Council by the king under his hand and not by any letters patent and the secretaries of state have ever been of the Council. And Sir Humphrey May is one of the Privy Council, and he sits as an assistant in the Court of Star Chamber, and that determines not his office of Clerk of the Court of Star Chamber. And there is a difference between these cases and Blake's Case in 3 El., Dy. 197; the Remembrancer of the King in the Exchequer made a baron if that court *quandiu se bene gesserit* voided the office.[3]

Fourth, it was not determined here whether one that has a general notice of a trust shall be subject to the trust, for My Lord Goring's counsel urged and stood much upon it that there ought to be a particular notice and a general report will never serve the turn. Dr. and St. 116; 6 rep. 29, Greene's Case; 22 El., 369, Dy.; 18 El. 346; 8 rep. 92, Francis's Case; 26 Hen. VIII, 9; D. and S. 149.[4]

Fifth, it was pressed by the lord Goring's counsel that, admitting that he had a particular notice of the trust, yet he ought not to be subject unto it:

First, because he comes in under the king, who cannot be subject to a trust. 12 Hen. VII, 12; 28 Hen. VIII, Dy. 8; Com. 238, 242; and 5 Edw. IV, 7;[5]

---

[1] Perhaps *Reynell v. Peacock* (1619), 2 Rolle Rep. 105, 116, 81 E.R. 688, 696.
[2] Stat. 5 & 6 Edw. VI, c. 16 (*SR*, IV, 151–152).
[3] *Rex v. Blage* (1561), *ut supra*.
[4] C. St. German, *Doctor and Student* (T. F. T. Plucknett and J. L. Barton, edd., 1974), Selden Soc., vol. 91; *Green v. Baker* (1602), *ut supra*; *Anonymous* (1580), 3 Dyer 369, 73 E.R. 828; *Bacon v. Bishop of Carlisle* (1576), 3 Dyer 346, 73 E.R. 778; *Milner v. Fraunces* (1609), 8 Coke Rep. 89, 77 E.R. 609, also 2 Brownlow & Goldesborough 277, 123 E.R. 940.
[5] *Lord Brook v. Lord Latimer* (1496), YB Mich. 12 Hen. VII, ff. 12, 13, pl. 7; *Abbot of Bury v. Bokenham* (1536), 1 Dyer 7, 73 E.R. 19, also 1 Anderson 2, 123 E.R. 321, Benloe 16, 123 E.R. 12; *Willion v. Berkley* (1562), 1 Plowden 223, 75 E.R. 339; YB Mich. 5 Edw. IV, f. 7, pl. 15 (1465), also Chancery Repts. Middle Ages, 154.

Second, in regard that this estate is determined by the surrender which was subject to the trust and My Lord Goring is in of a new estate from the king by his letters patent and a use, which, in law is but a trust, shall not lie upon a lord by escheat or any other who comes not in in privity of estate. 1 rep., Chudl. Case;[1]

Third, in regard the indenture imports no other than a personal agreement between the lord Brooke and John Verney, which, though it binds John Verney, yet it binds not the lord Goring. And there was vouched 14 Hen. VIII, 15; 21 Hen. VII, Brooke, 77; 16 Edw. IV, 9; 20 Hen. VII, 9; 3 Hen. VII, 14.[2] But My Lord Keeper's [COVENTRY's] opinion was that the lord Goring, notwithstanding the surrender and having of a new patent and coming from under the king, may notwithstanding be decreed in Chancery to execute the trust *quantam in se est*. And so it was agreed in the Case of Oldbury, where there was a surrender of the office and he came in under the surrender. Sixth, it was urged that the letters patent of 14 Jac. and also of 1 Jac., in which case upon the matter, no decree can be made whereupon the lord Brooke may take a benefit, for there is no reason to give recompense upon a void patent or to make a decree for the execution of a void patent. Whereupon, direction was given that a case should be made concerning the validity of the patent and presented to the judges assistant, which was done. And the judges, perceiving that the case would prove difficult, desired that the case might be referred to all the judges of England, which was done also. And [it was] solemnly argued twice. And, as I heard, the judges' opinion was that the patent of 24 July 1 Car. [1625] was merely void for want of a recital of the patent of 19 Eliz. and 25 Eliz., whereby the king might be truly informed how the case stood for these offices and the king, which this patent of 1 Jac. was granted, for anything that appears, conceived that there was no patent on foot concerning these offices and so the king was deceived in his grant. And 39 Hen. VI, 49; Com. 500, Grendon's Case; 6 Hen. VII, 14; 8 Hen. VII, 12; 8 rep. 55; 11 Edw. IV, 1; 1 rep. 45, 48, Alton Woods Case; *tempore* Hen. VIII, B., 350; 6 Edw. VI, Dy. 77; 3 El., Dy. 195; 3 Hen. VII, 6; Com. 331; 27 Hen. VIII, 28; 11 rep. 4; 3 El., Dy. 197; 16 Edw. III, *Breve*, 651; *Grants*, 53; 38 Hen. VI, 36, 37, B., *Patents*, 96; 2 rep. 54; Com. 455; 21 Edw. IV, 49; 2 & 3 P. & M., Dy. 116; 2 Eliz., Bendloe's Rep., Sir Thomas More's Case; and 32 & 33 El., Harrys and Winge's Case, that was adjudged in the very point upon a lease for years made to the same lessee without recitals of the first lease, were vouched by the counsel of both.[3]

---

[1] *Dillon v. Freine* (1589–1595), 1 Coke Rep. 113, 135, 76 E.R. 261, 305, also Popham 70, 79 E.R. 1184, 1 Anderson 309, 123 E.R. 489.

[2] *Southwall v. Huddleston* (1523), YB Hil. 14 Hen. VIII, f. 15, pl. 1, 119 Selden Soc. 139, 150; *Pigot v. Malpas* (1476), YB Pas. 16 Edw. IV, f. 9, pl. 6; YB Mich. 20 Hen. VII, ff. 8, 9, pl. 18 (1504); YB Mich. 3 Hen. VII, f. 14, pl. 20 (1487).

[3] YB Hil. 39 Hen. VI, ff. 48, 49, pl. 11 (1461); *Grendon v. Bishop of Lincoln* (1576), 2 Plowden 493, 75 E.R. 734, also Benloe 293, 123 E.R. 206; YB Hil. 6 Hen. VII, ff. 13, 14, pl. 2 (1491); YB Pas. 8 Hen. VII, f. 12, pl. 5 (1493), Chancery Repts. Middle Ages

And the better opinion of the judges also was, as I was informed by Henry Calthrop [1586–1637], that the *non obstante* in the patent of 14 Jac. And 5 Car. would not aid inasmuch as for the default of the recital of the patents of 19 Eliz. and 25 Eliz. his patents of 1 Jac. and 9 Jac. as they were in force where they are void and omit the patents of 19 Eliz. and 25 Eliz., as patents not being of force, where for anything appearing to the court, it stood in force.

Second, the patent of 14 Jac. is of the offices after the death of Fulke Grevill and Adam Newton so that, during their lives, they did not have the power to execute the office, the king supposing that Fulke Grenvill is the present officer and Adam Newton the succeeding officer after him, in which the king is deceived, on account of which, their patents are void so that, during their lives, there is a vacancy that is prejudicial to the commonwealth. And though a *non obstante* in their patent would give aid where the defect is in the form, yet not where the defect is in the substance. 4 rep. 35, Bozoun's Case; 2 El., Bendl. rep. 33; [. . .] annuity, 112; Stanf. 101; 20 Hen. VI, 8; 8 rep. 29, Prince's Case; 6 Jac., the Lord Beauchamp's Case; 8 rep., the Earl of Cumberland's Case; 6 rep., the Lord Chandois' Case, were vouched.[1]

But the judges never made any certificate of this case to the Court of Chancery. But, by the mediation of the Lord Keeper [COVENTRY] and the judges, it was compounded and the lord Goring to have the present possession, giving the lord Brooke £5500 and to John Verney £1100 and the lord Goring and John Verney make a surrender of their patent of 5 Car. And a new patent was granted to the lord Goring and another that he may nominate during their lives.

[Order of 30 October 1629: Public Record Office C.33/157, f. 73v.]

278; *Earl of Rutland v. Earl of Shrewsbury* (1608), *ut supra*; YB Trin. 11 Edw. IV, f. 1, pl. 1 (1471); *Attorney General v. Bushopp* (1600), *ut supra*; *Alington v. Cox* (1552), 1 Dyer 77, 73 E.R. 165; *Kempe v. Makewilliams* (1561), *ut supra*; YB Pas. 3 Hen. VII, f. 6, pl. 4 (1488); *Regina v. Earl of Northumberland (The Case of Mines)* (1567), 1 Plowden 310, 337, 75 E.R. 472, 512; YB Mich. 27 Hen. VIII, f. 28, pl. 13 (1535); *Curle's Case* (1610), 11 Coke Rep. 2, 77 E.R. 1147; *Hunt v. Coffin* (1561), 2 Dyer 197, 73 E.R. 435, also Jenkins 126, 145 E.R. 89; *Rex v. Burgesses of Wells* (1342), YB Hil. 16 Edw. III, Rolls Ser. 31b, vol. 7, p. 108, pl. 38, Fitzherbert, Abr., *Briefe*, pl. 651; *Rex v. Bishop of St. David's* (1376), YB Mich. 50 Edw. III, f. 26, pl. 8, Fitzherbert, Abr., *Graunt*, pl. 53; *Rex v. Abbess of Sion* (1460), YB Trin. 38 Hen. VI, f. 33, pl. 2, 2 Brooke, Abr., *Patentes*, pl. 96; *Chomley v. Hanmer* (Ex. 1597), 2 Coke Rep. 50, 76 E.R. 527, also Moore K.B. 342, 72 E.R. 617; *Wroth v. Attorney General* (Ex. 1573), *ut supra*; *Mount v. Hodgkin* (1556), *ut supra*; *Holt v. Roper (Moore's Case)* (1560), *ut supra*; *Harris v. Wing* (1590), *ut supra*.

[1] *Bozoun's Case* (1584), *ut supra*; *Anonymous* (1575), Benloe 33, 73 E.R. 955; W. Staunford, *Plees del Coron* (1557), f. 101; *Pilkinton v. Anonymous* (1441), YB Mich. 20 Hen. VI, f. 8, pl. 17; *The Prince's Case* (1606), 8 Coke Rep. 1, 77 E.R. 481; *Crofts v. Lord Beauchamp* (1486), YB Trin. 1 Hen. VII, f. 28, pl. 6; *Earl of Cumberland's Case* (1609), 8 Coke Rep. 166, 77 E.R. 726; *Duke of Chandos's Case* (1606), *ut supra*.

56

Hawton v. Duncombe

(Ch. 1629)

A trust to pay certain money was enforced against the trustee who had withheld the money through fraud.

British Library MS. Add. 25246, f. 88

Mistress Hawton, widow, plaintiff, against her brother Mr. Duncombe in Chancery.

Mr. Hawton and his wife join in a fine for [the] sale of lands for £5000, whereof she had a jointure. And it was agreed before the fine by indenture between the husband, Mr. Hawton, of the one part, and the brother of the wife of the other part, that the wife should have £1000, parcel of the sum of £5000 after the death of the husband, and that the husband should have the use of the £500, part of the said £1000, during his life and that the wife during the life of the husband should have the use of the other sum of £500 for her maintenance and that the said sum of £100 in the meantime should remain in the said Duncombe's hands in trust as aforesaid for all the said parties. The husband in the plague time in 1 Car. [1625–26] insinuates to Mr. Duncombe, her brother, (who was the party trusted) that his wife did elope from him and remained with the adulterer; and that she thereupon had forfeited by the equity of the Statute of Merton[1] the aforesaid sum of £1000, which came in lieu of her dower, as also the use thereof; the words of which statute are '*Si autem mulier abierit cum adultero, et remanet cum eo sive reconciliatione tunc amittet omnem actionem petendi dotam [?] suam*'.[2] Upon pretense whereof they kept from her the use of the £500 limited to her for her maintenance, although that she was only in the country for her safety in the great increase of the plague in the visitation time in the first year of the king [1625–26]. And during that time by reason of some agreement between the husband and Duncombe for £2000 allowed by Duncombe to the husband Mr. Hawton under his hand and seal releases to Duncombe, the party trusted as aforesaid (and who had the £1000), all and every the trust aforesaid, and the said stock of £1000 and all concerning the same. And the husband dies, and the wife survives.

The wife, Mistress Hawton, sues Mr. Duncombe, her brother, in Chancery for the said £1000 and for the use thereof due to her in her husband's life and for the said indenture upon the trust aforesaid and alleges combination between him and her husband in breach of the trust. And Duncombe, the defendant, de-

---

[1] *Cf.* Stat. 13 Edw. I, Westminster II, c. 34 (*SR*, I, 87).

[2] If, however, a wife goes away with an adulterer and remains with him without reconciliation, then she loses all actions for seeking her dower.

nies the one or the other. And she proves the release to him by her husband *in verbis conceptis* as well of the stock of money of the £1000 and of the use thereof concerning her, as of all the trust expressed in the indenture. And she proves the indenture itself.

Upon the hearing of which cause before the Lord Keeper COVENTRY, and for that the release was proved in Chancery to be by combination between the husband and the brother for £200 only paid to the husband by him, and so for the benefit of them both; and for that the indenture of trust was not produced, though it was proved, it was decreed that this single release to one of the grantees in trust upon the practice aforesaid was fraudulent and not conformable to the former trust. And, therefore, by decree, she was relieved upon proof of the trust, practice, fraud, scandal, and combination aforesaid against her brother who was the chief party trusted and the money deposited in his hands.

[Orders of 23 or 27 June and 19 November 1629: Public Record Office C.33/155, f. 1318v, C.33/156, f. 1119v, C.33/157, f. 233v.]

57

Countess of Peterborough v. Countess of Nottingham
Earl of Nottingham v. Countess of Nottingham

(Ch. 1629)

A bill in equity to avoid a confirmation of the defendant's jointure will be denied where the plaintiff received a substantial consideration for the confirmation and the plea of infancy can be made at common law.

Equity favors jointures, but disfavors perpetuities.

British Library MS. Add. 25246, f. 90

The countess of Nottingham, dowager, defendant, in two bills to avoid her jointure in Chancery.

The countess of Peterborough, daughter and heir to the lord of Effingham, who was son and heir to Charles, earl of Nottingham, sued by bill in Chancery for lands and tenements as heir general to the said earl, the countess dowager, his widow, to avoid her release and confirmation under her hand and seal made to the said countess of Nottingham for to confirm her jointure in respect that she was within age at the time of the said deed making and did it by the commandment of her grandfather, the earl of Nottingham, and in obedience to him. But the bill was dismissed: first, because she had £2000 lands of inheritance out of her grandfather's estate, the which was a sufficient recompense; secondly, for that she might have pleaded that plea of infancy at the common law.

The now earl of Nottingham, son to the said decedent, Charles, earl of Nottingham, having but one hundred marks of his father's lands to support his earldom, and he having made a deed after the death of his older brother to confirm the jointure made by his father to his said mother-in-law with covenants by the said deed from time to time to make any other assurance or conveyance to confirm her estate, he having after the making of the said deed found a deed of entail to entitle himself to the lands in jointure by a title that he knew not of before, and therefore he also sued the said countess by bill in Chancery to avoid the said jointure and his deed of release and confirmation. But that bill of the said earl was likewise dismissed.

First, for that that court of Chancery did favor jointures.

Secondly, for that the deed and covenants were strong against him notwithstanding any new title.

Thirdly, for that perpetuities were not favored in Chancery.

Fourthly, for that although that court would perhaps favor the apparent and immediate heir in tail, yet not a more remote or secondary heir, as the complainant was, who was the second in remainder after the death of the lord of Effingham without issue male of his body.

The Lord Keeper [LORD COVENTRY] therefore associating the two chief justices to him and conferring with them in the fifth year of King Charles [1629–30] and they being of the same opinion dismissed both the bills aforesaid (they being both heard on one day) and left the earl of Nottingham to sue at the common law and to avoid the jointure by the deed of entail if he could.

58

Barker v. Norton

(Ch. 1629)

After arbitrators awarded and the court of equity decreed that the mortgagee accept the late payment and interest that had been paid into court, the mortgagee refused to return the security etc. and was imprisoned for contempt of court.

British Library MS. Add. 25246, f. 91v

Mr. Barker, patentee *ad imprimendum solum etc.*, does mortgage the patent, his house, and all necessary implements and the stock of the printing instruments with the appurtenances to Mr. [Bonham] Norton[1] for £3000 at £10 *per centum* before the Statute[2] which reduced the interest to £8 *per centum*. And Mr. Barker does fail for non-payment and does exhibit his bill in Chancery upon the mortgage to redeem and pay the £3000 etc. And the cause was referred to Sir Eubald Thelwall and to Mr. Gerrard, the lawyer, who do order a new day of redemption

---

[1] D. L. Gants, 'Norton, Bonham (1565–1635), printer and bookseller', *Oxford Dictionary of National Biography*, vol. 41, pp. 156–157.

[2] Stat. 21 Jac. I, c. 17 (*SR*, IV, 1223–1224).

two years after for Barker and do further order and appoint that if Barker fail at the same day to pay the sum borrowed and the use thereof, that then Barker should pay £40 in the hundred for the whole sum borrowed as a penalty to him. And the said award was by deed under both their hands and seals.

Barker fails of payment at the second day, but tenders the silver a small time after. But Norton refuses, and Barker exhibits his bill in Chancery upon the mortgage and avers the tender of the money and of the use according to the Statute at the rate of £8 *per centum*. And the defendant alleges the first non-payment and the award of £40 *per centum* and the second non-payment, and he prays to be dismissed.

And the said cause, upon pleading as aforesaid, came to a hearing, and the Lord Keeper [LORD COVENTRY] referred the exposition of the said award to the arbitrators aforesaid, Sir Eubald Thelwall and Mr. Gerard, who, under their hands, declared their meaning, that Barker should not pay the £40 penalty for each £100, according to the words and letters of the said award, for that they did award only that as a penalty *in terrorem* to make Barker more provident to redeem the patent at the day etc.

And, thereupon, the Lord Keeper [LORD COVENTRY] decreed to Barker the patent, stock, and implements and decreed to Norton the £3000 upon the said mortgage and £10 *per centum* before the Statute and £8 *per centum* after the Statute but restrained Norton of the £40 *per centum* to the letter of the said award. And he decreed the patent and premises to Barker upon payment of the premises; and the money and use was brought into the Chancery by Barker. But Norton refuses and keeps all the instruments and implements and prints, and so [he] was in contempt and committed to the Fleet [Prison].

[Orders of 26 January, 9, 12, and 20 February, 20 March, 18 April, 23 June, 20 October, and 8 and 11 December 1629: Public Record Office C.33/155, ff. 551, 603, 668, 677v, 694v, 1125, C.33/156, ff. 422, 542, 579, 631, 645, 654v, 920, C.33/157, ff. 220, 256v, 260.]

59

Hulse v. Daniell

(Ch. 1629)

The jurisdiction of the courts of the counties palatine is limited to land and to local matters; therefore, personal actions cannot be sued there.

British Library MS. Hargrave 174, f. 24v, pl. 4

The bill being for a personal thing there, the court overruled the plea of the jurisdiction of the county palatine. And in the same cause, Mr. Page, to whom it was referred to certify, reported upon a view of precedents that the jurisdiction of county palatines was allowed between parties dwelling in the same county and for lands there and for matters local. And in the argument of the principal case, I cited the Case of Sir John Egerton v. Earl of Derby, 4 *Institutes*, 'County Palatine of Chester'.[1]

And upon long debate in the principal case, the plea was overruled, but without costs. See Hobart 77.[2]

[Other copies of this report: British Library MS. Hargrave 99, f. 63, pl. 19.]

[Orders of 24 October, 27 November, and 8 December 1629: Public Record Office C.33/157, ff. 52v, 174, 214.]

60

Anonymous

(Ch. c. 1629)

A bond given to enforce a contract to resign from a parsonage upon demand is valid and enforceable.

British Library MS. Add. 25246, f. 85v

A., patron of a parsonage, does present B. thereunto, and B., upon an agreement before presentation, does give his bond of £300 to A. with a condition to resign to A. within three months next after notice given to B. by the said A.; and B. is after[wards] inducted thereunto. And upon some cause, A. gives notice to B. that he must resign to him and to his use. But B. does not resign within the time limited in and by the condition of the said obligation. And thereupon A. sues the bond of £300, and B. pleads the Act and Statute of 31 Eliz.[3] to avoid all simoniacal presentments, contracts, leases, bonds, agreements, etc. and so demurs. And A., the plaintiff, joins in demurrer.

And upon the argument to[4] all the judges in the Common Pleas and by their opinions, it was adjudged no simony within the Statute, and the demurrer was overruled. And the patron, who was the plaintiff, had judgment.

And before execution B. exhibits his bill in Chancery to stay judgment and execution upon the cause and reasons aforesaid and to put the said A., the patron, to his oath. But the said bill was dismissed out of the Chancery upon the demurrer of A., the patron. *Et sic vide, et stude fraenum optimum ad captinandum et castigandum indomitos praesbiteros ad obedientiam Dei, amorem populi, et patroni vota correspondentiae.*

---

[1] *Egerton v. Earl of Derby* (1614), E. Coke, *Fourth Institute* (1644), p. 213, also 12 Coke Rep. 114, 77 E.R. 1390, 1 Eq. Cas. Abr. 137, 21 E.R. 940.

[2] *Owen v. Holt*, Hobart 77, 80 E.R. 227.

[3] Stat. 31 Eliz. I, c. 6 (*SR*, IV, 802–804).

[4] of *MS*.

This case may be compared to Doctor Bancroft's invention, the archbishop of Canterbury,[1] who gave lands in tail to Richard Bancroft, the remainder in tail to another cousin, and took a statute of £5000 of Richard Bancroft that [neither] he nor his issue should suffer a common recovery to bar the issue or displant the remainder, for in both cases the taker is compellable to a new law by their own agreement, bond, and statute, and not contrary to the law. *Ducit nolentes factum valentes trahit.*

61

Anonymous

(1629–1630)

In this case, a sum of money given to a master and an usher of a school was ordered to be given entirely to the schoolmaster.

Herne & Duke 69

£20 *per annum* [were] given to a schoolmaster and usher, *viz.* £13 6s. 8d. to the schoolmaster and £6 13s. 4d. to the usher. And [it was] decreed that the schoolmaster should have the whole £20.

62

Case of Chipping Sudbury, Gloucestershire

(Ch. 1629–1630)

In this case, the litigation expenses of the plaintiff in enforcing a charitable trust were reimbursed out of the recovery and the surplusage over the terms of the gift was given to other charitable uses.

Herne & Duke 69

The prosecutor's charges were allowed out of the money decreed. And the surplusage above the uses particularly appointed by the donor were decreed by the then Lord Keeper [LORD COVENTRY] to be disposed of to other charitable uses.

63

Rippon v. Thornton

(Ch. 1629–1630)

Lands can be given to a minister to read divine service.

---

[1] *Hunt v. Bancroft* (Ch. 1617–1621), Bacon's Reports 65, 118 Selden Soc. 486.

Herne & Duke 70

A decree made by commissioners for charitable uses for lands given to a minister for reading divine service [was] confirmed by the then Lord Keeper [LORD COVENTRY].

64

Case of Barnstable, Devonshire

(Ch. 1629–1630)

The Lord Chancellor can increase the amount of an award made by charity commissioners.

Herne & Duke 70

The Lord Keeper [LORD COVENTRY] enlarged a decree made by commissioners of charitable uses whereby £85 only was decreed. And his Lordship made it up £170 and decreed [it] accordingly.

65

Case of Wiveliscombe, Somerset

(1629–1630)

The building of a water conduit is not within the intent of a gift for the relief of the poor.

Herne & Duke 70

Monies given to the relief of the poor [and] paid out to build a conduit [was] adjudged a misemployment.

66

Anonymous

(Ch. 1629–1630)

The beneficiary of a trust who is to perform a charitable duty can be sued to enforce the trust without making the trustees parties to the suit.

Herne & Duke 71

Lands [were] conveyed to trustees in trust for another, who was to maintain a charitable use. The commissioners decree the lands against the *cestui que trust* and not against the trustees. And the decree [was] adjudged good though the trustees were not parties.

67

Anonymous

(1629–1630)

Notice of a charitable purpose that is given to the first purchaser of land will bind subsequent purchasers.

Herne & Duke 71

Notice given to the first purchaser, the *cestui que trust*, [was] adjudged good notice to the succeeding purchasers.

68

Anonymous

(1629–1630)

A public record, such as of an incorporation, is good notice to a purchaser of land of a charitable intention for the land.

Herne & Duke 71

The record of an incorporation of a school [was] adjudged a good notice.

69

Lucas v. Pennington

(Ch. 1629–1630)

In this case, the rights of the mortgagee of a copyhold and those taking under him were enforced against the mortgagor, his successors, and the lord of the manor where the debt was never repaid.

Nelson 7, 21 E.R. 776

5 Car. I [1629–30]. LORD COVENTRY. Lucas v. Joseph Pennington, William Pennington, Wright, and Noble.

The father of Wright, the defendant, being tenant of a copyhold estate held of Joseph Pennington as lord of the manor, mortgaged the same to Lucas, the plaintiff's father, upon condition to be void upon payment of a sum of money, which not being paid on the day, Lucas, the father, entered, and devised the same to the plaintiff. And he died seised. After whose death, the plaintiff enjoyed it. And the lord demanding a fine, he consented that the lord should have the profits for a certain time in satisfaction of the fine, who enjoyed the same accordingly. But he, having received out of the profits more than the fine amounted unto, refused to deliver the possession to the plaintiff, pretending that the estate was forfeited, in regard that Lucas, the plaintiff's father, was never admitted and had not paid any fine. And William Pennington, while his father, Joseph, was in possession under the aforesaid agreement to take profits in satisfaction of the fine, procured Wright, the defendant, to execute a release to him, but without any consideration expressed. And, then, he conveyed the premises to his father, who conveyed the same to Noble, another of the defendants. And all this was without any consideration.

Upon a bill exhibited, the defendant Wright answered that the mortgage was at first unduly obtained from his father upon his deathbed and a greater sum was expressed than was really borrowed and that, notwithstanding the said fraud, the whole money was really tendered at the day, and nobody was there to receive it, but Wright, the father, made no entry into his estate again after the tender and Wright, the son, executed a release to William Pennington.

The court held that, although such release had extinguished his entry, yet the same should enure to the benefit of him who had the former right in trust only and for the use of the plaintiff, and decreed the possession to him accordingly against the defendants and all claiming under them, and, likewise, that Joseph Pennington, the lord of the manor, should account for the profits since his entry, deducting only his fine.

70

Moyle v. Lord Roberts

(Ch. 1629–1630)

In this case, the court of equity, considering the great length of time since the bond in issue was made and the course of dealings between the plaintiff's decedent and the defendant, presumed the bond to have been paid, though not cancelled.

Nelson 9, 21 E.R. 776

5 Car. I [1629–30]. LORD COVENTRY.
About eighteen years before the bill was filed, Moyle, the father, became bound with one Rosecarrock in a bond of £200 conditioned for the payment of £100 to the Lord Roberts, the defendant, at a certain day long since past. Afterwards, the defendant purchased lands of the said Rosecarrock to the value of £500, which purchase was made about four years before Rosecarrock's death.

After his death, the plaintiff took out administration to him, and, being sued upon this bond, exhibited his bill for relief. And, in regard of the antiquity of the bond and for that Rosecarrock himself was never sued in his lifetime, it was presumed that the defendant did deduct the debt out of the purchase money and notwithstanding there were no proofs made of the payment of the money.

The court decreed that the defendant should be restrained from proceeding at law on the bond.

71

Fleetwood v. Charnock

(Ch. 1629–1630)

A surety has a right of contribution against a co-surety.

Nelson 10, 21 E.R. 776

Lord Coventry.
The plaintiff and defendant were jointly bound for a third person, who died leaving no estate. The plaintiff was sued, and paid the debt.

And he brought his bill against the defendant for contribution, who was decreed to pay his proportional part.

72

Gawle v. Lake

(Ch. 1629)

A court of equity does not have the jurisdiction to determine a modus decimandi.

Nelson 10, 21 E.R. 776

Lord Coventry.
The bill was to establish certain customs of tithing within a particular parish, the plaintiff alleging that there were such customs and setting them forth at large in his bill.

The defendant, by his answer, denied the customs, and alleged that it was not proper for a court of equity to determine whether there were any such customs or not, that the bill was in the nature of a prohibition at common law, and in a case where such a prohibition had never been granted or the custom tried.

And, therefore, the bill was dismissed.

[Other copies of this report: 1 Rayner 17, 2 Gwillim 436, 1 Eagle & Younge 370.]

73

Gifford v. Gifford

(Ch. 1629–1630)

In this case, the marriage settlement in issue was enforced in favor of a widow against a subsequent grantee and lessee.

Nelson 11, 21 E.R. 777

5 Car. I [1629–30]. LORD COVENTRY.

Gifford, the father, being possessed of a lease for years, taken in the name of another person in trust for himself, but determinable upon his own life and the life of his wife, did afterwards purchase the inheritance. And, upon the marriage of his son with the now complainant, he settled an annuity of £50 *per annum* upon her to be issuing out of the premises during the lives of him, the said Gifford, and his wife, in case the said complainant should survive her husband, and he conveyed the inheritance to the defendant, and he died. His son died, the widow of Gifford, the father, still living.

And now the son's widow exhibited her bill against the defendant to have the annuity decreed to her and the arrears ever since the husband's death and, likewise, against the person in whose name the lease was taken, who, to avoid the annuity, had assigned his interest to the said defendant, who claimed the lands by virtue of a grant from Gifford's father. And the same was produced not cancelled.

But it was decreed that neither the said grant nor the lease ought to prejudice the plaintiff but that she should have the annuities and the arrears and that the lands should be liable to a distress for the same.

74

Middleton v. Jackson

(Ch. 1629–1630)

A court of equity can settle the rates payable by the tenants to the lord of the manor.

1 Chancery Reports 33, 21 E.R. 499

The plaintiffs and defendants were to produce precedents for fines in cases of tenant right in what manner they had been assessed formerly by this court. The defendant now offering to give the plaintiffs a moderate year's value for a fine, this court, in the case of tenant right, conceiving the said offer to be fair and reasonable, decreed the defendants to pay the plaintiffs for the present one whole year's value of their lands for a fine, and, as the land rises or falls upon every alienation or death of the tenant or death of the lord, a moderate year's value and the defendants to give notice of every alienation at the lord's court. And the fine now assessed is not to be taken as a fine certain. And a Master of this court is to set the said fine.

The said Master assessed the defendants to pay for a fine to the plaintiff for every acre of land, according to the usual measure in those parts, which, in a tenant right, they shall hold of the plaintiff's manor, the sum of 7s., except it be a land called Moss Land, which he rates at 12s. the acre, which the defendant submitted unto, which this court decreed accordingly.

[Reg. Lib. 5 Car. I, ff. 353, 397.]

75

Peter v. Rich

(Ch. 1629–1630)

Co-sureties are equally liable to pay the debt of their insolvent principal debtor.

1 Chancery Reports 34, 21 E.R. 499

The plaintiff and defendant, with one Southcot and Grimes, became bound to the Lord Russell in two bonds of £1600 apiece for the payment of £800, £100 being purchase money. And the plaintiff and the defendant entered into two counter-bonds to the said Southcot for his indemnity. And the first bond of £800 was paid. And the plaintiff and defendant Richard Sheppard came to account, upon which the plaintiff appeared to have paid all his part of the said purchase money save £40, for which the plaintiff gave the defendant Rich alone a bond of £80, and, thereupon, was to be freed by the said defendants of the £800 bond, and was to give over the said purchase wholly unto them.

Yet, notwithstanding, £100 of the said purchase money being not paid, the plaintiff was compelled to pay the same, being formerly bound with the defendants in the said bond of £1600, together with £5 interest thereof, which said £105 this court conceived ought to have been paid by the said Sheppard as the residue of his part of the said purchase money. But the said Sheppard being insolvent, the said £105, in the opinion of this court, ought to be equally paid and borne by the plaintiff and defendant Rich. And [it was] decreed accordingly.

[Reg. Lib. 5 Car. I, f. 315.]

76

Huddlestone v. Lamplugh

(Ch. 1629–1632)

In this case, the marriage settlement in issue a specifically enforced in favor of the possession of the plaintiff.

1 Chancery Reports 36, 21 E.R. 500

This case is touching a lease of the manor of Little Hatley and other freehold lands made by Simon Perrot and Mary, his wife, 19 Eliz. [1576–77], to William Gibbens and Edward Gibbens for ninety years, contrary to the purport of a decree in the Court of Wards, by which the said Perrot had only power to make leases for twenty-one years if he had issue by his wife, as a tenant in tail he might do, and not otherwise.

The plaintiff insisted that the said lease was kept on foot by the plaintiff's father only to accompany the freehold and inheritance, and not for any profit to be made by the said lease. The plaintiff's father, 28 Eliz. [1585–86] by feoffment of livery and seisin, settled the premises to the use of the plaintiff immediately after the death of William Huddlestone, the plaintiff's father, who died in March 3 Car. [1628]. And the tenants attorned to the feoffees.

And the defendants insisted that the said lease was kept on foot by the said William Huddlestone for a benefit.

This court, on the first hearing, forbore to give judgment, but would advise with the judges touching the said estate made to the plaintiff and the assignment made on the defendant's behalf, being both done voluntarily and without any consideration, the one being his son and heir and the others the defendant Elizabeth's children, the said William Huddlestone's wife, born for the most part of them before the marriage in the lifetime of the plaintiff's mother, whether the said lease for years ought in equity to follow and attend the conveyance of the inheritance or no.

His Lordship [LORD COVENTRY], with several of the judges, did now declare that he, and other judges also to whom the case had been put by him, were all of opinion that it was just to decree that the said lease should be brought into this court and be assigned over unto the plaintiff. And he decreed the plaintiff to enjoy the manor and lands in the said lease contained against the defendants and the defendants to assign the said lease to the plaintiff.

And as touching Mrs. Elizabeth Huddlestone's, the defendant's, thirds, which she has recovered at law against the plaintiff and is kept out of possession thereof, His Lordship [LORD COVENTRY], in regard this point is not judicially before him, cannot make an order therein, the said Elizabeth having no bill in court.

[Reg. Lib. 5 Car. I, f. 796; 7 Car. I, f. 370.]

[Related cases: Huddlestone v. Huddlestone (Ch. 1631–1632), see below, Case No. 124.]

77

Tuphorne v. Gilbie

(Ch. 1629–1630)

A conditional estate pur autre vie granted as a security or pledge for an unpaid debt, by forfeiture, can become an asset of a decedent's estate.

1 Chancery Reports 39, 21 E.R. 501

The defendant Gilbie conveyed lands to the defendants Heyward and South and their assigns to the use of them, their heirs, and assigns during the lives of the said Gilbie and Elizabeth, his wife, and to the longer liver of them, with a proviso that, if the said Gilbie shall pay unto Thomas Bennet, the intestate, £120 in February 1628, then the estate to be void and the said Gilbie to reenter. And the

£120 not being paid, the estate became forfeited. And the testatrix, Anne Mansel, having paid divers debts for the said Thomas Bennet, for whom her husband stood engaged, she had the order of this court for the defendants Hayward and South to convey their interest to her, which they did.

And the tenants of the lands having been ordered to pay their rent and the estate of the said Anne Mansel in the said premises has been settled in the plaintiff, who is her executor, by the order of this court, but there being no decree in the cause, the plaintiff has exhibited this bill to have the said estate confirmed to him by a decree.

This court, with the advice of judges and a view of precedents of this court, whereby, in some special cases, the court has ordered the possession against an occupant, did declare that where, in a case of an occupant upon a general trust, this court did rest doubtful how to decree anything upon a matter of equity in opposition to a ground or rule at law.

But this court finds this case to be much differing from a general trust upon an estate granted *pur autre vie*, this being a conditional estate *pur autre vie* granted as a security or pledge for a debt, which being not paid, the estate, by forfeiture, becomes assets in the plaintiff's hands to pay the said Bennet's debts.

This court decreed the said lands to the plaintiffs and assigns absolutely during the continuance of the said estate for satisfaction of the said Bennet's debts, and the tenants to attorn *nisi causa*, and none was showed.

Vide the Statute of Frauds and Perjuries[1] as to estates of occupancy being assets.

[Reg. Lib. 5 Car. I, f. 357.]

78

Winchcomb v. Hall

(Ch. 1629–1630)

A court of equity will not consider the mental capacity of a grantor after a long period of time and after a grant to a bona fide purchaser for value.

1 Chancery Reports 40, 21 E.R. 501

The plaintiff seeks to have a conveyance of his father's estate set aside, which was made twenty years since, when he was eighty years old and *non compos mentis*.

This court was of opinion and declared that, after twenty years and two purchasers, it was not proper for this court to examine a *non compos mentis*, and did dismiss the bill.

[Reg. Lib. 5 Car. I, f. 385.]

---

[1] Stat. 29 Car. II, c. 3 (*SR*, V, 839–842).

79

Morgan v. Clark

(Ch. 1629–1630)

A court of equity can establish or confirm the extent of a glebe which was a part of an enclosure agreement.

1 Chancery Reports 41, 21 E.R. 501

By consent of the freeholders of Kingsthorp, the plaintiff enclosed lands there. And the defendant, being parson of the said church and seised in the right of his parsonage of some glebe within the plaintiff's enclosure, it was agreed between the plaintiff and defendant that the plaintiff and his heirs should enclose and keep in severalty the said glebe and that the defendant and his successors, parsons of Kingsthorp, should enjoy in lieu thereof freehold of the plaintiff's, being as good in quantity and quality as the glebe within the plaintiff's enclosures.

The plaintiff exhibited his bill to have the enclosures established by the decree.

The defendant confessed the agreement. But, because it is to bind the inheritance of the church, he desired a commission to examine the quantity and value of both lands, that the church might receive no prejudice, whereby it appears the lands in lieu of the glebe are full as good as the glebe.

This court decreed the plaintiff, his heirs, and assigns to enjoy the said glebe in severalty to their own use and that the defendant and his successors, rectors of Kingsthorp, and all claiming under them, the defendant, and his successors to enjoy the said freehold according to the said agreement.

[Reg. Lib. 5 Car. I, f. 445.]

80

Barker v. Zouch

(Ch. 1629–1630)

In this case, the change of trustees was not a revocation of a prior will.

1 Chancery Reports 42, 21 E.R. 502

The Lord Zouch, in June 1617, made his will in writing with a schedule annexed. And he thereby directed that his feoffees in trust for the manor of Greevil should make a lease thereof to the plaintiff and one Moor for eighty years, if either of them should so long live, at 5s. *per annum* rent, payable to the executors of the said Lord Zouch. And, he appointed Edward Montagu and Robert Fulnethy his executors. And many years after the said will and schedule, the said Lord Zouch, being desirous to change his executors, but fearing that change might impeach the said will or schedule, about two years before his death, made this memorandum and schedule at the end of the said will.

Memorandum: If, by law, this my last will may stand and be in force with this schedule thereunto annexed, that I revoke my executorship of Robert Fulnethy and Edward Montagu and do hereby appoint and constitute Sir Edward Zouch my only executor to perform this my will and schedule.

And, after the said memorandum was made, he resolved to change the feoffee in trust of the said manor of Greevil for some reasons, and, in 1625, caused the then feoffees or some of them to join with the said Lord Zouch in making a feoffment of the said manor of Greevil to the said defendant and one Arthur Worth and their heirs to the use of the said Lord Zouch and the defendant, Sir Edward Zouch, and others, until the Lord Zouch limit or order new uses thereof, which he never did, and he died.

And Sir Edward Zouch proved the said will etc., but he refused to assure a moiety of the said manor of Greevil to the plaintiff, James Barker, according as the said will and schedule directed, pretending the said feoffment, being made after the said will and schedule, was by law a revocation of the said will.

This court, having well advised and considered of this point, was of opinion that the said feoffment was in equity no revocation of the plaintiff Barker's moiety of the said manor of Greevil, but it ought to be settled on him, the said defendant Sir Edward Zouch having performed some part of the said will.

[Reg. Lib. 5 Car. I, f. 202.]

81

Wood v. Bury

(Ch. 1630)

A bond given to enforce an agreement to resign from a parsonage upon demand will be enforced if the purpose of the agreement is reasonable and legal.

Lincoln's Inn MS. Maynard 75, f. 43

At the hearing of the cause, the case was [as follows]. Bury had purchased the advowson of [*blank*] in the County of Essex, and having a daughter, there was a communication between Babington, the father [*blank*] Babington, a clerk, for marriage between Babington, the father, touching the marriage of the daughter of Bury with the son of Babington. And it was in consideration of this marriage agreed between them that when this church became vacant, that Bury would present Babington, the son, to it. Afterwards the church became vacant, Babington, the son, being at that time so ill that he could not attend to be instituted, and in the meantime, one Richardson, a stranger, had obtained a presentation from another stranger, by which there was a danger of usurpation, on account of which Bury presented Wood, the complainant, who at this time had the preferment of a curateship under Bury in Sydbury in Devon to the value of £20, which he relinquished. And he accepted the presentation by Bury in trust to relinquish to the use of Babington, the son. And for assurance he entered into an obligation of £600 conditioned to relinquish when he would be required by Bury to [do] it.

Afterwards, Bury sued the obligation at common law against Wood,[1] because he would not resign upon request.

Wood preferred a bill in Chancery to be relieved, surmising how Bury intended to draw him into resigning because he would not be content to grant him £60 *per annum* for four years. But upon the answer and the proof, the case appeared [to be] as above.

And SIR THOMAS COVENTRY, LORD COVENTRY, [Lord] Keeper etc., decreed that the bill should be dismissed.

First, he said that he disliked all trusts upon presentations.

Second, and [he said] that if one be presented upon trust for another, that he would not in Chancery relieve such trust by any means, though it be broken, to compel the person that was instituted etc. to resign.

Third, he disliked those bonds made with such conditions to resign when it will be required.

Fourth, and on account of that, if it be proved that originally there was any corrupt intention to make a gain by it or if afterwards it be proved that there was an application of it to the gain by the patron, then he would relieve the parson against such bond.

Fifth, but such a bond can be entered into for a good end, as to avoid a man who would be non-resident, or to avoid it if the parson should have another benefice, or when a man has a son at Oxford etc., who for age is not capable, of presenting another in the meantime and taking such a bond as above to the intent [that] when the son is capable to give [it] to him, this is not simony, and on account of that, against such obligation taken upon such a trust, he would not give any relief.

And on account of that [. . .] diversity, as he will not relieve a trust upon a presentation, so also if there be a bond to perform such a trust, he will not give relief against such bond, if the trust be not proved to be illegal. And on account of that in the principal case, he gave no relief to Wood, but he dismissed his bill because he could not prove any corrupt intention nor application.

Yet in fact he proved by one witness a demand, as above, but it was a single witness against two others on the part of the defendant, who proved the trust directly; and it was also the brother of the plaintiff, and the proof was on the behalf of the plaintiff, it was on his behalf to prove the illegality of the condition etc.

---

[1] *Babington v. Wood* (1630), Croke Car. 180, 79 E.R. 757, W. Jones 220, 82 E.R. 117, Hutton 111, 123 E.R. 1137, British Library MS. Lansdowne 1094, f. 55, pl. 2.

Nevertheless, the recorder, Serjeant *Finch*, urged that this is dangerous, because when such a bond is given [. . .][1] and those who will [. . .] the request will demand money etc. in so secret a manner that it will never be proved. And [?] the single witness accompanied with the presumption of the bond that bears evil intent was good proof.

Nevertheless, the decree was as above for the reasons above.

[Other copies of this report: Lincoln's Inn MS. Hill 125, f. 2.]

British Library MS. Lansdowne 1094, f. 59v, pl. 1

The case was in the King's Bench, and it was thus. The patron, before he presented, took an obligation from the incumbent that he at any time upon the request of the patron would resign his benefice etc. and for the refusal of the incumbent, the patron brought an action of debt. And it was adjudged that the action well lay because there did not appear to be any simoniacal contract in the case.

And now the incumbent sued in the Chancery to be relieved against this obligation. And it was overruled in the Chancery because Coventry, Lord Keeper of the great seal, would not relieve him against a legal bond, it not being alleged or surmised that there was any collateral matter of the paying of money or the performing of any simoniacal contract for which the obligation was made. But the obligation being adjudged good at the common law, he would not constrain or relieve him against it.

[Order of 14 June 1630: Public Record Office C.33/158, f. 653v.]

82

Anonymous

(Ch. 1630)

A court of equity will not reconsider the evidence presented in an ecclesiastical court in a suit there involving the probate of a will.

Lincoln's Inn MS. Maynard 75, f. 43v, pl. 1

On the same day [14 June 1630] upon a hearing of the case upon the bill and answer, it was that a legatee, who had a legacy by a will, preferred a bill for it, setting out a repeal of the will in the spiritual court but showing divers frauds and abuses in suppressing the testimony etc. by the commissioners there.

But the [Lord] Keeper [LORD COVENTRY] dismissed the bill without examining the frauds and abuses in the proceeding.

[Other copies of this report: Lincoln's Inn MS. Hill 125, f. 3, pl. 1.]

---

[1] ad il sound *MS*.

83

Jernegan v. Palmer

(Ch. 1630)

The question in this case was whether the series of contracts and conveyances in this case should be treated as a mortgage or not.

Lincoln's Inn MS. Maynard 75, f. 43v, pl. 2

Between Sir Henry Jerningham and others, the case in Chancery was that Sir Henry, seised of the manor of Morton Valence, entered into a treaty to sell it. And there was agreement for the price of £3500 and assurances were made and £2000 [was] paid, but if the vendee disliked it within one month and had given notice in writing, all would be for naught, and then the £2000 was to be repaid and the land reconveyed. And notice was given of dislike within the month.

Afterwards at the day [of performance], the £2000 was not [re]paid, but further day of six month's forbearance [was] given and the old covenants [were] released and new assurances [were] made that, if the £2000 and use etc. [was] paid etc., then the vendee would reassure. At this day also, the £2000 nor the use was not paid, but then Sir Henry and the vendee agreed upon the absolute purchase of the manor for £500 more, if the £2000 and the use was not paid upon a third day, which now also was given further by six months. And Sir Henry covenanted then to procure the tenants to attorn and to deliver the possession, if he did not pay the £2000 etc. and if the vendee paid £500 more. At this day the £2000 was not paid, but Sir Henry accepted the £500 and procured the tenants to attorn and delivered the possession and released the covenants of reassurance.

And, thus, at first was the case upon the evidence. And the opinion of the Lord Keeper [LORD COVENTRY] was against the plaintiff who preferred this bill for the £1000 which was abated in the process.

But then it was objected that the defendant himself in his answer said that after this last agreement [was] executed, the defendant admitted and offered to Sir Henry Jerningham that if he would repay the £2500 and the use, that he would have his land.

Upon this it was decreed that the defendant reconvey etc. (notwithstanding that this offer was refused by the plaintiff) and upon the repayment of the £2500 and the use and six months for payment etc. in which if he fail, then the land was decreed to the defendant, because the Lord Keeper [LORD COVENTRY] said, that this offer shows a conveyance [?] like a mortgage.

Yet it was objected that after the £500 [was] paid any lives were dead, to which it was responded that if it was a mortgage, then it is not material. And where after the bill and answer, the vendee was dead and not having any land held *in capite* except this, his heir of full age, who also was a party to the bill, by which he was forced to sue livery of all his land, sued, this charge was imposed upon the plaintiff, but if the defendant had held other land, then it was decreed only for the ratable part, *viz.* according to that which will be charged was augmented by the said land.

[Other copies of this report: Lincoln's Inn MS. Hill 125, f. 3, pl. 2.]

[Order of 11 November 1630: Public Record Office C.33/159, f. 126.]

84

Connock v. Rowe

(Ch. 1630)

A beneficiary of a trust can sue the surviving trustee for all that is due to him from the trust, and the surviving trustee can then sue the executors of the deceased trustee for contribution.

Lincoln's Inn MS. Maynard 75, f. 44, pl. 1

Richard Conock conveyed to the defendant and one Billings, deceased, certain lands and woods in Calstock in the County of Cornwall in trust, etc. and made them executors. They received the profits jointly. And it was decreed that the survivor answer [for] all to the plaintiff [J. Conock], who sued for legacies and *hospit*[*alitas*] appointed by the will of Richard Conock. And yet the report of the master was that Rowe in his answer said that he received only a moiety, but [it] being read, it was not a negative.

And Rowe was put over against the executors of Billings for contribution, because the Lord Keeper [LORD COVENTRY] said there is no reason that the plaintiff should be put to prove what one received and what the other.

[Other copies of this report: Lincoln's Inn MS. Hill 125, f. 4, pl. 1.]

[Order of 11 November 1630: Public Record Office C.33/159, f. 172.]

85

Horner v. Burwell

(Ch. 1630)

A court of equity requires the plaintiff to have two witnesses to testify against a defendant who answers directly under oath in order for the plaintiff to prevail.

Lincoln's Inn MS. Maynard 75, f. 44, pl. 2

On the same day [11 November 1630] in Dr. Burwell's case, he, being a fellow of St. John's [College] in Cambridge, received £260 from one Browne to renew a lease for him and to restore as much as should be left of it. And the charge of the bill preferred by one Horner, administrator *durante minore aetate* of the children of Browne, was that the doctor had bestowed only £66 for the lease from the college. And Dr. Burwell in his answer showed that Browne had lived seven years after this supposed delivery of the money and never questioned him, and he denied the receiving of the £260 [with an obligation] to account or [any] other sum 'to any such end and purpose as in the bill is untruly surmised'. And the proof of it was by only one witness, that he had received £260.

And upon this, the Lord Keeper [LORD COVENTRY] said that if a man denies a charge directly, then he would never make a decree upon [the evidence of] one witness because there [it would be] one versus one, but because here the doctor had denied the receipt of the money with a negative pregnant, therefore, he put the matter upon the oath of the doctor, he being in court, [so] that if he would directly deny etc., that then he will be discharged. But because he was not thus sworn, he was of the opinion that he should be charged.

But then it was moved that, this bill being preferred by administrators during a minority, now [?] pending the suit the infants were [come] of full age, and it [was] proved by a copy of the administration running to them, and [it was] proved to be a true copy by examination at the hearing.

Therefore, the Lord Keeper [LORD COVENTRY] wished to be advised by the judges whether the suit should abate.

[Other copies of this report: Lincoln's Inn MS. Hill 125, f. 4, pl. 2.]

[Orders of 4 and 11 November 1630: Public Record Office C.33/159, ff. 12, 43v.]

86

Fachell v. Lassells

(Ch. 1630)

In this case, an interlocutory order of quiet possession was granted to the plaintiff.

Lincoln's Inn MS. Maynard 75, f. 45, pl. 1

The bill was to discover by what title the defendant [?] made [?] frequent interruption, and it showed a sale by the father of the defendant to the plaintiff for valuable consideration and that the defendant had gained the evidences wherefore he presumed to make the interruption etc. And in proof, Lassels made no title except by one Metham from whom he could not [have been] conveyed[1] any title, and there was no proof of the coming of any evidences to the hands of the defendant.

---

[1] a que il ne poit conveyer *MS*.

Nevertheless [it was] decreed that the possession of the plaintiff will be established against the defendant until he shall show better matter upon a bill in this court.

Secondly, [it was held] that the defendant and the said Metham (a stranger to the suit but deposed in the cause as a witness, and there he deposed that he sold to the plaintiff the lands etc.) should be examined upon interrogatories touching the writings.

[Other copies of this report: Lincoln's Inn MS. Hill 125, f. 5.]

87

Anonymous

(Ch. 1630)

The question in this case was whether the arrearages of payments of an annuity to a husband and wife can be assigned to a third person by the husband and wife.

Lincoln's Inn MS. Maynard 75, f. 45, pl. 2

A covenant to pay an annuity to the husband and wife etc. was made with the friends of the wife; the annuity was in arrears; the husband being in debt, he, with his wife, assigned the arrearages in satisfaction of the debt, and he died.

First, the Lord Keeper [LORD COVENTRY] was of the opinion that the arrearages belong to the wife, and

Second, that her consent is not a bar to her.

Still it was offered to be proved that he would have starved if the debt had not been [made] because it was for meat and drink supplied to him in prison. But, nevertheless, it was ended by composition in court by assent. But the [Lord] Keeper declared his opinion, as above, yet it was said that the arrearages should have [?] been paid to the husband, and if they should [?] be paid, he could have disposed of them.

[Other copies of this report: Lincoln's Inn MS. Hill 125, f. 5v, pl. 1.]

88

Nash v. Preston

(Ch. 1630)

The widow of a bargainee is entitled to dower.

Croke Car. 190, 79 E.R. 767

A bill in Chancery was referred to JONES, Justice, and myself [CROKE], to consider whether one should be relieved against dower demanded etc.

The case appeared to be that J.S., being seised in fee, by indenture enrolled, bargains and sells to the husband for £120, in consideration that he shall re-demise it to him and his wife for their lives, rendering a peppercorn, and with a condition that, if he paid the £120 at the end of twenty years, the bargain and sale shall be void. He re-demises it accordingly, and dies. His wife brings [an action of] dower.

The question was whether the plaintiff shall be relieved against this title of dower.

We conceived it to be against equity and the agreement of the husband at the time of the purchase that she should have it against the lessees, for it was intended that they should have it re-demised immediately to them, as soon as they parted with it and it is but in the nature of a mortgage. And, upon a mortgage, if land be redeemed, the wife of the mortgagee shall not have dower. And, if a husband take a fine *sur cognisance de droit come ceo* and render back, although it was once the husband's, yet his wife shall not have dower, for it is in him and out of him *quasi uno statu*, and, by one and the same act. Yet, in this case, we conceived that, by the law, she is to have dower, for, by the bargain and sale, the land is vested in the husband and, thereby, his wife is entitled to have dower. And, when he re-demises it upon the former agreement, yet the lessees are to receive it subject to this title of dower. And it was his folly that be did not conjoin another with the bargainee, as is the ancient course in mortgages. And, when she is dowable by act or rule in law, a court of equity shall not bar her to claim her dower, for it is against the rule of law, *viz.* 'where no fraud or covin is, a court of equity will not relieve'.

And, upon conference with other the justices at Serjeants' Inn upon this question, who were of the same judgment, we certified our opinion to the Court of Chancery, that the wife of the bargainee was to have dower and that a court of equity ought not to preclude her thereof.

1 Equity Cases Abr. 217, 21 E.R. 1001

Easter [term] 6 Car. I.

If A., in consideration of £100, by bargain and sale enrolled, conveys to B. and his heirs to the intent that B. shall re-demise to A. for life, with a condition that, if A. paid the £100 at the end of twenty years, the bargain and sale should be void, and B. re-demises accordingly, and dies, his wife shall be endowed, for, though B. re-demised upon the former agreement, yet A. takes it subject to the title of dower. And it was his folly that he did not join another with the bargainee, as is the ancient course in mortgages.

[This was] agreed in Chancery by JONES and CROKE and, upon a conference with the other justices, certified accordingly.

Lord Nottingham, *Prolegomena*, p. 329

6 Car. I.

A bargainee of lands with a proviso for redemption at the end of twenty years re-demises to the bargainor and his wife for their lives, and dies.

It was adjudged: first, the wife of the mortgagee after redemption shall not be endowed generally; second, here, the wife of the bargainee shall be endowed, for it was the folly of the bargainor not to join another with the bargainee to prevent dower; third, there is no relief in equity against it, because the law gives the title, and, there being no fraud nor covin, equity will not relieve against it.

But I [Lord Nottingham] do not agree to this case.

89

Acland v. Atwell

(Ch. 1630–1632)

The patron of a prebend can prevent his prebendary from committing waste of the prebend.

3 Swanston 492, 36 E.R. 957

3 December 1630.

Forasmuch as the Right Honorable Lord Keeper [LORD COVENTRY] was this present day informed by Mr. *Noy*, being of the plaintiff's counsel, that the defendant, being one of the prebends of Dutton in the County of Devon, whereof the plaintiff is patron, the said defendant committed diverse great waste and spoil upon the houses, lands, woods, and timber trees of the said prebend, and, therefore, it was prayed that a writ of prohibition might be awarded against the defendant, as also a writ of assistance unto the sheriff of the county where the said lands do lie, to see that the defendant shall not commit any waste or spoil upon the houses, lands, woods, or trees belonging to the said prebend, and the said plaintiff's counsel now offered that he would show precedents in like cases, wherein such assistance had been granted, it is thereupon ordered by His Lordship that a writ of prohibition should be awarded against the defendant, inhibiting him thereby from doing or committing any waste or spoil upon the houses, lands, woods, or trees of the said prebend and the said plaintiff's counsel are to attend Mr. Justice Powis and Mr. Justice Croke with a draft of the said writ of assistance unto the sheriffs, who are entreated by His Lordship to peruse the same and see that the same be done according to the course of law and then the said writ is to issue out accordingly.

[Reg. Lib. 1630 A, f. 136.]

15 October 1631.

Whereas, by an order of this Court the 3d day of December last, a writ of prohibition was awarded against the defendant, inhibiting him thereby from doing or committing any waste or spoil upon the houses, lands, woods, or trees of the prebend in question, upon opening of the matter this present day unto this Court by Mr. *Rolle*, of the plaintiff's counsel, and upon the reading of two several affidavits, the one of G.G. and the other of B.G., it appeared that, although the said defendant had been personally served with the said writ of prohibition, yet he had committed waste upon the premises by rooting up timber trees growing upon the same, it is, therefore, ordered that, if the defendant shall not on the return of a subpoena to be served on him for that purpose show unto this Court good cause to the contrary, then an attachment is awarded against the said defendant to bring him into this Court to answer the said contempt.

[Reg. Lib. 1631 A, f. 25.]

20 November 1631.

After a recital of the preceding order, the Court being this day informed by Mr. *David*, being of the defendant's counsel, that the defendant caused but one timber tree to be felled, which he appointed for the reparation of the house, and that the same was not felled in any contempt to the said prohibition, it is therefore ordered, that, if the said defendant shall by the second return of the next term make affidavit that he caused the same to be felled for no other purpose but for the reparation of the said house, then the said contempt and attachment are discharged, and, in the meantime, the same are suspended.

[Reg. Lib. 1631 A, f. 173.]

2 December 1631.

After a recital of the preceding order, upon opening the matter this present day before the Right Honorable the Lord Keeper [LORD COVENTRY] by Mr. *Germin*, of the plaintiff's counsel, and upon the reading of both the said former orders, it was alleged that the said tree was not employed about the said house, as by the defendant pretended, but that the same was sold and that the defendant had also felled other trees, contrary to the said prohibition, it is, therefore, ordered by His Lordship that the said defendant making oath that he has felled but one timber tree upon the premises and that the same was employed in repairing the said house, then the said attachment is discharged, or, if the plaintiff shall make affidavit that the said tree was not employed about the said house or that the defendant has felled any other trees upon the premises since the said prohibition, then the plaintiff may proceed with his attachment against the defendant for the same.

[Reg. Lib. 1631 A, f. 192.]

26 January 1632.

On oath that the defendant has broken an order, an attachment is issued against him.

[Reg. Lib. 1631 A, f. 300.]

13 February 1632.

After recital of the order of the 2d of December 1631, upon opening the matter this day, Mr. *Duke*, being of the defendant's counsel, and upon the reading of the affidavit made by the defendant, it was alleged that, notwithstanding affidavit was made on the defendant's behalf, yet the plaintiff did, nevertheless, take out process of attachment against the defendant before the second return of this term, and caused the same to be served upon the defendant on Candlemas day [2 February] last when, as the defendant was burying the dead corpse of one A., he had him violently carried into a house by two bailiffs, who did not suffer him to bury the said dead corpse, but kept and detained him in prison until he had given good bond for his appearance, by means whereof the defendant did personally appear accordingly, it is thereupon ordered that the Six Clerks not towards the cause shall examine the same, and, if they shall find the same, this Court will then give good costs against the plaintiff.

[Reg. Lib. 1631 A, f. 338.]

22 February 1632.

After recital of the preceding order and of a certificate of the Six Clerk, attesting the accuracy of the former allegations, the plaintiff being unable to make it appear that the attachment was duly obtained, the attachment was discharged, the plaintiff was ordered to pay costs, and an attachment was ordered against the bailiffs.

[Reg. Lib. 1631 A, f. 396.]

Directions were afterwards given for examination on interrogatories relative to the alleged contempt in the process of attachment. But no order on the merits has been discovered.

2 Rolle, Abr., *Wast*, pl. 3, p. 813

Thus, if a prebendary waste the trees of his prebend, the patron can have a [writ of] prohibition. A prohibition was granted by the LORD COVENTRY, Lord Keeper, for the prebend of Catton in Devon.

90

Moor v. Lord Huntington

(Ch. 1630–1631)

The lord of a manor must hold courts and allow his tenants to transfer their copyhold lands to others.

Nelson 12, 21 E.R. 777

6 Car. I [1630–31]. Lord Coventry.

The defendant, being lord of several manors, did refuse to hold courts and grant admittances etc., whereupon the copyhold tenants exhibited their bill to be relieved.

And it was decreed that the defendant and his heirs should from time to time as occasion should require procure courts to be held for the said manors and suffer the plaintiffs and their heirs to make surrenders to such persons and for such uses as the copyholders should limit and direct and that the surrenderees should be admitted accordingly.

91

Lasbrook v. Tyler

(Ch. 1630–1631)

A court of equity will enforce the payment of alimony to a wife.

1 Chancery Reports 44, 21 E.R. 502

The plaintiff, on the behalf of the other plaintiff, Margaret, his sister, sought to be relieved against the defendant Tyler, her husband, for an allowance to be given her for maintenance for all the time she departed from him, which was a year and a half, which this court decreed, and also the benefit of a bond given before marriage.

[Reg. Lib. 6 Car. I, f. 329.]

92

Mayor of London v. Bennet

(Ch. 1630–1631)

In this case, the court of equity stayed the immediate repayment of a debt contracted on behalf of the crown that was due to the defendant creditor because it was impossible for the plaintiff, the debtor and surety for the crown, to repay immediately.

1 Chancery Reports 44, 21 E.R. 502

King James borrowed £100,000 of the City upon their common seal, and an Act of Common Council was made in London, by which the bonds were to be made in the names of the plaintiffs under their common seal for the payment of the said £100,000 and interest to such persons as would lend the same. And, amongst others, the defendant lent the plaintiffs at their request £1000, for payment whereof the plaintiffs became bound in £1500. And his now Majesty Charles I borrowed £60,000 more, and secured that and the £100,000 by a mortgage. And His Majesty, for further satisfaction of the lenders' debts and damages, agreed to sell lands in fee farm, which was accepted of and yielded to, and an Act of Common Council was made. But the defendant's said debt cannot receive such sudden satisfaction, and the defendant requires money not being to be raised so suddenly. And, at another Common Council, the City used all endeavors for the raising of the money, and they promised to deal with the defendant as well as any other of the lenders as to the speedy payment of his debt, yet the defendant proceeds at law against the plaintiffs upon the said bond.

This court granted an injunction.

This defendant offered divers reasons against the injunction.

But this court liked of none, there being a precedent where, in the like case, an injunction was granted. And this court ordered an injunction until a hearing.

[Reg. Lib. 6 Car. I, f. 649.]

93

Peacock v. Glascock

(Ch. 1630–1631)

A devise can constitute a payment of money due under a marriage settlement.

1 Chancery Reports 45, 21 E.R. 503

Weston Glascock, former husband of Anne, the plaintiff's wife, about fourteen years since, upon his intermarriage with the said Anne, became bound to one Boosey in a bond of £3000 to acknowledge a statute of £2000 within six months after his marriage with the said Anne to the said Boosey, defeasanced that, if the said Weston Glascock should not in a convenient time after the said marriage, before his death, convey to the said Anne freehold lands in Essex of the clear yearly value of £500 for her life for her jointure, then the said Weston should leave the said Anne at his death £1000.

And the said Weston did by his will devise to the said Anne lands to her and her heirs, agreed now in court to be £52 *per annum*.

But the said plaintiff insisted that the lands so devised were a voluntary gift of her said husband, and not in respect of the said bond of £3000 or jointure. And he produced two witnesses to prove the same.

This court, nevertheless, is clear of opinion that the said lands so devised were in lieu of the said Anne's jointure and that the said proofs are but mere conjectures, and, therefore, decreed the said bond of £3000 to be delivered up to be cancelled.

And, as to the lease of 1000 years of the lands claimed by the said Peacock and Anne, his wife, executors of the said Weston Glascock, the same was made over unto the defendant Ignatius Glascock by the said Weston, redeemable on payment of £373. And the said Weston, by his will, appointed all the rents and profits of the said land to Ignatius for payment of his debts and legacies until the said Thomas Glascock shall come to his full age. And, if the said Ignatius refuse to give a bond of £1000 to his executors to pay his said debts and legacies and discharge the said Anne of all debts due unto him, the said Ignatius, Weston Glascock, or to any other, then the said Anne should have the said rents, revenues, goods, and profits of the said lands to pay the said debts and legacies. Now, for that Ignatius refused to render the said bond of £1000 and for that, by his answer, he confesses the said lease was made to him in trust, and, as a security for the said £373, which, if he may have [been] damaged, and what money is owing to him from the said Weston, he will assign the said lease to the plaintiffs, and, for that all the debts and legacies are to be paid out of the said leased lands, it is ordered that the said plaintiffs paying first unto the said Ignatius his money due on the said lease and what money is due to him from Weston with damage which this court allows the said plaintiff again out of the rents and profits with the like damages, then the said lease shall be assigned to the said plaintiffs until satisfaction be made them for the debts and legacies and also for what they shall pay as aforesaid, and both parties to account before a Master.

And it is decreed that, after the said debts and legacies be paid, the plaintiffs shall take no further benefit of the said lease, but shall account to the said Thomas Glasscock, the heir, at twenty-one years of age, and declared the personal estate of the said Weston, bequeathed unto the said Anne by his said will, shall not be subject or liable to the said debts and legacies as aforesaid.

[Reg. Lib. 6 Car. I, f. 656.]

94

Drury v. Drury

(Ch. 1630–1631)

A co-heir can enter upon a lessee for non-payment of rent, thereby ending the lease, and the court can thereupon compel a partition among the co-heirs.

1 Chancery Reports 49, 21 E.R. 504

William Smith, seised of the manor of Coles, made a lease of the demesne thereof to one Clark for twenty years, and he died, leaving the reversion to descend to the plaintiff and the defendant William Drury, his co-heirs. And the said William Drury has entered into the whole manor. And the said defendant Clark is charged to be behind with his rent.

The defendant says that, without the consent of the plaintiff, he entered upon the defendant Clark for not payment of rent, and he conceives that, thereby, he has wholly avoided the lease, which being a point doubtful in law, whether the lease be wholly avoided or but for half, this court referred that point to the judges, who certified that a writ of partition be brought between the said co-heirs.

This court ordered the same according to the said certificate, and the defendant Drury shall answer to the plaintiff a moiety of the profits of the premises from the time of the avoiding the defendant Clark's lease, according to the just value of the lands.

[Reg. Lib. 6 Car. I, f. 74.]

95

Earl of Newcastle v. Earl of Suffolk

(Ch. 1630–1631)

Trustees are bound by conveyances of trust assets made by their beneficiaries.

1 Chancery Reports 50, 21 E.R. 504

The plaintiff claims the premises by deed in 11 Jac. [1613–14] executed by the late earl of Suffolk to Dame Judith Corbet, mother of the plaintiff's wife Dame Elizabeth, in consideration of a marriage between Henry Howard, Esq., the third son of the said late earl of Suffolk and the said Lady Elizabeth, daughter of the said Judith Corbet, and by fine levied thereupon by the said late earl and Dame Katherine, his then wife, and the defendant, the now earl of Suffolk, his son, unto the said Dame Judith Corbet with general warranty to and for the use and behoof of the said Henry Howard and the said Elizabeth, his then wife, for their lives, in part of her jointure.

The defendant insists that the said fine and conveyance ought not to take place or work upon the said lands and premises, for that, as touching part of the premises, *viz.* Tollesbury, Abshall, etc., there was a lease in 3 Jac. [1605–06] made by the said earl to Roger Pennel, his servant, for fifty years from Michaelmas then next, in trust for the said countess of Suffolk, under which said lease and trust, by agreement and permission of the said countess of Suffolk, the said William Howard received the profits of the manor of Tollesbury, having the inheritance thereof settled in him by deed from the said late earl, his father, and the said now earl, in avoidance of the plaintiff's title to the manors of Abshot, Salkot, and Wigborrow, did allege the like lease to be made to Pennel upon the same trust for the said countess dowager of Suffolk and that the same manors descended to him as son and heir to the said late earl, his father. And it was insisted that the said late earl had no estate in the manors of Wendon and Westbury at such time as the said fine and conveyance were made and levied, but that the interest thereof was then in Henry Speller and Michael Humphrey, and that Sir Henry Speller, being the survivor, granted and demised the same to the Lord William Howard and Marmaduke Moor for 500 years, and, afterwards, conveyed the inheritance to the now earl of Suffolk.

This court did, therefore, now declare that the said fine, wherein the said countess dowager of Suffolk is a party, is sufficient to bind the trust of the said lease made to Pennel, being for the said countess's use, and, howbeit the estate in law of the said manors of Wendon and Westbury was in the said Sir Henry Speller, yet the same was then in the said Sir Henry Speller and Michael Humphrey in trust for the said late earl of Suffolk and his heirs, for that it appeared he held the possession thereof and disposed thereof at his will and pleasure, and of part thereof, he made a lease of twenty-one years and several other leases. All which leases did precede the plaintiff's jointure, and are yet in being.

And it not appearing whether the said lease of 500 years made to the said Lord William Howard and Moor was made before the commencement of this suit or the process or letter served touching the same nor whether the lessees had any notice of the said trust, this court decreed that the plaintiffs and their assigns, during the life of the said Lady Elizabeth, shall enjoy all the lands in the bill against the defendants, their heirs, etc. But, if hereafter the lease of 500 years shall appear not to be made *pendente lite*, then it is decreed the said earl of Suffolk shall recompense and satisfy the plaintiff by reason of the said lease.

[Reg. Lib. 6 Car. I, f. 644.]

96

Notes

(Ch. 1631)

Witnesses; depositions in related suits; bills of review; res judicata.

British Library MS. Hargrave 30, f. 278, pl. 2

[1] Note [that it was] agreed in Chancery that when the depositions are published, still new witnesses[1] can be examined, and they are called *proves obornants*;

---

[1] proves *MS.*

but these witnesses are only for the explanation of the first witnesses.[1]

[2] Note [that] if a bill of review of a decree is preferred in this court, the defendant cannot plead this former decree against the plaintiff. But if the second bill is not a bill of review of the former decree nor recited to be so but is a new bill for to examine again the same matter formerly decreed, this decree is a good plea against him, because this matter decreed should not be reconsidered[2] except upon a bill of review.

[3] Note that [where] witnesses are examined[3] in a cause which afterwards is dismissed, their testimony will not be allowed to be used in another cause thereafter, because when the cause is dismissed, the testimony taken in this cause should not be thereafter used. And it was said thus to be resolved in the Lord Brooke's Case.[4]

[4] Also if A. as lessee for years exhibits a bill here and witnesses are examined but the term expires and this cause is not brought to a hearing but is pending and afterward the one in reversion exhibits a new bill for the same cause, the evidence taken in the former cause which is still pending shall not be allowed to be used in the latter cause.

97

Ramsey v. Goslin

(Ch. 1631)

A court of equity will not order specific performance of a contract to sell land where there was inadequate consideration plus fraud or surprise.

Lincoln's Inn MS. Maynard 75, f. 45, pl. 3

Gosnall being a young man and recently come from the university, an estate in land in Norfolk descended to him from his uncle, for which he covenanted for £1300 to make assurance to Ramsey and his heirs, where in truth the land was worth £400 *per annum*. And Ramsey preferred his bill in the Chancery for performance of the covenants, which now Gosnall refused to do. And upon proof, it appeared by one witness only that Gosnall never had a counterpart of the assurance it was in such great haste and [there were] other circumstances savoring of a surprise of the young man.

And the bill was dismissed without any discountenance [of the] covenants. And the Lord Keeper [LORD COVENTRY] gave the reason that when covenants

---

[1] Note, pl. 7 (1508), Keilwey 96, 72 E.R. 260.
[2] reveled into *MS*.
[3] testmoignes prise *MS*.
[4] Perhaps *Lord Brooke v. Lord Goring* (Ch. 1629), see above, Case No. 55; note that none of the reports of that case consider this point of the law of evidence.

are [made] to assure land and there is a great disproportion in the consideration, as in this case, still this is not cause for relief not to be awarded. But where there is fraud or surprise, there he will have regard to it. And for this cause, as here, there was not a fraud proved except by one witness, but a surprise appeared. Thus the bill was dismissed.

[Other copies of this report: Lincoln's Inn MS. Hill 125, f. 5v, pl. 2.]

[Orders of 25 January and 5, 7, 8, 12, and 22 February 1631: Public Record Office C.33/160, ff. 200, 235, 240v, 281, 283, 339v.]

98

Anonymous

(Ch. 1631)

In this case, a particular shipping contract was enforced.

Lincoln's Inn MS. Maynard 75, f. 45v, pl. 1

In Easter [term] 7 Car. [1631], before the Master of the Rolls [CAESAR] and [with] Justice JONES in court, [the case was that] a ship was let to freight for a certain sum per month and the account for the payment [was] to commence upon the loading of the ship. It was after this in February [that] the parties loaded the ship with pipestaves and remained there one month in the harbor, and then came a proclamation by which it was declared that pipestaves were illegal to be transported, being ammunition, then [in the] mean [time] between the unloading of them and the reloading of the ship, that was one or two months more, came an arrest of all ships, that none depart out of the harbor (this was when the duke of Buckingham went to Rochelle). And on account of that, the ship was [further] hindered from proceeding on the voyage [for] two months, and then it went. And upon the return, there was a suit for the freight from the time of the loading.

And the bill was exhibited here to discharge it because the first time it was necessarily stayed by the proclamation that inhibited the commodities. And also the other [?] time [was] by an act of state.

But it was decreed that he pay all because the prohibition by the state was upon the commodities and not upon the ship the first time, so that it was then the act of the plaintiff in loading them and it will be to his prejudice. And as to the second stay, it would not have happened except the first had been made, which was occasioned by their act and they, after the loading of the pipestaves, slacked their time for a month.

[Other copies of this report: Lincoln's Inn MS. Hill 125, f. 6.]

99
Giles v. Gesling
(Ch. 1631)

In this case, equitable relief was granted to a surety who was prevented from making certain repairs that he had contracted to do.

Lincoln's Inn MS. Maynard 75, f. 45v, pl. 2

Gesling, father of the defendant, farmed two mills from Bettisworth and covenanted to repair them. And Giles entered into an obligation of £100 as surety for Gesling to perform the covenants. Gesling, the father, assigned to the defendant. And he died and made him executor (but it was not thought material [whether] he be executor or assignee, because nothing appeared of the assets or of the assignment).

The mills fell into decay. Bettisworth put the bond in suit, and he had judgment, but it was deferred in consideration of £5 received and that [if] Gesling repair before Michaelmas, that he would not have the advantage of the judgment.

Giles came to repair and provided materials before Michaelmas, but he was hindered from repairing by Gesling, and an action was brought against him by Gesling for entering onto the land.

Upon this, the mills not being repaired, Bettisworth took execution out against Giles. And then he agreed with Giles orally that if he would pay £20 and repair the mills, that he would be discharged of reparation thereafter. And also he agreed that he would procure a license from Gesling, his tenant, to allow him to repair, after which Giles provided materials. But Gesling hindered him again and prohibited him etc.

And because the mills were not repaired, Bettisworth took out a new execution, and upon it, he levied £73 plus, and for relief Giles exhibited a bill against Gesling and Bettisworth. And it appeared that twenty marks would have repaired [the mills] at the time of the second agreement.

It was decreed that for all of the damage that Giles had sustained for the non-repairing, Gesling, being the principal and being an assignee, should make satisfaction to Giles and that Bettisworth retain as much of it as he had levied, as he was indemnified at the time of the agreement, because he agreed that Giles have leave etc. and, in conscience, he should not have more upon the bond than that which he was damaged [?] and for the future time he had discharged Giles, this was a breach on his part, that Giles did not have leave.

Note [that] the assignee [was] to save the surety harmless from his bond in this case. The [Lord] Keeper said it was no defense [?] whether [they were] ruinous at the time of the assignment or the death of the father or not. It was his fault to have taken an assignment of a ruinous house. But if he had assigned over before the suit, he would not be bound for more than that which fell down or became ruinous in his time.

[Other copies of this report: Lincoln's Inn MS. Hill 125, f. 6v.]

[Order of 5 May 1631: Public Record Office C.33/159, f. 479v.]

100

Nele's Case

(Ch. 1631)

The successor of a bishop is bound by a decree in equity against his predecessor in office.

Lincoln's Inn MS. Maynard 75, f. 46v, pl. 1

Where, upon a former hearing between Master Nele and others, it was referred to precedents whether a decree may be against a bishop and his successors and the bishop dies whether the successor bishop can avoid the decree without a bill of review. And no precedents were found.

Therefore, it was held by the Lord Keeper [LORD COVENTRY] and declared that the successor may not avoid [it].

Yet it seems to me that he can [have] judgment at common law.

[Other copies of this report: Lincoln's Inn MS. Hill 125, f. 7v, pl. 1.]

101

Earl of Suffolk v. Grenville

(Ch. 1631)

A defendant who was served with process but did not answer can give evidence.

A chose in action cannot be assigned at common law. A court of equity will not enforce an assignment that is not supported by consideration.

The terms of an instrument should not be proved by witnesses, but the instrument itself should be produced.

Lincoln's Inn MS. Maynard 75, f. 46v, pl. 2

Between the earl of Suffolk and Sir Richard Grenville and Mary his wife, defendants, before the Lord Keeper [LORD COVENTRY] assisted by justices HUTTON and WHITELOCKE, the case was [as follows].

A suit was pending between Mary, being a widow, and the earl of Suffolk in this court upon certain covenants made between the earl and friends of his wife for assurance of £600 *per annum* to Mary for a jointure in marriage with Sir Charles Howard. And [it was] decreed that assurance should be made accordingly and that the arrearages, being £2400, should be paid. But before the decree, there was a treaty of marriage between Sir Richard Grenville and the said Dame Mary. And he agreed that Mary should have the disposition of all of her estate, personal and real, and of this decree, notwithstanding the marriage. And the marriage was stayed until after the decree. And then by a writing proved by G. Cutford and two others to be sealed and delivered but the trust was [to be] disposed only by G. Cutford, *viz.* in trust for the said Mary and her assigns for her and her children.

Afterwards Sir Richard and Dame Mary married, but disputes arose between them. She and G. Cutford released the decree to the earl, who brought a bill upon this matter to be relieved against the former decree.

First, it was excepted that Cutford's [deposition] not be read because he was served with process [and] named [as] a defendant, but because he did not answer, an inquisition was referred to the six clerks, who certified that he could be examined. And upon this he was examined, and his deposition was read.

Second, the judges and the Lord Keeper [LORD COVENTRY] declared that the whole agreement, though it was by deed obligatory etc., with Mary was *ipso facto* void upon the marriage if one sues here for it in point of pernancy that one sues for it.[1]

And in this case, there was a decree that it did not lie in grant. But the judges and the Lord Keeper [LORD COVENTRY] said [?] that, in such a case, the way was to come into court and pray for an order to such purpose that a friend of the wife have the decree for her benefit assigned to him and then it would be good.

At the end it was referred at this point that Sir Richard Grenville and Dame Mary and G. Cutford should be examined again upon interrogatories, because the Lord Keeper [LORD COVENTRY] said the view of the deed of assignment to Cutford would give [?] great light to him, and it was suggested in the bill that Sir Richard Grenville had through violence broken the chests of the lady and burned the deed, which the lady upon her oath in her answer confessed and Sir Richard Grenville in his answer denied that he had done it.

[Other copies of this report: Lincoln's Inn MS. Hill 125, f. 7v, pl. 2.]

British Library MS. Hargrave 174, f. 18, pl. 2

16 June 7 Car. I.

The defendant, the Lady Grenville, while unmarried, had a decree against the earl of Suffolk, the plaintiff, for £600 *per annum*. Against which decree, the earl prayed to be discharged in respect of a deed of assignment of the benefit of that decree, [which was] made by the Lady Grenville before her marriage unto one Cutford upon a verbal agreement between the defendants before their intermarriage that she should have the power and sole dispos[ition] thereof, which Cutford and the lady had released to the plaintiff. And the plaintiff not having

---

[1] si un icy sues pur ceo in point de pernancy que un suer pur ceo *MS*.

the deed to produce and alleging [that] the defendant Sir Richard had gotten it and cancelled it and [the] defendant denying it, [it was] ordered that the defendants and Cutford be examined on interrogatories for discovery of the deed or a copy thereof. And, accordingly, they were examined.

But the matter being not at all cleared thereby nor [it appearing] what were the contents of the deed more than at the former hearing, the court declared they[1] had maturely considered the points in question and, conferring now together, did concur in one uniform opinion, that there was neither sufficient matter nor proof at the last hearing or now to bar the defendant Sir Richard of the said decree or [to] relieve the plaintiff and that [the] arrears of the £600 *per annum* decreed to the lady, being in its own nature a thing in action and so to be come by merely by the process of the court, cannot in law be assigned over so as the assignment to Cutford, if approved, was void in law and being so ought not to be maintained against the rule of law in a court of equity, no consideration appearing to support the same which should make it better in equity than at law, the said Sir Richard's verbal agreement in consideration of the said marriage being in subversion of the grounds of the law and [the] right of marriage, and that unless they agree and be settled by a legal assurance and [be] good in law, it was not fit for a court of equity to give any such power to a married woman as the lady pretended [to. And] whereas things in action, though not assignable, are sometimes turned over by letter of attorney, [the court all declared that, if it had been so there, yet presently by the marriage, the letter of attorney] ceased,[2] and that all covenants, promises, and agreements made by Sir Richard to his lady before marriage touching her disposal of her estate were extinguished by the marriage and that, if Cutford had had an effectual letter of attorney and the same had continuance, he could not in his own [name] release, as the release to the plaintiff was. And therefore, [that] being void, he remained a party interested and ought not by his own oath, being but a single witness, none but he swearing to the contents of the said deed, to be admitted a witness for that purpose, there being also other exceptions against him in respect of former and continued differences between Sir Richard and him. And the court held it very dangerous to admit the contents and sufferances of deeds to be proved by the testimony of one witness, the construction of deeds being the duty[3] of the court, and the fact touching [the] execution pertained only to the proof of witness[es]. And so the bill was dismissed, and Sir Richard had liberty to prosecute the decree against the earl of Suffolk.

[Other copies of this report: British Library MS. Hargrave 99, f. 56, pl. 1, 2 Freeman 146, 22 E.R. 1119, 3 Chancery Reports 89, 21 E.R. 738.]

---

[1] The Lord Keeper Coventry, Justice Hutton, and Justice Whitelocke.
[2] determined *MS*.
[3] office *MS*.

Nelson 15, 21 E.R. 778

26 July, 7 Car. I [1631]. Lord Keeper [LORD COVENTRY], Justice HUTTON, Justice WHITELOCKE.

The defendant the Lady Greenvill, whilst unmarried, had a decree against the earl of Suffolk for £600 *per annum*, against which decree the earl prayed to be relieved in regard there was a verbal agreement between Sir Richard Greenvill and the said Lady before marriage that she should have the sole disposal of the said £600 *per annum*, that, accordingly, before the said marriage, she by deed assigned the benefit of that decree to one Cutford, and that, afterwards, she and Cutford released the same to the said earl. But not having the said deeds to produce and alleging that Sir Richard Greenvill had got and cancelled the same, which he denied, it was ordered that he and Cutford should be examined upon interrogatories to discover the said deeds or copies thereof. And, accordingly, they were examined.

But the matter being not cleared by such examination or what were the contents of such deeds, the court was all of opinion that there was no sufficient proof to bar Sir Richard Greenvill from the benefit of the said decree, for that the arrears of the said £600 *per annum*, being in its own nature a thing of action and so to be merely recovered by the process of this court, cannot in law be assigned over to another so that, if the assignment to Cutford had been proved (as it was not), it would have been a void assignment in law and ought not to be supported in a court of equity, especially where no consideration appears to make it better in equity than it is at law. They were all of opinion that the verbal agreement of Sir Richard Greenvill, in consideration of the said marriage, was to subvert both the grounds of law and the right which was vested in him by the intermarriage, and, therefore, if such agreement is not settled by some legal assurance to make it binding in law, it is not fit to be maintained in a court of equity in order to give a married woman such a power as is now pretended.

It is true things in action are sometimes turned over by letter of attorney, but, if it had been so in this case, yet, presently, by the intermarriage, the letter of attorney had been revoked and determined and all covenants, promises, and agreements made by the husband to his wife before marriage relating to the disposal of his estate would be extinguished by the marriage, and, therefore, if Cutford had an effectual letter of attorney executed to him and the same could be produced, yet he could not in his own name seal such a release to the plaintiff, as he had done. The contents whereof appearing only on his single testimony, he ought not to be admitted as a witness, for he was a party interested and might justly be suspected of partiality because of former and continued differences between him and Sir Richard Greenvill.

And, therefore, the court held it dangerous to admit the sufficiency of a deed to be proved by the single oath of such a witness, especially since the construction of deeds was the proper office of the Court of Chancery, but the fact relating to the executing such deeds was proved by witnesses. So, the bill was dismissed, and Sir Richard Greenvill had liberty to prosecute the said decree against the plaintiff.

[Orders of 3 May and 16 June 1631: Public Record Office C.33/159, ff. 400v, 520, 653v.]

102

Countess of Suffolk v. Earl of Nottingham

(Ch. 1631)

A conveyance by a fine that was invalid at common law will be enforced in equity on behalf of one who gave consideration for it but not on behalf of a donee.

Lincoln's Inn MS. Maynard 75, f. 47

The countess of Suffolk sued the earl of Nottingham, and it was to have a jointure established to her and a lease for sixty years made to some of her friends confirmed and the inheritance settled upon her daughter by William, her former husband, the older brother of the defendant.

The case upon the opening was [that] Charles earl of Nottingham upon the marriage of the plaintiff with William, his oldest son, being seised in tail to him and the heirs male of his body of the manor of Blachinglea etc., covenanted to assure it to the use of William, his oldest son, for life, remainder to the plaintiff for life, remainder to the heirs male of William. And this was done in 39 Eliz. [1596–97]. But no fine nor recovery nor other conveyance [was] made in execution of it, but William entered notwithstanding and enjoyed it and leased it out. Charles died in 9 Jac. [1611–12]. William levied a fine to the use of the plaintiff for life and to the use of the lessee in trust for sixty years and limited the inheritance to the daughter of the plaintiff by himself. And because this fine was endeavored to be destroyed by a legal technicality,[1] *viz.* because no execution of the covenants of 39 Eliz. [1596–97] was had, William, by his entry, was a tenant by will and his lessee a disseisor, and thus the fine passed nothing but enured to the benefit of the disseisor:

First, it was resolved and decreed that no relief should be [given] to the daughter nor to the lessee for sixty years but it should be left to the [common] law because they were only voluntary conveyances nor was it upon preceding covenants, but they were contrary to them, it was by them [that] the male heir should be preferred not the female;

---

[1] nicety in ley *MS.*

Second, if there had not been a fine in the case, the Lord Keeper [LORD COVENTRY] said that it should be a shrewd[1] case to have relieved the plaintiff, the countess, because then the defendant [is] aided by the Statute *de Donis*;[2]

Third, but when a fine is levied which, as to this, is according to the intent of the first covenants, now it will not be subverted by any such defect in law, and on account of that the possession is established with the plaintiff for her life;

Fourth, but liberty was given to the defendant to bring some [people] to try the title for the inheritance now, for otherwise the witnesses may [?] be dead in the lifetime of the plaintiff perchance, and then it will be too late.

[Other copies of this report: Lincoln's Inn MS. Hill 125, f. 8v.]

103

Turberville v. Swame

(Ch. 1631)

Where consideration has been paid, a grantor must confirm the title of his grantee.

The king will confirm a grant as a matter of grace where equity requires it.

The defendant in this case accepted this grant from the crown with knowledge of the plaintiff's equitable rights and was thus bound thereby.

Lincoln's Inn MS. Maynard 75, f. 47v

The Lord Keeper [LORD COVENTRY], having the two chief justices [as] assistants with him, put the case, which by order was drafted on paper and delivered to the judges, and [it was] resolved by the advice of all of the judges of England. And he put it as follows.

Richard Tate was seised of the Priory of Horton in Kent in fee, and he sold it to William Mantell and Jane, his wife, and to the heirs of William Mantell. William Mantell in 1 & 2 Mar. [1554] was attainted of high treason, by which Jane became tenant for life, reversion in the Crown.

In 13 Eliz. [1570–71], Queen Elizabeth granted the said priory to one Matthew Mantell in tail.

And afterwards, in consideration of the manor of Knoll and other lands granted to her by the earl of Leicester and John Morley, the queen granted to them the said priory.

Upon this grant, there arose a question in law whether the patents were good because the former estate was not recited, but he said that he and the judges would not give a resolution of that point of [common] law but only of the equity because he and they admitted the patent to the earl [to be] void.

---

[1] shrode *MS*.
[2] Stat. 13 Edw. I, c. 1 (*SR*, I, 71).

On 11 July 24 Eliz. [1582], the earl and Morley, reciting the former letters patent, granted and surrendered them to the queen and the said priory to be held by the queen and her successors etc.

On 9 August 24 Eliz. [1582], the queen, in consideration of the said grant and surrender of the priory and of other lands of the value of £24 *per annum*, granted to the earl of Leicester and John Morley certain lands in Islington, being the lands in question.

This patent being void, yet the possession of the lands in question [. . .][1] now for the space of fifty years and came to the plaintiffs.

On 7 April 18 Jac. [1620], the plaintiffs being in possession, King James, in consideration of £500 paid to him, granted the lands in question to Sir Henry Spiller and others in trust for Pointer, rendering 12d. *per annum*, provided that if they were *in onere*[2] before any auditor etc. on January 15th etc., that then the grant would be void.

And in this part of the case, said the Lord Keeper [LORD COVENTRY], the cases drawn by both parties vary it. The plaintiff said that no moneys were paid; the defendants say the contrary. But he said in his private knowledge, he knew well that there was a tally struck for £500, but the truth of the case was that Pointer alleged service done to the crown in apprehending one of the traitors of the Powder Treason by which £500 was promised to him and in lieu of this, it was made to him. But he admitted that the £500 was paid.

The question was whether the plaintiffs should be relieved here against the patentees or not. And it was resolved and decreed that they should be relieved.

The case in brief was [that] the earl of Leicester granted the manor of Knoll to the queen. She, in consideration of this grant to the queen, granted Horton Priory to the earl in fee, which grant was defective for default of a recital; then the earl surrendered this priory to the queen, and in consideration of the said surrender, the queen granted lands in Islington to the earl in fee. And afterwards, the possession being with the assignees of the earl, King James granted the lands in question to Pointer in fee in consideration of £500, which was paid accordingly. And the assignees of the earl sue by English bill for relief against Pointer.

And [it was] decreed that they should be relieved because originally the earl was owner of Knoll and the queen and her patentees enjoyed it under the grant of the earl. And the queen, in recompense for this grant, granted Horton Priory to him. And if it should be taken away for a defect in the patent of the king, the subject would have no recompense for Knoll. And if the Crown enjoyed the lands granted or the patentees of the crown, reason goes that the subject also should enjoy that which the queen granted to him. And then when Horton was given back for the lands in Islington, they came in lieu of the other, *viz.* of Horton.

---

[1] msques al *MS*.
[2] In arrears.

And though there is no compulsory equity in any court of equity to force the king to confirm his grant, yet there is a remedy by way of appeal to the person of the king by way of petition, and the king, being informed of the truth, will have the patent amended in all conscience, because it is the intention[1] of the king that good conscience and right should be observed between him and his subjects as between subject and subject.

Thus, when the kings grant out the lands, the same equity remains against the patentee unless that there be anything in the patent to take away that equity. And thus [there] being now a case between subject and subject, this court now has jurisdiction. And here of necessity, the last patentees have knowledge of this matter of equity, because the possession was with it, and otherwise the patentees would not have taken their patent if the former had not been defective. And thus the consideration of the £500 paid will not alter the case in equity where the party is with knowledge.

And for these reasons, he declared that the judges have resolved, and he was of the same opinion, that the plaintiffs should be relieved. And the two chief justices assisting assented that this was their resolution. And HYDE said that it was the opinion of the greater part of his house in Fleet Street.[2] And RICHARDSON said that all of his house[3] were of this opinion. And he said that it was a patent of concealment (note the proviso *supra*), and it was to avoid the possession of the plaintiffs.

[Other copies of this report: Lincoln's Inn MS. Hill 125, f. 9v.]

104

Note

(Ch. 1631)

A court of equity will order a creditor who has been paid off by a surety to assign the debt to the surety so that the surety will be subrogated against principal debtor.

Lincoln's Inn MS. Maynard 75, f. 48v, pl. 1

The Lord Keeper [LORD COVENTRY] declared that it is the constant practice and rule that if a surety has paid the creditor, he will force him to assign the bond etc. to him for his relief against the principal but not if he has not satisfied him, thus he will not have relief against the creditor.

[Other copies of this report: Lincoln's Inn MS. Hill 125, f. 11v, pl. 1.]

---

[1] ment *MS*.
[2] Serjeants' Inn, Fleet Street.
[3] Serjeants' Inn, Chancery Lane.

105

Anonymous

(Ch. 1631)

A defendant cannot file a second demurrer to the same bill.

Lincoln's Inn MS. Maynard 75, f. 48v, pl. 2

The defendant, after a demurrer was overruled, demurred again to the same bill.

And for this reason without considering the cause of the demurrer, the Lord Keeper [LORD COVENTRY] overruled it, and gave 40s. costs, upon the motion of Mr. *Calthrop*.

[Other copies of this report: Lincoln's Inn MS. Hill 125, f. 11v, pl. 2.]

106

Anonymous

(Ch. 1631)

A party who had not seen the depositions that had been already taken was allowed to take depositions after publication.

Lincoln's Inn MS. Maynard 75, f. 48v, pl. 3

After publication, upon an affidavit that the defendant had not seen the depositions nor anyone for him, he obtained an order to examine two witnesses, who were examined accordingly, but the order was not ever entered. And now upon a similar affidavit, the Lord Keeper [LORD COVENTRY] ordered that if there were notes for the order in the book of the registers, the depositions may be used at the hearing.

[Other copies of this report: Lincoln's Inn MS. Hill 125, f. 12, pl. 1.]

107

Anonymous

(Ch. 1631)

A court of equity will not decree the forfeiture of an estate.

Lincoln's Inn MS. Maynard 75, f. 49, pl. 1

Upon a motion of *Jones* upon a report of Justice Jones, a decree [was] made that one will not be compelled to forfeit his estate, and this was reported upon a view of precedents.

[Other copies of this report: Lincoln's Inn MS. Hill 125, f. 12, pl. 2.]

108

Anonymous

(Ch. 1631)

The Court of Chancery will enjoin suits at common law for matters formerly adjudicated in the Chancery Court of the County Palatine of Durham.

Lincoln's Inn MS. Maynard 75, f. 49, pl. 2

At the motion of *Philips*, it [was] moved that there was a decree made in Durham in the Chancery there by Justice Hutton, chancellor of the bishop, and that an action was brought at common law that crossed this decree. And he prayed for an injunction from this court for a stay of the suit.

And the Lord Keeper [LORD COVENTRY] granted the injunction, but it was to stay only those suits that were contrary to this decree.

[Other copies of this report: Lincoln's Inn MS. Hill 125, f. 12, pl. 3.]

109

Anonymous

(Ch. 1631)

In this case, a pendente lite sequestration of the profits of a church was refused.

Lincoln's Inn MS. Maynard 75, ff. 49, 49v

On the same day [6 June 1631], in two cases, the Lord Keeper [LORD COVENTRY] denied a sequestration of the profits of a church in litigation between two persons after a clerk was inducted although the matter of the bill was that this induction was void by the acceptance of the first [?] benefice and even though it was paid on behalf of the clerk of the king.

Sequestration of the profits of a parsonage [was] moved for the clerk of the king [?] because no damages may be recovered. And at an earlier day, it was denied, and now it [was] proved again and denied again because the clerk was not inducted. But in a case of Newton, where the clerk of the king was inducted and also the clerk of the common person and the clerk of the common person refused to appear to a *quare impedit* brought by the king, there was a precedent read from 16 Jac. [1618–19] where, in such a case, a sequestration was granted. Note [that] there was a bill pending here in the court.

[Other copies of this report: Lincoln's Inn MS. Hill 125, f. 12v, pl. 1.]

110

Anonymous v. Lord Walden

(Ch. 1631)

An infant defendant should appear by a guardian ad litem and not simply ignore writs of process issued against him.

Lincoln's Inn MS. Maynard 75, f. 49, pl. 4

A bill was preferred against Lord Walden, who it happened was an infant. And he stood out all process of contempt, and a serjeant at arms was ordered against him. Now it was moved that he was an infant of fourteen years and that on account of it, [the suit] should be stayed.

The Lord Keeper [LORD COVENTRY] [said that] he should appear by guardian [*ad litem*] and pray his [non]age, and if there is cause, he shall have it. But he should first appear. The court should not take notice of the infancy until he appears. And the Lord Keeper [LORD COVENTRY] said that he had made a decree against an infant under fourteen years in this court.

[Other copies of this report: Lincoln's Inn MS. Hill 125, f. 12v, pl. 2.]

111

Anonymous

(Ch. 1631)

A bond given for the expenses of finding a vicar is enforceable unless the contract was simoniacal. A simoniacal bond is not enforceable.

Lincoln's Inn MS. Maynard 75, f. 49, pl. 5

On the 8th of June, a bill was exhibited for relief against a bond for £30. The defendant in his answer showed that it was for defraying expenses about the procurement of a vicarage for the plaintiff and that he had expended £30, as he believed.

Bacon moved for an injunction because it is a quasi penal bond until accounting.

And [at the] hearing of the cause, the Lord Keeper [LORD COVENTRY] [said], if there was no intent of simony, it is reason[able] that he should be paid for his charges; if it is simony, I will not ever give relief for a bond given [for a] simoniacal contract for money against the bond *in odium simoniacae*.

[Other copies of this report: Lincoln's Inn MS. Hill 125, f. 12v, pl. 3.]

112

Anonymous

(Ch. 1631)

Where the parties to a bill in equity live in Chester, they should sue in the Court of Exchequer of the County Palatine of Chester and not in the High Court of Chancery.

Lincoln's Inn MS. Maynard 75, f. 49, pl. 6

On the same day [8 June 1631], a bill was exhibited in Chester in the Exchequer there, and, for the same cause, a new bill here. And the defendant demurred, claiming a privilege, because he dwells in Chester. And afterwards the plaintiff proceeded in the exchequer there in Chester, and he had a decree for himself. And the defendants sued the plaintiff at common law. And special matter was reported by Sir John Mitchell [Master in Chancery], and on the part of the defendant, it was ordered that the proceeding in the exchequer there waived the bill here, it being for the same cause. And though it was said on the part of the plaintiff that the proceeding there was after the demurrer and that the decree in Chester could not aid against a suit at common law, still the Lord Keeper [LORD COVENTRY] declared that he would dismiss the bill in that he declared that where parties dwell in Chester it is a cause to demur to the bill here.

But if there is [?] a suit at common law prosecuted by the defendant here, then it is a transitory action because the party plaintiff in this court here cannot have aid in Chester against this suit that is at common law because there the privilege will not take place. But being informed that here there were more defendants in this court than in Chester, therefore the Lord Keeper [LORD COVENTRY], at the end [?], upon this cause only, overruled the demurrer unless better cause be shown etc.

Query the point *supra* when the plea comes after the report because of this the master was not to consider.

[Other copies of this report: Lincoln's Inn MS. Hill 125, f. 13.]

113

Anonymous

(Ch. 1631)

A court of equity will not refer a matter to a Master to determine a question of law.

Lincoln's Inn MS. Maynard 75, f. 49v, pl. 1

On the same day [8 June 1631], it was moved to refer to the consideration of a master whether any matter [was] confessed in the answer [to] ground an injunction. And the Lord Keeper [LORD COVENTRY] declared that he would not make such a general reference. He said [that] now the masters grant all injunctions. And he said so in another cause, but if the matter be open, he will refer the truth of it to a master, [it] being contained and expressed in the order of reference.

[Other copies of this report: Lincoln's Inn MS. Hill 125, f. 13v, pl. 1.]

114

Anonymous

(Ch. c. 1631)

An interlocutory injunction will be granted to restore possession of the res in litigation to the party who had it at the beginning of the dispute.

Lincoln's Inn MS. Maynard 75, f. 49v, pl. 3

On the same day [8 June 1631], one moved for an injunction to settle possession with the defendant upon a bill here, as it was four years before [?] the bill and now is. And it was denied at first [on the] part of the defendant but otherwise for the plaintiff.

But, at the end, the Lord Keeper [LORD COVENTRY] granted the injunction.

[Other copies of this report: Lincoln's Inn MS. Hill 125, f. 14, pl. 1.]

115

Anonymous

(Ch. c. 1631)

Where executors are directed to pay legacies at a convenient time, this means at a reasonable time, not at their unfettered discretion.

Lincoln's Inn MS. Maynard 75, f. 50, pl. 1

On the same day [8 June 1631], it was moved [that] Sir Richard Smith appointed divers executors and bequeathed divers legacies in certain and others out of the residue of his estate after legacies and debts. And as to the manner of the distribution, he left this to the discretion of the executors and [ordered] that the legacies should be paid in such convenient time as the executors should appoint.

And the Lord Keeper [LORD COVENTRY] said that the executors cannot pay at what[ever] time they please, but they are bound to pay in a convenient time. And therefore he ordered that, upon a bond[1] to save them harmless, they should pay etc. because three years [had] passed etc.

[Other copies of this report: Lincoln's Inn MS. Hill 125, f. 14, pl. 2.]

---

[1] caution *MS*.

116

Anonymous

(Ch. c. 1631)

The question in this case was whether the beneficiary of a trust can sue in equity against a third party for possession of goods without making the trustee a party.

Lincoln's Inn MS. Maynard 75, f. 50, pl. 2

On the same day [8 June 1631], Mr. *Clarke* moved a case, to which there was a demurrer, *viz.* the party to whose hands the goods had come was sued by the *cestui que use* without making the trustee who had the interest in [common] law a party to the bill, and the suit was to have the goods upon etc. And it was admitted a good cause for demurrer because the party cannot have any discharge unless the party that has the interest in law be made a party to the bill. However, [the case] was adjourned to hear counsel on both sides.

[Other copies of this report: Lincoln's Inn MS. Hill 125, f. 14v, pl. 1.]

117

Anonymous

(Ch. c. 1631)

The question in this case was whether a party can examine witnesses after the publication of the depositions where the commissioner was ill and the party had not seen the depositions.

Lincoln's Inn MS. Maynard 75, f. 50, pl. 3

On the same day [8 June 1631], in a case, after publication and the cause being set down for hearing, it was moved that upon affidavit that the defendant had not examined any witnesses because the commissioner was ill and also he had not seen the depositions nor [had] anyone for him. And because the cause had not come to hearing nor publication by the ordinary course but by special order and a great estate depended upon it, *viz.* £700 *per annum*, therefore he prayed that he could examine.

The Lord Keeper [LORD COVENTRY] denied [it], but importuned why out of the ordinary course [. . .] to name the witness. And then it appeared that he wished to cross-examine the witnesses of the other party. The Lord Keeper [LORD COVENTRY] said that he would not ever grant a cross-examination, and causes were to be ruled by justice not by the [. . .] of them. However, at the end he ordered that the defendant bring him the names of the witnesses, but he did not give an order one way or the other whether he would give liberty of examination etc.

[Other copies of this report: Lincoln's Inn MS. Hill 125, f. 14v, pl. 2.]

118

Anonymous

(Ch. 1631)

The question in this case was whether a defendant-appellant can post a bond to perform the decree and receive back the money that was deposited in court.

Lincoln's Inn MS. Maynard 75, f. 50, pl. 4

At the same day [8 June 1631] at the seal, [*blank*] that a party will not have an appeal until he has deposited the money with the commissioners, and now it was moved that the money was deposited with the commissioners and he offered security to perform etc. if it pass and find [?], and he prayed that he could have the money back.

The Lord Keeper [LORD COVENTRY] [said that] as the statute had limited a course though [. . .] I alter it.

[Other copies of this report: Lincoln's Inn MS. Hill 125, f. 15, pl. 1.]

119

Anonymous

(Ch. c. 1631)

Depositions from a former suit can be used in a second suit against a party to the first suit by a person who was not a party to the first suit.

Lincoln's Inn MS. Maynard 75, f. 50v, pl. 1

It was ordered by the Lord Keeper [LORD COVENTRY] that where a bill was preferred against J.S. and after depositions were examined in this cause, another, a stranger [to the suit], preferred a bill against him, and this stranger moved that the depositions in the other cause should be used in his cause, and a day was given to show cause why they should not; it was so ordered. And now the Six Clerks asked [what was] the course, and the opinion of the Lord Keeper [LORD COVENTRY] was that the depositions could not be used against the stranger if he did not require [them]. But when he required [them, there is] no inconvenience to use them against the party.

[Other copies of this report: Lincoln's Inn MS. Hill 125, f. 15, pl. 2.]

120

Champernon v. Champernon

(Ch. c. 1631)

In this case a new trust was declared on behalf of the beneficiary of another trust that had been frustrated by the neglect of the trustee.

Lincoln's Inn MS. Maynard 75, f. 50v, pl. 2

Dame Elizabeth Champernon had part of the rectory of Modbury and the manors of Modbury Upton and Penquit in the nature of a jointure. And the case was Sir Richard Champernon, her husband, took a lease from the College of Eton for the lives of Dame Elizabeth his wife, Henry Champernon the defendant, and John Champernon. And he conveyed it to William Bastard and others in trust for the dame during her life and afterwards for Sir Richard. And then upon the marriage of Henry Champernon, the feoffees and Sir Richard and the lady assigned all of their interest upon the condition of reassigning the manors and part of the rectory to Roger Warre etc. in trust for the lady; the residue was in trust for Henry Champernon and his wife. And the lady was to pay to Henry Champernon the third part of the rent and he the entire rent to the College. Henry Champernon for lack [?] of money, without any combination, which was charged but not proved, allowed the rent to be in arrears, by which the original lease was forfeited, and an entry was made by the College. And Henry Champernon [was] forced by the College to take a new lease or to lose all, by which he took a new lease for twenty-one years.

The Lord Keeper [LORD COVENTRY] decreed that the lady should enjoy [it] for all of the term if she live [so long and] that it should be renewed at the end of the term at the charge of Henry Champernon. But afterwards to accommodate the renewing from time to time, it was referred to Sir Robert Rich [Master in Chancery].

[Other copies of this report: Lincoln's Inn MS. Hill 125, f. 15v.]

121

Arnold v. Barrington

(Ch. 1631)

A contract to make a marriage settlement is specifically enforceable in a court of equity.

Dickens 5, 21 E.R. 167

24 November 1631.
John Arnold, the plaintiff's brother, being seised of copyhold lands and having issue, two daughters, Elizabeth and Catherine, and intending to make a pro-

vision for Elizabeth, his eldest daughter, surrendered part of the lands to the use of the said Elizabeth and another part thereof to Thomas Barrington for the payment of his debts. And, the residue, being of the value of £500, he left unsurrendered to descend to Catherine, his youngest daughter, as heir by the custom of the manor.

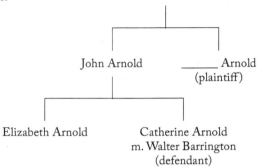

After the surrender, John Arnold made his will whereby he confirmed the surrender and directed the plaintiff to have the care of the marriage of his daughter, and appointed him executor.

Afterwards, a clandestine marriage was effected between the defendant Walter Barrington and the said Catherine. And, upon the marriage, the defendant Walter Barrington promised to make a jointure of lands of £60 a year, and entered into a bond to the defendant Catherine in the penalty of £1000 for the performance of the agreement.

Sometime after, the said Walter Barrington and Catherine cancelled the bond.

The plaintiff filed his bill to have the benefit of the bond, stating that no provision was made for Catherine, and, in case of the death of Walter Barrington, she would be left destitute.

Upon reading the answer, it appeared the marriage was had, and the promise made, and the bond given, and afterwards cancelled.

It was decreed that the defendant Walter Barrington should by Wednesday then next convey lands in fee simple worth £60 a year free from encumbrances unto the trustees for the said Catherine in lieu of jointure for her life.

[Reg. Lib. [1631–32], f. 864.]

122

Snelling v. Flatman

(Ch. 1631)

An issue out of Chancery can be directed to justices of the peace to certify a person's good behavior.

Dickens 6, 21 E.R. 168

A [writ of] *supplicavit* [issued] against the defendant. He took exceptions to the articles as not being sufficient on which to ground a *supplicavit*, they being too general. And he produced a certificate of his good behavior. The plaintiff averred the contrary.

The court ordered the two next justices of the peace in the neighborhood to call the said parties before them and to examine into the truth of the articles and the certificate and that the question of the *supplicavit* should be stayed in the meantime.

[Reg. Lib. [1631–32], f. 431.]

123

Spyer v. Spyer

(Ch. 1631–1632)

A court of equity can appoint commissioners to settle boundaries of lands.

Nelson 14, 21 E.R. 777

7 Car. I [1631–32]. Lord Coventry.

The bill was to make a partition and settle boundaries between lands which were freehold and other lands held in borough English. The defendant appearing, it was ordered that a commission should be directed to certain persons as well to take the defendant's answer as also to set forth the meets and bounds and to return terrars and boundaries, which was done accordingly and by consent of the parties.

The court decreed the boundaries and that the same should be ratified and confirmed to all intents and purposes as if the same had been judicially pronounced upon a full hearing in court.

124

Huddlestone v. Huddlestone

(Ch. 1631–1632)

A court of equity can appoint commissioners to settle lands to be held in dower.

1 Chancery Reports 38, 21 E.R. 500

The said Elizabeth [Huddlestone], having exhibited her bill and therein setting forth that she had obtained several recoveries at law for her dower in the premises in question, but the defendants detain the possession from her so that the plaintiff Elizabeth has been kept without her means since the death of her husband, the defendant insisted that the thirds allotted to the plaintiff out of the lands in Yorkshire was unequal, and Commissioners had allotted her the third part of the said lands for her dower, and, therefore, she ought to be concluded thereby.

This court ordered a commission.

[Reg. Lib. 7 Car. I, f. 370.]

[Related cases: Huddleston v. Lamplugh (Ch. 1629–32), see above, Case No. 75.]

125

Levington v. Wotton

(Ch. 1631–1632)

In this case, the Court of Chancery had priority of suit, and the defendants were ordered to answer the plaintiff's bill of complaint.

1 Chancery Reports 52, 21 E.R. 505

That an injunction might be granted by this court, it was insisted by the plaintiff that this court has priority of suit, Sir James Levington having exhibited four several bills in this court, one for the execution of a trust, two against Carrant and others to discover secret estates which had been made and for producing letters patents and writings touching the lands in question, and the fourth against the defendant Wotton upon a private agreement with him and others, for a full eighth part of the whole land when first the said Sir John Levington entertained and presented the suit to his late Majesty.

And the said injunction being not dissolved, two informations have been this term exhibited in the Duchy Chamber on a claim of divers acres of marsh ground and the information by Dacombe against the plaintiff and others on pretense of a trust devolved upon him and Ma. Carrant, wherein he is a competitor for the same lands with the now plaintiff, grounded upon the same patent. And to one of these informations, notwithstanding a plea and demurrer thereto, the relators have obtained an injunction out of the duchy for dividing and plowing the said lands, and staying of suits, as well at common law as in all other courts, and possession to remain with the relators. And the lands, for which the plaintiff in this court prays relief, are lands gained from the sea, and belong as well to the Crown as the duchy, and held of His Majesty's manors of East Greensteed and Enfield in Middlesex, and are granted in fee farm.

His Lordship [LORD COVENTRY], upon reading the order made in the Duchy Court, ordered that, if the defendant do not show better matter, this court will maintain and continue the injunction granted in this court, and, at the time of showing cause, all the letters patents and the certificate heretofore made by His Lordship and other lords referees unto His Majesty touching this matter and all proceedings both in this court and the duchy are to be ready.

This court upon reading the order of the Duchy Chamber, being, as aforesaid, to enjoin this and other courts to stay proceedings touching the marsh grounds, nothing then was said by the court of the defendants' competitors and pretenders to the marsh grounds to oppose the jurisdiction of this court, but that the same of right ought to be maintained notwithstanding the injunction of the Duchy Court.

His Lordship [LORD COVENTRY] does not conceive it any doubtful question, whether in case any lands (at first being Duchy, and after granted from the Crown by the king's letters patents in fee simple or fee farm under the great seal and duchy seal) are not upon a trust and other equitable causes to be debated and held plea of in this court. And, upon a complaint made to His Majesty on the plaintiff's behalf, 5 June, 7 Car. [1631], touching the premises, His Majesty was graciously pleased to refer the consideration of this cause to the Lord Keeper, Chancellor of the Duchy, and Chancellor of the Exchequer, who were to take such course for his relief as they should think fit in justice and equity, which they did, and certified their proceedings to His Majesty, which certificate His Majesty approved of.

And His Lordship [LORD COVENTRY] does still maintain and continue the injunction granted by this court, and granted a new injunction against all that are since made defendants. And, whereas the defendants have pleaded the jurisdiction of the Duchy Court and will not answer in this court, His Lordship overruled them all as to the point of the jurisdiction of the Duchy.

[Reg. Lib. 7 Car. I, ff. 360, 388.]

126

General Rule of Court

(Ch. 1631–1632)

All writs of process to be made upon any contempt must be made out in the proper county where the party against whom the same process issues shall be dwelling, unless he shall be then in or about London, in which case, it may be directed into the county where he shall then be, so that it may be served upon him there.

1 Chancery Reports 55, 21 E.R. 506

Ordo Curiae.

The Lord Keeper [LORD COVENTRY] finding much inconvenience and prejudice to fall upon divers of His Majesty's subjects, who are suitors in this court, by the undue proceedings of such as sue out the process of the court upon contempts, the same oftentimes running out to a commission of rebellion or to a serjeant-at-arms before the party against whom the process is made out has had notice of the precedent process issued forth against him, which is occasioned by reason that the process is oftentimes made into a county where the party is not resident and, when it is made into the right county, by reason of an unusual neglect and want of care of the prosecutor to get the same executed, the Sheriff returns a *non est inventus* or a *proclamari feci* and sometimes the return is made by others in the Sheriff's name in an ordinary course, His Lordship, therefore, to remedy such inconvenience and abuse hereafter and to prevent the vexation of the subjects in this kind, does think fit and order that all process hereafter to be made upon any contempt be made out in the proper county where the party, against whom the same process issues, shall be resident or dwelling, unless he shall be then in or about London, in which case, it may be directed into the county where he shall then be, that it may be served upon him there. And every suitor who prosecutes process of contempt against any of His Majesty's subjects shall do his best endeavour to procure the said process to be duly executed and the supposed contemners to be apprehended thereby. And, if any be hereafter arrested upon a proclamation or commission of rebellion or by the serjeant-at-arms and shall make it appear unto this court that the prosecutor has not done his best endeavor to have had the first and precedent process duly executed, then that party so offending shall pay unto the other very good costs.

127

Petty v. Styward

(Ch. 1631–1632)

There is no right of survivorship among co-obligees of a debt.

1 Chancery Reports 57, 21 E.R. 506

The defendant Nicholas Styward and one Simeon Styward, whose executor the plaintiff is, lent £2500 to Sir Thomas Glenham, £1450 of the said money being the proper money of the said Simeon, and the £550 residue was the defendant's money. And, for security, the said Sir Thomas Glenham mortgaged lands to the said Simeon afterwards and the defendant Styward and their heirs, redeemable at a day prefixed upon payment of £2630. The said Simeon, before the day of redemption, made his will, and disposed of the said £550, and therein recited that the £1450 was delivered by him to the said defendant, his father, which appeared by a note under both their hands, and that, if the said lands should be redeemed by payment of the said £2500 with interest, then the said £1450 with its interest should be delivered into the plaintiff's hands for the uses in the said will. The very day of redemption, the said lands were redeemed, and the whole money and interest paid to the defendant, which the said defendant claims by survivorship.

This court is clear of opinion that, by equity in a case of this nature, there ought to be no survivorship, in respect the same was but a mortgage and the money was repaid at the day. And the note under both the said parties' hands and the will of the said Simeon shows plainly a trust each in the other and an intention that, if the money was repaid, either of them should have his money again with interest. And he decreed the defendant to pay to the plaintiff the £1450 and interest so by him received.

1 Equity Cases Abr. 290, 21 E.R. 1052

If two persons advance a sum of money by way of mortgage and take the mortgage to themselves jointly and one of them dies, when the money comes to be paid, the survivor shall not have the whole, but the representative of him who is dead shall have a proportion.

[Reg. Lib. 7 Car. I, f. 93.]

128

East Grinstead Paupers v. Howard

(Ch. 1632–1635)

The Court of Chancery can correct defective decrees made by charity commissioners.

Herne & Duke 72

[It was] resolved by the Lord Keeper [LORD COVENTRY] upon [an] appeal to alter or confirm a decree made by commissioners upon the Statute of Charitable Uses[1] [that] the decree is not perpetuated[2] and not be to altered but by act of Parliament and is to remain in the Petty Bag, and it is in his power to make a decree good where it is defective.

Tothill 29, 21 E.R. 114

My Lord [COVENTRY] declared that, when he had altered or confirmed the decree made upon the Statute 43 Eliz., the decree is to be perpetual and then to remain in the Petty Bag. And it is in his power to make [a] decree good, which is defective [as to] how far a purchaser shall be bound.

129

Floyer v. Strackley

(Ch. 1632)

In this case, the court of equity, after several actions at common law, awarded the plaintiff quiet possession of certain land.

British Library MS. Hargrave 99, f. 203, pl. 349

There having been in this case several verdicts and nonsuits in [actions of] ejectment on either side, the court, after a verdict at law and a writ of error brought, awarded a new trial and quieted the possession in the meantime and stayed the proceedings on the writ of error and, after the trial, decreed the land to the then plaintiff in Chancery.

Nelson 13, 21 E.R. 777

7 Car. I [1631–32]. LORD COVENTRY assisted by all the judges.

The plaintiff exhibited his bill to be quieted in the possession of certain lands, which he had purchased of the daughter of one Pyke. He being now, about twenty years after his said purchase, disturbed by one Stephen Pyke, who pre-

---

[1] Stat. 43 Eliz. I, c. 4, s. 10 (*SR*, IV, 970).

[2] *Sic* in all printed editions.

tended a title as heir at law to Pyke, and born of the same father and mother with the daughter, which was proved by several witnesses, and, thereupon, he had recovered some verdicts at law, but the place where he was pretended to be born was a mean house and but seven miles distant from the dwelling house of his mother.

And, forasmuch as those verdicts were grounded on depositions formerly taken in this court, where the record of the bill and answer could not be found and the witnesses which were produced at the trial were of indifferent credit and because, on the death of the father, an office was found, whereby the daughter was returned heir and no claim was made by the son for several years after and for that several persons, as the Lord Chief Justice Popham and others, claimed under the title of the daughter and, at the last trial of her title, the jury were substantial and credible persons, and declared that, for twenty years and upwards, the daughter was reputed the right heir, therefore, the possession was decreed to the plaintiff.

[Order of 21 February 1632: Public Record Office C.33/161, f. 387v. Note also British Library MS. Hargrave 174, f. 16v.]

130

Maynard v. Lord Middleton

(Ch. 1632–1633)

In this case, the judge in the Court of Chancery, acting as an arbitrator, entered his award in the order book of the court.

Nelson 18, 21 E.R. 778

8 Car. I [1632–33]. LORD COVENTRY.

There being several differences arising between the plaintiff and defendant and they having petitioned the king therein, His Majesty recommended to the Lord Keeper to compose the same, who, having heard what was alleged on both sides, made a writing in the nature of an award, and decreed the same without a bill or answer. And, in the decreeing part, it was mentioned that, upon reference from His Majesty and upon the submission of the parties, it was ordered and decreed that all the said parties, their heirs, executors, and administrators should justly observe and perform all and singular the articles, clauses, and things therein mentioned according to the true intent and meaning of the said order and decree. And, in some places before the decreeing part, it is only said that it was 'ordered' so and so; in other places, it is 'ordered and declared'; and, in other places, it is 'ordered, adjudged, and declared'.

But, not long afterwards, the parties, agreeing, did petition the court to decree it, which was done accordingly.

131

Marston v. Marston

(Ch. 1632–1633)

A court of equity can order a devisee to specifically perform the conditions of the devise.

Nelson 24, 21 E.R. 780

8 Car. I [1632–33]. LORD COVENTRY.

The father both of the plaintiff and the defendant, being seised of a copyhold estate, surrendered the same to the use of his will, and he devised it to the defendant, who was his eldest son, paying his debts and so much money to the plaintiff, his sister, for her portion when of age, but, if he failed to pay the portion, then she was to have as much of the copyhold estate as did amount to the value of her portion. She afterwards came of age, and the defendant refused to pay the portion. Whereupon the homage allotted to her as much of the said copyhold lands as they adjudged to be the value of her portion, but the defendant, being admitted, refused to surrender the same.

Thereupon, the plaintiff exhibited her bill to have her portion or the said allotment decreed to her.

And the court gave a day for the payment of the portion, and, if he failed, then, he was decreed to surrender the allotment to the uses declared in the will.

132

Throgmorton v. Wagstaff

(Ch. 1632–1633)

In this case, a surety sued his principal's widow to make her pay her deceased husband's debt, she having assets.

1 Chancery Reports 59, 21 E.R. 507

The plaintiff seeks to be relieved against engagements entered into by him as surety for the defendant's late husband, the said defendant having sufficient [assets] of her husband's estate to discharge the same. And the plaintiff insisted to have leases for other lives whereof the testator was seised at the time of his death (and on which the said defendant entered as an occupant) to be assets in equity.

This court, in respect the plaintiff did not get a case made of this point by such a time, ordered the defendant to be discharged of and from the plaintiff's further demands.

Vide for this point the late Statute of Frauds and Perjuries.[1]

---

[1] Stat. 29 Car. II, c. 3 (*SR*, V, 839–842).

[Reg. Lib. 8 Car. I, ff. 59, 154.]

133

Sibson v. Fletcher

(Ch. 1632–1633)

After a long period of nonclaim on a debt, a court of equity will presume the debt to have been paid off, and will order the mortgage deed to be cancelled.

1 Chancery Reports 59, 21 E.R. 507

The defendant had a mortgage of the lands of one Briscoe, 14 Jac. [1616–17], which lands the plaintiff since purchased, which mortgage money was payable three years after, and the said Briscoe has had the possession of the lands ever since the making of the said deed of mortgage, until 21 Jac. [1623–24], at which time he sold to the plaintiff, who was never interrupted until now of late. The defendant sets the mortgage on foot, pretending the money was unsatisfied. Now, for that the defendant did not upon the plaintiff's purchase, although he saw the possession altered from Briscoe to the plaintiff, make any claim to the land, nor give any notice of his mortgage, and the defendant has since purchased lands of Briscoe and paid him money, so as, in all presumption, this mortgage money is satisfied, and possession has been seventeen years in Briscoe and the plaintiff.

This court was fully satisfied that there is nothing due on the said sleeping mortgage, and decreed the deed of mortgage to be delivered up to be cancelled.

[Reg. Lib. 8 Car. I, f. 529.]

134

Stoit v. Ayloff

(Ch. 1632–1633)

Inter-spousal contracts are void in law and in equity.

1 Chancery Reports 60, 21 E.R. 507

The defendant, after the marriage of his wife, promised payment to her of £100. And, since, they are separated. The plaintiff's bill is to charge the defendant with the £100.

But the debt being sixteen years old and the promise made by a husband to a wife, which this court conceives to be utterly void in law, [the court] would not relieve the plaintiff.

[Reg. Lib. 8 Car. I, f. 530.]

135

Harding v. Countess of Suffolk

(Ch. 1632–1640)

In this case, the court of equity specifically enforced the payment of an annuity.

1 Chancery Reports 61, 21 E.R. 507

The plaintiff's suit is for a rent charge of £200 *per annum*, granted by the late earl of Suffolk with the privity and consent of the said countess, 15 March, 7 Jac. [1610], to Sir John Townsend, deceased, during the life of the plaintiff Katherine, to be issuing out of the manor of Walden in trust and for the use of the plaintiff Katherine, which annuity was duly paid with the consent of the said countess all the lifetime of the said late earl. But the countess, after the said earl's death, sought to avoid the said annuity, pretending a precedent lease made by the said earl, 4 Jac. [1606–07] for many years yet to come to certain persons in trust for the said countess of the said manor and lands out of which the said rent issues and because the premises charged with the said rent lay intermixed, that the plaintiff could make no distress for recovery, the plaintiffs are remediless at law.

For the avoiding of which lease, the plaintiff produced a fine levied by the said late earl and the now earl in Michaelmas term 13 Jac. [1615] of the said manor and lands of Walden. And, though no indenture could be produced to lead the use of the said fine, yet they all alleged that the said fine was to the use of the said countess for her jointure and that she enjoyed the same by virtue of the said latter conveyance, and not by the said lease, and so the said rent charge ought not to be impeached.

And it did not appear that the said lessees for the countess ever made entry or claim by virtue of the said lease since the fine.

This court, at the first hearing upon this matter, declared that the said lease and fine were both considerable, it being then objected that, howsoever it were, the plaintiff ought not to be relieved in equity, for that there was no consideration for the said rent charge which might move a court of equity to relieve the plaintiff any further than the law would relieve him.

The Lord Keeper [LORD COVENTRY] took time to peruse all the pleading in this cause before he would deliver his judgment.

Then the plaintiff petitioned the king's most excellent Majesty, who referred the consideration thereof to the Lord Privy Seal and some others of the Lords of the Privy Council, before whom the matter was debated at large. But no end being made by them, the plaintiff petitioned the Lord Keeper, informing him of the said reference and that it appeared to the referees that the countess had an indenture made by the late earl to lead the uses of the said fine and that the said Lords Referees were of opinion that the said indenture being material should be produced by the countess, which the Lord Keeper ordered to be brought into court, which the countess still refused to do.

So the Lord Keeper and Lord Privy Seal, now hearing the cause upon the merits thereof and having maturely advised thereof, are clear of opinion that, albeit no cause were proved, yet, in respect the plaintiff's suit is upon a trust, they may and ought to be relieved, for that the suit is not to make up or amend any validity of the deed in point of law, the deed being valid and good enough. But the suit is to have the trust performed, for which the plaintiff cannot sue at law, and to be relieved against the confounding of metes and bounds, so that one manor is not known from the other, which is usually relieved in this court. But, as touching the said lease, their Lordships declared that, if it could not be impeached, the plaintiff could not be relieved. Their Lordships conceived that, unless some entry or claim were made to avoid the said fine in 13 Jac. [1615], the said lease, in 4 Jac. [1606–07], is thereby bound up in law, and cannot be set on foot to avoid the plaintiff's rent charge, so that the plaintiff ought to be relieved in equity, both against the said rent charge and arrears.

But their Lordships further declared that, if the countess bring in the said lease and deed and can thereby avoid the fine, then that may alter the case, but, if she cannot avoid the fine, then it must be decreed as aforesaid.

And their Lordships ordered the countess should leave with the Register of the court the points on which she will insist for avoiding the said fine or upholding the said lease against the said fine, and both parties are to prepare for that purpose. And their Lordships declared that, if a decree shall pass against the countess and she not yield obedience thereto, then all the manor of Walden shall be subject to a sequestration for the satisfying of the said decree.

The said deed and lease being produced and the defendant's points to avoid the fine being as follows, *viz.*, in these words. The countess having lands of good value of her own inheritance and [being] dowable of the earl's lands, joined in a fine at the earl's request of her own land and part of his land, in lieu whereof the earl made a lease of divers lands in the County of Essex to Roger Pennel for divers years yet in being in trust for the countess, and after[wards] granted the said rent charge to Sir John Townsend of part of the said lands leased. The earl died. This rent is neither in law nor equity, as the said countess conceives, to be laid on the said lease lands during the lease.

The earl during his life, and the countess since his death, enjoyed the lands so leased by permission of the said Pennel as tenant at will to him, in which case, no fine levied by the earl can debar Pennel, and [it is] not like to Saffyne's Case,[1] where the termor is put out of possession, and then a fine is levied, in which case, he is tied to the claim, but not here.

---

[1] *Saffyn v. Adams* (1605), 5 Coke Rep. 123, 77 E.R. 248, Croke Jac. 61, 79 E.R. 50.

Also (though it needed not) Pennel within the five years made entry and claim.

The earl, being seised of some lands in possession and of the lands leased to Pennel in reversion, levied a fine of both. This fine works distributively for part in possession, part in reversion, and does not turn the estate of Pennel into a right, and, consequently, does not enforce him to any entry to avoid the fine.

The countess, within five years after the fine in the behalf of the lessee, made an entry and claim, and did the like within five years after the earl's death.

And the countess being heard upon the said points, none of them could be proved, nor could prove that Pennel ever sealed a counterpart of the said lease or ever accepted of the said lease or ever so much as knew that the said lease was made unto him or that Pennel ever had possession of such part of the premises as were out of lease or that he or any for him made any entry into the same nor that he received or claimed by virtue of any lease or estate made to himself any rents of such lands contained in the said lease as were demised to undertenants, but, such as he received, he received as servant to the earl.

So, upon the whole matter, their Lordships declared the points insisted on by the said countess to avoid the said fine and support the said lease were not made out. And they are of opinion that the said lease was a sleeping lease and that no fruit or use was made thereof, either before the said fine or after, and is bound up in law by the said fine and proclamation and nonclaim of Pennel, and it cannot be set on foot to avoid the plaintiff's rent charge. But the possession, which the countess had of the said manor since the death of the said earl and now has, is by and under the said fine and the indenture leading the use thereof, directed by the indenture of uses now produced, by which the same are limited to the said countess for life in remainder after the said earl for her jointure. And, therefore, the plaintiff ought in equity to be relieved, both for the said annuity and arrears, and they decreed the same accordingly.

[Reg. Lib. 8 Car. I, f. 502.]

3 Chancery Reports 88, 21 E.R. 737

June 1635. Countess of Suffolk v. Harding.

Upon a bill of review, the defendant had a decree for £1800 and £200 *per annum* out of a manor, which the now plaintiff pretends not to be worth £50 *per annum*, and to charge the countess with the rent and arrear, who was no party to the grant of the rent charge. And, therefore, she brought a bill of review.

The answer was that the value was no new matter and that it was not excepted to in the former suit, and, therefore, she is now remediless, as in the case of an executor, who, if he do not plead at first that he has not assets, he shall not afterwards, when the debt is decreed against him, be admitted to plead not assets.

It was ordered that, if the countess give not security to perform the order of the court, the bill is to be dismissed.

1 Chancery Reports 138, 21 E.R. 531

Harding v. Earl of Suffolk.

The late earl of Suffolk granted an annuity of £200 *per annum* out of the manor of Walden. But the defendant refuses to pay the said annuity, pretending there is no manor known by the name of Walden *tantum*, but only a farm of £80 *per annum*.

Now, for that the defendant chiefly endeavored to prove that the manor of Walden, *alias* Chippen Walden and Brook Walden are two distinct manors and that there is no manor of Walden *tantum* and, if any, it is Walden *alias* Chippen Walden and the same only liable to the annuity, the value thereof being but £80 *per annum*, and the plaintiff proved that the great manor of Walden, which the defendant calls Brook Walden, was the manor meant to be subject to the said annuity, this court, with the assistance of the judges declared and are of opinion that, if there be two manors known by the name of Walden called Walden and sometimes distinguished with an *alias* and the one of them of small value and the other of a much greater, that it is a good averment in law that the greater manor should be liable to the rent charge.

[Reg. Lib. 15 Car. I, f. 553.]

136

Egerton v. Egerton

(Ch. 1632)

In this case, the bond in issue to observe the obligee's will was not broken by the obligor's entry into certain lands after the obligee's death.

W. Jones 265, 82 E.R. 138

Trinity term 8 Car.

In the case in Chancery between Sir Rowland Egerton and Randall Egerton, a point in law was referred to Chief Baron Davenport, Hutton, and Jones, Whitelocke, and Croke, which was thus. Sir Rowland Egerton entered into a statute to Sir John Egerton, his father, that was defeasanced upon a condition if Rowland Egerton observed, fulfilled, and accomplished the last will and testament of the said Sir John Egerton and will pay and content all of the bequests and legacies according to the intent and true meaning of the said testament and last will. Sir John, being seised of the lands *in capite* in the counties of Chester and Stafford, devised it by his last will to Edward Egerton in fee. And he gave divers legacies. And he made Lady Egerton his executrix. And he died. After his death, Rowland Egerton entered in the third part of the land.

And the question was whether the statute was forfeited.

DAVENPORT, HUTTON, and CROKE were of the opinion that it was not forfeited. But JONES and WHITELOCKE [held] *e contra*. And they made a general certificate that, by the opinion of the major part, it was not forfeited.

And, thus, it was decreed.

[Earlier proceedings in this case: Croke Jac. 346, 79 E.R. 296, 2 Bulstrode 218, 80 E.R. 1074.]

137

Vendal v. Harvey

(Ch. 1633)

A receiver and accountant in the Exchequer can be sued in the Court of Chancery and cannot remove the suit into the Court of Exchequer.

There can be simultaneous suits in equity for the same thing in both the Court of Chancery and the Court of Exchequer.

British Library MS. Hargrave 174, f. 26

The same day [that] the plaintiff's cause was to be heard in the Chancery, the defendant caused the plaintiff's counsel in Westminster Hall as they were going from the Chancery bar to be served with an injunction out of the Exchequer to stay that suit, which the plaintiff's counsel declared to the court. And thereupon, the defendant not attending, a further day was appointed, and the defendant [was] ordered to attend them, which accordingly he did. And by the declaration of the plaintiff's counsel and the defendant's not denying it, the case upon the service of the injunction being as aforesaid, the court appointed two several orders made by Chancellor Ellesmere to be read. By one of which it appeared that an officer of the customs house being served with a subpoena to answer bills here, he would not answer thereunto but procured an injunction out of the Exchequer to stay those suits and served it, and it was ordered here that the plaintiffs here should and might proceed with their suits notwithstanding their injunction, and by another of the said orders, he was committed for having served the plaintiffs' counsel here with the said injunction, this court taking the same to be a counter plea and a great derogation to the authority of this court.

And the Lord Keeper [LORD COVENTRY] declared to the defendant here [that he] might fully proceed so with him by giving [an] order [that] the plaintiff's counsel should proceed and by committing him. Yet he was willing to hear what could be said on either side that the cause might be relieved as [was] just and asked the defendant if he would waive the injunction and proceed in the cause.

To which he answered [that] he had not counsel and desires some to be assigned, which the court assented to and offered another day for his counsel to be heard so as he would be content [and] the plaintiff's counsel might be heard at the same time, which the defendant refused, affirming [that] it was not in his power to waive his injunction. And though the court admonished him, those speeches gave the court just cause to examine on interrogatories how it was that he had not power of his own suit, he coming in on a contempt by the defendant still refusing to give way that the plaintiff's counsel should be heard, the court ordered the plaintiff's counsel to open the case, which was done accordingly.

And then the court [again] offered the defendant, that if he desired to be heard therein, another day to be assigned for his counsel to be heard so as he would consent, the matter might then be freely debated on both sides, which the defendant Harvey not accepting, [the] Lord Keeper [LORD COVENTRY] declared the same no ground that this court should give any way to the said injunction, for if it be pretended that the defendant, being a receiver, ought not to be sued here, the question has been overruled by a multitude of precedents upon great deliberations in the time of the lord keepers, Sir Nicholas Bacon, Sir Thomas Bromley, Lord Ellesmere, and other chancellors and keepers. And since his lordship sat in this court, upon consideration of those precedents and [a] conference with Sir John Walter, chief baron, and the rest of the barons, one Clarke was ruled to answer and did answer here, who pleaded [the privilege of the Exchequer, being an officer there. And one Vernon, who pleaded][1] the like plea of privilege, waived it and answered here. And his lordship declared that if the privilege of the Exchequer were allowable where the suit is against an accountant and another person not privileged, as it is here, there can be no color to oust this court or any other of the jurisdiction of the cause by reason [of] one of the defendant's being privileged.

[And] whereas it was objected [that] the Exchequer had the priority of suit in this cause, it was answered [that] that did not appear and that the plaintiffs here were strangers to the suit in the Exchequer. And there were frequent precedents where the defendant in our court of equity has been admitted to a cross-suit in another court of equity without expecting the event of the first suit. For if the plaintiff in the first suit [abate][2] or be dismissed, the defendant has no help there but by his cross-suit. And the Exchequer has suffered new suits there touching matters judicially settled here. And this court has done the like by the Exchequer.

And to the objection of the inconvenience to have the same matters either [between] the same parties or divers to depend in several courts [at the same time, because the court] might differ in opinion and the orders clash, it was answered [that] his lordship always used, that if anything of difficulty that has been heard in the Exchequer comes before him, to be assisted by some of the barons.

And his lordship declared further that he did not conceive [that] any suit in equity between party and party was maintainable but by reason of privilege

---

[1] from British Library MS. Hargrave 99, f. 64, pl. 23.
[2] survey *MS*.

and that privilege holds not unless all defendants be privileged. And, therefore, as this court does not hinder the proceedings in the Exchequer, so it does order, notwithstanding the said injunction, the plaintiffs [to] be at liberty to proceed herein.

And the defendant, his counsel, etc., are enjoined by this court not to move in the Exchequer or [to] do anything to hinder the proceedings in this court, to which purpose the plaintiff may take an injunction here. And as concerning Harvey's contempt, the punishment thereof his lordship will advise further, wherefore he is to attend *de die in diem* until license to depart according to a recognizance [now acknowledged] for that purpose.

[Other copies of this report: British Library MS. Hargrave 99, f. 64, pl. 23.]

2 Freeman 162, 22 E.R. 1131

7 February 8 Car. I [1633].

The same day that the plaintiff's cause was to be heard in Chancery, the defendant caused the plaintiff's counsel in Westminster Hall, as the were going to the Chancery bar, to be served with an injunction out of the Exchequer to stay the suit, which the plaintiff's counsel declared to the court. Whereupon counsel not attending, a farther day was appointed, and the defendant was ordered to attend then, which accordingly he did.

And, by the declaration of the plaintiff's counsel and the defendant's not denying it, the case upon the injunction being as aforesaid, the court appointed two several orders made by Chancellor Ellesmere to be read, by one of which it appeared that an officer of the Custom House, being served with subpoenas to answer bills there, would not answer thereunto, but procured an injunction out of the Exchequer, and served it. [It was] ordered there that the plaintiff might proceed, notwithstanding the said injunction and, by another, committed for the contempt of this court.

And the Lord Keeper [LORD COVENTRY] declared that so it might be done in this case, but he would hear the defendant's counsel and that, upon hearing the cause, it might be dismissed or retained, as was just. And he asked the defendant if he would waive the injunction and proceed in the cause. To which he answered that he had no counsel and desired time to advise. The court was willing that his counsel should be heard, if also the plaintiff's counsel might be heard, which the defendant refused, pretending he was not able to waive the injunction, which the court denied, since it was his own suit. But the defendant still refusing, the court ordered the plaintiff's counsel to open the cause, which was done accordingly. And the defendant was allowed another day for his counsel to defend so that the matter of this cause might be freely debated on both sides, which the defendant refused.

Whereupon the LORD COVENTRY declared that the court would not give way to this injunction, for, if it be pretended that the defendant be a receiver of the Exchequer, that has been overruled by multitudes of precedents, upon great deliberation in the time of the Lord Bacon, Sir Thomas Bromley, and Ellesmere, and other Chancellors and Keepers and since his Lordship was Keeper, upon the precedents, and upon conference with Chief Baron Walter and the rest of the barons.

Nelson 19, 21 E.R. 779

8 Car. I [1632–33]. LORD COVENTRY.

On the same day in which the plaintiff's cause was to be heard, his counsel, as they were going to the bar, were served with an injunction out of the Exchequer. And the court being acquainted therewith, the defendant was ordered to attend, who was so far from denying the service of the injunction, that he owned it was done by his direction.

Thereupon, the court appointed two orders made by the Lord Chancellor Ellesmere to be read, by which it appeared that an officer of the Custom House being served with a subpoena to answer a bill, he refused, and procured an injunction out of the Exchequer to stay the suit. But it was ordered that the plaintiff should and might proceed in the suit, notwithstanding such injunction, and the party was committed for serving the same, the court taking it to be a great derogation to their authority. And, therefore, the court asked the defendant if he would waive his injunction and proceed in the cause, to which he answered that he desired counsel might be assigned to him, which was done accordingly. And another day was appointed for counsel to be heard on both sides, at which day, the defendant insisted that it was in his power to waive the injunction. And, thereupon, the court examined him on interrogatories how it was that he had not power in his own suit, he coming in on a contempt, and ordered the plaintiff's counsel to open the cause, which was done.

And the defendant still insisting on the injunction, the court decreed that they would not suffer it, for, if it was pretended that the defendant being a receiver ought to be sued in his proper court and not elsewhere, that had been overruled by many precedents upon great deliberation in the time of Sir Nicholas Bacon, Sir Thomas Bromley, the Lord Ellesmere, and other Chancellors and Keepers of the Great Seal. And in the present Lord Keeper Coventry's time, one clerk was ruled to answer after he had pleaded the privilege of the Exchequer, and he did answer accordingly. And this order was made upon conference with Sir John Walter, Chief Baron, and the rest of the Barons of the Exchequer. And the court declared that, if the privilege of the Exchequer was to be allowed where the suit was against an accountant only, yet there was no color of allowing it where the suit was against another person not privileged, as in this case.

And whereas it was objected that the Exchequer had the priority of suit in this cause, it was answered that did not appear and that the plaintiffs here were strangers to any suit in the Exchequer and there were many precedents where the defendant in one court of equity has been admitted to a cross-suit in another court of equity, without expecting the event of the first suit, for, if the plaintiff in the first suit should discontinue or be dismissed, the defendant has no help there but by a cross-suit, and the Court of Exchequer has allowed new suits to be brought there concerning matters which have been judicially determined here. And this court has done the like by the Exchequer.

And, as to the objection of the inconvenience to have the same matters and between the same parties or others to depend in several courts at the same time, because the courts might differ in opinion and the judgments clash, it was answered that, where any matter of difficulty arises in a cause which has been heard in the Exchequer and, afterwards, came into this court, that the Chancery calls some of the Barons to assist.

[Orders of 31 January and 7, 8, 9, 11, and 12 February 1633: Public Record Office C.33/164, ff. 255v, 271, 275v, 276, 378v, 279v.]

138

Anonymous v. Clerke

(Ch. 1633)

A privilege to sue and to be sued in a particular court is not available unless all of the co-defendants are so privileged.

2 Freeman 162, 22 E.R. 1131

One Clerke was ruled to answer, upon pleading the privilege of the Exchequer, being an officer there, and he did answer, and so did one Vernon upon the like plea. And the LORD COVENTRY said that, in case the privilege were allowable where one single accountant there was sued here, yet it is no plea where the bill is against an accountant and another, as here, for there is no color for it, neither in this case nor any other.

And whereas it was objected that the Exchequer had the priority of suit in this case, it was answered that did not appear and that the plaintiffs here were strangers to the suit in the Exchequer. And there are frequent precedents where the defendant in a court of equity has been admitted to a cross-suit in another court of equity without expecting the event of the first suit, for, if the plaintiff in the first suit surcease or be dismissed, the defendant has no help here but by his cross-suit. And the Exchequer has suffered new suits there touching matters judicially settled here, and this court has done the like by the Exchequer.

And His Lordship [LORD COVENTRY] declared that he did not conceive any suit in equity between party and party was maintainable in the Exchequer but by reason of privilege, and that privilege holds not unless all the plaintiffs or defendants be privileged. And, therefore, as this court does not hinder the proceedings in the Exchequer, so it does order, notwithstanding the said injunction, the plaintiffs be at liberty to proceed here. And the defendant and his counsel are enjoined not to move in the Exchequer to hinder the proceedings of this court, for which purpose the plaintiff here may take an injunction. And, as for the defendant's contempt, His Lordship [LORD COVENTRY] will advise farther, and the defendant to attend here *de die in diem* according to a recognizance to that purposes.

Nelson 20, 21 E.R. 779

And the court declared that a privilege does not hold unless all the defendants were privileged, nor then neither, for, as this court does not hinder the proceedings in the Exchequer, so that court is not to obstruct the proceedings here by any injunction. Therefore, the plaintiff shall be at liberty to proceed. And the defendant's counsel was enjoined by this court not to move in the Exchequer or to do anything to hinder the proceedings here for which purpose the plaintiff may take an injunction. And, as concerning the contempt of the defendant and the punishment thereof, the court advised farther, and ordered him to attend *de die in diem*.

139

Case of East Grinstead

(Ch. 1633)

Where rents from lands lying in several counties are given to a single charitable use, the charity commissioners in the county where the charity is located can supervise the gift.

A rent charge to a charitable use that was extinguished by the doctrine of merger can be revived by charity commissioners.

A rent charge to charitable uses remains when the land is sold to a purchaser for value without notice.

Land given to charitable uses that is sold to a third party for value without notice passes free of the intended charitable use; a purchaser from the first purchaser is bound by the latter's notice or lack thereof.

Herne & Duke 72

These points were resolved by the LORD COVENTRY:

First, that whereas Robert, earl of Dorset, had granted a rent charge of £330 *per annum* out of divers [of] his manors and lands in London and several counties for maintenance of an almshouse in East Grinstead erected by himself, first, that, if a rent be granted out of lands in several counties for maintenance of charitable uses in one county, the commissioners in that county where the charitable use is to be performed may make a decree to charge the lands in other counties to pay an equal contribution of charge in payment of the said rent, and there needs not several inquisitions in each county for that the rent is an entire grant by the deed or will.

Second, if the devisees of a rent charge or the grantees thereof to a charitable use do purchase part of the lands out of which the rent is issuing or all the land, although, in extremity of law, the rent charge is extinguished, yet, if the commissioners decree the rent to be revived and settle it upon others to maintain the charitable use, the rent is revived by the said decree.

Third, if a rent charge be granted out of land to a charitable use and the land is afterwards sold for valuable consideration of money or land to one that had no notice of the rent, yet the rent remains, for that the purchase was of another thing that was not given to the charitable use.

Fourth, by the Statute,[1] the parties interested are to have notice from the commissioners of the time and place of their sitting to execute the commission. Yet, if the commissioners make a decree without giving such notice to the parties interested, it is good. And, if the parties upon their appeal do take exception, that they had not any notice of the time of the executing of the commission from the commissioners, that shall not avoid the decree, unless they show withal in their exception, that for lack of such notice, they lost the benefit of such an exception to the commissioners or some of them or of such a challenge to a juror, expressing the cause in certain. And, if the Lord Keeper adjudge the cause shown to be a sufficient exception and challenge, the decree or orders of the commissioners shall be annulled and reversed without further examination, for the intent of such notice to be given is that the parties interested may make their lawful challenges to the commissioners or jurors, as the Statute allows them.

Fifth, [it was] resolved that the notice which a purchaser of lands given to charitable uses ought to have ought to be certain, and a general notice is not sufficient. As if land given to charitable uses be intended to be sold by act of Parliament and when the bill is read in the House of Parliament, it is there spoken unto and declared that the land is chargeable with a charitable use and recompense is offered otherwise to assure the charitable use then by that land and afterwards the bill does not pass and the land is sold to one of the members of the House that spoke unto the bill for money, yet this notice in Parliament is not sufficient notice within the intent of the Statute, because it was not known to such a purchaser but as a Parliament man in another capacity.

Sixth, if a purchaser of land given to charitable uses for consideration of money has legal notice of the use and afterwards sells the land to another for money, who has no notice of the use, this second purchaser shall hold the land chargeable with the charitable use, for that the first purchaser held it so and the second purchaser coming under his title must hold it subject to the charges the first purchaser held it, for that he claims under him. But, if the first purchaser

---

[1] Stat. 43 Eliz. I, c. 4, s. 1 (*SR*, IV, 968–969).

had no notice of the use, then is the land discharged of the charitable use. And if he afterwards sell it to another for money that has notice of the use, yet he shall not hold it subject to the charitable use, for that the land was discharged thereof upon the first purchase.

Seventh, that if a rent charge be granted to a charitable use out of lands in several counties, the commissioners are to charge this rent by their decree upon all the lands in every county, according to an equal distribution, having regard to the yearly value of all the lands chargeable with the rent and cannot by their decree charge one or two manors with all the rent and discharge the residue in other counties or places, for that their decree will then be contrary to the will of [the] founders or donors.

140

Rowe v. Inglett

(Ch. 1633)

A purchaser with notice of a devise cannot hold the land in question against the devisee.

Lincoln's Inn MS. Maynard 75, f. 51, pl. 1

The father of the plaintiff [was] possessed of a lease for years terminable upon three lives, of Joan his wife and two strangers. He granted so much of the term that shall be left at the time of his death to Newsam in trust for his wife (which grant, in truth, was void). Afterwards he devised the term to his wife, remainder to the plaintiff, and he made his wife executrix and Inglett overseer of the will, who wrote the will and was cognizant of it. And the testator died. The wife renewed the lease and granted it to one Brewen, with whom she married. And Brewen and his wife granted it to Inglett for £320.

And yet because Inglett [was] privy to the will, even though the wife did not assent to the legacy and Inglett came in upon valuable consideration, the decree [was] against Inglett by Justice BERKELEY.

[Other copies of this report: Lincoln's Inn MS. Hill 125, f. 16.]

[Order of 25 October 1633: Public Record Office C.33/166, f. 198v.]

141

Anonymous

(Ch. 1633)

A party whose commissioner divulged the contents of a deposition before publication will be held in contempt of court.

Lincoln's Inn MS. Maynard 75, f. 51, pl. 2

Glanville moved for an attachment against one who placed a commissioner to be present at the examination of the evidence to the intent that afterwards he could the better disprove it.

And upon an affidavit that he had confessed, it was ordered accordingly.

[Other copies of this report: Lincoln's Inn MS. Hill 125, f. 16v.]

142

Eyres v. Taunton

(Ch. 1633)

Where a debtor of a judgment debtor and the heir of the judgment debtor are jointly garnished for the judgment debt, the court can proceed against the former in the absence of the latter.

An issue out of chancery will be tried by a common law jury.

Croke Car. 295, 79 E.R. 859

Trinity Term, 7 Car. I. Roll 590.

[There was a] *scire facias* in Chancery upon a recognizance of £200 by one Cawley, who was returned dead, whereupon a second *scire facias* issued against the heir of Cawley and against the tenants of the lands and tenements of Cawley which he had *tempore recognitionis vel postea*, whereupon the sheriff returned the defendant Taunton terre tenant of such lands and omitted to return anything concerning the heir.

Upon this, the defendant pleads that the said Cawley had nothing in the said lands at the time of the said recognizance or ever after. And upon this, they were at issue in Chancery. And it was sent thither to be tried. And it was tried, and found for the plaintiff that Cawley was seised etc.

After a verdict for the plaintiff, *Mallet*, for the defendant, moved in arrest of judgment, because nothing was returned concerning the heir, *viz.* that there was not any heir or that the heir had nothing; therefore, no judgment shall be given, for it is a non-return of the sheriff, and not a mis-return, and it is not aided by the 32 Hen. VIII, c. 30, or 18 Eliz., c. 14, or 21 Jac. I, c. 13, or any of the Statutes of Jeofails.[1] The reason he alleged that no judgment ought to be given was because the terre tenant, without the heir, was not to be charged, and, therefore, the heir ought to be summoned, and, until the heir be summoned or that it be returned that there is not any heir to be summoned or that the heir has not any lands to be charged, the terre tenant ought not to be charged, for the heir might have a

---

[1] Stat. 32 Hen. VIII, c. 30 (*SR*, III, 786–787); Stat. 18 Eliz. I, c. 14 (*SR*, IV, 625); Stat. 21 Jac. I, c. 13 (*SR*, IV, 1221).

release to plead or other matter to bar the execution and his land is rather to be charged than the land of the terre tenant, for the heir shall not have contribution against the terre tenant as the terre tenant shall have. Also, if the heir be within age, the parol shall demur, and the terre tenant shall have advantage thereof. And, therefore, there being nothing returned concerning him, he moved that no judgment ought to be given.

RICHARDSON, Chief Justice, JONES, and BERKELEY, justices, held that the return was not good, because the plaintiff names and sets forth that there is an heir and there is no return *quoad* the heir, so, as to him, it is *quasi breve album*, and no return, and it is not aided by any statutes.

But I [CROKE] was of a contrary opinion, because the defendant has omitted to take advantage thereof, for, having pleaded and the issue being found against him, he shall not now take advantage for not returning the heir to be summoned, for it may be that there is not any heir or that the heir has no land or may not be found. *Vide* 17 Edw. II. *Execut.*, 139b; 18 Edw. II, *ibid.*, 142,[1] that the terre tenant in a *scire facias* shall not be warned until it be returned that there be not any heir or that the heir is warned and comes not in. *Vide* 3 Hen. IV, 10, a *scire facias haeredi et terre tenenti*;[2] the sheriff returns such a terre tenant warned, and speaks nothing of the heir, yet the terre tenant was enforced to answer. And after, *ad informandum curiam* whether there was an heir, it was ordered that a new *scire facias* should be awarded.

The Case of Bowyer v. Rivett[3] was cited by Justice JONES that, in a *scire facias* against the heir and terre tenant, he is charged only as terre tenant, and, by pleading *riens per descent*, and found against him, the execution was of the moiety of his land, and not of all, as the heir should have been charged upon a false plea.

Croke Car. 312, 79 E.R. 873

It was moved again by *Mallet*, for the defendant, in a stay of judgment, whereas the plaintiff, the last term, procured a new *scire facias* out of this court directed to the Sheriff of Gloucester to summon the heir of Cawley, because he had not made any mention in his former return of the heir, and, thereupon, this writ issued out of the court, *ex officio curiae ad informandum curiam*, and the sheriff had returned that Cawley had not any lands in his bailiwick which descended to his heir nor any heir within his bailiwick etc. that yet no judgment ought to be given:

First, because this *scire facias* ought not to have been awarded to the Sheriff of Gloucester but upon a *testatum* that the first *scire facias* was awarded to the

---

[1] Trin. 17 Edw. II, Fitzherbert, Abr., *Execucion*, pl. 139 (1324); Mich. 18 Edw. II, Fitzherbert, Abr., *Execucion*, pl. [142] (1324).

[2] YB Hil. 3 Hen. IV, f. 10, pl. 9 (1402).

[3] *Bowyer v. Rivet* (1626), Benloe 162, 73 E.R. 1026, 3 Bulstrode 317, 81 E.R. 264, W. Jones 87, 82 E.R. 45, Palmer 419, 81 E.R. 1151, Popham 153, 79 E.R. 1252, Paynell K.B. 25, British Library MS. Hargrave 30, f. 213v.

Sheriff of Middlesex, where the recognizance was first acknowledged, for, being grounded upon a record, he ought first to sue the *scire facias* there, and, upon a return that there is not any heir there, then to have this in another county. And he cited the Book of Entries, 500, and 2 Edw. III, 20.[1]

Sed non allocatur, for true it is the first *scire facias* upon a recognizance to have execution ought to be in the county where it was acknowledged, but, when it is sued there and the party returned dead, it may be sued against the heir or terre tenant in any county where the party surmises he has land. Also, this *scire facias* is *ex officio curiae* and in favor of the party and there is no reason he should take exceptions to it.

The second exception was taken to the return of the writ, for it is returned that there is not any heir within his bailiwick, where it ought to have been that there is not any terre tenant and that there is not any heir generally.

Sed non allocatur, for the return upon the first *scire facias* shows what lands he had, and it shall not be intended there be more lands when no heir is found there, and the sheriff has no authority to enquire into other counties.

The third exception, that the return upon the second *scire facias* in Chancery, whereupon the plea is pleaded and issue joined, was insufficient for the reasons before alleged and the trial [was] ill.

But now all the court agreed, although the return had been better if it had found who was heir and that he was warned or that there was not any heir in the said county, yet it is well enough, for, as 17 Edw. II, tit. *Execution*, 139, anciently, the *scire facias* was only against the terre tenant and the heir was not charged in the *scire facias* but as terre tenant and, if the return be not good or formal, yet it is aided by the Statutes of Jeofails and the mis-return or insufficient return of the sheriff also, *quoad* the heir, because he is not named in the return, is but a discontinuance, which is aided by the Statute of Jeofails.

Wherefore RICHARDSON, JONES, and BERKELEY, agreed that there was not any cause after verdict to stay judgment, whereto I [CROKE] assented.

The fourth exception, that it was not a good trial by *nisi prius*, for, issue being joined in Chancery and the record delivered into the King's Bench to be tried, it ought there to have been tried, and not by *nisi prius*.

But all the court was against it, for, an issue, being joined between party and party, may well be tried by *nisi prius* out of this court, and so are many precedents. Wherefore judgment was given for the plaintiff.

---

[1] YB Hil. 2 Edw. III, f. 20, pl. 7 (1329).

143

Symonds v. Green

(Ch. 1633)

In this case, various entailed lands and manor lands were properly described and included in the grant in issue.

Croke Car. 308, 79 E.R. 868

Sir George Symonds against Sir Michael Green and William Green, his son.

The Lord Keeper [LORD COVENTRY] being assisted by HUTTON, Justice, and JONES, Justice, in former hearings, and by me [CROKE] in this last hearing, it was decreed that, whereas Sir William Green was seised in fee of the manors of Great Milton and Little Milton and the reputed manors of Great Chilworth and Little Chilworth in the parish of Milton and of divers lands in Chilworth, purchased 30 Eliz. of Sir Michael Dormer, and of other lands purchased 1 Jac. I, which one Ives occupied together until 3 Jac. I, and then, in consideration of the marriage of Sir Michael Green, his son, with one Millesent Reade, with whom he had £4500, covenants to stand seised of the said manors of Great Milton and Little Milton and of divers particular closes by name in Chilworth and of all his other lands, tenements, and hereditaments to the said manors appertaining or used and occupied with them to the uses following, *viz.*, of the manor and premises, to the use of himself for life, without impeachment of waste, and, after, of such a manor and some of the closes by name, to the use of Anne, his wife, for her jointure, and of other the particular closes before mentioned to the use of Millesent for her life for her jointure and, after the decease of Sir William, Anne, and Millesent, to the use of the said Sir Michael Green and the heirs male of his body, with a remainder to his right heirs. Afterward, Sir Michael Green and Sir William Green joined in a bargain and sale of the manors of Milton and Chilworth and all the lands thereto appertaining or reputed as part of the same or within the same. And they levy a fine by the name of the manors and ten messuages, 600 acres of land, 200 *prati*, and 700 of *pasturae*, which quantity comprised as well the freehold lands as the manors.

The question was whether the parcels of land divided from the manor by the entail and the freehold land lately purchased should pass by this mortgage.

And they all resolved that the lands entailed, which were parcel of the manor, shall not be said to be severed from the manor, for the freehold never being severed, but remaining entire in Sir William Green during his life, shall pass as parcel of the manor at the time of the mortgage and that the freehold bought in and occupied with the manor, although it was but for two years before the mortgage, may pass, being said and reputed parcel and by that name. And the fine is well enough guided by the indenture for the manors and for the freehold purchased, although they were not *in rei veritate* parcel of the manor. And a little time is sufficient for the gaining a reputation.

Wherefore it was decreed that Sir George Symonds should enjoy the manor and the freehold purchased and that Sir Michael Green and his son should make further assurance at the cost of Sir George Symonds and that this indenture is a sufficient declaration of the uses of the fine as it was declared by all the said justices and by the Lord Keeper himself.

144

Townley v. Sherborne

(Ch. 1633)

Where there are two or more trustees and one of them receives all or the greater part of the profits and afterwards dies or becomes insolvent, his co-trustees shall not be charged for the receipts received by him in the absence of fraud or bad faith.

J. Bridgman 35, 123 E.R. 1181

Saturday the sixth day of June, in the ninth year of the reign of King Charles, between Francis Townley, Esquire, plaintiff, [and] Edward Sherborne, executor of Richard Mountford, deceased, executor of Thomas Challoner, deceased, defendant.

Upon hearing and debating of the matter, as well on the fifteenth as the eighteenth of June last, the court being assisted with Mr. Justice HUTTON, and Mr. Justice JONES, upon the plaintiff's bill of review for the reviving and reversal of a decree made in a cause wherein the said Richard Mountford, deceased, executor of Thomas Challoner, was plaintiff against the now plaintiff, and Thomas Forster, Esquire, concerning the sum of £1700, raised out of the rents and profits of certain lands and tenements in Linsted, Ardingley, and Worth in the County of Sussex, in trust for the said Thomas Challoner during his minority, and which the now plaintiff by the decree of this court was to pay in case the said Foster should fail to pay the same, several matters were offered by the plaintiff's counsel for the reversal of the said decree, as namely, that the now plaintiff was decreed to pay the sum of £1700 as raised out of the profits of the infant's lands settled upon an account made up by the said Forster with the said Thomas Challoner, the infant, after he came to age, whereto the plaintiff Townley was neither party nor privy, nor ever consented nor ought to be bound thereby, and, secondly, that the said plaintiff is by the said decree made liable to the payment of all the profits raised out of the said infant's estate, whereas he never received any profits at all, and, although he gave some acquittances, yet the same were only for the three first half years and no more, and were but to balance an account, the monies disbursed amounting to as much as the receipts, and there being three other co-trustees with him, the plaintiff's counsel conceived that he ought not to be charged with more than he himself received, especially for that the other parties trusted and who received the profits were or were reputed to be men of ability and responsible.

Touching which last point, being that whereon the plaintiff's counsel chiefly insisted for the reversal of the said decree as against the now plaintiff, it appeared unto this court that Challoner, father of Thomas, the infant, did heretofore make a lease of the said lands to one Weeks for five and thirty years, and, afterwards, conveyed away the reversion to Thomas Challoner, his brother, and, after the death of Francis (according to an award made between the said Weeks and Thomas Challoner, the brother, who was uncle to Thomas, the infant) the lease of five and thirty years, and the reversion in fee simple were to be assigned to parties trusted by the said Weeks and one Barbara Challoner, mother of the said infant, and by the said Thomas, the uncle, the lease to be in trust for Weeks for life, the remainder to Barbara for life, the remainder to Thomas, the infant, and the reversion in fee to be in trust for the said Thomas, the infant, but upon the limitation or condition that the said Thomas, the infant, when he came of age should make some assurance to Thomas, the uncle, according to the award, wherein, if he failed, then the trust limited to him should cease and the trustees should be seised for Thomas, the uncle.

In pursuance whereof the now plaintiff and the said Forster were trusted together with one Langworth and Lovell to take the estate in the lease, and did take an assignment thereof from Weeks the 12th of June 9 *Jacobi* [1611]. And all the trustees sealed the counterpart, and, the same day, the now plaintiff and Forster assigned their moiety in the said lease to one Mr. Peacock and Robert Forster, who were not privy nor acquainted therewith, and, on the thirteenth of June, the ninth of King James, the said Thomas Challoner, the uncle, passed over the inheritance to the now plaintiff and Thomas Forster, whereby it was probable that the said assignment made by the now plaintiff and Thomas Forster of their interest in the moiety of the lease was to keep the same from being extinguished. After which assurance so made, Weeks, during his life, and Barbara, after him during her life, received the profits of the said lands. And Barbara, in the year of our Lord 1614, died.

And it appeared that, soon after the death of the said Barbara, *viz.* 23 of March 12 *Jacobi* [1615], Langworth, one of the trustees of the lease being dead, whereby his interest in the moiety survived in Lovell, that Thomas Challoner, the uncle, procured the said Lovell to assign over his interest in the said lease, to the said Thomas Challoner, the uncle, liable to the said trust, as by a copy of the assignment now read appeared. And it appeared by the confession of the now plaintiff and by his answer to the former bill and by the acquittances now produced that the now plaintiff joined with the said Thomas Forster in giving acquittances for the three first half year's rents. But it did not appear that he ever received any after, or gave any more acquittances, but it does appear by the proofs that the said Thomas Challoner, the uncle, who had the assignment from Lovell, did receive the rents of the tenants, and paid the same over to the said Thomas Forster and that, when the infant came of age, he called the said Thomas Forster, and Thomas, the uncle, to an account, and that they did account and that the said Thomas Forster did then deliver him a book of account, which the defendant now produced in court, by which it did appear, that, for the three first half years, the rents were received by the said Thomas, the uncle, and, by him, paid to the now plaintiff and the said Thomas Forster for the use of the infant, but, for all the subsequent time, the same were received by the said Thomas Challoner, the uncle, and, by him, paid to the said Thomas Forster alone, who (as was not now denied) was at the time of such receipts generally taken to be of great ability and responsible, as it also appeared by the proofs, that the said infant, after he came of age, had declared the said Thomas Forster to be his debtor, and did by his will read in court give the said sum of £1700 to the said Mountford as a debt owing by the said Thomas Forster solely, not mentioning the now plaintiff.

Upon all which, this court was fully satisfied that the now plaintiff received no penny of profits after the three first half years. But whether he ought to be charged with all that the said Thomas Forster received, being a co-trustee with him, in respect the said Forster is now declined in his estate (as is conceived), this court somewhat doubted and, although a precedent was produced wherein this court had charged parties trusted but only according to their several and respective receipts, and not one for the other, yet, in respect the defendant's counsel opposed the same, alleging many precedents to be on the other side.

And the Lord Keeper [LORD COVENTRY], conceived the case to be of great consequence and thought not fit to determine the same suddenly, but to advise thereof, and desired the lords, the judges, assistance to take the same into their serious considerations and to assist him with their advice therein, whereby some course might be settled that parties trusted might not be too much punished, lest it should dishearten men to take any trust, which would be inconvenient on the one side, nor that too much liberty should be given to parties trusted, lest they should be emboldened to break the trust imposed on them, and so be as much prejudicial on the other side. And the Lord Keeper [LORD COVENTRY] and the lords the judges assistants afterwards conferring together and upon mature deliberation concerning the case, to be of great importance, His Lordship was pleased to call unto him also Mr. Justice CROKE, Mr. Justice BERKELEY, and Mr. Justice CRAWLEY, for their assistance also in the same, and appointed precedents to be looked over, as well in this, as in other courts, if any could be found touching the point in question; whereupon several precedents were produced before them, some in this court and some in the Court of Wards, where parties trusted were chargeable only according to their several and respective receipts, and not one to answer for the other; but no precedent on the contrary was produced to them.

Whereupon His Lordship [LORD COVENTRY], after long and mature deliberation on the case and serious advice with all the said judges, did this day in open court declare the resolution of His Lordship and the said judges that, where lands or leases were conveyed to two or more upon trust, and one of them receives all or the most part of the profits, and after died or decayed in his estate, his co-trustees shall not be charged, or be compelled in this court, to answer for the receipts of him so dying or decayed, unless some purchase, fraud, or evil dealing appear to have been in them to prejudice their trust; for they being by law joint tenants or tenants in common, every one by law may receive either all or as much of the profits as he can come by and it being the case of most men in these days, that their personal estates do not suffice to pay their debts, prefer their children, and perform their wills, they are enforced to trust their friends with some part of their real estate, to make up the same, either by the sale or perception of profits; and if such of these friends, who carry themselves without fraud, should be chargeable out of their own estates for the faults and deficiencies of their co-trustees, who were not nominated by them, few men would undertake any such trust. And if two executors be and one of them waste all or any part of the estate, the *devastavit* shall by law charge him only, and not his co-executor; and in that case, *aequitas sequitur legem*, there having been many precedents resolved in this court that one executor shall not answer nor be charged for the act or default of his companion. And it is no breach of trust, to permit one of the trustees to receive all or the most part of the profits, it falling out many times that some of the trustees live far from the lands, and are put in trust out of other respects than to be troubled with the receipt of the profits.

But His Lordship [Lord Coventry] and the said judges were of opinion that, if two trustees were, and one of them without warrant of the party that trusts him, or of a court of equity, assigns his estate, and the assignee does receive the profits, and becomes non-solvent, he that made the assignment shall answer it for him, but the other original trustee shall answer for no more than what he receives himself, because the assign comes not in by him or his assent or appointment and that, in case, if the original trustee, that did not make the assignment, receive the whole profits, and become non-solvent, neither the assignor nor the assignee shall be answerable for them, and, if an obligation be made to two in trust and one of them release the whole debt, as, by law, he may, this shall not charge his companion for any part, and, albeit, in all presumption, this case has often happened, yet no precedent has been produced to His Lordship or the judges, that, in any such case, the co-trustee has been charged for the act or fault of his companion, and, therefore, it is to be presumed that the current and clear opinion has gone that he is not to be charged (it having not until of late been brought in question) in a case that, by all likelihood, has frequently happened. But His Lordship [Lord Coventry] and the said judges did resolve that, if, upon the proofs or circumstances, the court be satisfied, that there be *dolus malus* or any evil practice, fraud, or ill intent in him that permitted his companion to receive the whole profits, he may be charged though he received nothing.

And His Lordship [Lord Coventry] and the said judges did declare that, in this particular case, they did not find any material proof against Mr. Townley, to make his case worse than the general case aforesaid, but rather better, except only for the three half years rent, which he joined in acquittance with Mr. Forster, for the receipt of the profits alone by Mr. Forster is no breach of trust in Mr. Townley, and Mr. Challoner, when he came of full age, took Mr. Forster for his debtor. And, therefore, it is ordered and decreed, that so much of the said decree as charges Mr. Townley with any more of the profits than the three half years, for which he joined in acquittance, shall be reversed. But, as for those three half year's profits, if the same were not disbursed or employed for the use of Mr. Challoner, then, for so much thereof as has not been so disbursed or employed, the said complainant Mr. Townley ought to be answerable. And the defendant may call the plaintiff before Mr. Page, one of the Masters of this court, to audit the account touching these three half years, if any difference be thereabouts. And lastly, it is ordered, that the recognizances given on the plaintiff's part to perform the order of this court be discharged.

Croke Car. 312, 79 E.R. 872

Townley v. Chalenor
Upon a bill of review to reverse a decree there, the Lord Keeper [LORD COVENTRY] required the assistance of Justice JONES, by whom the decree was made, and of Justice HUTTON, Justice BERKELEY, Justice CRAWLEY, and myself [CROKE].

The case was that, Thomas Foster and Townley being assignees in trust of a lease to the benefit of Chaloner, an infant, Thomas Foster took all the profits, and was in arrear upon account £1500. And, being unable to satisfy, the question was whether Townley, agreeing to this assignment by sealing the counterpart thereof and joining with Foster in acquittances of the rents for a year and half (but never more meddled), shall be charged only for that wherein he had joined in the acquittances or for all the residue.

And it was resolved that Townley, being but a party intrusted, shall not be answerable for more than came to his hands, for it was the default of him who put them in trust to repose trust in one who was not able to pay and, he being the party trusted as well as Townley, Townley shall not be compellable to satisfy his defect. Wherefore, it was resolved that that part of the decree whereby he was charged to pay what Thomas Foster could not ought to be reversed.

145

Minn v. Hinton

(Ch. 1633)

A claim in a declaration must be pleaded with specificity.
The Court of Chancery does not have the equivalent of a bill of Middlesex.

Croke Car. 329, 79 E.R. 888

George Minn against Anthony Hynton, bailiff of the liberty of the Dean and Chapter of Westminster.

The plaintiff declares as Clerk of the Hanaper in an action upon the case. Whereas one Robert Treswell, 16th February, 4 Car. I [1629], was bound to him in an obligation of £100 which was not paid and whereas he, for the obtaining of the said debt, 12th March, 5 Car. I [1630], being Clerk of the Hanaper in Chancery, prosecuted an attachment of privilege directed to the Sheriff of Middlesex to attach his body, returnable 15 *Paschalis* in Chancery, *ad respondendum* the said George Minn *in placito transgressionis*, which writ he prosecuted *ea intentione* that the said Robert Treswell, so being arrested, upon his appearance, should put in good bail to answer him to his said bill by him to be put in for the recovery of his said debt upon the said obligation, which writ afterward, *viz.* 13th March, 5 Car. I [1630], was delivered to the sheriffs of Middlesex to execute and that they, the same day, directed their warrants under their seals to the bailiff of the liberty of the Dean and Chapter of Westminster to arrest him, which warrant, 14th March, 5 Car. I [1630], was delivered to the defendant, bailiff of the said liberty, to execute and that he, by virtue of the said warrant at Westminster, within the said liberty, upon the 25th March, 5 Car. I [1630], arrested the said Robert Treswell and had him in his custody and that, afterwards, before the return of the writ, *viz.* 8th April, 6 Car. I [1630], to delay the plaintiff of his suit and to defraud him of the recovery of his debt, let him out of his custody and to go at large against the plaintiff's will and had not his body at the day and that, afterward, *se eloinera*, and, because he is delayed in his suit and loses his debt etc.

The defendant pleads thereto that the said Robert Treswell found sureties for his appearance, Arthur Squibb and J.W., and, at the day of the return of the writ, the defendant returned *cepi corpus*, and that, before the habeas corpus to bring him to the bar, he the said Robert Treswell died. *Et hoc etc.*

The plaintiff replies that he did not take the said Arthur Squibb and J.W. sureties for his appearance *modo et forma*. And, hereupon, it was demurred.

And this was referred to Justice JONES, Justice BERKELEY, and to myself [CROKE] to consider of this demurrer. And, after argument by counsel on both sides, we resolved that this declaration was not good.

First, because he does not say of what liberty he is bailiff or whether he has execution and return of writs; otherwise, there is no color to charge him, and, therefore, it ought to be specially shown. And of this opinion was JONES. And I [CROKE] agreed with him. But BERKELEY doubted thereof, because, being bailiff of a liberty, it cannot be intended another liberty, and he admits it in his plea, by making him a warrant to arrest.

Secondly, because he alleges that he had an attachment of privilege to arrest him for trespass, intending after his appearance to declare in debt, which cannot be, for it is abusing the process of the court. Nor can it be so in any court but in the King's Bench, and, there, the reason is because, when he appears and puts in bail, he is supposed to be *in custodia mareschalli*, and [one] declares against him *in custodia etc.* But so it is not in any other court.

Wherefore they all held that the declaration for this cause was not good and that judgment ought to be against the plaintiff. And so we certified that the declaration was ill and the causes wherefore.

146

Jolly v. Anthill

(Ch. 1633)

A court can refer a matter back to arbitrators for them to consider further evidence and to amend their award.

British Library MS. Hargrave 174, f. 72v, pl. 2

Where the arbitrators, [who] by their own confession had exceeded their authority, erred in not doing according to their proofs unwittingly incurred,[1] the plaintiff had demanded their award of the defendant to [be] amend[ed] for the plaintiff's avail and right. The court referred it back to the arbitrators to review the pleadings and proofs, and [they] amended their award.

[Other copies of this report: British Library MS. Hargrave 99, f. 109, pl. 138.]

Lord Nottingham, *Prolegomena*, p. 306

6 July, 9 Car. I.

If any corruption in arbitrators or a refusal to hear the parties be suggested, the court will examine the suggestion and relieve against the submission bond, as by sending the parties back to the arbitrators, if they have not been fully heard, as was done.

[Order of 6 July 1633: Public Record Office C.33/163, f. 761v.]

147

Mayor of Bristol v. Whitson

(Ch. 1633–1634)

A devise of land for charitable purposes can be made to a municipal corporation.

---

[1] Sic in MS.

Herne & Duke 74

A man devises money to a charitable use to be bestowed amongst poor people and the other of his goods to be employed for such uses as his feoffees shall think fit. [It was] resolved by the Lord Keeper [LORD COVENTRY] and the certificate of two judges that although Bristol be a corporation, yet the devise to them is good.

[Other copies of this report: Tothill 33, 21 E.R. 115.]

Public Record Office C.33/166, f. 70

14 November 1633. Mayor, Burgesses, and Commonalty of the City of Bristol *et al.*, plaintiffs; Rachel Whitson, executrix of the will of John Whitson, *et al.*, defendants.

Upon the hearing of the matter this present day in the presence of counsel learned on both sides, the scope of the plaintiffs' bill being as well to discover the omissions out of the inventory exhibited by the executrix of some part of the estate, real and personal, of the testator and to have her pay in what is remaining in her hands and to yield a just and true account of the whole according to the trust in her reposed by the said testator as also to settle by decree the lands and tenements in question and such parts of the overplus, both of his real and personal estate, his debts, legacies, and funeral charges being satisfied and discharged for the maintenance of charitable uses according to a deed of feoffment made by the said John Whitson, deceased, of his said lands and in such sort as he himself by his last will and testament in writing has appointed and that the defects of and in the said deed, if any be, may be supplied in equity and the said overplus employed accordingly. And forasmuch as the said defendant, Mrs. Whitson, by her counsel, affirmed that she has been always ready to account and has set forth her account by her answer upon oath, the said plaintiff did offer no proof against the same, it is therefore ordered that the Right Reverend Father in God, George, lord bishop of Bristol (who is entreated by the Lord Keeper), Sir Robert Poyntz, Knight of the Bath, and Sir Gilbert Jones, doctor of the laws and chancellor of the said lord bishop, or any two of them shall have power to take the said Rachel's account wherein the £400 is to be allowed and made good to the overplus, which by her answer she would defalk as given her by the testator in his life time and also £107 more. And the said defendant Rachel is to deliver a schedule of all debts, bills, bonds, specialties, and mortgages unsatisfied and yet owing to the said estate and all counterbonds and other securities and annuities, debts, and legacies yet payable are to be looked unto and allowed by the said referees as shall be thought meet for the indemnity of the executrix. And likewise, the said commissioners shall take the account of such of the complainants as have intermeddled with any receipts of rents, profits, or other duties touching or concerning the estate of the said testator since his death. To the end that the overplus rehting in the hands of the defendant Rachel and resting in the hands of the complainants or any of them may be all put together that then two parts of the whole may be employed according to the will and appointment of the said testator. In taking of which accounts, the plaintiffs are to be allowed all sums of money, annuities, payments, and disbursements touching and concerning the execution of the said will as the said commissioners or any two of them shall conceive fit and reasonable and the residue remaining to be paid to be employed and disposed as aforesaid. And as touching the said other defendants and coheirs, his Lordship will be pleased to consider of the said will which is to be brought unto him with the case now vouched by Mr. Attorney General and thereupon will give further order herein as shall be fit.

Public Record Office C.33/166, f. 134

9 December 1633. Mayor, Burgesses, and Commonalty of the City of Bristol *et al.*, plaintiffs; Rachel Whitson, executor of the will of John Whitson, *et al.*, defendants.

Whereas, upon the hearing of this cause in open court the 14th of November last, the right honorable the Lord Keeper did then after long debate of the matter give some directions and settled some points in this cause but, as touching the surplusage of the testator's lands given by his will unto the said City of Bristol, his Lordship did then forebear finally to determine that point and wished that his Lordship should be attended with the will of the testator and a case then vouched by Mr. Attorney General, and accordingly his Lordship having been attended with the said will and case and with certain precedents made in cases of like nature and his Lordship having advisedly perused and considered of the same is doubtful whether the bequest of the testator, being so general as it is, be within the limitations or extent of the Statute of 43 Eliz. whereby his Lordship may have power to settle the same. And therefore, his Lordship does think fit, before he make a dispositive order herein, to have the advise of judges thereupon and, to that purpose, does order that Mr. Justice Hutton, Mr. Justice Jones, Mr. Justice Croke, and Mr. Justice Berkeley be attended herein, who are desired by the Lord Keeper to take this case into consideration and certify his Lordship their opinions therein whereupon his Lordship will give a final and settled order therein.

Public Record Office C.33/166, f. 338v

12 February 1634. Mayor, Burgesses, and Commonalty of Bristol *et al.*, plaintiffs; Rachel Whitson, executrix of the will of John Whitson, *et al.*, defendants.

Upon opening of the matter this present day by Mr. Attorney General, being of the plaintiff's counsel, in the presence of Sir John Finch, knight, the queen's attorney, being of the defendant's counsel, and upon the reading of an order of the 14th of November last taken upon the hearing of the cause and showing forth of a certificate thereupon made by the referees in this cause, it was alleged that the referees having taken the matter into consideration have certified the sum of £2400 and odd pounds to be in the hands of the defendant Rachel Whitson, which was humbly prayed may be brought into court and divided according to the intent of the former order, whereupon the defendants' counsel alleged that there are several mistakes in the certificate and the defendants have just exceptions thereunto which the defendants desire they may be heard, it is thereupon ordered that the defendants shall set down their exceptions in writing to the said certificate and within these two days present the same to his Lordship, who thereupon will be pleased to appoint a day for the hearing of counsel on both sides therein.

Public Record Office C.33/166, f. 297

20 February 1634. Mayor, Burgesses, and Commonalty of the City of Bristol *et al.*, plaintiffs; Rachel Whitson, executrix of the will of John Whitson, *et al.*, defendants.

Whereas, upon the hearing of this cause the 14th of November last, the taking of the defendant Rachel's account was referred unto the lord bishop of Bristol and others and whereas the said referees did make a certificate and returned the same into this court, the plaintiffs by their counsel moved the right honorable the Lord Keeper upon the same the 12th of this month desiring the £2400 and odd pounds certified to be in the hands of the defendant Rachel Whitson might be brought into court and divided according to the intent of the order upon hearing, but the defendants' counsel then alleging that there were several mistakes in the certificate and the defendant had just exceptions thereunto, it was ordered that the defendants should set down their exceptions in writing to the said certificate and within two days present the same unto his Lordship, who thereupon would be pleased to appoint a day for the hearing of counsel on both sides therein and the defendant having set down her exceptions in writing and presented the same unto his Lordship and his Lordship having considerately perused the same was pleased to appoint the solicitors on both sides to attend and accordingly Mr. Meredith, chamberlain of Bristol, on the behalf of the said plaintiffs, and Mr. Pester, on the behalf of the defendants, now attending and upon reading of the said certificate and the defendants' exceptions thereunto and hearing what could be alleged and offered on either side, his Lordship declared that as touching the money certified and confessed to be in the hands of the defendant Rachel, there is no color [?] but that ought to be paid in by her. And therefore, it is ordered and decreed that according to the order upon hearing, the defendant Mrs. Whitson shall upon Lady Day [25 March] next pay unto the plaintiffs two parts of the money so confessed to be in her hands to be divided according to the order upon hearing. But as touching the other points controverted and whereunto exceptions are taken, it is ordered that a commission be awarded unto the former referees to examine witnesses upon oath for the clearing of any the points so excepted unto. And for their better proceedings therein, it is ordered that the commissioners shall, as they shall see cause by virtue of the said commission, examine the said defendant Rachel upon oath to any points they shall think fit for the clearing of any doubts. But as touching Mr. Danvers's deed of mortgage for £200, for that the defendant pretends that, by the testator's private journal, it appears the money was received in the testator's life time and a great part of the books are written by one Haynam servant and cash keeper to the testator, who is now beyond the seas and can by his oath clear that point, his Lordship does order that the deciding of that point be respited until the said Haynam shall come over that he may be examined therein. And as touching the £270 mentioned in the certificate to be disbursed by the plaintiffs in repairing a house for poor children and the plaintiffs affirm the same reparations were put in hand by the testator in his life time, his Lordship declared for what was done by the testator in his life time and not paid for was a debt chargeable on him and so the same will rest on his executor, but the clearing of that point will also fall within the compass of the said commission to be examined. And lastly, whereby the order upon the hearing the plaintiffs are to be allowed all sums of money, annuities, payments, and disbursements touching and concerning the execution of the said will, as the commissioners or any two of them should conceive fit and reasonable and the residue remaining to be paid and to be employed and disposed as aforesaid, it was humbly prayed on the plaintiffs' behalf that, according to the intent of the said order, upon hearing, the ch rges expended by the plaintiff may be deducted out of the whole money so to be paid unto the plaintiffs by the said Rachel and the residue to be divided as aforesaid, his Lordship leaves the same to the consideration of the referees to do therein as they shall think just and fitting.

148

Meechett v. Bradshaw

(Ch. 1633–1634)

An assignment of a debt made bona fide cannot be reached or vacated by the creditors of the assignor after the subsequent bankruptcy of the assignor.

Nelson 22, 21 E.R. 779

9 Car. I [1633–341]. LORD COVENTRY.

The plaintiff was bound for the defendant in several sums of money, and, in order to indemnify him, the defendant, by letter of attorney, assigned to him several debts, and covenanted not to release the same or any part thereof. Afterwards, the defendant, being a tradesman, became a bankrupt, and the rest of his creditors came in and compounded and were paid out of the residue of his estate not assigned to the plaintiff by the letter of attorney as aforesaid.

Afterwards, the defendant intending to receive some of the money which he had assigned to the plaintiff before he had committed any act of bankruptcy and combining with some of the creditors who had compounded to share the money which he had assigned to the plaintiff, he exhibited his bill to be relieved and to have the letters of attorney confirmed.

And the court, being satisfied that the assignment was made *bona fide* and before any act of bankruptcy, did decree that the creditors who had compounded ought not to claim or have any share of the money or debts assigned and that the letters of attorney should be confirmed to the plaintiff against the defendant and all claiming under him.

149

Lake v. Prigeon

(Ch. 1633–1634)

A deputy register to a bishop cannot purchase his office.

Nelson 27, 21 E.R. 781

9 Car. I [1633–34]. Lord Coventry.

The defendant, being Register to the bishop of Lincoln, did for a sum of money grant the deputation thereof to the plaintiff for a certain term of years, who enjoyed the same for some time, but was turned out before the term expired. And the defendant, having got the agreement in writing, refused to deliver it to the plaintiff, so that he could have no remedy at law.

And, therefore, he exhibited his bill for relief here, to which the defendant demurred, and, for cause, set forth the Statute 5 & 6 Edw. VI, prohibiting the sale of any Office of Justice or the Deputation thereof.[1] And he averred that the office of Register concerned the administration of justice. And for that the plaintiff, by his bill, had confessed that he had given money or contracted for it contrary to the meaning of the Statute, therefore, he was disabled to execute the same.

And the demurrer was held good.

150

Rigault v. Clobery

(Ch. 1633–1634)

A prisoner in a debtor's prison can be given a day writ to go and give evidence to a commissioner in Chancery appointed to take an account.

---

[1] Stat. 5 & 6 Edw. VI, c. 16 (*SR*, IV, 151–152).

1 Chancery Reports 67, 21 E.R. 509

This cause, being a matter of account, was referred to commissioners to determine, which they could not do without the plaintiff's attendance. It was prayed that His Lordship would grant the plaintiff liberty to attend the said commissioners.

His Lordship [LORD COVENTRY] considered that he cannot grant any other than day writs, it being resolved by the judges that granting liberty to prisoners in execution by other writs is against the law. But His Lordship is content he shall from time to time have such and so many day writs as shall be needful for his attendance on the commissioners without paying any fees, either for the making or sealing of them.

[Reg. Lib. 9 Car. I, f. 730.]

151

Plomer v. Lady Plomer

(Ch. 1633–1634)

A husband is not liable for the torts of his estranged wife.

In this case, the debtor plaintiff was not held liable for the tort of the creditor defendant's daughter, who stole the money payable to the defendant at the time of payment.

1 Chancery Reports 68, 21 E.R. 509

The plaintiff bringing £100 to pay to the defendant, one Margaret Smith, the defendant's daughter, snatched £20 out of the £100, and went away therewith. The defendant would enforce the plaintiff to pay the said £20, pretending so much due to her by the plaintiff.

This court saw no cause to charge the plaintiff therewith, and, for that the said defendant Margaret Smith lives apart from her husband and has so done for many years and will not answer the plaintiff's bill, this court would not charge her husband with the said £20 in regard of their living apart, but that the said Margaret Smith ought to answer the same. And the court ordered that the defendant, Lady Plomer, should not take advantage against the plaintiff for the same, but expect until the plaintiff can recover the same from the said Margaret, and the plaintiff is to prosecute the said Margaret with process of contempt for her answer. And [the court] granted the plaintiff an injunction against the defendant.

[Reg. Lib. 9 Car. I, f. 457.]

152

Lake v. Philips

(Ch. 1633–1637)

Where co-defendants plead a privilege to be sued in another court, all of the defendants must be so privileged.
Parol evidence is inadmissible to vary the terms of a deed.

1 Chancery Reports 69, 21 E.R. 509

The defendants have pleaded the privilege of the Court of Exchequer and that they ought not in respect thereof to be drawn to answer the plaintiff's bill in this court, albeit the constant precedents of this court were to the contrary.

This court ordered the defendants to show cause why the plea should not be overruled.

The defendants produced a precedent in 16 or 17 Eliz. [1573–75], Nott *contra* Hutton.

And the Lord Keeper [LORD COVENTRY] declared he had heretofore seen that precedent, but had also seen very many precedents in this court to the contrary. But however it were in point of precedent, yet the defendant's plea being insufficiently pleaded, therefore and for that neither by law nor by any precedent any more than only one plea is to be admitted to the jurisdiction of a court, therefore, in this case, the plea being insufficiently pleaded, the defendant ought to answer. Besides, this suit at the exhibiting of the bill was a joint suit against Sir Nicholas Fortescue, who for aught appearing, had no privilege in the Exchequer. And, though Sir Nicholas Fortescue being dead, yet, when the court was at the first duly and lawfully possessed of the plea, his death ought not to give any more privilege to the other defendants to draw the cause from this court than they should have had at the beginning or while he lived. And, therefore, His Lordship [LORD COVENTRY] does adjudge the defendant's plea to be insufficient, and he ordered the defendants to make a direct answer to the plaintiff's bill in this court.

[Reg. Lib. 9 Car. I, f. 135.]

1 Chancery Reports 110, 21 E.R. 522

Lake v. Philips and Lake.

Lands are by deed of trust expressly mentioned to be conveyed to the plaintiff. But the defendant produced proofs that it was intended the plaintiff should not have power to alienate, which this court would not regard in respect that the proof was contrary to the said deed of trust and that it carried no probability, the feoffees being enjoined by the said deed to convey to the plaintiff, which goes beyond all testimony. And [the court] decreed the premises to be conveyed to the plaintiff.

[Reg. Lib. 12 Car. I, f. 418.]

153

Kennedy v. Lady Vanlore

(Ch. 1633–1634)

In this case, the plaintiff's suit was barred by former decrees of the court and by the Statute of Limitations.

1 Chancery Reports 70, 21 E.R. 510

This case is upon a plea and demurrer, *viz.* that the plaintiff, by his first bill, pretending that Sir John Kennedy, his brother, had transferred his right in equity, touching the lands in question to him, and prayed relief in equity against Ferrers, Gosson, and Johnson, who sold the said lands by virtue of the decree of this court, and against Sir Peter Vanlore,[1] who purchased the said lands, which bill, in October 19 Jac. [1621], was dismissed. After which, Sir John Kennedy being dead, and the plaintiff insisted himself to be relieved, both by the said deed and as heir and administrator to his said brother, did 21 Jac. [1623–24] exhibit his bill against the said Sir Peter Vanlore in his lifetime to be relieved for the said lands or the overplus of the value thereof. To which bill the said Sir Peter put in his plea and demurrer, setting forth the several orders and decrees touching the same and the purchase and consideration by him paid, being £10,000, for a reversion depending upon the life of the Lady Ewer, which plea and demurrer was reported insufficient by a Master of this court.

Yet, at the arguing of the same afterwards in this court, the said plea and demurrer was 25 February 22 Jac. [1625] adjudged sufficient and the bill dismissed, and the dismission was signed and enrolled. After which the said Sir Peter by deed, 3 Car. [1627–28], conveyed the said lands to the defendant, the Lady Vanlore, his wife, during her widowhood, and after to his children and grandchildren, many of them infants, and after[wards] he died.

After which the plaintiff exhibited another bill against the said Lady Vanlore and Sir Edward Powell for the aforesaid lands and also two mills, and [for] fifty acres of meadow, which the plaintiff insists was not in Sir Peter Vanlore's purchase made from Ferrers, Gosson, and Johnson, and also for £2000, which the plaintiff insists that the said Sir Peter did not pay of his purchase money, which is still in Sir Peter's hands. To which bill the said defendants pleaded and demurred as aforesaid, and the Master again reported the same insufficient; yet the court again adjudged the same sufficient, and dismissed the bill.

Since which, the plaintiff exhibited a new bill against the defendants and the children and grandchildren of the said Sir Peter for the said lands, mills, meadow, and the £2000. To which they pleaded as before. And the Master reported

---

[1] V. Larminie, 'Vanlore, Sir Peter (c. 1547–1627)', *Oxford Dictionary of National Biography*, vol. 56, pp. 122–123.

the same insufficient. And, thereupon, the cause was debated and heard at large. And, the first day of June, an order was made reciting the whole substance and progress of all the business and proceedings in this court touching the said lands at Tunbridge, as well in the time of the now Lord Keeper, as in the times of His Lordship's predecessors, the Lord Ellesmere, Lord Verulam, and the Lord Bishop of Lincoln, by which it was then ordered that the plaintiff should by the first day of the last term produce precedents where this court has heretofore given relief for matters in equity mentioned in orders before any judicial order and decree made for recovery thereof and also to search whether the decree mentioned in the said order were signed and enrolled and show what matter he could for maintaining this bill.

The main points now insisted on by the plaintiff to maintain his bill were that Sir Peter Vanlore was no party to the suit between Sir John Kennedy and the feoffee and that Sir Peter came in and purchased *pendente lite* and that the lands were not sold at a full value as they were then worth at the time of the sale and that the said Lord Ellesmere was not acquainted with the purchasers according to the intention of the former orders and that the decree whereupon the said sale was grounded was after[wards] reversed and that, upon a hearing before the late Lord Chancellor Bacon, being then assisted by the Lord Chief Justice of the Common Pleas and Mr. Justice Dodderidge, the court was of opinion that Sir Peter should have his money again, but not the whole benefit of his bargain. And, therefore, it was then decreed that Sir John Kennedy should pay as well the said £10,000 purchase money as also so much as Sir Peter paid to the said Lady Ewer for the possession with interest within a year following or else the lands were decreed to the said Vanlore, which decree not being drawn up and enrolled, a commission was ordered to issue to survey the said lands and Sir Peter to be paid what he was out of purse with interest, either by some part of the lands or money. And the plaintiff also insisted that the said lands were worth £1200 *per annum* and that Sir Peter paid but £10,000 for the same and many other reasons were offered by the plaintiff for maintenance of the said bill.

But His Lordship [LORD COVENTRY], having heard the matter debated at large and advisedly considered of the orders which were made in the times of his predecessors, does find that, because the Lord Ellesmere, who decreed the lands to be sold, did by his order provide that His Lordship should be made acquainted with the sale and purchasers that the lands might not be sold at an under value and because there is no notice made to appear, therefore, it is alleged that the purchasers came in *pendente lite*, whereas, by order of 4 December 13 Jac. [1615], that because the order for sale of the lands was not an absolute order and decree, the purchasers would not deal, and then the Lord Ellesmere made the said order an absolute decree, and, thereupon, the said lands were sold to the said Sir Peter, upon which His Lordship conceives that the Lord Ellesmere took notice of the sale and purchasers. And this court finds that the Lord Bacon undertook the cause as an arbitrator only, and awarded Sir John Kennedy to pay Sir Peter

£17,000 or else Sir Peter to enjoy the said lands, which arbitrament not taking by Sir John Kennedy, the matter was heard in open court again, and, the Lord Bacon being assisted with the judges aforesaid, it was decreed that Sir John Kennedy should pay to Sir Peter Vanlore his money with interest in a year or else the estate of Sir Peter was thereby decreed. Which decree Sir John Kennedy did not draw up nor enroll. And the said Sir Peter conceived he had no cause to do it. And this court finds by the order of 23 January 17 Jac. [1619] by which Sir Peter was to take a proportion of land for his money, upon a survey to be taken, was made by the said Lord Bacon alone without consultation had with the judges, who assisted His Lordship formerly, and was repugnant to the decree made by the court, assisted as aforesaid, without a bill of review. And so this court sees no cause why the said latter order should be any ways binding.

This court, therefore, in regard of the decrees and dismissions aforesaid and in regard the defendants claim under Sir Peter Vanlore and have had so long possession and he claimed as a purchaser for valuable considerations by the decrees of this court and his estate established by so many decrees as aforesaid and for that the mills and fifty acres of meadow which the plaintiff claims, pretending they are comprised in the general words of the original conveyance under which the plaintiff claims, it sufficiently appears that the same were not comprised in the said plaintiff's conveyance, but were conveyed upon a second purchase thereof made by Sir Peter of the Lady Hunsdon for valuable considerations. And for the main purchase, the same was but a reversion depending upon a contingency. And, if the Lady Ewer had lived as by course of nature she might, the said Vanlore had had a very near bargain. And, besides, this court does conceive that it stands with the rule of justice that, if lands be bought in reversion expectant upon death and the tenant for life die, a purchaser by the decree of this court, after such proceedings, as aforesaid, shall not then be drawn to take his money again with interest notwithstanding the pretense of *pendente lite* and that this suit is not well brought. And, as for the £2000, if it were not paid by Sir Peter to the said Ferrers etc., it is barred by the Statute of Limitations.[1]

[Reg. Lib. 9 Car. I, f. 193.]

154

Anonymous

(Ch. 1634)

A bequest of chattels is a gift of only those chattels in the testator's possession at the time when the will was made.

---

[1] Stat. 21 Jac. I, c. 16 (*SR*, IV, 1222–1223).

3 Swanston 400, 36 E.R. 924

Easter term 1634.

Mr. Andrew Gray, a bencher of the Inner Temple, having two daughters and having concluded a marriage for the eldest, gave unto her a moiety of all his goods and household stuff, and the other moiety to his other daughter, to have them after his death.

Those only pass which are in specie at the time of the gift. And, if any of them be lost, decayed, or changed, and others bought and brought in their place, they do not pass in law or equity.

155

Warreyn v. Eltham Inhabitants

(Ch. 1634)

Where land and a house are given to charitable uses, the lessee may use the timber thereon to keep the house in good repair but any other use of the timber is a waste for which the lessee is liable.

Court costs can be awarded for prosecuting a breach of a charitable trust before charity commissioners and for an appeal therefrom.

A lease of lands given to charitable uses at a rent that is less than the fair rental value is a breach of trust and may be declared void by charity commissioners; also, the charity commissioners can order such lessee to pay to the charity the full rental value of the land.

Herne & Duke 79

The case was thus. Land was given in the time of Henry VIII, being then of the value of £3 *per annum*, to the parishioners of Eltham [Kent] to repair the highways there. This land improves to be of the value of £11 *per annum*. Divers of the parishioners, being vestrymen there, demise this land and house upon it to Warreyn for fifty years at £3 rent *per annum*. Warreyn cuts down timber trees growing upon the land and repairs the house with part and sells and otherwise disposes of the residue and pays the £3 rent yearly, which is bestowed in repair of the highways. The commissioners decree Warreyn to pay damage for cutting down three trees and that his lease should be void and surrendered up to be cancelled and to pay the surplusage of the true value of the land as it was improved at the time of the lease for the time he enjoyed it and that divers of the parishioners, naming them particularly, should be trustees to the said land for the best profit of the charitable use and that such a number should enfeoff others of the parishioners to continue the number of the trustees by the decree appointed.

And upon Warreyn's appeal to the Lord Keeper [LORD COVENTRY], the decree of the commissioners was confirmed in all things, and [it was] resolved:

First, that the cutting down of the trees was a waste for which Warreyn should pay damages according to the value of them and bestowing but part upon the house, not being able to prove the quantity; it was fraud in him to color his disposing [of] the residue otherwise. But, if he had bestowed all or the greatest part of the trees in the repair, it had been no waste.

Second, it was resolved that commissioners may give costs to the party which prosecutes a commission to reform a breach of trust in a charitable use and the Lord Keeper may increase these costs if the party aggrieved complain without cause.

Third, the lease being made at an under value is a breach of trust and fraud to deceive the charitable use of the true value of the land. And the commissioners may decree the lease to be void and surrendered and that the lessee shall pay the true profits of the value of the charitable use above the rent reserved.

And lastly, the commissioners may by their decree enable persons, as trustees, to have [an] interest in the lands given to charitable uses and to demise the same according to the improved value.

156

Seymour v. Twyford Paupers

(Ch. 1634)

Interest is payable on money wrongfully detained from a charitable use.

Herne & Duke 80

Money was given to charitable uses and detained a long time as concealed. The commissioners upon the said Statute[1] decreed the money to be paid with interest after the rate of £8 *per centum*. And this decree was confirmed by the Lord Keeper [LORD COVENTRY].

So in the case of Lady Montagu of Ilford and the inhabitants of Barking in Essex, Sir Charles Montagu, her husband, gave by his will £10 to the poor of Barking and made his wife executrix and died; she kept the money above twelve years in her hands, and the commissioners decreed her to pay £20 for the detaining [of] this money, for use and principal; and Lord Keeper COVENTRY confirmed this decree about 12 Car. [1636–37].

Public Record Office C.33/166, f. 660

10 July 1634. Edward Seymour, Esq., plaintiff; Paupers of Twyford in the County of Southampton, defendants.

---

[1] Stat. 43 Eliz. I, c. 4 (*SR*, IV, 968–970).

The matter in question having received hearing in this court the last term in the presence of the counsel learned on both parts, it appeared that by inquisition taken at Winchester the 18th of June 9 Car. [1632] before Sir Henry Mildmay and others, commissioners by virtue of a commission to them directed upon the Statute of Charitable Uses when it was found by the oaths of twelve men that Sir John Seymour, knight, deceased, had in his hands the sum of £120 given by the late Queen Elizabeth as a stock towards the relief of the poor people of Twyford as appeared by his bond dated the 6th of November 32 Eliz. [1590] and that it had been detained forty years and more and that the plaintiff being his son and heir and administrator had assets left to the value of £2000 and that during all the time aforesaid, neither the said Sir John nor the now plaintiff did ever dispose of any the profits of the said £120 for the relief of the said poor people and therefore they assessed for damages £280, which was decreed accordingly, and that all the several sums of money, gifts, and stock of cattle mentioned in the said inquisition should be forthwith delivered to persons in trust in the decree named to be by them disposed of until some land might be bought with all or part thereof and that the whole profit thereof should be to the use of the said poor people and decreed further that the lands should be purchased in the name of Sir Henry Mildmay and seven others as feoffees to the use of the poor of the parish and that if it should happen that there should be but four of the feoffees living, then the survivors should elect four more that there might be a perpetual continuance of the use, which said decree being returned and of record in the Petty Bag, the plaintiff put in his exceptions to the said decree and the said defendants made answer to the said exceptions and witnesses were also examined thereupon and after debate had of the matter and the proofs and depositions of witnesses read in the cause, his Lordship did for the present forebear to give his final order and decree in this cause. But having since advisedly considered thereof and finding by the proofs made in the cause and the acquittances produced and read in court, amongst which the one was an acquittance under the hand of the late lord archbishop of Canterbury that the said Sir John Seymour did in his life time pay in £60 to the dean and chapter of Winchester to whom the said bond was made to the use of the said poor people, and his Lordship finding by the decree that the commissioners did allow damages as if the £120 principal had been still entire but nevertheless the commissioners had taxed the said dafages but at £280, which was but little more than the moiety of the damages from 32 Eliz. [1590] to this time and reckoning according to the several statutes of ten and eight *per centum* and therefore, there being £280 taxed by the commissioners, His Lordship [LORD COVENTRY] conceived the moiety thereof ought to be abated in respect the moiety of the principal was paid.

It is therefore ordered and decreed that the said plaintiff shall pay unto the said defendant the said £140 for damages and £60 for principal *in toto* £200 and for so much of the said overplus of the principal and damages, the decree of the court to stand reversed, but for all the rest, the same is hereby confirmed.

And it is further ordered that, upon payment of the said money, the said bond is to be delivered up unto the plaintiff to be cancelled.

157

Anonymous

(Ch. 1634)

Where a grantor gives the grantee the power to execute the conveyance to himself however he chooses, the first grant executed is the one that operates to effect the conveyance.

2 Rolle, Abr., *Uses*, pl. O, 5, p. 787

Michaelmas [term] 10 Car.

If a man, in consideration of natural affection and of money, give, grant, bargain, sell, enfeoff, and confirm land to B. in fee by a deed indented with a letter of attorney in the deed to make livery and the deed is afterwards enrolled within six months, it will pass as a bargain and sale notwithstanding the letter of attorney in the deed because the feoffor had given to the feoffee an election to execute the estate one way or the other and it is the way that first executed the estate that will stand.

[It was] said by Justice BERKELEY that he so held this same term in Chancery with the Lord Keeper [LORD COVENTRY].

158

Mauter v. Fotherby

(Ch. 1634–1635)

Where legacies are paid to adult legatees, the court can provide for a proportional repayment in case the decedent's estate is insufficient to pay the infant legatees their legacies when they come of age.

Nelson 25, 21 E.R. 780

10 Car. I [1634–35]. LORD COVENTRY.

Legacies were devised to be paid to children when they came to their several ages of twenty-one years.

Some of them who were of age applied to this court for their legacies, but the court being not satisfied whether the estate would be sufficient to discharge all the legacies to all the children, some of them having not then attained their ages of twenty-one years, did decree that those legatees who were of age should receive their respective legacies, but that they should make retribution respectively out of the same if the court should think fit so that the younger children who were not of age and who were to be paid last might have a proportionable part and share in case the estate should not be sufficient to answer the full of every legatee's part.

159

Hutchings v. Strode

(Ch. 1634–1635)

Where one purchases a manor with knowledge of a copyhold right in another person, he cannot destroy the copyhold by purchasing a prior lease of the same land.

Nelson 26, 21 E.R. 780

10 Car. I [1634–35]. Lord Coventry.

Sir Thomas Phillips, being seised, *inter alia*, of several parcels of land for which the plaintiff seeks relief, did *anno* 9 Jac. [1621–22] lease the same to certain persons for 500 years, and, afterwards, *viz. anno* 22 Jac. [1624–25], grant the same by copy of court roll to the plaintiff, who was admitted and paid a fine and held the same for lives. Afterwards, Strode, the defendant, purchased the manor house and the demesnes, and got the lease assigned to persons in trust for himself, and then claimed these lands as parcel of the demesnes, alleging that the copyhold estate was destroyed.

And the plaintiff claiming them as ancient copyhold, the court was of opinion that his grant being before the defendant Strode's purchase ought not to be prejudiced by the lease, especially if the same were ancient copyhold lands and not parcel of the demesnes.

However, the court directed a trial at law whether the lands were copyhold or not and the lease not to be given in evidence at the said trial. And there was a verdict that the lands were not copyhold. But it appearing to the court that the lands had been ancient copyhold lands and for that Sir Thomas Phillips, in a survey of the manor, had mentioned the same as parcel of the copyhold of the said manor and for that the plaintiff had for several years enjoyed the lands quietly as copyhold, notwithstanding the said lease, and it also appearing that the plaintiff's estate was known to the defendant at the time he purchased the demesnes and that he bought it but as an estate in reversion, therefore, the plaintiff was decreed to hold it according to his grant. And the defendant was ordered, notwithstanding the verdict, to pay good costs both here and at law.

160

Barnes's Case

(Ch. 1634)

A sole surviving executor of a will can act alone to administer the decedent's estate.

W. Jones 352, 82 E.R. 185

Michaelmas term 10 Car.

A case out of the Chancery was referred to Jones, Croke, and Berkeley. One Barnes was seised in fee of lands in Essex, and he devised them to his wife for life and that, after the death of his wife, [they were] to be sold by his executors for the payment of his debts and legacies, and he made two executors. And he died. One of the executors died; the wife died. And the question was whether the surviving executor could sell.

And the three justices certified the Lord Keeper [Lord Coventry] under their hands that, by the law, the executor could sell the land.

Vide 4 & 5 Eliz., Dyer, f. 219.[1]

161

Marsh v. Kirby

(Ch. 1634–1635)

In this case, the birth of a posthumous child defeated a remainder to remote devisees.

1 Chancery Reports 76, 21 E.R. 512

Julius Marsh, deceased, by his will, devised the rents, issues, and profits of all his messuages during his interest therein to his wife for life and, if she died before the expiration of his said interest, then the same to come amongst all his children equally and that his wife should not sell. And the said testator, conceiving his wife to be with child, devised to the child she then went with a lease of two houses. And he ordered a moiety of the profits thereof to be put out by the overseers of his will as a stock for the benefit of such child and the other moiety for her maintenance until age or marriage. And, by his will, farther, he declared that, if all his children should die before marriage or age of twenty-one years, then the premises devised to his children should remain to brothers' and sisters' children. And four of the testator's children died before marriage or the age of twenty-one years. And Alice, who was not born at the time of the testator's death, only is living.

This court, on reading the will, does conceive that the collateral line have nothing to do with the estate of the testator during the life of the said Alice, the daughter, and dismissed the plaintiff's bill.

[Reg. Lib. 10 Car. I, f. 253.]

---

[1] *Danne v. Annas* (1562), 2 Dyer 219, 73 E.R. 484.

162

Lake v. Lake

(Ch. 1634–1635)

The payment of a devise of a sum of money that was also charged by a deed on lands is a satisfaction of the charge, the devise and the charge being the same.

1 Chancery Reports 77, 21 E.R. 512

This case is touching a double portion. This court conceived the £500 was included in the will, though charged by deed on lands.

[Reg. Lib. 10 Car. I, f. 246.]

163

Coles v. Emerson

(Ch. 1634–1635)

A bond not sued on for a very long period of time will be deemed to have been paid off, and a court of equity will order it to be cancelled.

1 Chancery Reports 78, 21 E.R. 512

The bill is against a bond of £60 entered into in *anno* 1612 to pay £30 at nine days' end, which was never sued until now, although the defendant was always necessitous and a prisoner and the plaintiff a man of worth.

This court conceived the said money to be satisfied, it not being demanded in twenty-two years, and decreed the bond to be delivered up to be cancelled.

[Reg. Lib. 10 Car. I, f. 170.]

164

Carpenter v. Tucker

(Ch. 1634–1635)

A bond not sued on for a very long period of time will be deemed to have been paid off, and a court of equity will order it to be cancelled.

1 Chancery Reports 78, 21 E.R. 512

This case is touching a bond of £100 entered into 9 Jac. [1611–12] to Charles Tucker, deceased, which is twenty-two years since, which bond was left in the hands of one Orpwood, as a void bond, the money thereby payable being long since satisfied, as the plaintiff insists, forasmuch as the said bond is of such antiquity and the defendant Tucker's father, the obligee, lived until about seven or eight years past and never demanded the money nor had any interest therefor, and the bond is but lately come to the defendant Tucker's hands, who is his father's executor.

This court does conceive that the said bond has been satisfied, and ought not, either in equity or good conscience, after so long time, to be put in suit against the plaintiff, and decreed the same to be cancelled, and, if judgment be entered thereon, the same to be vacated.

[Reg. Lib. 10 Car. I, f. 228.]

165

Lady Savile v. Savile

(Ch. 1634–1635)

In this case, the court of equity enforced the local custom of succession to a decedent's personal property.

1 Chancery Reports 79, 21 E.R. 512

The bill is to discover the personal estate of Sir Henry Savil, deceased, late husband of the plaintiff Dame Mary, and to have her moiety of the same, according to the custom of the Province of York. It is observed that, when anyone living or dying within the said Province has a wife and no child at his death, being possessed of a personal estate of goods, they are to be equally divided into two parts, the one part whereof to the party dying without issue and the other part to his wife over and above her jewels and wearing apparel. And the plaintiff also prays relief against an assignment of certain mortgaged lands, unduly gotten from her husband a little before his death.

The Lord Keeper [LORD COVENTRY], after deliberate hearing of the matter and proofs, took time to advise touching the custom, and heard the counsel several times. And, having taken all the particulars of the cause into consideration and finding the demands to be great on both sides and the parties wholly submitting the same to His Lordship, His Lordship [LORD COVENTRY] decreed that the said defendant, John Savil, shall pay to the plaintiff the sum of £900 in full satisfaction of all demands upon the said bill.

Vide a late statute 4 William and Mary; this custom was altered.[1]

[Reg. Lib. 10 Car. I, f. 45.]

---

[1] Stat. 4 Will. & Mar., c. 2 (*SR*, VI, 372).

166

Revet v. Rowe

(Ch. 1634–1635)

In this case, the court of equity construed a will and ordered the distribution of a decedent's estate.

1 Chancery Reports 80, 21 E.R. 513

The case is that Sir John Hayward, being seised in fee of certain houses and lands in Tottenham, settled the same on his daughter Mary and the heirs of her body and, for default of such issue, the remainder to him the said Sir John Hayward. The said Mary, his daughter, married with the defendant, Sir Nicholas Rowe, and had issue by him, Mary, her daughter, and died, which said Mary, the granddaughter to Sir John Hayward, died without issue.

And so the said lands in Tottenham do belong to the defendant Sir Nicholas Rowe, as tenant by the curtesy of England. And the said Sir John Hayward, being seised of the reversion of the said lands and houses in Tottenham in fee to him and his heirs, by will, devised the same, if his grandchild died without issue, to his wife during her life, in case she should be alive after the curtesy determined and, after her decease or if he should not then be living, then to the plaintiff, being his only sister's eldest son, and to the heirs of his body. And he devised his lands in Felixtown in the County of Essex, both fee and copyhold, to his wife for life, and, after[wards], to the said Mary, his grandchild, and the heirs of her body, but, if she should die without heirs of her body, then the same to the plaintiff and to the heirs of his body. And he surrendered the said copyhold to the use of his will.

And the said Sir John Hayward, being possessed of a lease of a house in Great St. Bartholomew's, devised the same to his said grandchild Mary in case she should be then living at the time of his decease. Otherwise, he gave the same to the defendant Hanchet, whom he made sole executor, with a proviso, in case his grandchild should be living at the time of the said Sir John's decease, then, his executor should account to the said grandchild for the profits and rents of the said house, as to one moiety of the same, at the age of twenty-one years or marriage, and the said Hanchet to retain the other moiety to himself. And the said Sir John, having a mortgage of £1300 upon some lands in Kentish Town, desired in his will that his executor should purchase the same out of the residue of his estate. And then he did give the same to his said grandchild and the heirs of her body. And, thereby, he also desired his executor to apply the profits thereof to the performance of his will and for the benefit of his said grandchild, and account to her for the same at the age of twenty-one or marriage, retaining £20 *per annum* for his pains therein. And, if his said grandchild Mary died without heirs of her body, then he devised the same to the plaintiff and the heirs of his body, and the account thereof to be made to him the said plaintiff or his heirs. But, in case the said purchase should not be made, then his executor should take the said £1300 and apply the same for the benefit of the said grandchild, and be accountable to her for it at the age of twenty-one or marriage, reckoning himself 20 marks *per annum* for his pains, and, if she died before marriage, then he devised the said money and profits to such uses as in his will. And he gave all his books and a moiety of the residue of his goods and chattels and debts to his said grandchild, in case she should be married, and the other moiety to the plaintiff. And, soon after, the said Sir John Hayward died.

And the said Hanchet, his executor, possessed himself of the said £1300 as also of the books and other personal estate of Sir John. Since which time, the said Mary, the grandchild, died before her marriage or twenty-one years of age, by reason whereof and of the said will, the plaintiff claims the deeds and writings of Tottenham and Felixtown as also the moiety of the rents and profits of the house in St. Bartholomew's, which ought to have been accounted for to the said grandchild, and also the £1300 on the mortgage and the profits thereof, as also the books and moiety of the residue of the other goods, chattels, and debts.

This court, assisted with judges, on perusal and due consideration had of the said will, are clear of opinion that £1300 and the profits thereof since the death of the said grandchild, as also the books and residue of the goods, chattels, and debts of the said Sir John Hayward do in right and equity, according to the said will, belong to the plaintiff and that the lease of the house of St. Bartholomew's belongs to the defendant Hanchet, the executor. And they decreed accordingly.

[Reg. Lib. 10 Car. I, f. 405.]

167

Nott v. Smithies

(Ch. 1634–1635)

A testamentary gift that is in violation of a local custom is void and unenforceable.

1 Chancery Reports 84, 21 E.R. 514

The suit is to have a proportionable part of a lease and the profits thereof, according to the custom of the City of London, which the testator, Edward Sewster, the plaintiff's father, by his will, has directed the defendants, Smithies, his executors, to convey the same to the defendants, George and Edward Sewster, his sons.

This court, on reading the deed made to the said executor, whereby it appeared it was in trust to the use of the last will of the said testator, declared that the said deed of trust made to the said executor is contrary to and against the custom of London and that the plaintiff Elizabeth, being a daughter, ought according to the custom to have her part of the said lease and profits thereof.

1 Equity Cases Abr. 152, 21 E.R. 951

If a freeman of London makes a deed of trust of a term for years to the use of his will, and he, by will, declares it to J.S., this deed and declaration will be void, being against the custom.

[Reg. Lib. 10 Car. I, f. 402.]

168

Scott v. Wray

(Ch. 1634–1635)

Arbitrators can amend their award in order to explain their original intention.

1 Chancery Reports 84, 21 E.R. 514

The parties in this cause did refer the differences between them to arbitrators, who made their award, by which award, it was awarded that Roger Whittey should have such and such lands. And it was provided by the said award that, if any doubts arose, the arbitrators were to interpret and expound the same. The defendant Wray found a defect in the said award, *viz.* that the said Roger Whittey should have the said lands, and not that the said Roger Whittey and his heirs should have the said lands. So, it was insisted that the said Roger had but an estate for life. Whereupon three of the four arbitrators only living, by a writing under their hands and seals, did declare they meant the lands to the said Roger and his heirs forever and that the word heirs' was left out by a mistake. The said Roger, being in possession of the said lands, conveyed the same to the plaintiff Scott and his heirs.

The defendant, claiming by an old deed of entail, seeks to eject the plaintiff out of the premises.

This court, upon the perusal of the said award and explanation thereof and of the depositions of two of the said arbitrators, who are all that are living, who depose that it was intended that the said Roger and his heirs forever should have the land, considering that the award was long since made and executed on both parts, and His Lordship [LORD COVENTRY] calling to his assistance Mr. Justice CROKE and Mr. Justice CRAWLEY, two reverend judges, took their opinion touching the point in question for decreeing the said award and explanation thereupon, the arbitrament being voluntary and without the direction of this court, but executed on both sides, are all clear of opinion that this court ought in point of justice and equity to ratify and confirm the same by decree accordingly and that the plaintiff Scott and his heirs do enjoy the said lands against the defendants and all claiming etc., according to the said award and explanation as aforesaid.

[Reg. Lib. 10 Car. I, f. 348.]

169

Byat v. Pickering

(Ch. 1634–1635)

The universities have a privilege of suit among their members.

1 Chancery Reports 86, 21 E.R. 515

This court declared the privilege of the University of Cambridge ought to be maintained, and not to be infringed by this court.

[Reg. Lib. 10 Car. I, f. 767.]

170

Bates v. Micklethwait

(Ch. 1634–1635)

A bond bought by one person in another person's name is property owned by the purchaser.

1 Chancery Reports 86, 21 E.R. 515

Dr. Bates, by his will, appointed that his estate, being £2500, be divided into two parts, and he bequeathed one-half thereof to the plaintiff and the other to the plaintiff's son, an infant, out of which estate, £700 was in bonds taken in the said infant's name.

The question is whether the said money in the infant's name, as aforesaid, shall be accounted part of the testator's personal estate disposed by his will.

This court is of opinion that it is part of the personal estate, and to be divided as aforesaid.

[Reg. Lib. 10 Car. I, f. 869.]

171

Arundel v. Trevillian

(Ch. 1634–1635)

Marriage brokage bonds are void and unenforceable.

1 Chancery Reports 87, 21 E.R. 515

The plaintiff did enter into a bond or bill of £100 to the defendant, formerly promised by the plaintiff to the defendant for effecting a marriage between the plaintiff and Elizabeth, his now wife, which was effected accordingly.

But this court, utterly disliking the consideration whereupon the bill was given, the same being of dangerous consequence in precedents, upon reading precedents, wherein this court had given relief in the like cases against bonds of that nature and taking notice of other precedents of the like nature, thought it not fit to give any countenance unto specialties entered into upon such contracts, and decreed the said bill to be cancelled.

[Reg. Lib. 10 Car. I, f. 402.]

172

Geofrey v. Thorn

(Ch. 1634–1635)

A bond not sued on for a very long period of time will be deemed to have been paid off, and a court of equity will order it to be cancelled.

1 Chancery Reports 88, 21 E.R. 515

A bond of £300 penalty without a condition, entered into by the plaintiff to the defendant to save the defendant harmless against a bond of £200, the said bond being twenty-three years old and not sued in that time, [was] decreed to be delivered up to be cancelled.

[Reg. Lib. 10 Car. I, f. 590.]

173

Blackwell v. Redman

(Ch. 1634–1635)

Gambling debts are void and unenforceable.

1 Chancery Reports 88, 21 E.R. 515

The plaintiff, being a linen draper, was by the defendant drawn to play at dice at the house of the defendant Axtel. And the defendant Buller having won about £50 of the plaintiff, which was done by false dice, brought thither by the defendant Redman, the defendant Redman did lend to the plaintiff several sums of money, amounting in all to £40, which the said Buller likewise won from the plaintiff. The defendant Redman insists that he did dissuade the plaintiff from playing after he had lost the said £50, and was unwilling to lend him any money, yet the plaintiff importuned him, who after that gave a bill under his hand for the payment thereof in a few days, and yet, afterwards, got the said bill away from the defendant. And the same money lent to the plaintiff was money paid by the said Buller unto the plaintiff for a debt due unto him from Buller.

Yet it appearing that the said several sums so lent to the plaintiff by the defendant Redman was but the same money which the said Buller had formerly so won of the plaintiff and lent divers times over by the said Redman for the said Buller and all gotten again by the said Buller and it did not appear that the said Buller was really indebted to the said Redman in any sum nor that he did ever recover or had satisfaction for the said £40 from Redman, this court was of opinion that the said monies were unduly gotten from the plaintiff, who can have no remedy at law for the same against Buller, he being beyond the seas. And this court decreed a perpetual injunction against Redman's proceedings for the £40 and that the plaintiff shall be discharged from the said action for the £40 and of the said £40.

[Reg. Lib. 10 Car. I, f. 609.]

174

Arundel v. Arundel

(Ch. 1634–1635)

Where a deponent gives his direct testimony but dies before the cross-examination, the court can allow the deposition to be admitted into evidence.

1 Chancery Reports 90, 21 E.R. 516

A witness was examined for the plaintiff, and he was to be cross-examined for the defendant. But, before he could be cross-examined, he died, yet this court ordered his depositions to stand.

[Reg. Lib. 10 Car. I, f. 668.]

175

Caldwell v. Wheat

(Ch. 1634–1635)

An erroneous execution of a judgment by a judgment creditor's executors can be quashed by a court of equity.

1 Chancery Reports 90, 21 E.R. 516

The plaintiff became bound to one Critchlow in a recognizance of £600 for the payment of £300, upon which the said Critchlow took forth a [writ of] *levari facias* directed to the Sheriff of Middlesex to levy the said debt upon the lands and goods of the said plaintiff. Whereupon the Sheriff returned they had no lands nor goods. And, after[wards], Critchlow died. And the defendants being executors, without suing forth any *scire facias* upon the said judgment, took forth execution directed to the Sheriffs of London. And the plaintiff was taken in execution in London, and is a prisoner in the Fleet [Prison] upon the same.

Therefore, the said execution being illegally gotten and the plaintiff wrongfully imprisoned, it was prayed that a [writ of] *supersedeas* may be awarded to the Warden of the Fleet for the enlarging of the plaintiff.

This court referred it to the judges for their opinion, what, in a case of this nature, this court may do in law touching the granting of a *supersedeas* to the Warden of the Fleet for enlarging the plaintiff.

The judges are of opinion that the execution taken forth by the defendant against the plaintiff upon the recognizance does appear to be erroneous by the record, in regard no *scire facias* has been taken forth to the defendant. And therefore, according to the proceedings of other courts of justice, a *supersedeas* may be granted to discharge the said execution, which according to the said judges' opinion, this court granted accordingly for discharge of the said execution.

[Reg. Lib. 10 Car. I, ff. 319, 328, 400.]

176

Dymand v. Walton

(Ch. 1635)

Where a gift to a charitable purpose is fully performed, any surplus money will be disposed of by the court.

Lincoln's Inn MS. Hill 125, f. 19v, pl. 2

7 February 10 Car.

Houses were given to a charitable use, *viz.* to repair a church. The lands are of far greater value than will suffice. The court will dispose of the surplus.

177

St. John v. Wareham

(Ch. 1635)

The conveyance in issue in this case was an absolute purchase and not a mortgage.

73 Selden Soc. 202

16 June, 11 Car. I.

The defendants, for £3000, conveyed the lands to Sir Richard Grobham and his heirs. Sir Richard made a lease to Wareham, rendering to him and his heirs £230 *per annum*. And this lease was for seven years with a *nomine poenae*, distress, and clause of re-entry and a proviso that, if Wareham and his heirs should within seven years be desirous to re-purchase and signify the same to Sir Richard Grobham, his heirs, and assigns, and pay them £3000, then he and they to assure to Wareham.

Lord Coventry, Richardson, Chief Justice, and Croke decreed the money to the heir of Sir Richard Grobham, and not to the plaintiff, St. John, who was his executor, and justly, for this was not the case of a mortgage, but of an absolute purchase, for the proviso could not turn it to a mortgage. But it was a mere collateral agreement, for which there was no remedy in equity after the seven years.

[Other copies of this report: 3 Swanston 631, 36 E.R. 1001.]

178

Morris v. Darston

(Ch. 1635–1636)

In this case, a conveyance was construed according to the intent of the grantor, and an inconsistent provision was disregarded.

Nelson 30, 21 E.R. 781

11 Car. I [1635–36]. Lord Keeper Coventry.

One Curtis, the father of Margery, now the wife of the plaintiff Lambeth and who married one Price, her first husband, did in consideration of the said marriage and of a sum of money paid unto him by Price, the husband, settle certain lands on the said Price and Margery, his wife, for life, remainder upon the heirs of their two bodies lawfully to be begotten, remainder to the right heirs of the said Price forever.

Price, afterwards, settles the said lands upon the defendant Darston and his heirs in trust and for the use of himself for life, remainder to the heirs of his body, and, for want of such issue, to Margery and the heirs of her body, and for want of such issue, to the plaintiff Morris and the heirs male of his body, with several remainders over to other persons.

Price died without issue. And Margery, afterwards, married with the other plaintiff Lambeth, who exhibited his bill to have the premises reconveyed to him and his wife according to the uses limited in the last deed.

And, at the hearing, his counsel insisted that the limitation in that deed, *viz.* to Darston, the trustee, and his heirs with a remainder to the heirs of the body of Price was inserted only through the ignorance of the writer, for, if those words had been omitted (as they ought), then the plaintiff Margery would have an estate tail, as was intended by the said Price, her first husband, otherwise, she had but an estate for life, which she had before by the settlement of her father.

But the defendant's counsel insisted that the clause was inserted by Price on purpose to bar his widow from doing any act to prejudice those in remainder and for that Price was likely to have no issue by Margery and did, afterwards, die without issue.

It was decreed that she should have the lands for life, remainder to her issue if she should have any and that, if the plaintiff Lambeth should have any issue by her which should die, then he to be tenant by the curtesy and hold the same during his life. And a conveyance was directed to be drawn for that purpose and to bar Margery to prejudice the estates in remainder.

179

Town of Market Rasen v. Brownlow

(Ch. 1635–1636)

A charity, having a decree against several parcels of land, can levy the entire amount against any of the parcels, and, then, commissioners in Chancery can be appointed to determine the amount of contribution the other land owners must pay.

1 Chancery Reports 91, 21 E.R. 516

A decree upon the Statute of Charitable Uses[1] being made for the Town of Raisen and the defendant possessing some part of the lands which is liable to the payment of the money decreed, the defendant insists to pay but his proportion of the money, there being several other persons that have lands in their occupations chargeable with the said charitable use, yet the plaintiff lays the whole decree upon the defendant's lands.

This court declared that a decree being made on the behalf of the said town, the town may lay the whole upon any one they shall find liable to the payment thereof and that the defendant must pay the whole money decreed, which, when done, a commission shall issue to examine in whose possession any of the lands liable and chargeable with the money decreed and the commissioners to apportion each party's payment with such proportional part of the charges the defendant has been put to.

[Reg. Lib. 11 Car. I, f. 482.]

---

[1] Stat. 43 Eliz. I, c. 4 (*SR*, IV, 968–970).

180

Alisbury v. Troughton

(Ch. 1635–1636)

A party cannot be arrested in a civil case when he comes into court to put in a pleading.

1 Chancery Reports 92, 21 E.R. 517

The defendant was arrested at the plaintiff's suit as he came about putting in his answer, and was imprisoned. And, after[wards], several other actions charged upon him were all discharged, it being done in breach of the privilege of this court.

[Reg. Lib. 11 Car. I, ff. 23, 37, 46.]

181

Bidlake v. Lord Arundel

(Ch. 1635–1636)

In this case, the court presumed the purchase price for land to have been paid, the date for payment having been long since past, and the court enforced a bond for quiet enjoyment.

1 Chancery Reports 93, 21 E.R. 517

Matthew Arundel, seised of the rectory of Lowdiswel, 10 Eliz. [1567–68], demised the same to Philip Sture, grandfather of the plaintiff, and Richard Sture, the plaintiff's father, for their lives, remainder to Grace Sture, afterwards wife to William Newton, for her life at the rent of £14 *per annum*. And 34 Eliz. [1692], for £600, the said Arundel absolutely sold all the said premises to the said Richard Sture and his heirs with a warranty against him and his heirs. And, on 31 January 34 Eliz. [1692], the said Arundel entered into a recognizance of £1000 for quiet enjoyment.

And, afterwards, Richard Sture received the rents, and was the reputed owner thereof. And the inheritance descended to Philip Sture, his son, but the freehold rested in the said William Newton in the right of Grace, his wife. And they entered and paid the rent for divers years to the said Philip until he died, and, after his death, the rent was paid to the plaintiff until the said Grace died. Upon whose death, the defendant, the Lord Arundel, entered into the premises on the pretense of an entail on Sir Matthew Arundel and his heirs male by the gift of Queen Mary, the reversion remaining in the Crown. And, thereby, he would avoid the said conveyance, by which means the said recognizance became forfeited, the said rent of £14 not being paid since the payment of £600. And Sir Matthew Arundel, having sold divers lands subject to the said recognizance, made leases in trust to secure against the said recognizance. And yet, notwithstanding the said entail, the defendant offers to pay what money she can prove due to her or can make appear was duly paid by the said Richard Sture to the defendant's father, as this court shall adjudge, without insisting upon whether assets descended to him from his father or no, but to confirm the plaintiff's estate in the premises. The defendant refused, having made a lease of the premises for three lives, and so it is not in his power.

This court declared the said £600 was paid above forty years since, and the same is expressed in the indenture, and, after so long time, it is not to be expected that precise proof should be made of the payment thereof, but it is to be presumed it was a good payment. This court further declaring that, as this case now stands, this court cannot order the said premises to be settled with the plaintiff, nor the value thereof, neither can the court go beyond the penalty of the said recognizance.

But this court took time to consider farther on the case. And, now again, the court declared the case to be very hard on the plaintiff's part, yet, beyond the penalty of the recognizance, this court could not go, but wished the plaintiff to take a competent sum, which the plaintiff consenting to, His Lordship's decree for a final end of this cause was that the defendant should pay the plaintiff £850 in full discharge of the recognizance and of the plaintiff's claim to the premises.

[Reg. Lib. 11 Car. I, f. 349.]

182

Feltham v. Davy

(Ch. 1635–1636)

A plaintiff in an action to enforce a contract must prove the agreement in issue.

1 Chancery Reports 95, 21 E.R. 517

This court is of opinion that, the plaintiff having made no proof of the agreement in question, that the defendant's answer must be taken to be true, and so dismissed the bill.

[Reg. Lib. 11 Car. I, f. 519.]

183

Pope v. Day

(Ch. 1635–1636)

In this case, the Court of Chancery made an order contrary to a final judgment at common law where a lessee who was himself in default got a judgment on the lessors's bond and levied on the lessor's surety.

1 Chancery Reports 95, 21 E.R. 518

The plaintiff lets the defendant a lease at £3 *per annum* rent and to enter upon default of payment of the rent in twenty days. The plaintiff gives a bond for the defendant's quiet enjoyment of the premises and performing of the covenants. The defendant fails in the payment of his rent. The plaintiff enters. And the defendant sues the bond, and gets judgment, and takes the plaintiff's surety in execution, who pays the defendant £21.

This court ordered the defendant to repay the said £21 to the plaintiff.

[Reg. Lib. 11 Car. I, ff. 38, 40.]

184

Hartwell v. Ford

(Ch. 1635–1636)

The term 'lawful age' in a will means twenty-one years.

1 Chancery Reports 99, 21 E.R. 519

This case is touching a term of years of the premises in question, which the plaintiff claims as executor to Charity Ford, forasmuch as there arises a great question upon the will of Lionel Ford, whether the plaintiff as executor to Charity Ford, who made her will and died at the age of eighteen years, has right to the premises by virtue of the said will or whether the same belongs to the defendant Locket, who married Mary, the heir of William Ford, the eldest, which said defendant took administration of the goods of William Ford, the younger, brother to the said Charity unadministered or whether the same does belong to the sister's children of the said Lionel Ford or to some other, for that the said Lionel having given by his will the said lease and profits to the said Charity, his daughter, for a term in the said will expressed, he gave the residue and remainder of the said lease, after the said term given to the said Charity, to his son William, his executors, and assigns.

Now, the words of the will upon which the question arises are these, *viz.*:

> and, if it happen my daughter Charity to die before that she shall have accomplished the years of a lawful age, then the whole profits of the premises to remain and be wholly to William, my son, and, if my son William die before the like lawful age, then all the profits of the said premises to remain to Charity, my daughter, surviving, and, if the said Charity, my daughter, and William, my son, die before the like lawful age, as aforesaid, having no issue of their bodies lawfully hereafter to be begotten, then all the whole term of the said lease with the profits etc. I give and devise to all my sister's children to be equally divided and distributed amongst them.

Which said will His Lordship [LORD COVENTRY] and the judges having considered of and debated the case, the question arising in the case being whether the said Charity, who died at eighteen years of age, was to be deemed of full age, according to the words of the will and meaning of the testator, His Lordship [LORD COVENTRY] and the judges are of opinion that a lawful age in general words (unless it be in a particular case, as guardian in socage) must be construed and taken twenty-one years. And, therefore, are all of opinion that the said remaining term, according to the construction of the will, belongs neither to the plaintiff nor the defendant, but to all the sister's children of the said Lionel Ford.

[Reg. Lib. 11 Car. I, f. 341.]

185

Aynsworth v. Pollard

(Ch. 1635–1636)

A trust will not be enforced where the circumstances of its creation are suspicious and the proof of it is inadequate.

1 Chancery Reports 101, 21 E.R. 519

Thomas Hall deceased, having only one child, the plaintiff, made his will and three executors in trust for the use of the defendant Mary Pollard, whom he intended to have married. And, by his will, after debts and legacies, he gave the residue of his estate to his executors in trust for the said Mary Pollard. Two of the executors declared by their answer that the trust was for the said Mary Pollard, but the third executor declared he conceived the trust was for the plaintiff and that the said Hall declared no trust in him for the said Mary Pollard.

It being doubtful to which of them this trust is, it was referred to a judge, who certified.

He conceives that, in extremity, there is no trust proved according to the will, but it appearing that the said Mary Pollard was a lewd woman and had abused the said Hall, this court, in respect the trust was not proved according to the letter of the will, think it not fit to relieve the said Mary Pollard on her bill for the surplus of the said Hall's estate, this court much disliking that the estate of the said Hall should be given away from his own child to the said Mary Pollard, who has and had a husband living at the time of the said will. And the court dismissed Pollard's bill, this court, with the said judge, conceiving that, after debts, legacies, and executor's charges paid, the overplus of the estate should go and accrue to the plaintiff Aynsworth, the said Hall's only child. And the court decreed accordingly.

[Reg. Lib. 11 Car. I, f. 413.]

186
Woodward v. Huland
(Ch. 1636)

Bonds entered into in fraud of a marriage settlement are void and unenforceable.

Lord Nottingham, *Prolegomena*, pp. 259, 351

2 January, 11 Car. I.

The father draws his son into bonds just before marriage, and conceals those bonds from the wife's friends.

COVENTRY, Keeper, decreed the bonds to be delivered up or released.

187
Case of Sutton Colefield, Warwickshire
(Ch. 1636)

The evidence in a case before the charity commissioners can be heard by different commissioners from those who make the decree.

Where an endowment to charitable uses increases, the entire additional value is to be given to that charitable purpose.

If the first purchaser of land had no notice of a charitable use imposed on the land, then the land is discharged of the use, and it shall remain discharged in all the subsequent purchasers' hands, although they had notice of the use.

Where the visitors of a charity are the trustees also, the charity commissioners may reform any abuse of the charitable use.

Herne & Duke 82

First, it was resolved that it is not material that the commissioners who were present at the time the evidence was given and of the taking of the inquisition be present at the making of the decree, for if any or all of them are absent at the making of the decree who were present at the time of the taking of the inquisition and evidence, the decree is good, if it be made by four commissioners or more. And, if it appears by the return that the names of four commissioners were affixed to the inquisition and four other commissioners to the decree, all is good.

Secondly, [it was] resolved, if lands of the value of £3 *per annum* be given to maintain a schoolmaster and in the deed it is expressed that the said £3 shall be only employed to maintain that use and no other use is expressed in the deed and afterwards the land increases to a greater value, all the increased rent shall be employed for maintenance of that charitable use, because it does not appear that the donor had any intention that the profits of his land should be employed to any other use and, at the first, he gave so much as the land was worth.

Thirdly, [it was] resolved, if land given to [a] charitable use be sold for money to one that has notice of the use, this notice did make the land chargeable with the use in all other purchaser's hands, although the other purchasers had no notice of the use, because they take the land charged with other encumbrances as the first purchaser held, but, if the first purchaser had [no] notice of the use, then is the land discharged of the use, and it shall so remain in all the purchasers' hands, although they had notice of the use.

Fourthly, [it was] resolved, if land of the value of £3 *per annum* is given to a charitable use, which is paid accordingly, and afterwards the land increases to a better yearly value, if the increased value be not also paid to the charitable use, that is [a] breach of trust, which the commissioners may reform, if no other use of employment of the revenue be expressed in the donor's deed.

Fifthly, [it was] resolved, if land be given to a corporation or other particular persons to perform a charitable use and the donor appoint them visitors also of the use according to his intent, if the said visitors do break the trust, either in detaining part of the revenue, misemploying, or any other ways defrauding the charitable use, this may be restored by decree of the commissioners, notwithstanding the Statute of 43 Eliz.,[1] which disables commissioners to meddle with lands given to charitable uses where special visitors are appointed, for the intent of the Statute is to disable commissioners to meddle with such a case where the land is given to persons in trust to perform a charitable use and the donor appoint special visitors to see these trustees to perform the use according to his intent; if the trustees defraud the trust, the commissioners cannot meddle, but the visitors are to perform it; but, where the visitors are trustees also, there the commissioners may by their decree reform the abuse of the charitable use.

188

Newell v. Ward

(Ch. 1636–1637)

A subsequent purchaser takes the land subject to a prior devise of which he had knowledge.

Nelson 38, 21 E.R. 784

12 Car. I [1636–37]. Newell v. Ward and Brightmore.

One Ward, being seised of an estate in fee, devised £20 to the plaintiff's wife to be paid unto her at her age of twenty-one years. And he devised the said lands unto William Ward and his wife for life upon condition that the said William, his executors, administrators, or assigns should pay all his debts and legacies. And, after the decease of the said William Ward and his wife and the survivor of

---

[1] Stat. 43 Eliz. I, c. 4, s. 3 (*SR*, IV, 969).

them, then he devised the inheritance to their son Edmond Ward and the heirs of his body with several remainders over, and he made the said William Ward his executor, and he died.

Afterwards, he and his wife and son join in a conveyance of these lands to the defendant Brightmore. Then William Ward died, leaving no personal estate.

And, now, the plaintiff being of age and married to Newell, she and her husband exhibited a bill against the widow of William Ward and against the purchaser Brightmore for her legacy, alleging that the said purchased lands ought in equity to be liable to the payment thereof during the life of the widow, who confessed the will and the sale to the other defendant Brightmore, but that her husband left no assets and that she was neither executrix nor administratrix.

The other defendant Brightmore insisted that the lands were not liable to pay this legacy, because, by the limitation over to Edmond Ward and the heirs of his body after the death of his father and mother, the condition in the will was destroyed and, therefore, that a purchaser's estate was neither liable in law nor equity to pay the debts and legacies, although he had notice thereof.

But the court was of opinion that the lands were liable in equity. And, therefore, the purchaser was decreed to pay the same with damages and costs, and, when paid, he was to take his remedy against the other defendant, the widow, for the profits received, which the court declared were likewise liable to pay this legacy. And she was decreed to pay the same to the purchaser, for which purpose he was to have the benefit of this decree.

189

Greenhill v. Church

(Ch. 1636)

An arbitral award can be set aside by a court on the grounds of fraud or corruption.

3 Chancery Reports 88, 21 E.R. 737

11 February 1635[/36].

The bill was to be relieved against an award submitted to by the parties and bonds given to perform it.

The court declared they would neither confirm nor overthrow such awards, unless circumvention or corruption were proved, but, otherwise, if the award was made by order of the court.

190

Rex v. Cage

(Ch. 1636)

Whether an office to find whether a person was underage or not was properly taken by an escheator or not is a question of law and not a question of fact.

W. Jones 389, 82 E.R. 204

Easter term 12 Car.

The king brought a *scire facias* against Cage to repeal a special livery, in which the question was whether the King's Attorney [General] could aver against an office returned [into] the Petty Bag [that] it was not taken before the Escheator, but it was put in by another and to have it resolved.

The Lord Keeper [Lord Coventry] took the assistance of Jones, Croke, Crawley, and Berkeley.

And, after divers arguments at the bar in court, upon a private conference at Durham House, it was agreed and resolved by the Lord Keeper [LORD COVENTRY], JONES, CROKE, and BERKELEY that it could not be tried by a jury, but upon examination in court; if there was any such thing, it could be redressed.

CRAWLEY was of a contrary opinion. But, afterwards, he agreed to the first opinion.

And, upon this, the Lord Keeper [LORD COVENTRY] advised Mr. Attorney [General Bankes] to waive the former demurrer and to take issue upon the age of Cage, *scil.* whether he was of full age or underage.

191

Popham v. Lancaster

(Ch. 1636–1637)

A court of equity can settle the rents and taxes payable by the tenants to the lord of the manor.

1 Chancery Reports 96, 21 E.R. 518

The defendants, being tenants of the manor of Newby in the County of Westmoreland, held of the plaintiff, complain that the steward of the said manor sets too high a rate on their lands and tenements, and insist that their fines ought to be assessed according to the ancient rent after such proportion as had been used as the lord and tenants could agree. And they submit to this honorable court for their fines.

This court, finding there has been a variation of the fines, so as the same were not certain, and upon perusal of precedents by the defendants produced, and especially the case between Middleton and Jackson, 5 Car. I, before mentioned,[1] decreed that an improved year's value in a moderate way shall be given and accepted from the tenant to the lord for a fine.

[Reg. Lib. 12 Car. I, f. 477.]

192

Porter v. Emery

(Ch. 1636–1637)

In this case, the equity of redemption survived the reconveyance in issue, and came to the plaintiff.

1 Chancery Reports 97, 21 E.R. 518

Thomas Brett, 7 Jac. [1609–10], being seised in fee tail of the farm called Phelow, mortgaged the same to Thomas Emery, father of the defendant, for £300, 9 February 8 Jac. [1611], the said premises being then in lease to one Sacked. The said Brett granted the premises to Edward Emery and his heirs, brother of the said Thomas, in trust for the said Thomas. And the said Brett did thereby covenant at all times then after to make further assurance to the said Edward Emery, his heirs, and assigns, which assurance was made with the intent that the said Edward should immediately after reconvey the said premises to the said Brett and his heirs upon condition that, if the said Brett or his heirs or assigns should not pay the said £300 and interest at the time prefixed, then the said Edward might reenter. And the 10th of February, being the next day after, the said Edward sealed a reconveyance unto the said Brett with a covenant therein that, if the said Brett or his heirs or assigns did pay the said £300 and interest, according to the said condition, that then the said Edward should quit the premises.

And, in Easter term following, Brett suffered a recovery. And the said Brett, after the said conveyances so made and reconveyed, received the rents. And, about 13 Jac., Brett died. And, by a will, he bequeathed the premises to the plaintiff and his heirs, and desired the said Thomas Emery to release the said mortgage, the plaintiff paying him what money was due. And the said Edward Emery also died, and his estate descended unto the said Thomas Emery, who also died. And the defendant claims the premises as son and heir of the said Thomas, his father, and he purchased the interest also of the heir of the said Brett.

Now, the question being how the recovery suffered as aforesaid did work, whether only to the first conveyance made to the said Edward Emery or whether to the conveyance and reconveyance made to Thomas Brett, this court, with the assistance of the judges, declared that, in law and equity, the said recovery did

---

[1] *Middleton v. Jackson* (Ch. 1629–1630), see above, Case No. 74.

work and inure to the uses in the said reconveyance and that the benefit of the said redemption belonged to the plaintiff, and decreed the same accordingly.

[Reg. Lib. 12 Car. I, f. 475.]

193

Baldwin v. Procter

(Ch. 1636–1637)

A bond made many years before and not enforced will be barred by the creditor's laches.

1 Chancery Reports 102, 21 E.R. 520

The plaintiff Baldwin's suit is to be relieved against the defendant upon a statute of recognizance of £2000 entered into by John Colby, the defendant Colby's father, deceased, to Sir Francis Baldwin deceased, conditioned to pay an annuity of £140 *per annum* and another of £60 *per annum* to the said Sir Francis Baldwin and his Lady during their lives, which recognizance the plaintiff, as administrator of Sir Francis Baldwin, has extended upon lands descended unto the said defendant Colby for arrears of the annuity, and also to have the decree of this court for confirmation of the said extent.

This court would not relieve the plaintiff, but dismissed the bill.

And the defendant Colby's bill being to be relieved against the said extent and to have the said statute or recognizance and defeasance to be delivered up to be cancelled, it appearing to this court that the said recognizance was entered into 7 Jac. [1609–10] for payment of the money out of the lands which were sold by Colby, the father, for £3150, and that Sir Francis and his Lady joined in a fine with him in 12 Jac. [1614–15] and, at the same time, Colby, the father, purchased lands in Yorkshire in the name of the said Sir Francis, and the interest thereof continued in him until within four months of John Colby, the father's, death, to whom the said Sir Francis did then convey the same and, in all probability he would not have conveyed if the recognizance had not been discharged or if the said Yorkshire lands had continued in him as a security for the payment of the said annuities and it did not now appear that, after Colby, the father's, death, any part of the said annuities were paid to the said Sir Francis or, after Sir Francis's death, to his Lady and Sir Francis never extended the said statute in all that time and, though it appeared that the said annuities were often demanded of the relict of Colby, the father, and she desired to be forborne, which the plaintiff Baldwin insists was yielded unto, in respect the said relict was daughter-in-law to the Lady Baldwin, yet it also appeared, that, when the said Yorkshire lands were extended by a statute, junior to the recognizance in question and the said Mary, the relict, was instigated by the said Lady to set on foot the statute in question to save the lands from the junior extent, the said Mary, the relict, refused, affirming the same was satisfied by her husband, upon all which, this court was fully satisfied that the said statute or recognizance being so ancient and no payment proved of the annuities since the said re-assurance of the said Yorkshire lands from Sir Francis to Colby and the recognizance in all this time never set on foot until now by an administrator *de bonis non* and that the same was proffered to be delivered up for a small sum and for the rest of the reasons, as aforesaid, the same ought in all equity to be discharged, this court decreed that the defendant Baldwin do vacate the same.

[Reg. Lib. 12 Car. I, f. 222.]

194

Hales v. Hales

(Ch. 1636–1637)

After a very long period of time of no interest being paid or demanded, a court of equity will presume the debt to have been paid off and order the mortgage to be cancelled.

1 Chancery Reports 105, 21 E.R. 520

The suit is to be relieved against an ancient mortgage, which has slept sixty years, the plaintiff being a purchaser of the premises from Sir Edward Moor, who enjoyed the same about fifty-seven years. But the defendant Pett has set on foot an old sleeping mortgage, pretending [it] to be made by the said Sir Edward Moor to John Pett, father of the defendant, Thomas Pett, and his heirs of the premises in 20 Eliz. [1577–78] for security of £800.

Now, it appears that the said Pett, father of the defendant Thomas Pett, died forty years since, and, in all that time, there was never any interest paid or any demand at all upon the said mortgage until of late. And the defendant had confessed, as the plaintiff did prove, that all the mortgage money was paid and that, about five years since, the defendant offered for a small matter to release his claim in the premises unto Lettice Moor, the heir general of the said Sir Edward Moor.

And in respect the plaintiff and those whom he claims under have enjoyed the premises for sixty years last past, this court decreed the plaintiff and his heirs shall hold the premises in question against the defendant and all under him and that a *vacatur* be entered upon the enrollment of the said mortgage.

[Reg. Lib. 12 Car. I, f. 578.]

195

Dennis v. Nourse

(Ch. 1636–1637)

Where a bond debt was entered into many years before and the creditor was in possession of the debtor's land, a court of equity will presume the debt to have been paid off and order the bond to be cancelled.

1 Chancery Reports 106, 21 E.R. 521

A statute was entered into of £180 in 37 Eliz. [1594–95] to the defendant's father for a debt not yet satisfied.

The conusee held lands of the conusor several years, and, for other reasons, this court is clear of opinion that the said debt, if any ever were due upon the said statute, was fully satisfied and, therefore and in regard of the said statute's antiquity, that a *vacatur* be made thereof and it discharged.

[Reg. Lib. 12 Car. I, f. 475.]

196

Cole v. Peyson

(Ch. 1636–1637)

A life tenant can be forbidden to commit waste by cutting down trees and plowing up meadows and pastures.

1 Chancery Reports 106, 21 E.R. 521

The bill is to restrain the defendants, who are tenants for life, from the felling of timber trees and the plowing up of ancient meadow and pasture ground.

The defendants demurred for that, in the lease, the timber trees are not excepted in particular words. And they crave the judgment of the court if the timber trees do not pass in the grant as part of the said freehold.

This court, in regard the defendants have but an estate for their lives and in respect the defendants have cut good timber trees and cleaved them for fuel, granted the injunction to continue against the felling of timber and the plowing of ancient pasture.

[Reg. Lib. 12 Car. I, f. 485.]

197

Tryon v. Mitchell

(Ch. 1636–1637)

A debt merges into a judgment by confession, giving the debtor the defense of res judicata to a subsequent writ of extent to enforce the original debt.

1 Chancery Reports 107, 21 E.R. 521

The defendant entered into a bond to the plaintiff, which the defendant insists is paid by perception of the profit of Strelly Park taken by virtue of an extent for the king upon the said bond.

It now appearing to the court that, after the said bond was entered into and long before the said extent, the defendant gave the plaintiff a judgment for his said debt. Therefore, this court now declared that, in point of law, the said extent was void, because the bond did *transire in rem judicatam*. And yet nevertheless, if the said defendant would have proved that any profits had been taken by the said extent, this court would have relieved the defendant for the same. But, failing of such proof, this court ordered the defendant to pay the £100 on the said bond with damages.

[Reg. Lib. 12 Car. I, f. 228.]

198

Smith v. Smith

(Ch. 1636–1637)

A court of equity can compel the specific performance of a defective conveyance of copyhold lands.

1 Chancery Reports 108, 21 E.R. 521

This court declared that they would help a defect in a surrender.

[Reg. Lib. 12 Car. I, f. 99.]

199

Hayn v. Nelson

(Ch. 1636–1637)

The guardian of an infant's estate must account for his administration of it and pay interest.

1 Chancery Reports 108, 21 E.R. 521

The defendant, for any monies which he has put out belonging to the plaintiff as her orphanage money, shall account and pay interest after such rate as is allowed for orphanage money by the Court of Orphans and no more.

[Reg. Lib. 12 Car. I, f. 220.]

200

Southcot v. Southcot

(Ch. 1636–1637)

An old annuity in a marriage settlement that was not enforced for a long period of time will be barred by the defense of laches.

1 Chancery Reports 108, 21 E.R. 521

Thomas Southcot, the plaintiff's grandfather, being seised of lands and marrying Thomasin, the cousin and heir of Sir Peter Carew, who, upon that marriage, did convey the premises after his and his lady's death to the use of the said Thomas Southcot and his heirs. And, having by her three sons, George, the plaintiff's father, Thomas, and Peter, the said Thomasin died. After whose death, Thomas, the plaintiff's grandfather, married Elizabeth Fitz-Williams, by whom he had seven sons, which the defendant was one. After which, Thomas, the grandfather, for provision for his younger children, granted the annuity in question unto the defendant, being his second son by the second wife. After which Thomas, the grandfather, settled all the premises aforesaid, except the manor of Moon-Sattery, on the defendant and the other sons by the said Elizabeth to the disherison of the plaintiff's father, who was the eldest son of the said Thomas, who conveyed the said Moon-Sattery, charged with £300 *per annum* to the said Elizabeth, unto the defendant George.

And, after the death of Thomas, the grandfather, finding himself aggrieved by the disherison, he commenced a suit in the Court of Wards, which was referred and settled. Releases were sealed on both sides, and there was no mention of the said annuity. And it was not intended by Thomas, the grandfather, that he should have any benefit of the said annuity when he had conveyed all or the greatest part of his lands away from the plaintiff's father to him.

And the same having so rested and never questioned in all this time from 33 Eliz. [1590–91] until now of late and the point of the annuity is in reference from His Majesty to four of the Lords of the Council, wherefore and for that the said deed of annuity is an old sleeping deed newly started up after forty years, there is no cause to compel the plaintiff to bring in the said annuity, and [the court] granted an injunction for the staying of the suit at law for the said annuity.

[Reg. Lib. 12 Car. I, f. 198.]

201

Bracken v. Bentley

(Ch. 1636–1637)

A remainderman's administrator can require the life tenant of the goods to put up a bond as security for the delivery of the goods in due course.

1 Chancery Reports 110, 21 E.R. 522

Goods and a library [were given] to the defendant for life and, after, to the defendant's daughter and her heirs forever. The plaintiff married the daughter, who is since dead, so as the plaintiff, as administrator, seeks to compel the defendant to give security to deliver the goods to the plaintiff after the defendant's death or the value thereof.

This court decreed the same accordingly. And a commission is awarded to the Master to examine upon oath such witnesses as shall be produced before him.

[Reg. Lib. 12 Car. I, f. 388.]

1 Equity Cases Abr. 78, 21 E.R. 891

A. had the use of goods and a library for life, remainder to the plaintiff's wife, who was dead. But he, as her administrator, brought his bill to have the goods etc. secured to him after the death of A., which was decreed accordingly.

202

Mostian v. Nurse

(Ch. 1637)

Exceptions to the credibility of witnesses must be made in writing and filed with the court.

British Library MS. Harley 1576, f. 229, pl. 1, 2

If either party will question the credit of the other's witnesses, he shall first set down his exceptions in writing against those witnesses and acquaint the court therewith to give allowance of examination in that behalf as there shall be cause, and what is otherwise done is not to be allowed. And therefore [the] examination of [the] credit of [the] witnesses by Nurse, [the] defendant, against Mossan [was] disallowed.

If a bill be exhibited to be relieved against a mortgage and the mortgage [is] denied by answer and [the] plaintiff [is] put to [his] proof, [the] mortgagee shall not be allowed costs.

[Orders of 27 April and 7 June 1637: Public Record Office C.33/172, ff. 221v, 333.]

203

Sambroke v. Ramsey

(Ch. 1637)

A person is bound by a trust imposed upon and accepted by his ancestor.

British Library MS. Harley 1576, f. 233v, pl. 2

The father, in his sickness being seised of lands in fee, imposes by word a trust on John Ramsey, his heir apparent, to pay to his son George £200 for a portion. And [he] dies leaving the lands to descend and no other portion to his son George, but John promised the father to pay the portion. John refusing to pay, George exhibits his bill against him, and there was made a decretal order that John should pay unless he showed cause the first day etc., before which day, John dies and leaves the lands to Roger as his heir. George revives the suit against Roger. George died; the plaintiff, his executor, revives the suit again.

The Lord Keeper [LORD COVENTRY] declared that the ancestor's promise binds not the heir without a bond wherein the heir is named but, the lands being left to the plaintiff[1] with a trust to pay the £200, decreed that the defendant pay the £200 with the damages.

[Orders of 27 October and 3, 9, and 15 November 1637: Public Record Office C.33/174, ff. 45v, 60v, 197v, 229v.]

204

Wiseman v. Capel

(Ch. 1637)

Where an executor contracts to sell the decedent's land and dies before making a conveyance, the executor's administrator will not be compelled to specifically perform the contract.

Where a joint tenant sells his interest and dies before making a conveyance, the surviving joint tenant will not be bound by it.

Where a husband is possessed of a lease in the right of his wife and he contracts to assign it to another and dies before he does it, this will not bind his widow.

1 Rolle, Abr., *Chancerie*, pl. U, 1, 2, p. 380

If a man, possessed of a lease for years as executor to J.D., agrees for good consideration to convey it to J.S. and, afterwards, he dies before he does it intestate and, then J.N. takes letters of administration of the goods of the first testator, he is not liable in equity to convey it according to the agreement of the executor though

---

[1] Sic in MS.

the executor, during his time, had the power to dispose of it at his pleasure because the administrator comes paramount to this agreement and he is to dispose if for the soul and for the payment of the debts of the first testator.

Easter [term] 13 *Caroli* in Chancery between Sir Gamliel Capell, defendant, at the suit of Sir Robert Wiseman, decreed by the Lord Keeper [LORD COVENTRY], he having the opinion of Justice JONES, BERKELEY, and CRAWLEY in the same case, as he said, their opinions being accordingly.

Thus, if two joint tenants are of a lease for years and one agrees to assign his moiety and he dies before he does it, this agreement will not bind the survivor in equity because he comes paramount to the agreement.

Easter [term] 13 *Caroli* in Chancery in the said case of Wiseman, agreed by the Lord Keeper [LORD COVENTRY], and he said that it was also the opinion of the three judges, and he said also that so was their opinion that, if a husband be possessed of a term in the right of his wife and he agrees to assign it to another and he dies before he does it, this will not bind his wife in equity.

205

Ireland v. Payne

(Ch. 1637)

A trust of a lease cannot be entailed.

Pollexfen 25, 86 E.R. 500

12 October 13 Car. I.

The term was thus limited, as to one moiety, to Elizabeth Godden, and the other moiety to John Ireland and Joan Godden for so many years of the term as Elizabeth Godden shall live, and, after her death, the whole premises to remain to John Ireland and Joan Godden and to the children of their bodies to be begotten for the residue of the term. Afterwards, John Ireland and Joan Godden intermarry, and have issue of their bodies, Joan. And then John Ireland died, and Joan, his relict, intermarried Humphrey Payne, and, afterwards, died without other issue.

The question was whether Joan Ireland, the daughter, has any and what estate by this trust.

The Lord Keeper [LORD COVENTRY], assisted with two judges, did all of them declare that there was no entail in law of the lease and that Joan Ireland, the daughter, had no joint estate with her mother therein. And, therefore, the bill was dismissed.

1 Chancery Reports 111, 21 E.R. 522

Elizabeth Godden, being possessed of a lease of 100 years, by her deed dated 7 August 2 Car. I [1626], in consideration of a marriage between John Ireland, the plaintiff's father, and Joan Godden, daughter of the said Elizabeth, did assign all her remaining term in the premises to Thomas Ireland, the plaintiff's guardian, and Walter Noble in trust, *viz.* the one moiety of the said premises to the use of the said Elizabeth Godden for so many years of the term as she should live and the other moiety to the use of John Ireland and Joan Godden for so many years of the term as the said Elizabeth Godden should live and, after the decease of the said Elizabeth, the whole premises to come to John Ireland and Joan Godden and to the children of their bodies to be begotten for all the residue of the said term of 100 years. And shortly after the sealing of the said last deed, John Ireland and Joan Godden intermarried, and had issue the plaintiff. And the said John Ireland afterwards died. And the defendant afterwards intermarried with the defendant Pain and afterwards died, having no other issue than the plaintiff, who ought to enjoy the said lease for the remaining term.

This court, upon consideration of the assignment and the uses therein and with the assistance of the judges, did now declare that they were all of opinion that there was no entail in law of the said lease, neither had the plaintiff any joint estate with her mother therein, and so dismissed the plaintiff's bill.

[Reg. Lib. 13 Car. I, f. 21.]

206

Lewis v. Owen

(Ch. 1637)

New interrogatories can be exhibited for the examination of new witnesses at any time before publication of the evidence.

Dickens 6, 21 E.R. 168

7 November 1637.

The question was whether, after a joint commission was executed, new interrogatories might be exhibited to new witnesses.

The Master of the Rolls [DIGGES], upon a conference with the Lord Chancellor [LORD COVENTRY], was of opinion that new interrogatories might be exhibited into court for the examination of new witnesses at any time before publication, although there had been a joint commission executed.

207

Blackston v. Master of Hemsworth Hospital

(Ch. 1637)

Where rents from lands are given to a charitable use, the charity is entitled to receive the full value, even though the trustees made leases for less than the full rental value.

Herne & Duke 96

Robert Holgate, late archbishop of York,[1] by his will, dated 27 April 1555, did devise to Sir William Peters, etc., whom he made executor of his will, and their heirs divers houses and lands in Yorkshire to the intent to erect an hospital in Hemsworth [Yorkshire] for one master and twenty brethren and sisters to continue forever and directed an allowance to each of them, being about the then value of the lands and authorized his executors to sell his goods and divers of his lands and that the executors should keep no goods or profits besides their charges in their hands but bestow the same to the glory of God and the health of his soul. The surviving executors proved the will and became seised, and, 17 March 3 & 4 P. & M. [1557], renting a license to erect the said hospital, ordered a common seal, etc., settled 100 marks *per annum* upon the master and brethren, the lands being worth £500 *per annum*. The executor sold the lands, reserving only 100 marks *per annum* to the hospital.

[In] 11 Jac. [1613–14], the vicar and churchwardens of Hemsworth exhibited a bill in Chancery against such as had the lands. And upon the hearing, Sir Edward Philips, Master of the Rolls, increased the 100 marks *per annum* to £100, declaring that he did not conceive that the defendants' fines with proclamations barred the charity. Afterwards, the master, brethren, and sisters of the hospital, conceiving the former bill to be exhibited by practice, exhibited their bill against the possessors of the land and did set forth that the lands were given to the hospital and that, in breach of trust, the lands had been conveyed away in fee farm, reserving upon all but 100 marks *per annum* to the hospital.

The defendants answered and set forth their titles and claimed the lands, some by descents and others by conveyances and fines for valuable considerations.

The Lord Ellesmere and the judges declared that there had been an apparent breach of trust and that the hospital had been abused by being kept from what, by the donor, was meant unto them, *viz.* the land itself and not only a dry rent, being appointed by the donor for the good and benefit of the hospital. Neither did his Lordship conceive that the fines with proclamations ought to be a bar to the said charitable use and that all the purchasers claiming under the trust, which was broken, and there being a violent presumption that they had notice

---

[1] H. L. Parish, 'Holgate, Robert (1481/2–1555)', *Oxford Dictionary of National Biography*, vol. 27, pp. 641–643.

of the trusts, as well [as] that they that sold the said lands, could not make any title but by the will of the said archbishop, as also for that they did all pay rents to the said hospital.

And in 12 Car. I [1637], this matter came again in question before the Lord Keeper Coventry, who directed a commission to be awarded upon the Statute of Charitable Uses.[1]

The commissioners made a decree for the whole lands, to which exceptions were put in by one Brigg, who claimed under a purchase made by one Mr. Wymarke, who, pretending the crown was entitled to the lands, had obtained a patent thereof from Queen Elizabeth as concealed lands.

The Lord Keeper [LORD COVENTRY], assisted by Judge HUTTON, Judge JONES, and Judge BERKELEY (no color of proof being offered that the same were concealed lands, as His Lordship [said], but only the patent itself), His Lordship [LORD COVENTRY] did see no cause to give allowance to the patent to overthrow a charitable use. And His Lordship [LORD COVENTRY], having perused the evidences, confirmed the decree as to all but some chantry lands in the patent, which were not the archbishop's, and that the hospital should hold the lands forever. But, because the exceptant had laid out much money in building upon the hospital lands, he should have a lease for one-and-twenty years, at £120 *per annum* being above [the old rent of] £50 *per annum*, increase of what had been formerly paid to the hospital, the lands being above £150 *per annum* above the old rent of £70 *per annum* reserved to the hospital, and so would be worth £130 to the lessees above the rent which they should pay for it, and a lease was made accordingly.

[Later proceedings in this case: Chancery Repts. 1660–1673, Case No. 156.]

[Orders of 4 February and 22 May 1637: Public Record Office C.33/171, ff. 152, 161v, 352v.]

208

Sandys v. Blodwell

(Ch. 1637)

The Statute of Limitations period does not begin to run on an account until the account is closed.

W. Jones 401, 82 E.R. 210

Michaelmas term 13 Car.

A matter out of Chancery was referred to me [Jones], Croke, and Berkeley between George Sandys, K.B., and one Blodwell. An account was made between

---

[1] Stat. 43 Eliz. I, c. 4 (*SR*, IV, 968–970).

Freeman Sandys, testator, and one Blodwell, both being merchants, and the said Blodwell acknowledged £1200 to be in arrear; but Freeman claimed more. Before the entire account ended, Freeman died. His executor exhibited a bill in Chancery against Blodwell, and he pleaded in bar the Statute of Limitations.[1]

And we certified that it was not a bar because the account was not ended and also it was between merchants.

209

Robsart v. Turton

(Ch. 1637–1638)

A court of equity will specifically enforce a marriage settlement.

1 Chancery Reports 112, 21 E.R. 523

The plaintiffs seek relief for portions given them by the will of Arthur Robsart. This court, before they would make any decree, directed that the validity of the revocation of the deed of 15 Eliz. [1572–73] should be tried, whether a revocation or not, which, on a special verdict, was found no revocation. But the defendant produced a deed of 24 Eliz. [1581–82] made by the said Arthur Robsart, but without any seal thereunto, purporting a covenant for him and his heirs to stand seised after his death of a moiety of the premises to the use of the said Dorothy, his son's wife, for her life, and supposed to be made before his revocation, which deed of 24 Eliz. [1581–82] was to be produced to the plaintiff, who, having seen it, insisted it worked no alteration in the case as to the point of revocation.

This court, thereupon, referred the consideration of the said deed to three judges and that, if they certified that the said deed made no alteration as to the said revocation, then no trial should be had on that deed.

The said judges certified that Arthur Robsart, by the deed of the 15th Eliz. [1572–73], did limit to himself but an estate for life, with a remainder to Robert Robsart, the son, in tail, with several remainders over, but, by the proviso, he left to himself a power to alter the estates then settled, if he should afterwards grant any estate in fee simple or fee tail of those lands or any part thereof. And, afterwards, according to his power, the said Arthur conveyed an estate in fee simple by making a lease and grant of the reversion in fee, under which the plaintiff claims, which was the case already adjudged upon a special verdict, before which time this deed of 24 Eliz. [1581–82] was made by the said Arthur, and not mentioned in the former suit. But the said judges were of opinion that the said deed of 24 Eliz. [1581–82] intervening makes no alteration of the case to interrupt the power of revocation, for that it is but a covenant of Arthur's for him and his heirs to stand seised of one moiety of the lands to the use of the wife of the said Robert

---

[1] Stat. 21 Jac. I, c. 16 (*SR*, IV, 1222–1223).

for her life for her jointure, and meddles not at all with the estate of inheritance then in fee simple or fee tail, and so, being not pursuant to the power, it is of no force to that purpose which the defendant would extend it to make an interruption of the power of revocation.

This court decreed two parts of the said three parts to the plaintiff, according to the judge's certificate.

[Reg. Lib. 13 Car. I, ff. 94, 195, 247, 357.]

210

Wroughton v. Hubbart

(Ch. 1637–1638)

The question in this case was whether a certain fund could be reached by the creditors of an insolvent decedent.

1 Chancery Reports 114, 21 E.R. 523

Sir Giles Wroughton, the plaintiff, being seised of the manor of Broodlinton, sold the same to Glanvil for £8000, which £8000 was to be disposed of, *viz.* £2000 to pay Sir Giles's debts, £3000 put to interest for the benefit of Sir Giles and his Lady during their lives, to secure £240 *per annum* to them for their lives, and £500 apiece to be paid to the plaintiffs Katherine and Gresham at their marriage, and the £240 *per annum* to abate for so much as the interest of the portions came to from the time of payment, and the other £3000 to be at the disposition of the said Mr. Wroughton, the testator. And the sum of £3000 apiece was accordingly paid to the said Mr. Thomas Wroughton. And it was agreed that, if the said Sir Giles and his Lady die before the plaintiffs Katherine and Gresham were married, then they are to have £40 *per annum* for maintenance apiece until their marriage, and then the £500 apiece to be paid them. And the Lady Wroughton is since dead. And the said Thomas Wroughton, in March 12 Car. I [1636–37], made his will, and gave the plaintiffs Katherine and Gresham £500 apiece, and made the defendant executor, and he died. And, ever since the sale and agreement aforesaid, Sir Giles received the £240 *per annum* for the interest of the £3000. And, since Mr. Wroughton's death, for one-half, until June last, the defendant has refused to pay the same under pretense of the testator's debts and want of assets.

And, therefore, the plaintiffs, for the £240 *per annum* secured by the £3000, the security being in the said Thomas Wroughton's name, and to have the £500 apiece, have exhibited their bill.

The defendants insist that the testator died greatly indebted to several by statutes and other specialties and the testator's estate besides this £3000 will not satisfy his debts. And the creditors have a suit depending against the defendant for their debts. And Mary and Elizabeth, two of the testator's children, have a bill in this court for £400, which they claim out of the testator's estate as money given them by Mrs. Brown, their mother's aunt.

Now, the main point insisted on by the plaintiff was that, according to the original agreement, touching the £3000 to be put out at interest for Sir Giles and his Lady, [it] ought to remain entire, and not to be touched or impeached by any of the creditors.

[Reg. Lib. 13 Car. I, f. 219.]

211

Fermier v. Maund

(Ch. 1637–1638)

A court of equity can forbid waste by plowing up ancient pasture land.

1 Chancery Reports 116, 21 E.R. 524

This court would not give way to the plowing up of ancient pasture, although it was insisted on that the nature of the ground was for tillage and had been formerly plowed.

[Reg. Lib. 13 Car. I, f. 339.]

212

Lady Hatton v. Jay

(Ch. 1637–1638)

A court of equity will forbid the enforcement of a bond that was made a very long time before, even though payment was often demanded.

1 Chancery Reports 117, 21 E.R. 524

In regard of the antiquity of the statute of £500 wherein the Lord Cromwell was bound to John Jay, the defendant's father, was set on foot by the said defendant, as administrator to his said father, forty years after the entering therein, all the proceedings were stayed until cause [be] shown.

The defendant insists that the defendant's father forbore prosecution, for that Sir Edward Cook,[1] who purchased divers of the lands liable thereto, did from time to time promise to satisfy the said debt. And the defendant, since his father's death, which is eighteen years since, has often demanded of Sir Edward

---

[1] A. D. Boyer, 'Coke, Sir Edward (1552–1634)', *Oxford Dictionary of National Biography*, vol. 12, pp. 451–463.

Cook the said debt, which he promised to discharge. But failing, the defendant, ten years since, gave the statute to an attorney to take out execution thereon. And, until about two years past, he could not get the same out of his hands. And it appears by letters from the Lord Cromwell, all dated in the same month the statute bears date, that he importuned the defendant's father to lend the money on the statute.

This court ordered the plaintiffs to bring their bill to stay proceedings on the statute.

[Reg. Lib. 13 Car. I, f. 306.]

213

Palmer v. Keynell

(Ch. 1637–1638)

The terms of a marriage settlement will be specifically enforced by a court of equity.

1 Chancery Reports 118, 21 E.R. 524

The case is that, before the marriage between the defendant and Agnes, his late wife, grandmother of the plaintiffs, the defendant agreed that the said Agnes should after marriage by will or otherwise dispose of £500. And for the performance, the defendant gave a bond for £1000 that the said Agnes before her death appointed the said £500 to be disposed of amongst the plaintiffs, her grandchildren. But the said defendant procured his said wife Agnes to consent that the said bond should be cancelled. To be relieved notwithstanding was the plaintiff's suit.

And a decree was pronounced that the said £500 should be divided according to the said agreement of Agnes with interest, which decree was allowed by the Master of the Rolls [DIGGES].

But the Lord Keeper [LORD COVENTRY] refused to sign the same upon some point in law then seeming doubtful to His Lordship, which point being now debated, which, at the first hearing, was not insisted on, the substance thereof being that, upon releasing the said bond, the said defendant did sign a note of writing, that notwithstanding the said note was released, yet the said defendant would permit and suffer his said wife to dispose of the said £500, so as he might first be acquainted therewith, which note the defendant would avoid upon these words, *viz.* 'so as he might be first acquainted with it', which the defendant supposes to tie his agreement to a condition.

But this court, upon reading the said note, is satisfied that the same ought not to receive that construction, but to be binding to the defendant, and confirmed the first decree.

[Reg. Lib. 13 Car. I, f. 643.]

214

Mills v. Mills

(Ch. 1637–1638)

In this case, the terms of the trust in issue were specifically enforced.

1 Chancery Reports 119, 21 E.R. 525

This case is touching two leases, one of sixty and the other of 1000 years, of lands purchased by Roger Mills, father of the defendant Roger Mills, in the name of John Mills and the defendant Roger, his sons, which the said Roger claims by survivorship, John being dead, the inheritance thereof being in the said Roger, and after descended and came to John.

By the order [at] f. 409, it appears that Roger Mills, the plaintiff Elizabeth Mills's grandfather, she being daughter of John Mills, eldest son of the said Roger, having issue two sons as aforesaid, *viz.* John, his eldest, and Roger, his youngest, conveyed the lands to John, his eldest son, and the heirs male of his body and, for want of such issue, to the heirs female of the said John.

This court, as touching the two leases of sixty and 1000 years, upon reading the deed of uses, is of opinion and declared that the defendant Roger, the son, had no power to redeem the lands settled on the female heirs of the said John by payment of the £500 in the proviso of the said deed of uses mentioned, he having neither wife nor son. And, if he had such power, yet the non-payment of the £500 within the time limited, he having notice thereof, made the estate of the heir female absolute, and, therefore, the said lease ought to wait on the inheritance. And [the court] decreed accordingly.

[Reg. Lib. 13 Car. I, ff. 409, 606.]

215

Morgan v. Seymour

(Ch. 1637–1638)

A surety is entitled to contribution from co-sureties and to subrogation against the principal debtor.

1 Chancery Reports 120, 21 E.R. 525

The plaintiff with Sir Edward Seymour, the defendant, [was] bound with Sir William St. John for the proper debt of the said St. John to the defendant Rowland in a bond of £200 for the payment of £100. And the said Rowland sued the plaintiff only on the said bond.

The plaintiff seeks to have the said Seymour contribute and pay his part of the said debt and damages, the said St. John being insolvent.

This court was of opinion that the said Seymour ought to contribute and pay one moiety to the said Rowland, and decreed Rowland to assign over the said bond to the plaintiff and Seymour to help themselves against the said St. John for the said debt.

[Reg. Lib. 13 Car. I, f. 438.]

216

Norwood v. Norwood

(Ch. 1637–1638)

In this case, the court enforced the payment of a legacy of a marriage portion even though the devisee married without the assent of a third party contrary to the condition of the legacy.

1 Chancery Reports 121, 21 E.R. 525

The plaintiff's bill is for a £400 portion left her to be paid to her at the age of twenty-one years or day of marriage, so as she married with the assent of the trustees and her mother and eldest brother. The defendant insists that the plaintiff is about marrying without the assent aforesaid, and refuses payment of the said portion, and offered several reasons against the payment.

But this court declared it just and reasonable that the said £400 with damages should be paid to the plaintiff.

[Reg. Lib. 13 Car. I, f. 560.]

217

Vintner v. Pix

(Ch. 1637–1640)

A marriage without consent will not defeat a legacy on a condition of dutiful behavior.

Where legacies are payable successively, the executor may not pay the first whole legacy if there are not sufficient assets to pay the rest, but all of the legacies must abate proportionally.

1 Chancery Reports 121, 21 E.R. 526

Richard Pix, by will, of which he made the defendant his executor, gives to his two daughters, Elinor and Alice, £200 apiece to be paid at their ages of twenty-one years or days of marriage. And the testator gave the said Elinor and Alice £200 more by a marginal note in his will with this clause, 'if they behave themselves dutifully to their mother'. And the said Alice died. And the said Elinor is her administratrix. And Elinor marries the plaintiff without the consent or liking of the said defendant, her mother.

This court declared that, the £200 positively given by the said will, the defendant ought to pay the same to the plaintiff. But, as touching the £200 given to the said Elinor and Alice by the marginal note in the will upon their dutiful behavior to the defendant, she having married herself without the consent of her mother as aforesaid, [the court] referred that point to the judges.

The judges certified that the £200 in the marginal note mentioned, as well as the £200 in the body of the will, do belong to the plaintiff Elinor, her marriage notwithstanding, and that the first letters of administration of the estate of Alice sued out by the plaintiff, administratrix of Alice, are yet in force, the letters of administration granted to the defendant being subsequent to the plaintiff's letters of administration.

[Reg. Lib. 13 Car. I, ff. 443, 505.]

1 Chancery Reports 133, 21 E.R. 529

The defendant, an executor, having paid a legatee her portion of £400, the Master, in his report, thinks it against law that an executor should pay some legacies and leave the rest of the legatees unpaid, but everyone should lose in proportion.

The defendant executor insists that the legacies were not all due at one time, but some sooner and some later, as the children were in age, one before the other. And the eldest daughter had a preferment offered her, and so [there was] no reason that she should lose the occasion for want of her portion, which this executor, by the will, was constrained to pay her.

This court would be satisfied what the law is when several legacies are given, the first being due and the rest not until in a time after, whether the executor may pay the first if there be not assets to pay the rest. This court referred this matter to the judges of the Prerogative Court.

The judges certified and were of opinion that, by law, the executor may not pay the first whole legacy if there be not sufficient [assets] to pay the rest.

This court, reading the will and the proviso in it for the supplying of the legacies out of the real estate if the personal [estate] will not suffice, does conceive it equitable and just that the executor ought to have carved equally and given each one his ratable part. And, therefore, it must lie upon the executor to make the rest of the legacies good in a proportional way, and the executors and legatees to make themselves whole out of the real estate, the proviso appointing it.

In regard the legacies are to be made up out of the growing receipts and not upon and out of a plentiful estate and that the executor by his forwardness in paying legacies must now bear it out of his own purse, this court sees no cause to allow the legatees damages for the same.

[Reg. Lib. 15 Car. I, ff. 18, 219.]

218

Hale v. Lady Carr

(Ch. 1638)

A trustee of an infant's estate is liable to pay interest on money held in trust, but, if a prudent investment of the trust fails, the trustee is not liable for the loss.

3 Swanston 63, 36 E.R. 781

25 January 1637[/38]. Sir Edward Hale's and the Lady Car's Case.

If a man be trusted with money as executor or otherwise for children's portions, though no interest be reserved, yet interest in some measure shall be paid while it is in his hands. And, if he let it out to such men as are trusted and esteemed by others to be men of worth and ability, if any loss happen, he shall not bear the loss thereof.

219

Cotton v. Heath

(Ch. 1638)

A contingency upon a contingency is valid and enforceable.

Pollexfen 26, 86 E.R. 500

First heard 1 May 14 Car. I, and, 6 and 16 June following, [it was] adjudged.

Robert Cotton, possessed of a term in lands, devised the profits and occupation thereof to Lettice, his wife, for eighteen years, and, afterwards, that Edmond Cotton, his son, should have the premises during his life, and, after his death, willed that his eldest issue male of his body should have the profits and occupation of the premises during his life. And he made Lettice, his wife, his executrix, and died. And Lettice proved the will, and assented to the legacy.

The eighteen years expire. And Edmond Cotton enters, and has issue Roger, his eldest son. And then he makes a feoffment with warranty of the premises unto Thomas Butler and his heirs, whereupon Richard Woodcock, who was seised in fee of the reversion of the premises, entered for a forfeiture.

The question was whether the feoffment and entry had destroyed the executory devise of the premises to Roger Cotton or not.

The Lord Keeper [LORD COVENTRY] desired the opinion of three judges in the point, two of which certifying their opinion that the executory devise to Roger Cotton was not destroyed by the feoffment and the Lord Keeper being of the same opinion, the estate was decreed to Roger Cotton according to the devise.

1 Rolle, Abr., *Devise*, pl. L, 3, p. 612

8 May 14 Car. Upon a reference out of the Chancery to Justices Jones, Croke, and Berkeley between Cotton and Heath for them to resolve.

If A., possessed of a term for years, devisees it to B., his wife, for eighteen years and, then to C., his eldest son, for life, and then to the eldest issue male of C. for life, even though C. did not have any issue male at the time of the devise and the death of the devisor, yet, if he had issue male before his death, this issue male will have it as an executory devise because, even though it be a contingency upon a contingency and the issue not *in esse* at the time of the devise, yet, inasmuch as it is a limitation to him only for life, it is good and the same as Manning's Case.[1] [This was] without question.

1 Rolle, Abr., *Extinguishment*, pl. F, 4, p. 937

If A., possessed of a term for years, devises it to his wife for eighteen years and, afterwards, to B., his eldest son, for life and, afterwards to the eldest male issue of B. for life and he dies and, after the eighteen years, B. enters and is possessed and, afterwards, C., his eldest male issue, is born and, afterwards, B. makes a feoffment in fee of the land and dies, this will not destroy the estate of C., he being born before the feoffment. [This was] by the said justices [Jones, Croke, and Berkeley] resolved, and so certified accordingly. And it was then said that the opinion of the Lord Keeper [Lord Coventry] was agreeing.

73 Selden Soc. 105

8 May 14 Car. I.

A term was devised to the wife for eighteen years, remainder to C., his eldest son, remainder to the eldest issue male of C. for life. Though C. had not any issue male when the testator died, yet, if any issue male be after born, he shall take, though it be a contingency upon a contingency, because, at most, it was but an estate for life which interposed.

And so it was resolved by Jones, Croke, and Berkeley, upon a reference out of Chancery.

[Other reports of this case: 1 Eq. Cas. Abr. 191, 21 E.R. 981.]

220

Peacock v. Thewer

(Ch. 1638)

Land given to charitable uses that is sold to a third party for value without notice passes free of the intended charitable use.

---

[1] *Manning's Case* (1609), 8 Coke Rep. 94, 77 E.R. 618.

A rent charge to charitable uses remains when the land is sold to a purchaser for value without notice.

An occupier of land burdened by a rent charge in favor of a charitable use is liable for any arrearages during the time of his occupancy only.

Herne & Duke 84

Lands are given to a charitable use. If a purchaser buys these lands, not having notice of the charitable use, it shall not bind the purchaser. But, if the rent be given out of lands to a charitable use and a purchaser purchases the lands for money, not having notice of the charitable use, yet he shall pay the rent, for that he does not purchase it but the land out of which the rent issues it.

But he shall not pay any more arrearages of the rent than what was incurred during his time of purchase, but every occupier and owner must answer the arrearages for his own time.

See below, Parkhurst's Case and the Inhabitants of Woodford and Barnard Hide's Case, before.[1]

Tothill 33, 21 E.R. 115

If lands be given to a charitable use, to dispose an overplus, if the purchaser had no notice, [it] cannot bind him. But, if [a] rent issue out of land, the purchaser must pay it, but [it] will not charge him to pay arrearages before [his] purchase, nor lay it upon one, nor excuse the other.

Public Record Office C.33/176, f. 47v

29 October 1638. Richard Peacock and Timothy Axtell, *ex parte* the Parish of Redbourne in the County of Hertford, and Henry Lloid, clerk, plaintiffs; Edward Thewer, Robert Whitley, and Seth Sladman, defendants.

The matter in question between the said parties coming this day to be heard in the presence of counsel learned on both sides, the scope of the plaintiffs' bill being to be relieved touching the rent of £10 *per annum* and the arrearages thereof for twenty-five years past charged to be issuing out of certain lands late the possessions of Sir Richard Read, deceased, which £10 *per annum* was by the last will of the said Sir Richard devised to such uses as by his will is directed and the lands pretended to be chargeable with the payment thereof is now in the possession of the defendant, forasmuch as it was affirmed on the defendants' behalf that the defendants are possessed but of a small parcel of the lands pretended to be liable to the payment of the said £10 *per annum* and the defendants are purchasers for a valuable consideration of the said lands and had not any notice of the charitable use and they became purchasers but lately and ought not to be charged

---

[1] *Woodford Inhabitants v. Parkhurst* (Ch. 1640), see below, Case No. 261; *Hide v. Gillingham Parishioners* (Ch. 1628), see above, Case No. 34.

with any arrears before their purchase, this court declared that, as to the point of notice, it was not material to be proved, for the lands be chargeable with the rent and, the defendants buying the lands, they must take the same chargeable with the rent whether they had notice or not. But where the plaintiffs' suit is to have arrearages which become due before the defendants' purchase, this court sees not how to order the same against them for such arrearages as happened before their several purchases but that these must be required from such persons as then held the lands. And in respect it was now alleged that the parties did heretofore refer the examining and ending the differences unto Mr. Serjeant Heath and Thomas Mutas, Esq., this court conceives that course very fit to be prosecuted and does therefore order that the said former referees be again attended herein, who are to call before them as well the now defendants as also all such as they shall conceive and find ought to be contributory to the payment of the said rent of £10 *per annum*. And thereupon and upon hearing also what could be offered on the behalf of New College in Oxford to settle a final end between the parties and for the referees' better light herein, they are to look upon the proofs already taken and shall be armed with a commission to examine such witnesses on either side for the clearing of any doubts as they shall think just and fit.

221

Tanfield v. Davenport

(Ch. 1638)

A court of equity can require a husband to make a reasonable jointure for his wife before decreeing a devise to her to be paid.

2 Cooper *tempore* Cottenham 244, 47 E.R. 1151

Martis, 27th November 1638, LORD COVENTRY. Robert Tanfield and others, plaintiffs v. James Davenport and others, defendants.

Upon opening of the matter this present day by Mr. *Fountaine*, being of the plaintiffs' counsel, it was alleged that Sir Henry Robinson, knight, deceased, having two daughters unmarried, by his will, devised to each of them £2500, and made the plaintiff Robert his executor in trust for the benefit of the said daughters and to employ his estate to the best use. And, about Christmas last, he died, his youngest daughter being fifteen years of age. And the defendant James, being second son to the Lord Chief Baron [Sir Humphrey Davenport][1] and a widower and having a son and heir by his former wife, by secret means and fair promises, so far prevailed with the youngest of the said daughters that he persuaded her

---

[1] D. X. Powell, 'Davenport, Sir Humphrey (c. 1566–1645)', *Oxford Dictionary of National Biography*, vol. 15, pp. 265–266.

to go away with him in the night season, and, forthwith, intermarried in private without the knowledge and consent of the plaintiff Robert or any of her friends.

And, now, the said defendant does refuse to settle a competent jointure upon his said wife or to make any fitting provision for her and her children in case she shall have any out of the said portion, and, nevertheless, does prosecute the said plaintiff in the Court of [*blank*] for the said portion.

Now, in regard the plaintiff is but an executor in trust and is willing to pay the said portion, as the estate will bear, so as the defendant will settle a competent jointure upon his said wife or otherwise provide for her and such children as he shall have by her out of the said money, it was humbly prayed that the said suit in the ecclesiastical court may be stayed by an injunction of this court and that the said plaintiff may not be forced to part with the said portion until the said defendant has performed a competent jointure to his wife and settled the said portion for a future provision for his said wife and such children as he shall have by her, and the rather that the defendant's wife's sister is lately dead and there does accrue near £1500 more to the defendant by her death and, if the defendant shall purchase lands with his said wife's portion, the same, by law, will descend to his son by his first wife or, in case he shall die before any provision made, the defendant's wife and such children as he shall have by her are likely to be unprovided for.

It is, therefore, ordered by His Lordship [LORD COVENTRY] that the said parties shall attend Mr. Page one etc. [a Master in Chancery] to the end that he may mediate and settle an indifferent deed between them if he can for a complete provision to be had and made for the defendant's wife and for the children as she shall have, and, in default thereof, certify where the fault is and what he thinks fit to be done. And it is ordered that, if the said defendant, upon notice hereof, shall not show good cause to the contrary at the second general seal, then, an injunction is awarded against the said defendant, his counsellors, doctors, proctors, attorneys, agents, and solicitors for stay of all proceedings concerning the said portion until the said Master shall have either settled the main business concerning the portion or this court shall give other order in the cause. And, in the meantime, the proceedings in the ecclesiastical court are stayed by order of this court.

Tothill 114, 21 E.R. 140

14 Car. [1638–39].

The defendant sues in the ecclesiastical court for a portion due to his wife. This court orders an injunction to stay proceedings there until he shall make a competent jointure.

[Reg. Lib. B 1638, f. 114.]

222

Leigh v. Winter

(Ch. 1638)

An executory deed can be defeated by a later deed.
A condition not to marry without consent is not enforceable after the party bound has reached full age.

W. Jones 411, 82 E.R. 215

Sir Francis Leigh assured by a fine certain manors and tenements to the use of himself for life, remainder to Woolly Leigh, his son in tail with a proviso of revocation if his son marry without his consent. Afterwards, by an indenture made between him and the grandmother of the said Woolly of the part of his mother, he rehearsed the said proviso and the power in it contained and the recital of certain considerations given to the said Sir Francis Leigh:

now, therefore, it is agreed by and between the said parties, and the said Sir Francis Leigh has covenanted, granted, concluded, and agreed, and, by these presents does for him, his executors, and administrators, covenant, grant, promise, and agree to and with the said Bridget Winter, the grandmother, that the said Sir Francis Leigh shall not, nor will revoke, make void, or determine any of the uses or estates limited or appointed to or for the said Woolly Leigh or his heirs by the indenture aforesaid, nor shall, nor will have, use, or execute any power of revocation, determination, or making void, or any way concerning the same, without the licence and consent of the Lord Coventry, Lord Keeper, first had in writing, and does also grant and agree that any revocation or declaration by him to be made touching the revoking, determining, or making void the said uses or estates or any of them without such assents, shall be void, frustrate, and of none effect.

Upon a suit in the Chancery between the said Sir Francis and Bridget Winter, the grandmother, and the said Woolly Leigh, the Chief Justice BRAMPSTON and JONES were called to the Court of Chancery. And they declared their opinion that, by the said second indenture, the power of revocation, that was absolute in the first indenture, was restrained and that the said Sir Francis Leigh could not revoke without the consent of the Lord Keeper, because the power was executory, that, by the subsequent agreement, by the indenture could be defeated and determine the deed conditional.

Also it was agreed by the Lord Keeper [COVENTRY] and the said justices that, if the elder son of a man, at his full age of twenty-one, marry without the consent of the father, the father had no remedy.

223

Wentworth v. Young

(Ch. 1638–1639)

A gift of land goes to the heirs of the donee, but a gift of money goes to the next of kin.

Nelson 36, 21 E.R. 783

14 Car. I [1638–39]. Lord Keeper COVENTRY.

The plaintiff married the defendant's daughter, with whom he had £1500 in marriage. And his wife afterwards dying and leaving issue two daughters, he entered into articles with the defendant that as well the £1500, which he had in portion with his wife, as £1500 more, which he gave out of his own estate, should be secured for them by a purchase of lands or leases of lands and paid unto them at their ages of twenty-one years or marriage.

The court was of opinion that, if the money had been laid out in lands pursuant to the articles and the children had died before the time of payment, the lands would have gone to their heir. But, since it was in money and if they both should die before it became payable, it should go to the father and to his executors or administrators.

224

Sherbourn v. Houghton

(Ch. 1638–1639)

The palatinate courts of Lancaster have jurisdiction over suits between parties dwelling there, for lands there, and for local matters.

Nelson 37, 21 E.R. 783

14 Car. I [1638–39].

The bill was to be relieved upon a trust. The defendant pleaded the jurisdiction of the Duchy, but he was ordered to answer.

So, where the bill was for a personal thing and the defendant pleaded the jurisdiction of the County Palatine, it was referred to Mr. Page, to search precedents and certify the court, who reported upon view of precedents that the jurisdiction of the County Palatine had been allowed between parties dwelling in the same and for lands there and for matters local.

And, in the argument of the principal case, the 4th Institutes was cited in a case between Sir John Egerton and the Earl of Derby,[1] concerning the jurisdic-

---

[1] *Egerton v. Earl of Derby* (1614), 12 Coke Rep. 114, 77 E.R. 1390, 1 Eq. Cas. Abr. 137, 21 E.R. 940, E. Coke, *Fourth Institute* (1644), p. 213.

tion of the County Palatine of Chester. And, upon a long debate, the plea was overruled.

225

Marston v. Marston

(Ch. 1638–1639)

A minor, obvious misdescription of land being conveyed will not invalidate an otherwise good conveyance.

1 Chancery Reports 123, 21 E.R. 526

The plaintiff, as heir in tail, makes title to lands. And the defendant makes title for her life for her jointure by deed and fine, which fine is mistaken, for that the lands do lie in two parishes within the City of Coventry, *viz.* part in Trinity Parish and the other parcel in St. Michael's Parish, and that the fine is only of the lands in Trinity Parish.

But it not appearing that any of the lands in the deed of jointure and fine, which did both agree in names and quantities, do lie out of the said Trinity Parish, nor anything else appearing to invalidate the said jointure, His Lordship [LORD COVENTRY] dismissed the bill, and confirmed the Master of the Rolls [DIGGES] and the judge's order.

[Reg. Lib. 14 Car. I, ff. 676, 725.]

226

Maundy v. Maundy

(Ch. 1638–1639)

An inofficious will will be set aside.

1 Chancery Reports 123, 21 E.R. 526

The question in this case being touching the validity of the will of Thomas Maundy, late husband to the defendant Joan, by which will, the lands of the said Thomas are settled on the said Joan and her issue, out of the name and blood of the said Thomas, her husband, which will the plaintiff insists was contrived by the defendant Joan contrary to the intent of the testator and against certain notes written by him in his lifetime, by which he had settled the inheritance of the said lands on the plaintiff and his heirs after the death of the said Joan. And the plaintiff proves that the testator intended to prefer him, being of his name and blood, and drew notes for his will, whereby he gave the lands to Joan for life and, after[wards], to the plaintiff and his heirs. But the testator left the perfecting of his will to the defendant Ayleworth, an attorney, who prevailed with the testator to let the will be as he [the attorney] should pen it.

This court, it appearing the said Joan declaring to several that she had the lands but for life and this court conceiving the testator to be but weak in regard he left it to the discretion of the said attorney, declared and is of opinion that the said will was a very inofficious will, seeking to prefer strangers before name and blood.

[Reg. Lib. 14 Car. I, f. 1247.]

227

Rowe v. Lord Newburgh

(Ch. 1639)

A person not in privity cannot sue to enforce a marriage settlement.

W. Jones 415, 82 E.R. 217

Hilary term 14 Car.

Sir Henry Rowe exhibited his bill in Chancery against Sir Edward Barrett, knight, lord Newbury, and the Chancellor of the Exchequer,[1] because Sir Edward Barrett, the defendant, upon the marriage of Lady Mildmay, now the wife of Sir Henry Mildmay and daughter of Alderman Holyday and niece to the plaintiff, *scil*. daughter of his sister, promised to assure lands to the value of £500 *per annum* for the jointure of the said wife (and the promise was made to the said alderman) and, afterwards, in default of issue of his body in tail, to Sir Henry Mildmay in tail. And he made a note in writing to this purpose. And the said promise was made beyond twenty years past. And the alderman made his wife his executrix, and he died. And the wife was married to Lord Warwick. And he surmised that the said writing came to the hands of the defendant.

The said defendant denied that he had the said writing. And, further, he demurred upon the bill, principally because the plaintiff was not privy that, by the law, he can sue in this case.

The Lord Keeper [LORD COVENTRY] called to himself the Lord Chief Justice Brampston and Justice Jones, and the matter was well debated again. And the precedents were viewed in this case. And they resolved that Sir Henry Rowe, the plaintiff, was not enabled to sue in this case, but the executor of the alderman or Sir Henry Mildmay and his wife could sue. And, thus, they declared their opinion to the counsel of the plaintiff.

---

[1] R. Wisker, 'Barrett, Edward (1581–1644/5)', *Oxford Dictionary of National Biography*, vol. 4, pp. 43–44.

Second, another thing was moved, whether this promise was bound by the Statute [of Limitations].[1] And it seemed to them that it was. But they did not declare their opinion absolutely.

228

Thynn v. Cary

(Ch. 1639)

A conveyance by a fine will bar a claim where a person has the right in equity in the land itself but not where his right in equity is only against the person in respect of the land.

W. Jones 416, 82 E.R. 218

Hilary term 14 Car.

Sir Thomas Thynne and Warren Townsend, as heirs to Dame Knivet, exhibited a bill to be relieved in equity against John Cary, Esq., against a conveyance obtained by indirect means from the said Dame Knivet.

And the defendant pleaded a fine with proclamations and non-claim of the said lands for five years.

And it was referred for a view of the precedents.

And, in the Christmas holidays, the matter was debated at Durham House. And it seemed to them that it was a bar.

And by the request of the Lord Keeper [LORD COVENTRY], the Chief Justice requested the opinion of Chief Baron Davenport, Croke, Trevor, Berkeley, Crawley, Weston, and Henden. And they were of the same opinion. And the Chief Justice reported it to the Lord Keeper.

79 Selden Soc. 506

Sir Thomas Thynn supposed himself to have a right in equity to some lands, whereof, by his bill, he charged Cary to have obtained a conveyance from the Lady Knivet by some indirect means.

Cary pleaded in bar a fine with proclamations and non-claim.

And, by the opinion of all the judges, Sir Thomas Thynn was barred.

The differences are these, where a man has the right in equity in the land itself and where his right in equity is only against the person in respect of the land. In the first case, a fine will bar, not in the latter.

[Other copies of this report: 2 Swanston 610, 36 E.R. 748.]

---

[1] Stat. 21 Jac. I, c. 16 (*SR*, IV, 1222–1223).

229
Bery v. Burlace
(Ch. 1639)

A grant of a remainder of a lease is void at common law.

W. Jones 416, 82 E.R. 218

Hilary term 14 Car.

Richard Bery, being possessed of a parcel of lands called Combemantyn in the County of Devon, for the term of 1500 years, made his will in these words, 'I give and bequeath to Humphrey, my son, my lease of Combemantyn Park, after the death of my brother Nicholas Bery'. And he made his wife Katherine and the said Nicholas his executors. And he devised to them all the rest of his goods and chattels, and he died. And they proved the will 3 May 1588.

Nicholas Bery enjoyed the premises during his life. On 3 July 42 Eliz. [1600], the said Humphrey Bery, by indenture, reciting the original lease and devise by the said will, did grant and assign the premises to Francis Lane and Richard Coffyn for 99 years if Prudence, the wife of the said Humphrey, should so long live, to begin after the death of the said Nicholas Bery. And the said Humphrey Bery did further by the said indenture for natural love and affection to Nicholas, his son, grant and assign to the said Nicholas, the son, the remainder of all the aforesaid lands to have and to hold the same lands to the said Nicholas Bery, his son, his executors, administrators, and assigns immediately after the death of the said Nicholas, the uncle, and Prudence Bery for and during all the rest and residue of the said 1500 years, which should be then to come and unexpired at the time of the decease of the said Nicholas, the uncle, and Prudence with power of revocation upon tender of 5s. to Nicholas, the son.

First, whether the grant by Humphrey to Nicholas, the son, Nicholas, the uncle, being then living, be good.

Second, whether the grant by Humphrey to Nicholas, the son, be good if Nicholas, the uncle, had been then dead.

This case was referred by order from the Chancery to Chief Justice BRAMPSTON, JONES, and BERKELEY, and they certified as follows. 'According to an order of the 3d of December last, we have heard counsel of both sides, and have taken consideration of the case agreed upon by counsel of both sides made upon the will of Richard dated 21 March 1583 and the deed of 30 July 42 Eliz. [1600] made from Humphrey Bery, the father, to Nicholas, the son, in the order mentioned, and we are of opinion upon the said case that the said grant made to Nicholas, the son, is not good in law.' Subscribed by Brampston, Jones, and Berkeley, and so certified to the Chancery.

230

Pensterd v. Pavior

(Ch. 1639)

An executor can be ordered to carry out a testamentary gift to a charitable purpose by purchasing lands to endow a charitable trust. Such a trust is to be endowed out of the personal estate of the testator.

Herne & Duke 87

A. devises £20 *per annum* to a preaching minister and makes his wife executrix and dies, leaving lands and assets in goods. The executrix refuses to buy lands or a rent of that value.

The Lord Keeper [LORD COVENTRY] and two judges decree the executrix to buy lands to that value and to assure it for the charitable use.

Tothill 34, 21 E.R. 115

A. devises £20 *per annum* to a preaching minister [and] dies, leaving lands and assets. The defendant will not pay it accordingly.

The court with the judges charges her, out of the assets, to buy lands to perpetuate it, she having but a third part of the lands, and so ought not to be chargeable with any more.

Public Record Office C.33/176, f. 623v

2 July 1639. Robert Pensterd, clerk, Thomas Canter, and Richard Adney, plaintiffs; Ellen Pavior, Ralph Kinnaston, Margaret, his wife, S. and [*blank*] Challoner, defendants.

Whereas upon the hearing and debating of the matter in the presence of counsel learned on both sides upon the 27th of June last the substance of the plaintiffs' suit appearing to be that whereas Roger Pavior, gent., deceased, being in his lifetime seised in fee of divers messuages, lands, tenements, and hereditaments with their appurtenances in the towns or parishes of Trevannant and Alberbury in the County of Salop and of divers messuages and tenements in Standon in the County of Hertford of the yearly value of £100 or thereabouts and being possessed of a great personal estate did in December 10 Car. [1634] make his will and thereby give unto the Parish of Drayton of which the plaintiff Robert is minister and the other plaintiffs are church wardens £20 *per annum* forever towards the maintenance of a preaching minister in the said parish and devised to the said Ellen, his sister, all his said messuages, lands, and tenements and the residue of all his personal estate his debts and legacies being discharged and thereof made her sole executrix and died the first of February then next following, after whose decease the inheritance of the premises did descend to the defendants Margaret, Elizabeth, and Mary as cousins and coheirs of the said Roger

Pavior. And the said Ellen Pavior proved the will and took upon her the execution thereof and entered into the premises and possessed herself thereof and of all the personal estate of the said Roger. But she, the said Ellen, and the other defendants do now refuse to pay the £20 *per annum* so devised towards the maintenance of the said minister as aforesaid or to secure the payment for the future. And the defendant Ellen having by her answer set forth that the third part of the premises did after the death of the said Roger descend to the other defendants and they entered accordingly into the same and do enjoy and receive the profits thereof and confesses the devise of the said £20 *per annum* for the maintenance of a minister as aforesaid and the other defendants having by there answer set forth that, before the bill was exhibited, they sold the reversion of part of the premises to Sir Richard Newport and his heirs, this court was clear of opinion that the said Ellen so long as she lived ought to pay the said £20 *per annum*, she having the land and personal estate. But the court not being fully satisfied how the personal estate should be wholly charged for the future with the payment of the said £20 *per annum*, the Lord Keeper held fit that the will of the said Roger should be brought unto his Lordship, who would thereupon be pleased to consider and take advice upon the same and so give such final order and decree therein as he should find fit.

And now His Lordship [Lord Coventry] having this day accordingly with the assistance of Mr. Justice Berkeley deliberately considered of the matter and of the said will, His Lordship with the advice and opinion of the said judge does think fit the said Ellen in respect she has assets and has not in her answer pleaded or set forth that she had not assets sufficient to satisfy the said £20 *per annum* ought to be chargeable with and pay the same out of the personal estate of the said Roger and all the arrearages thereof and do order and decree the same accordingly. And, for the more sure settling and securing of the said £20 *per annum* for the future towards the maintenance of a minister according to the will of the testator, it is ordered and decreed that the said Ellen shall out of the personal estate aforesaid procure and cause a sufficient and legal grant to be made of lands to some persons in trust for the payment of the £20 *per annum* forever according to the will of the said testator and the said plaintiffs and defendants are to attend Sir Thomas Milward for the naming of fitting persons to whom the said land shall be granted as aforesaid who is thereupon accordingly to name them and agree the assurance or direct the same as he in his judgment shall think fit.

231

Pember v. Kington Inhabitants

(Ch. 1639)

The maintenance of a preaching minister is not within the words of the Statute of Charitable Uses, but it is within the policy and intent of the Statute, and such a use will be upheld by the court.

Herne & Duke 86

Money was given to maintain a preaching minister. This is no charitable use named in the Statute.[1] Yet, by the Lord Keeper [LORD COVENTRY] and two judges, it was decreed to be good and the use a charitable use within the equity of that Statute. And the executor was ordered to pay that money to the charitable use for maintenance of it.

Tothill 34, 21 E.R. 115

[Upon a question] whether money given to maintain a preaching minister be a charitable use, the Lord Keeper and the judges did decree, notwithstanding it is not warranted by the Statute to be a charitable use, that the same shall be paid by the executor to such maintenance.

Public Record Office C.33/176, f. 623

6 July 1639. Francis Pember, plaintiff; Inhabitants of the Parish of Kington, defendants.

Upon opening of the matter this present day unto the right honorable the Lord Keeper [LORD COVENTRY] by Mr. *Grosvenor*, being of the defendants' counsel, and upon reading of an order of the 16th of May whereby Mr. Justice Jones, Mr. Justice Croke, and Mr. Justice Bartlett were desired to consider and certify their opinion whether a gift for maintenance of a preacher be comprehended within the meaning of the Statute for Charitable Uses, it was now alleged the said judges have not made their certificate and the matter in reference to them is only concerning £200 given for the maintenance of a preacher and there are divers other sums of money decreed to the defendants upon the said Statute that have no dependence or relation to the said matter referred as aforesaid, and therefore it was prayed that the said decree might be confirmed in all things saving the matters which are referred to the judges as aforesaid, it is ordered that the plaintiff having notice thereof shall by the beginning of the next term show what cause he can why the decree should not be confirmed as was now desired. And where it was prayed that the prosecutors for the said charitable use might be allowed and satisfied their costs out of the £62 given by the said commissioners for

---

[1] Stat. 43 Eliz. I, c. 4, s. 1 (*SR*, IV, 968–969).

the damages for the money due to the said charitable use, His Lordship [LORD COVENTRY] does order that the said commissioners do consider and settle what costs shall be allowed to the said prosecutors as they shall think fit.

232
Bramble v. Havering Paupers
(Ch. 1639)

A married woman cannot make a will.
An arbitral award to pay a void devise will be set aside.

Herne & Duke 90

A married woman makes a will and devised 30s. *per annum* out of some of her own lands to a charitable use; the heir submits himself to an award and is bound to perform it; the arbitrators do award the payment of it. Yet, by decree, the heir is discharged to pay it and that the devise was void *ab initio*. So [it is] of an infant and other persons disabled in law to make a will or to devise lands.

[Other copies of this report: Tothill 34, 21 E.R. 115.]

233
Mayor of London's Case
(Ch. 1639)

A misnomer of a donee of a devise to a charitable purpose can be corrected by the court.

Herne & Duke 90

Lands were devised to the Mayor and Chamberlain of London to the use of the master and governors of the Hospital of St. Bartholomew, London. [It was] resolved that the devise is good, although the corporation be not incorporated by that name but by the name of Mayor and Commonalty, for the intent of the devisor shall be observed and it appears that the devisor intended to give it to the Corporation of London. Also, the will is to maintain a hospital, which is a charitable use and which the law ought to favor.

234
Gorges v. Chancey
(Ch. 1639)

Choses in action or upon trust can be disposed of by a married woman without the agreement of her husband.

British Library MS. Harley 1576, f. 233v, pl. 3

The husband and wife living asunder, the husband, Sir William Chancey, did agree with her friends to allow her £170 6s. 8d. *per annum* as alimony for her maintenance. She saved £200 and delivered it to one Gibbs to place out at interest, she to have the interest during her life and, afterwards, the plaintiff to have [the] interest and principal. The money was lent out, [and] security was taken in the name of the defendant, Toby Chancey, who released the debt, lent the party's obligors more money, and took security in his own name for all. The lady devises by her will the money to the plaintiff and dies.

The defendant Chancey was decreed to pay the money with costs and damages to the plaintiff, grandchild of the said wife, Dorcas Chancey. The defendant objected that his father, the husband, by his writing gave authority to the said Lady Dorcas, his wife, to dispose only of the estate which she then had or after[wards] should have in possession, and this deed is dated in July 1634, but the money was placed out in 1631. But the court was there of opinion and so declared that for things in action or upon trust, a married woman might dispose of the same without the assent of her husband. Toby then assented to pay the £200 without further suit so [long] as costs and damages might be spared. And [it was] decreed accordingly.

1 Chancery Reports 125, 21 E.R. 527

The bill sets forth that, whereas the Lady Dorcas Chansey, grandmother to the plaintiff, being possessed of the sum of £200, in October 1631, delivered the said £200 to one Gibbs on trust to be put out at interest to the end she may receive the interest for her life and, after, the same to remain to the plaintiff's use, and the principal to be to the plaintiff's use forever. Which was put out accordingly in the name of Toby Chansey, the defendant aforesaid, for the purpose aforesaid, and the bonds were delivered to the said Toby Chansey, who received the interest during his life. And about a month before her death, she gave the said bonds and monies due by the same to the plaintiff, according to her former declaration. And the said Toby Chansey, being only trusted, as aforesaid, but minding to gain the said money for himself, released the said bonds. And the said Lady Chansey being dead, the defendant Toby refused to pay the said money and interest to the plaintiff, and insists that Sir William Chansey, his father, did by deed in 1634 give a power to the said Lady Dorcas Chansey, his wife, to dispose of all her estate, which she had then in possession or at any time should be possessed of unto him this defendant Toby Chansey and not otherwise. And, thereupon, the said lady continued them in the defendant's name until her death. In 1635, the said Gibbs caused the said Lady Chansey to make her will, whereby she gave her estate to the plaintiff's mother, and made her executrix, but, afterwards, revoked that will, and gave her estate to the said Toby Chansey.

And the defendant insisting that, there being a separation between the said lady and her husband, Sir William Chansey, the said Sir William agreed to allow her £170 *per annum* as alimony for her maintenance. And she did save and get the said £200 in question out of the said alimony, and being a married woman had now power to dispose thereof by will or otherwise at her death without the assent of her husband, he having authorized her to dispose thereof by will to the defendant Toby, her son. But, forasmuch as she had by her will taken upon her to dispose the same otherwise, such gift and will ought by law to be void.

This court was clear of opinion, and so declared, that, for things in action or upon a trust, a married woman might by will dispose of the same without the assent of her husband. And, therefore and in regard it appeared that the said lady did declare that the said £200 should be and go after her decease to the use and benefit and towards the benefit and for a portion for the said plaintiff, her grandchild, and that the same for that purpose was put forth in the defendant Toby's name in trust, this court was fully satisfied that the said £200 with damages and costs ought to go and be paid to the plaintiff, according to the declaration of the said lady.

Tothill 97, 21 E.R. 134

Michaelmas term 14 Car.

A married woman, being separated, having an allowance of £200, she improved it. And she disposed of it by her will.

[Order of 12 November 1639: Public Record Office C.33/177, f. 226v.]

235

Willoughby v. Earl of Rutland

(Ch. 1639)

A devise to a creditor is a satisfaction of the debt.

Nelson 38, 21 E.R. 783

15 Car. I [1639–40].

The earl of Rutland bequeathed £500 to the plaintiff to be paid unto her at the age of twenty-one years or day of marriage. But, before either, the defendant paid the said £500 to her father upon condition he would make it £1000, which he covenanted to do.

And, afterwards, by his will, he devised unto his said daughter £1000 to be paid unto her at the respective times as aforesaid. And he died without mentioning that he devised the said £1000 in pursuance of the aforesaid covenant. And, now, after her father's death, she exhibited her bill against the defendant for the £500.

But it was dismissed.

236

Harrison v. Lucas

(Ch. 1639–1640)

A court of equity can give a remedy where the plaintiff has no remedy at common law.

1 Chancery Reports 125, 21 E.R. 527

The Statute of Limitations[1] was pleaded and overruled. And this court with the judges were of opinion that the plaintiff had no remedy at law, but made a decree for the plaintiff.

[Reg. Lib. 15 Car. I, f. 236.]

237

Isham v. Cole

(Ch. 1639–1640)

After a long period of time, a bill to redeem a mortgage will be barred by the defense of laches.

1 Chancery Reports 127, 21 E.R. 527

Edward Hill, for £130, surrendered lands to the use of the said Edward Hill and his wife for their lives, remainder to the plaintiff and her heirs and assigns forever, to which the defendants do entitle themselves and detain the same from the plaintiff.

The defendants insist that the said Edward Hill, for £207, in July 3 Jac. [1605], demised the premises to one William Sparry for ninety-nine years, and Sparry, 15 Jac., for valuable considerations, granted the same to John Sparry. And he, in 3 Car. I [1627–28], assigned the same to Anthony Cole, the defendant. And the said defendant Cole confesses that, in the deed from Hill to William Sparry, there is a proviso of redemption.

And, although it appeared by articles that there was a good consideration of money besides natural affection which induced the said Edward Hill to surrender the premises to the plaintiff's use and it being proved by one witness that the said William Sparry about twenty-four years since told him he was fully satisfied and paid all his debts due from the said Edward Hill, which moved the court to conceive that the plaintiff had good cause of relief, yet, in regard it is thirty-three years since the mortgage from Hill to the said William Sparry, this court does hold it a dangerous precedent to relieve mortgages after so long an elapse of time. But this court proposed, in respect of the badges of equity, which this

---

[1] Stat. 21 Jac. I, c. 16 (*SR*, IV, 1222–1223).

cause bears on the plaintiff's part, to do something for the plaintiff, which the defendant consented to do.

[Reg. Lib. 15 Car. I, f. 329.]

238

Wyard v. Worse

(Ch. 1639–1640)

An executor of a will can seek the advice and guidance of a court of equity as to the administration of the decedent's estate and have a discharge by the court.

1 Chancery Reports 129, 21 E.R. 528

Elizabeth Wyard, the plaintiff's mother, lent one Wellington £200; for security whereof with interest, [he] made to several trustees an annuity of £20 *per annum* out of lands for the use of the said Elizabeth, provided that, if the said Wellington, at any time, repaid the said £200, then the annuity to cease. Which rent was paid to the said Elizabeth accordingly, who, afterwards, by her will, bequeathed the said annuity to the plaintiff and the heirs of his body, with remainders over, subject to the said proviso. And he made the defendant executor, who, many years, received the said annuity, and paid the same to the plaintiff. But, the said Wellington being dead, his son and heir paid the said £200 to the defendant, and discharged the said annuity.

And, since, the defendant has paid the interest of the £200 to the plaintiff, but refused to pay the £20 to the plaintiff, lest he might be after questioned for the same after the plaintiff's decease by the heirs of the plaintiff's body or by those in remainder if the plaintiff should die without issue. Whereas, in case the said annuity had not been redeemed, the same had been only at the plaintiff's disposal, and so ought now the £200, which cannot be entailed by the laws of this realm, which this court referring to a Master, who certified the truth to be as aforesaid, this court decreed the £200 to be paid to the plaintiff, and, for payment thereof, this court does discharge the defendant.

[Reg. Lib. 15 Car. I, f. 328.]

239

Naylor v. Baldwin

(Ch. 1639–1640)

A fraudulent deed of settlement will be set aside by a court of equity.

1 Chancery Reports 130, 21 E.R. 528

The several points insisted on in this cause are *viz.* that Richard Baldwin, the defendant, being seised in fee of several lands and tenements, in July 1630, made a voluntary conveyance, by which he sold the premises to Abraham Hays and his heirs in trust to the use of his son Thomas Baldwin, remainder to another son, Richard, remainder to Katherine, his daughter, and her heirs forever, with a proviso that the yearly rents and profits of the premises should be paid to Anne, his wife, for the maintenance of his children and the raising of their portions, and, after[wards], a full third part to be for a jointure for his said wife. After which deed was made and before enrollment thereof, a lease of the said premises was made by Richard Baldwin to the defendant Tirril for the securing of £400 lent by Tirril to the said Baldwin with a clause of redemption at the end of three years. And to confirm the said lease, Baldwin and his wife acknowledged a fine to the said Tirril. And the said Hays, afterwards, conveyed the premises to Rothwel and his heirs, another defendant, subject to the said trust. And Baldwin, in August 7 Car. I [1631], became indebted to the plaintiff Naylor in a £240 bond for wares, which he sued to judgment. And the said Baldwin, 7 Car. I [1631–32], was indebted to the plaintiff Noell in a recognizance of £240 for plate and jewels and to the plaintiff Bourne in £100 on bond, which is sued to judgment. Conceiving Baldwin had a good power to let leases and that he was seised in fee of the premises, 7 Car. I [1631–32], [he] let a parcel of the premises to one Goodwin for the consideration of £40 for forty-one years at 40s. *per annum* rent to build. And the defendant Parsons, taking the lease to be good, bought the same of Goodwin for £69, and, now finding his lease to be insufficient, dares not go on with his building. And both the sons being dead and the daughter of Baldwin married to the defendant Higgins Baldwin, they received the rents.

So the creditors not being satisfied of their money have exhibited their bill for relief. The plaintiff insists that the said deed of settlement is fraudulent, and made to deceive creditors.

This court ordered the said deed to be set aside and that Tirril shall not stand upon the forfeiture of his lease otherwise than to help him to his just debt and damages together with the £39 10s., which was also lent upon security of that lease, provided it appear upon taking an account that the same was agreed to be secured by the said lease. Otherwise, this court will not give way to the hedging in of other debts.

And, as for the debts due by wares which were put upon the said defendant Baldwin and of which he could not make half the money, this court, not favoring contracts of that kind, ordered the Master to make allowance as he saw cause.

And as for Mrs. Baldwin's dower, unless she has barred herself totally by levying the fine, this court makes no order therein at present, but declared that, if she levied the fine only to secure the lease, no debt could bar her except Tirril's debt on the lease. And this court ordered the lease to stand good.

[Reg. Lib. 15 Car. I, f. 430.]

240

Magdalen College, Oxford v. Crook

(Ch. 1639–1640)

A badly drafted will will be construed according to the intent of the testator.

1 Chancery Reports 134, 21 E.R. 529

Sir Simon Bennet devised all the coppices and wood grounds and all and singular the premises and all woods and underwoods (except timber trees) to his wife for life, and, after her death, he limited the same with the timber trees to trustees that they for two years should pay the profits of the premises to the plaintiff and they to bestow the same in building the College, and, after[wards], he limited the reversion and fee simple of the premises to the plaintiff and their successors forever, the said woods, underwoods, and timber trees excepted. Now the question is, as the exception is made of the woods, underwoods, and timber trees, whether the soil is not excepted also from the plaintiff.

This court is clear of opinion that the intent of Sir Simon was that the whole, as well the soil as the said woods, underwoods, and timber trees, do pass by the said will.

[Reg. Lib. 15 Car. I, f. 229.]

241

Popham v. Desmond

(Ch. 1639–1640)

A court of equity will not enforce a debt that was due and payable a long time before where the circumstances suggest that it has been paid off.

1 Chancery Reports 135, 21 E.R. 530

The plaintiff was the sole daughter and heir of Sir Sebastian Harvey and administratrix of Sir James Harvey, her grandfather, of the goods unadministered by the said Sir Sebastian Harvey. And Sir Thomas Gresham,[1] 21 Eliz. [1578–79], for money borrowed, entered into a statute of £2000 for payment of £1000 to Sir James Harvey. And Sir Thomas Gresham conveyed the said premises to his wife and her heirs and, by his will, declared she should pay all his debts. And 23 Eliz. [1580–81], an act of Parliament was made, that his wife should be charged with all his debts, and, if she paid not the same, then commissioners were to sell so much of the premises as would pay the same. And the Lady Gresham, 39 Eliz.

---

[1] I. Blanchard, 'Gresham, Sir Thomas (c. 1518–1579)', *Oxford Dictionary of National Biography*, vol. 23, pp. 764–771.

[1596–97] died, and the premises descended to Sir William Read, and, on 19 Jac. [1621–22], he died, and the premises descended to the defendant, who refuses to pay the said debt.

So, the suit is to have the said premises sold for the payment of the said debt and damages according to the act.

And it appeared that this bill was exhibited in pursuance of a certificate made by the two Lord Chief Justices and Lord Chief Baron upon the plaintiff's petition to the Lords Commissioners for the sale of the premises, in which certificate, the said judges thought fit and declared that the plaintiffs should take their course by bill in this court, or, otherwise, that it may appear whether the money mentioned in the defeasance of the said statute was then due and unpaid or no and whether there was cause to sell the said manors and lands, it being the forty-sixth year after the said money ought to have been paid, and whether any demand had been made thereof or no.

Now, for that there is no mention of the debt in the inventory in the Prerogative Court by Sir Sebastian Harvey of the goods of Sir James Harvey, his father, to whom the said debt was first due and for that it appeared that, as there was originally a clear debt not to be denied, there was also a greater quantity of lands subject to the same if it had not been paid, and for that the same debt grew due above fifty years past and the plaintiff has not made unto this court any such proof of any demand or pursuit of or for recovery of the said debt, by which this court might declare any opinion that the said debt is unsatisfied or however the said manors and lands or any part thereof ought to be sold for the payment thereof or that any relief ought to be given to the plaintiff for the same, especially after so many descents to several heirs and purchasers thereof by others, all of them as well heirs as purchasers, strangers to the payment of the debts of the said Sir Thomas Gresham, this court dismissed the plaintiff's bill.

[Reg. Lib. 15 Car. I, f. 220.]

242

Askwith v. Chamberlain

(Ch. 1639–1640)

A decedent's debtor who is made the executor of the will must pay his debt into the estate.

1 Chancery Reports 138, 21 E.R. 530

A debtor made executor shall not extinguish his debt, but the same is to be taken as part of the testator's personal estate.

[Reg. Lib. 15 Car. I, f. 309.]

243

Booth v. Peckover

(Ch. 1639–1640)

The question in this case was whether an award made by the king should be entered in the court order books or be tried at common law.

1 Chancery Reports 138, 21 E.R. 530

The bill is to have an award made by the king decreed. The defendant demurred, and insisted the matter ought to be tried at law.

This court declared His Majesty is the royal fountain from which all streams flow. *Quaere.*

[Reg. Lib. 15 Car. I, f. 404.]

244

Goddard v. Goddard

(Ch. 1639–1640)

A bill of review can be barred by the defense of laches.

1 Chancery Reports 139, 21 E.R. 531

Upon a bill of review to reverse a decree 22 Jac. [1624–25], the plaintiff, for error, says the cause was referred to four commissioners, and but three certified, and also that the lease, which the plaintiff now insists on, was not then in issue, and the plaintiff never consented to the certificate.

This court upon reading the proofs, it appeared by depositions of two witnesses that there was an agreement for settling the differences and, in regard the decree was so long since and nothing was done against the same in all this time, being sixteen years, this court would not reverse the decree.

[Reg. Lib. 15 Car. I, f. 248.]

245

Bourman v. Wild

(Ch. 1639–1640)

The Court of Chancery can adjudicate the jurisdiction of the Court of the Cinque Ports.

1 Chancery Reports 140, 21 E.R. 531

This court overruled the jurisdiction of the Cinque Ports.

[Reg. Lib. 15 Car. I, ff. 253, 266.]

246

Church v. Roper

(Ch. 1639–1640)

An arbitral award can be specifically enforced by a court of equity.

1 Chancery Reports 140, 21 E.R. 531

The plaintiff and defendant referred the differences in question to the arbitration of Mr. Hades and Mr. Lovelace, who made an agreement or award therein as to the lease of the farm in question to be surrendered to the defendant upon terms. But the plaintiff did insist upon allowance for improvements of the said farm, which matters the said Hades and Lovelace not being so able to judge of, they nominated five other persons. Which four or three of them were to settle the matter of improvements, which the plaintiff and defendant assented unto, and bound themselves to stand to their award. The plaintiff performed his part of the said award made by Hades and Lovelace. And three of the five said arbitrators made their award, and awarded £120 to be paid by the defendant to the plaintiff for his improvements and for the surrendering of his said lease. But the same [was] not delivered to the defendant punctually, whereby the plaintiff might take a remedy thereby in point of law. And although the defendant insisted that the same was an extrajudicial award and void in law, yet, the same was but part of the award made by Mr. Hades and Mr. Lovelace, and the defendant had a benefit thereby, and gained possession of the said farm and otherwise.

And this court conceived that the award made by three of the said five arbitrators nominated by the said Hades and Lovelace was made in pursuance of the award of Hades and Lovelace and in consummation thereof and was and ought in equity to be deemed as an entire award with theirs, which was in part executed. And after the plaintiff has lost his lease and paid his rent and is left remediless for his money intended him, this court is clear of opinion that the award made by the said three arbitrator's ought in all equity to be performed by both parties, and decreed accordingly.

[Reg. Lib. 15 Car. I, f. 436.]

247

Bishop v. Bishop

(Ch. 1639)

A court of equity will specifically enforce a contract to arbitrate a dispute.
A court of equity will not order a perpetuity.
A defendant cannot be forced to make discovery of anything against himself that would result in a penalty.

1 Chancery Reports 142, 21 E.R. 532

The bill is to have an award decreed and performed. It was voluntarily referred to Mr. Justice Croke by the parties, plaintiff and defendant, to end the difference between them, who made his award. And the bill also charges the defendant to make a discovery of the breach of the said award.

The defendant insists that the said award was merely voluntary and extrajudicial and made without the directions of this court and that both parties did rely upon their bonds mutually given for the performance of the said award. And, as to the bond entered into for the performance of the award and the pretended breach thereof, the defendant insists it is put in suit by the plaintiff at law and that the defendant is not bound by law to answer upon oath any such matter against himself as may be any evidence to bring him within the penalty of the said bond.

Now, as concerning the said award, forasmuch as the plaintiff has performed the same, His Lordship [LORD COVENTRY] declared it was a proper suit in this court to compel the defendant to perform in on his part, although the said award were not made originally by any direction of this court.

The defendant insisted that the part of the said award was chiefly insisted upon in the said bill which did bar the defendant, being tenant in tail, from that power which the law gives him, the bill charging that Sir Thomas Bishop, father of the plaintiff and defendant, was seised to him and his heirs male, with the fee expectant of divers lands in Henfield, and the plaintiff conceiving he had been seised of the lands in Henfield, conveyed the same to the defendant and his heirs male of his body, having the fee in himself and there being a deed of gift made of the testator's goods at Henfield unto the defendant in trust for the testator's wife, the mother of the plaintiff and defendant, and, after her decease, in trust for the defendant.

That difference arising about the said estate tail, Mr. Justice CROKE awarded the defendant to enjoy a former estate tail settled upon him and the heirs male of his body by the said testator and the plaintiff to confirm the said estate tail at the charge of the defendant and that the defendant should do no act to debar or discontinue the said estate tail or the remainder of the plaintiff without the plaintiff's consent, except it be for a jointure for his wife.

His Lordship [LORD COVENTRY], to this part of the award, declared it was absolutely against the constant course of this court to decree a perpetuity or give any relief in that case. And, as to that point, he held the defendant's demurrer to be good. But, as to the performing the said award, this court ordered the defendant to answer, and overruled the demurrer.

And, as touching the bond for the performance of the award, His Lordship [LORD COVENTRY] saw no color that the defendant should discover anything against himself whereby to charge himself with the penalty of the bond.

[Reg. Lib. 15 Car. I, f. 59.]

1 Chancery Cases 40, 22 E.R. 683

An award was confirmed in part, and made void in part.

Tothill 17, 21 E.R. 110

Mich. 15 Car. [1639].

A voluntary award was decreed. But some part being to bind a tenant in tail not to alien, the court would not decree that, but gave relief against the award, being to make a perpetuity. And a man is not bound to answer as to cause him to be subject to the penalty of a bond. And the Statute of Limitation[1] (as this case stands) is overruled.

248

Bales v. Procter

(Ch. 1639–1640)

A recovery will bar an estate tail without a fine.
In this case, the defense of laches barred the plaintiff's claim.

1 Chancery Reports 144, 21 E.R. 532

The bill is to be relieved for messuages, which the plaintiff insists are descended to him in tail, which the plaintiff's father, 18 Eliz. [1575–76], suffered a recovery to one Garnet and John Bales and their heirs and covenanted to levy a fine the same year in consideration of £20 to be paid to him, and also to be relieved for two annuities of £6 *per annum* to be granted out of the said premises by the said recoverors during his life, which the plaintiff insists was not paid, and so the premises ought to descend to him in tail.

The defendants insist that they are purchasers for a valuable consideration, and plead and demur, for that a recovery will bar an estate tail without a fine, so as the only point of equity in the plaintiff's bill is for non-payment of the said £20 and the two £6 *per annum* annuities, supposed to be in 18 Eliz. [1575–76], which the defendant Procter, being a purchaser at the first hand, hopes he shall not be now compelled to prove payment of, being sixty-five years since the annuities were due and thirty-one years since the death of the plaintiff's father, who all his lifetime never complained of it. And, in 12 Jac. [1614–15], a fine was levied by Fairclough against Bull and others then in possession and another fine to the defendant and his trustees by one Sambrook, under which fines, the defendant claims. And, in 12 & 13 Car. I [1637], the plaintiff was nonsuited on an [action of] ejectment brought, and the defendant Hansley and his wife claim under the said recovery and a fine levied in 6 Jac. [1608–09] of the messuages.

---

[1] Stat. 1 Jac. I, c. 16 (*SR*, IV, 1222–1223).

This court dismissed the plaintiff's bill.

[Reg. Lib. 15 Car. I, f. 719.]

249

Ford v. Stobridge

(Ch. 1625 × 1639)

A surety has a right of subrogation against his principal debtor.

Nelson 24, 21 E.R. 780

Lord Coventry.

The plaintiff was bound as surety for the defendant, and the debt was recovered against him. And he, having no counter-bond, brought his bill to recover the debt and damages against the defendant, which was decreed accordingly. *Quod nota.*

250

Gwynn v. Edmonds

(Ch. 1625 × 1639)

A person who was a witness to a conveyance will be estopped to deny the validity of that conveyance.

Nelson 28, 21 E.R. 781

Lord Keeper Coventry.

Rowland Owen, being seised in fee of the premises in question, made a lease thereof to the defendant Edmonds for twenty-one years, and, afterwards, he granted the reversion to the plaintiff Gwynn. The term expired, but Edmonds refused to deliver the possession, alleging that, before Rowland Owen had any estate or interest in the premises, one Owen ap John was seised thereof in fee, and made a lease to the said Edmonds for twenty-one years. And, afterwards, he granted the reversion to one Griffith Edmonds, brother to the defendant, who released his right to the defendant. And he affirmed that the first lease made by Rowland Owen was only to prevent suits at law which might arise, for that, after the said release, Griffith Edmonds had delivered the deed, *viz.* the grant of the reversion, to the said Rowland Owen, who was heir at law to Owen ap John, the grantor, and that the acceptance of the lease from Rowland Owen ought only to be an estoppel during the term.

But it appearing to the court that Griffith Edmonds, the grantee of the reversion and under whom the defendant claimed by virtue of the said release, had made a feoffment of the premises to the plaintiff Gwynn *anno* 7 Jac. [1609–10], which was executed by livery and seisin and to which the defendant Edmonds was a witness, and for that the defendant's title by the release was never set on foot until the lease was expired, therefore, the possession was decreed to Gwynn and his heirs, according to the grant of the reversion to him by Rowland Owen as aforesaid.

251

Lippiat v. Neville

(Ch. 1625 × 1639)

In this case, a lord of a manor was ordered to admit a tenant who had a defective title, inasmuch as the lord had admitted other tenants under the same defective title and the tenant was already in possession.

Nelson 32, 21 E.R. 782

Lord Keeper COVENTRY and Justice HUTTON.

The father made a settlement of a manor, reserving only an estate to himself for life, remainder in tail to his son, the defendant. And, afterwards, he married a second wife, and settled part of the said manor on her. And then he died, his wife surviving, who enjoyed it for the greatest part of her life, during which time, she granted several copyhold estates to the tenants who enjoyed the same under such grants. And, among the rest, she granted a copyhold estate to one Smith for his life, and, after his death, she granted the reversion to the plaintiff Lippiat. But not long before her death, the defendant, who was tenant in tail, brought an [action of] ejectment against her, but he confirmed the estates which she had granted to the tenants by signing their copies.

Upon the death of the said Smith, who was one of the said copyhold tenants, the aforesaid Lippiat, who had the grant of the reversion, desired to be admitted. But the defendant, being lord of the manor, refused it, whereupon he exhibited his bill to be relieved.

And, in regard Smith had enjoyed it all his lifetime and for that the defendant had confirmed the estates of the other tenants, the court decreed that the plaintiff should be admitted and hold his estate likewise according to the grant made by the widow.

252

Cosin v. Young

(Ch. 1625 × 1639)

Where there was a gift of land obtained by fraud, the donees will be ordered to convey the land to the person who was defrauded.

Nelson 33, 21 E.R. 782

Lord Keeper Coventry.

The plaintiff, Cosin, delivered several sums of money to one Young to put out at interest for his use, who informed the plaintiff that he had put the money out accordingly, and had got the securities in his possession, when, in truth, he had purchased copyhold lands in his own name with the money, to which he was admitted. And, afterwards, he surrendered the same to the use of himself for life and, after his decease, to the use of the defendant Fuller, who was his sister's son, and to several other of his nephews.

Afterwards, when this practice was discovered, Young entered into a statute to Cosin, the plaintiff, conditioned to surrender all his copyhold estates to him. And he, accordingly, did surrender the same. But, before the plaintiff was admitted, Young, the surrenderor, died. And, in regard Fuller was presented to be his next heir, Cosin, the plaintiff, was denied to be admitted, whereupon he preferred his bill to be relieved.

And the fraud plainly appearing and that all Young's estate would not satisfy the plaintiff and for that Young did declare a little before he died that his nephews, the Fullers, being then infants, should surrender when they came of age, the court decreed the plaintiff to hold the lands until that time and that the defendants should surrender to him when they came of age.

253

Gird v. Togood

(Ch. 1625 × 1639)

After a long period of time, an equity of redemption can be barred by the defense of laches.

Nelson 34, 21 E.R. 783

Lord Keeper Coventry.

Anno 13 Jac. I [1615–16], lands were mortgaged. And the mortgage being long since forfeited, the plaintiff, as executor to the mortgagor, did in the year 1643[1] bring a bill to redeem.

---

[1] Sic in MS.

But, after so long a time and the lands being settled on the son of the mortgagee upon his marriage, the court would give no relief, but decreed the defendant to hold the same. And for that there were some lives expired since the mortgage so that the estate was of better value than when first mortgaged, the court ordered the defendant to pay some money for the same.

And for that the executor was directed by the will of the mortgagor to pay the surplus money after the principal debt and interest was satisfied to such uses as therein mentioned, he was decreed to pay the same accordingly and that the defendant should hold the lands against him, but not against the heir, because he was no party to the bill.

254

Jones v. Baugh

(Ch. 1625 × 1639)

A debtor can petition a court of equity to set aside a voluntary trust made by him so that he can pay off his creditors.

Nelson 35, 21 E.R. 783

Lord Keeper COVENTRY.

The plaintiff was possessed of a lease for years. And he made a voluntary conveyance thereof to the defendant in trust for himself, his wife, and children. The wife died leaving children.

And the plaintiff, being much in debt and having no estate to pay the same besides this lease, exhibited his bill to compel the defendant to join in a sale of the interest thereof to raise money for the payment of his debts and for his maintenance and, with all consenting, that a reasonable part thereof should be deducted and remain in the hands of the defendant for the portions of the children suitable to their mother's fortune, which was decreed accordingly, and the Master [was] to ascertain the portions. And the defendant was discharged of the trust save only as to the children.

255

Neville v. Broughton

(Ch. 1640)

A specific clause in a will prevails over a general clause.

1 Chancery Reports 145, 21 E.R. 533

This court declared that a general clause in a will ought not to prejudice a particular devise.

[Reg. Lib. 16 Car. I, 1640–41, f. 504.]

256

Peyton v. Green

(Ch. 1640)

After a very long period of time, a defendant can prove his accounts by his own oath where no other evidence exists.

1 Chancery Reports 146, 21 E.R. 533

This court ordered that, in regard the account in question is of twenty years' standing, the defendant shall prove his account by his own oath, for what he cannot prove by books and cancelled bonds, for that, after so many years, his own oath must be accepted as a proof in this case.

[Reg. Lib. 16 Car. I, 1640–41, f. 569.]

257

Leach v. Dean

(Ch. 1640)

Where a father conveys land to his son upon no valuable consideration and, afterwards, sells the same land to a third person, the court will order the father and the son to convey the land to the purchaser for value.

Tender of performance is a good performance of a contract.

1 Chancery Reports 146, 21 E.R. 533

The plaintiff's suit is to be relieved upon articles of agreement for the purchase of lands from the defendant Richard Dean, who, before the said articles had by deed conveyed the premises to the defendant Roger Dean, his son.

This court with the assistance of the judges declared that the said deed of uses so made to his son Roger, as aforesaid, being a voluntary conveyance and the said Richard Dean selling the premises to the plaintiff for valuable considerations, the said voluntary conveyance was a fraud and that the tendering of the purchase money by the plaintiff was as good a performance of the contract on his part as if the money were paid. And, as for the defendant Roger Dean, it is but just that he should be in the same case as his father, as if his father had never made the conveyance. And [the court] decreed the articles to be performed.

But, as to the voluntary conveyance, the same is not hereby impeached as between the father and the son for any advancement or any other thing thereby settled on the said son, other than making good the said articles of agreement aforesaid, but the trustees are to be paid their debts and engagements out of the purchase money.

[Reg. Lib. 16 Car. I, 1640–41, f. 577.]

258

Pickering v. Keeling and Pickering

(Ch. 1640)

Equity will not aid a volunteer.

1 Chancery Reports 147, 21 E.R. 533

Thomas Pickering, deceased, father of the defendant Thomas Pickering, and the defendant Thomas Pickering, by deed 16 Jac. [1618–19], settled lands to several uses charged with an annuity or a rent charge of £20 *per annum* to be paid to the plaintiff. But the defendants, having gotten seised of the said lands and got the said deed into their hands, refuse to pay the said annuity.

The defendants insist that the said deed is void in law by reason of a former deed made 21 Jac. [1623–24] for valuable considerations, whereby the said lands were conveyed in fee without any rent charge.

This court upon reading the said deed, the plaintiff not proving that the said annuity was granted upon any valuable consideration whereby this court might be induced to set up and make good the said deed in equity, this court saw no cause to relieve the plaintiff herein, but dismissed the bill.

[Reg. Lib. 16 Car. I, 1640–41, f. 292.]

259

Press v. Hinchman

(Ch. 1640)

No act of a present incumbent of a church can bind his successor.

1 Chancery Reports 148, 21 E.R. 534

The bill is to have a lease of the parsonage of Portland heretofore made by one Green to one Peers, under whom the plaintiff claims, made good and confirmed to the plaintiff according to a decree made by the consent of the defendant Steedly whilst he was there the incumbent. And the defendant Hinchman is the now the incumbent. And the plaintiff would have him bound thereby, and compelled to confirm the same, which this court, on reading the decree, saw no cause to do, this court being clear of opinion that the act of a present incumbent cannot bind his successor, and so [the court] dismissed the plaintiff's bill.

[Reg. Lib. 16 Car. I, 1640–41, f. 325.]

260

Barkley v. Southcot

(Ch. 1640)

A secret trust will not be enforced where the purpose of the trust fails.

Lincoln's Inn MS. Hill 125, f. 19v, pl. 3

8 February 1639[/40].

The plaintiff, being the elder brother and intending to go into Ireland, was persuaded by his mother to enfeoff some friends of her to the use of herself for life, remainder to one of the defendant's brothers in tail [?], but [there was] no consideration, but the pretense was to prevent a forfeiture [?] by the plaintiff. And she promised that it should lie dormant and not prejudice. The plaintiff returned, married, and had issue.

He exhibited a bill, and was relieved. But an annuity was settled on the younger brother for his life £4 on trust that this he had not disposed of himself [?] to [. . .] etc.

261

Woodford Inhabitants v. Parkhurst

(Ch. 1640)

A purchaser of land taking title in the names of his infant children is the equitable owner of the land and can grant a rent charge out of the land to charitable uses.

An imperfect conveyance of an interest in land to charitable uses is perfected by the Statute of Charitable Uses.

A rent charge to charitable uses remains when the land is sold to a purchaser for value without notice.

A rent charge to charitable uses that was extinguished by the doctrine of merger can be revived by charity commissioners.

A rent charge is liable to distraint, and contribution lies against previous owners.

Herne & Duke 91

Sir Henry Leigh did purchase copyhold lands in Woodford [in Essex] in the name of two of his younger sons and their heirs, they being within age and, by his will, devises to Sir William Martin and other parishioners of Woodford and their heirs a rent charge of 40s. *per annum* out of this copyhold land for relief of the poor there and dies. Sir William Martin purchases this land and enjoys it for many years and then sells the land unto Parkhurst and his heirs. Parkhurst has notice of the charitable use between the surrender and his admittance. The commissioners decree Parkhurst to pay all the arrearages since Sir Henry Leigh's death.

And upon his appeal, the lord keeper [FINCH] resolved these points:

First, that the rent is well devised, although Sir Henry had nothing in the land in strictness of law, for that the estate in law was in the children, yet Sir Henry making the purchase and enjoying the land as owner and receiving the profits of it, he shall be said in equity to have power to dispose to a charitable use. Also, it being objected that there wanted a surrender to enable him to devise, the lord keeper said yet the devise was good enough and shall be said a good 'gift, limitation, and appointment' within the Statute in favor of charitable uses.[1]

Secondly, [it was] resolved that the rent, although it was extinct in law by Sir William Martin's purchase, yet, by the commissioners' decree, it is revived.

Thirdly, [it was] resolved, the rent is not extinct by this purchase, although he had no notice of the same, for that the purchase is of another thing than was given to the charitable use.

Fourthly, [it was] resolved that the rent is a charge which goes with the land in whose hands soever it comes and a distress may be taken for the arrearages upon the ter tenant for the time it was in arrears in other's hands and the owner's remedy, to have contribution against all others that enjoyed the land before him, is by suit in chancery. And here Parkhurst, by the decree, had contribution against all others that enjoyed the land charged and suffered arrearages to accrue in their time.

Lastly, [it was] resolved that the notice of the rent given to Parkhurst after the surrender and agreement for the purchaser and before his admittance was a sufficient notice within the Statute, if notice in this case had been requisite, for that Parkhurst was no complete and absolute purchaser before admittance, so of notice given to a purchaser of a charitable use chargeable upon the land mean between his agreement and sealing of the writings before the perfecting of the settling of the estate in him by attornment, livery, or enrolment of the deed of conveyance.

262

St. Nicholas v. Harris

(Ch. 1641)

In this case, the contract in issue to pay an annuity was enforced.

---

[1] Stat. 43 Eliz. I, c. 4, s. 1 (*SR*, IV, 968–969).

1 Chancery Reports 149, 21 E.R. 534

The bill is to be relieved against a bond of £300 entered into by the plaintiff Elizabeth conditioned that, if she did pay Timothy £15 *per annum*, during the plaintiff's life, then the said bond to be void. But the plaintiff pretended that the said bond was for the performance of an agreement, which was by the death of the said Timothy become impossible to be performed, and so the bond ought to be discharged.

Upon reading the proofs, this court would not relieve the plaintiff against the said bond, and ordered the plaintiff to pay the £15 *per annum* and arrears with damages to Timothy's executor.

[Reg. Lib. 17 Car. I, 1641–42, f. 206.]

263

Swain v. Wall

(Ch. 1641)

Where co-sureties become liable to pay the debt of their principal debtor and one of them is insolvent, the remaining co-sureties are liable only for their agreed upon proportionable share.

1 Chancery Reports 149, 21 E.R. 534

The plaintiff and defendant and one Jorden, 16 Jac. [1618–19], became jointly bound in a bond of £500 to the City of London for the payment of £310 in February then next, which £300 was employed by one Shadwell for procuring the place of Serjeant at Arms, which place, afterwards, Shadwell assigned to one Hunt for a good consideration, which Hunt, by direction and agreement of the said Shadwell and the plaintiff and defendant Jorden, entered into several counter-bonds unto the plaintiff and Jorden and Wall, for their indemnity from the said bond of £500, entered in to the City of London. And, thereupon, it was agreed that, if Hunt failed to pay the said debt to the City, then the plaintiff and Jorden and Wall should pay their respective parts of the said debt to the City. And Hunt died possessed of the said place insolvent, so as the plaintiffs Jorden and Wall were only liable to pay the said debt. And the City calling in the said debt, Wall was not able to pay his said share, and the plaintiff and Jorden, in 1622, took up £300 of one Ducket and Bates, and were bound unto them in several obligations for the re-payment thereof. And therewith, they paid the said debt to the City, and, afterwards, Jorden became insolvent, so as the plaintiff, on the behalf of himself and Jorden and Wall, was forced to pay the said £300 to Ducket and Bates and all interest. And Wall being afterwards of sufficient estate to pay his rateable part of £300 and interest paid by the plaintiff as aforesaid, so the bill is that the defendant Wall may pay to the plaintiff a moiety of the £300 and interest, Jorden being insolvent.

The defendant Wall insisted that the said defendant Wall was not bound in the bonds given to Ducket and Bates, but only in the first bond, wherein the plaintiff and Jorden and the defendant Wall were bound. And, by the agreement, they three were to bear their respective parts of the said £300 in case Hunt failed. Besides, the first bond being delivered up and the debt paid, the defendant conceives himself totally freed thereof.

This court upon hearing the proofs is satisfied that the said defendant Wall ought to pay to the plaintiff the third part of the said £300, and did decree the said defendant to pay £100. And, as for the damages for the same, forasmuch as the plaintiff, both by bill and replication, does only desire a rateable part of the principal money and the said damages by him paid, which was £300 and damages but for nine months, this court saw no cause to order more. And [the court] so ordered the said £100 and damages only for nine months.

But the plaintiff insisted that there are precedents to enforce the defendant to pay a moiety of the said £300 and damages.

The court ordered precedents to be produced for that purpose.

The plaintiff produced a precedent in 5 Car. I [1629–30] between Peter, plaintiff, and Rich and Sheppard, defendants, by which the said defendant Rich, in respect the other defendant Sheppard became insolvent, was ordered to pay the plaintiff Peter Cosverty with the said Rich and Sheppard a moiety of the debt and damages there in question.

Mr. Justice Hutton was to consider of this matter.

Mr. Justice HUTTON thinks fit the defendant shall pay the £100 and £7 10s. for nine months' damages, and, if the plaintiff has recovered or received anything towards the said £107 10s. of the counter-security before mentioned, he is to allow the same to the defendant.

This court confirmed the judge's order.

[Reg. Lib. 17 Car. I, 1641–42, ff. 16, 148, 252, 315.]

264

Perryman v. Dinham

(Ch. 1641)

Where a judgment debtor is in prison for the debt, yet the judgment creditor can still have a writ of sequestration against the land that secures the debt unless the judgment debtor pays the amount due.

Chancery Reports 152, 21 E.R. 535

The defendant being committed to the Fleet [Prison] for not performing a decree, a [writ of] sequestration was granted, and the plaintiff was put into possession of the lands. The defendant insists that the plaintiff ought not to have the lands, the defendant being in prison, it being a double execution.

But the plaintiff insisted that, as this case is, where money is lent upon security by lands, the plaintiff ought to have the lands until the defendant has paid the money and interest.

This court, with the assistance of the judges, were satisfied that the plaintiff's holding the lands was just and equitable and that the plaintiff ought to have the lands absolutely assured or else be satisfied the money and damages and costs due to the plaintiff before the defendant be discharged of his imprisonment and that, in the meantime, the plaintiff do hold the lands, but, if the defendant will assure the lands, then he is to be discharged from his imprisonment.

[Reg. Lib. 17 Car. I, 1641–42, f. 585.]

265

Thomas v. North

(Ch. 1641)

Where a testator makes a devise of land and, afterwards, mortgages that land, the mortgage operates as a revocation of the devise.

1 Chancery Reports 153, 21 E.R. 535

Nicholas Holmes, being possessed of the premises in question, in April 1631, made his will, and devised all his messuages to the plaintiff Nicholas Thomas, his godson, and to his heirs forever. And the said Nicholas Holmes, in December 1633, mortgaged the said premises to the defendant North for £200 to be repaid at three years' end. And, before the three years' end, the said Holmes fell sick, and declared he would not alter his said will.

But the defendant John Holmes claims the premises as uncle and next heir to the said testator Holmes, and has entered on the premises, taking advantage of the forfeiture. And he brought a suit into this court against the mortgagee, and had a decree for the equity of redemption, and did accordingly redeem the same, and disposed thereof.

The defendant insisting that, in case such a will was made, the said will can be no bar to the defendant's said title as heir, in respect the testator did mortgage the premises after the making of the will, if any were, which was a revocation thereof, he having but a conditional estate, and the plaintiff did not make it appear that there was any other subsequent will made or a new publication of the said former will after the said Nicholas mortgaged the premises.

This court saw no ground to give the plaintiff any relief, and dismissed the plaintiff's bill.

[Reg. Lib. 17 Car. I, 1641–42, f. 558.]

266

Maggeridge v. Grey

(Ch. 1641)

Where trustees for a charity refuse to act, the Court of Chancery can appoint substitute trustees.

Nelson 42, 21 E.R. 785

The plaintiff's husband had left a considerable sum of money which he directed to be paid to certain persons in order to buy lands for the endowment of a hospital.

But the persons to whom it was to be paid refusing to undertake the trust, the court [Lord Keeper LITTLETON] ordered other trustees to perform the same and that several persons of quality might elect poor people qualified according to the will of the donor to be placed in the hospital and that the trustees should have the power to displace and remove such who did not conform themselves to the rules of the hospital, though there was no such provision in the donation.

267

Martin v. Brockett

(Ch. 1641)

Where a person promises to pay a sum certain after his death and then sells his assets, a court can order the purchaser to retain the purchase money and pay it over to the obligee when it comes due.

Nelson 43, 21 E.R. 785

The defendant was to pay the plaintiff's wife £300 after his death. He sold his estate. And the plaintiff and his wife preferred a bill to have the money secured to them after the defendant's death.

And the court [Lord Keeper LITTLETON] decreed that the money should be retained in the purchaser's hands and to be paid as aforesaid and that he should be protected against the defendant for the same.

268

Joyce v. Osborne

(Ch. c. 1641)

A charitable trust for the benefit of a vicar will be enforced according to the conditions of the trust, even though the donor was mistaken as to who can choose the vicar.

Nelson 40, 21 E.R. 784

The father of the defendant was seised of a rectory impropriate, and, as he apprehended, of the perpetual donation of the vicarage, the endowment whereof was very small. And the vicarage house being very much in decay, he conveyed another house and lands to trustees and their heirs for the better maintenance of the vicars etc. And conceiving the vicarage to be donative, he did, in the said conveyance, appoint how the vicars should be qualified, and directed the trustees and their heirs to make a lease of the said house and lands for eighty years to the incumbent for the time being, if he should so long live, which was accordingly done. And his appointment was observed for some time.

But the donor being mistaken in his title, for the vicarage was presentative, and not donative, and, by this means, the right of presentation being fallen to the king by lapse, the plaintiff was presented under that title. But the defendant excepted against him in regard he was not qualified according to the appointment in the deed. And, thereupon, the trustees refused to make a lease unto him of the said house and lands, whereupon he exhibited his bill to be relieved.

The court declared that the qualification required by the deed was occasioned through the ignorance of the donor, who thought the vicarage to be donative, but that the benefit of the gift and the arrears thereof ever since the plaintiff had been incumbent ought to redound to him, for, in cases of charitable uses, the charity is not to be set aside for want of every circumstance appointed by the donor. If it should, a great many charities would fail.

Now, in this case, it was appointed that none should enjoy this house and lands but such as came into the vicarage by the donation of the defendant's father and his heirs, in which he was mistaken, for the vicarage was presentative. And, if so, it is impossible that anyone should enjoy this charity, there being other circumstances limited by this grant, *viz.* that the vicar for the time being was to have no other benefice and they were obliged to residence; otherwise, they were not to enjoy this charity.

The plaintiff was decreed to hold it under those conditions and the trustees were to make a lease to him accordingly. And whereas the defendant intended to proceed against the plaintiff to remove him by an [action of] *quare impedit*, the court declared that the plaintiff should have the benefit of the decree no longer than he could maintain his title to the vicarage.

269

Thompson v. Stanhope

(Ch. 1642)

A court of equity will reform a clerical mistake in a deed.

British Library MS. Harley 1576, f. 233, pl. 4

For satisfaction [. . .] security of £1004, [it was] agreed that the defendant would devise to the plaintiff certain lands and [*blank*] redevise for twenty years, rendering for the first ten years of the twenty-one £100 *per annum*. The redevise was made, but in the reservation, it was mistaken, rendering for the last years £100 where it should have been for the first years. And for one year the rent was paid. The court relieved the mistake and [ordered] that the rest should be paid notwithstanding it was to the contrary and notwithstanding that [there was] no proof of circumvention, yet it was charged to have been done by fraud.

270

Smith v. Hopton

(Ch. 1642)

A decedent's debts are to be paid out of his personal estate and any lands directed to be sold for the payment of his debts before his heir is liable for them.

1 Chancery Reports 155, 21 E.R. 536

Sir Owen Smith did borrow of Humphrey Beddingfield £1707, and, for the security thereof, he made a lease of the lands in Wighton and Walsingham for 100 years. And also, being otherwise indebted and for the payment thereof, the said Sir Owen, 9 Car. I [1633–34], conveyed other lands to one Saunders. And, afterwards, in August 9 Car. I [1633], reciting the last deed, he conveyed to trustees several lands to the use of Sir Owen for life and, afterwards, to the use of Sir Thomas Hopton and Arthur Hopton and their heirs the said lands and premises on trust to sell the same for the payment of debts and legacies. The said Sir Owen, in 1637, died without issue, whereby the reversion in fee of the leased premises descended unto Thomas Smith, the plaintiff's father, as uncle and next heir to the said Sir Owen. And, at the death of the said Sir Owen, £678 of the £1707 remaining unpaid, the said Thomas Smith and the plaintiff, to save the forfeiture, paid the same to the said Beddingfield. And the plaintiff, as heir to the said Sir Owen and his surety, was forced to pay divers of his debts. And the plaintiff's father died, and the plaintiff is both their heir and executor, who was, at the request of the said Sir Owen Smith, bound as surety for him in several obligations.

And the plaintiff's suit is, first, to compel the defendant, the Lady Smith, being executrix of the said Sir Owen Smith, who has possessed herself of his personal estate, to reimburse the plaintiff the said £672 paid by the said Thomas Smith, the said plaintiff's father, and the plaintiff out of the personal estate of the said Sir Owen, it being a debt mentioned in the deed aforesaid.

And the plaintiff insisted that, in case there be a personal estate sufficient to satisfy debts, the same ought not to lie upon the heir, whom, though this court will not discharge against the creditors, yet this court has often relieved against the executor and administrator for a reimbursing of such debts as he should so pay, so far as the personal estate will extend. And the plaintiff insists to have the £672, if not out of the personal estate, then out of the sale of the said lands appointed to be sold as aforesaid and, also, to have satisfaction for the debts for which the plaintiff was bound for the said Sir Owen Smith.

This court ordered the plaintiff to produce precedents where relief has been given to an heir against an executor or administrator touching the said £672.

The defendant confessing the charge of the bill to be true, this court was of opinion that the defendant, the Lady Smith, being privy to the trust aforesaid, is liable to satisfy the debts of the said Sir Owen so far as the land which she purchased of the said Owen Smith will extend.

[Reg. Lib. 18 Car. I, 1642–43, f. 404.]

271

Thomas v. Porter

(Ch. c. 1643)

Where the verdict on an issue out of chancery is contrary to a verdict in an action at common law, another issue out of chancery will be granted.

British Library MS. Hargrave 99, f. 203, pl. 350

After verdicts in ejectment for a forfeiture by waste, the court granted an injunction and after[wards] awarded a trial [as to] whether the waste were willful or not and after that another trial, because [there was] trial against trial.

272

May v. Crips

(Ch. 1645)

A contract to make a lease is not assignable.

British Library MS. Harley 1576, f. 229, pl. 3

Crips, [who was] seised in fee, leased to Rice Ellis for fifteen years at [a rent of] £22 and [for a] fine [of] £50. And by the indenture of lease, the lessor, for him [and] his heirs, covenanted with the lessee, his executor, administrator, and assigns that he and his heirs should and would at the end and expiration of the five first years at the request of Ellis, his executor, administrator, and assigns in that behalf made and, at their costs, make or cause to be made up the term of ten years then remaining unexpired the number of fifteen years. Ellis assigned his term. Five years expired. The assignee requires a new lease and, being denied, exhibits a bill against the lessor to have the covenant performed.

The defendant demurred because the covenant in law is not assignable and is collateral [and] not within the Statute. The plaintiff's counsel insisted [that] it was not collateral and, if so, yet is such a covenant as in equity shall wait on the interest.

The bill [was] dis[missed] by the commissioners [of the great seal] in Hilary vacation 20 Car. [1645].

[Order of 17 February 1643: Public Record Office C.33/184, f. 558.]

273

Mere v. Mere

(Ch. 1645)

Depositions taken de bene esse before the defendant filed an answer to the bill of complaint were admitted into evidence in this particular situation.

British Library MS. Harley 1576, f. 229, pl. 4

The bill being to perform an agreement to settle lands in consideration of marriage, the bill came in 11 July, and before the bill came in, *viz.* [?] 9 July, the plaintiff, on oath [that he] had served process and the defendant appeared not but was in contempt, got an order to examine witnesses *de bene esse*, and took forth a commission and examined witnesses. About a year after, the defendant moved for a commission, and the counsel being on both sides heard, the defendant had [an] order for a commission, and it was then ordered publication to pass and that the witnesses examined *de bene esse* should be published. But [there was] no notice taken of the evidence [?] of the witnesses *de bene esse* for aught appeared by the [*blank*] nor consent of the defendant that they should be published.

The cause coming to [a] hearing and the witnesses *de bene esse* being called to be read, exception was taken because they were examined before answer but no notice [was] given at the time of their examination but [*blank*] they ought to be read in regard [that] the defendant was in contempt, and in regard of the defendant's contempt, the court concluded to have read them but forbore it for that time but referred it to the six clerks, before whom the case appeared as before and that the order for examination was before the bill. They certified the proceedings [to be] irregular yet in regard of the said order, the examin[ations] to stand.

At the second day for hearing, the counsel for the defendant excepted to the reading of them. But on debate, the court allowed the examinations though [there was] no notice to the clerk, a party, and though then it was made [to] appear by affidavit that the order was on misinformation for the solicitor that served the process, who did not serve it till the evening of the return of the process and undertook to procure an appearance for the defendant but did not but pretended a contempt and took [an] attachment and procured the said order of examination of the witnesses on [the] suggestion of a contempt as aforesaid. And it was [*blank*] that though the order did not express in words that notice should be given of the examination to the other party, yet it was employed and then it was the very case of [*blank*] against the [*blank*] Company of Cordwainers ruled by the Commissioners [to hold the great seal] that Michaelmas term that unless [they] were given the depositions *de bene esse* taken before [*blank*] should not be used, yet the court allowed[1] the depositions in this case of Mere.

Then it was objected that no witnesses *de bene esse* ought to be read unless [an] affidavit were now made that they were dead. The rule was, after some debate, allowed, the debate being whether the plaintiff ought to make [it] appear to the court that the witnesses were dead or that the defendant ought to make it appear to the court [that] they were living, whereupon the plaintiff himself having made [an] oath that at the execution of that commission, he could not get them to be examined but that, as he believed, they were either dead or in the armies, the court allowed the reading of the depositions though it was [*blank*] he had not deposed any endeavor to find them or to serve them with process and it was his own oath [*blank*] on hearing proof on both sides [*blank*] who served the subpoena was [the] solicitor commissioners and [*blank*] the court directed a trial touching the matter, be an agreement or not, reserving the equity, but ordered the depositions *de bene esse* to be read at the trial which [. . .].

[Orders of 25 November and 5, 10, 15, and 23 December 1645 and 17 and 21 February and 7 April 1646: Public Record Office C.33/186, ff. 60, 83, 91v, 107v, 108v, 183v, 207v, 228.]

---

[1] altered *MS*.

274

Wright v. Moor

(Ch. 1645)

Past dealings in trade is a sufficient consideration to support a contract between merchants.

1 Chancery Reports 157, 21 E.R. 536

This court declared they could not relieve the plaintiff against a bond freely and voluntarily entered into without compulsion or restraint, though no consideration or fraud was used for it. And this court looked upon it as entered into upon some consideration, there having been dealings between the plaintiff and defendant in trade, and would not relieve the plaintiff against the judgment had thereon, but dismissed the bill.

[Reg. Lib. 21 Car. I, 1645–46, f. 485.]

275

Wiseman v. Roper

(Ch. 1645–1649)

A contract entered into in order to restore family harmony is enforceable without any further consideration.

In this case for specific performance of a contract, the court refused to hold the defendant in contempt of court because the plaintiff's affidavit was insufficient to show any contempt.

1 Chancery Reports 158, 21 E.R. 537

The defendant Roper, by articles between him and Sir Thomas Wiseman, the plaintiff's father, reciting that, whereas there was a marriage lately had between the plaintiff, nephew of the defendant Roper, and Anne, his wife, without the privity, consent, or good liking of the said Thomas Wiseman, did as well in consideration of the defendant's natural love and affection to the plaintiff, as for the regaining of the good will and affection of the said Sir Thomas to the plaintiff and his wife, they did covenant with the said Sir Thomas Wiseman to convey within one month after the death of Sir Anthony Roper, the defendant's brother, unto the plaintiff and Anne, his wife, or the survivor of them and the heirs of the plaintiff the manor of Haber with the appurtenances, reserving an estate to the defendant for his life, and that, in case the said manor, which was then the inheritance of the said Sir Anthony Roper, should be alienated by Sir Anthony, so that the same should not descend unto the defendant, then the defendant would assure other lands of that value, and, if no lands of that value should descend to the defendant from the said Sir Anthony, then the defendant would secure £4000 to be paid immediately after the defendant's death to the plaintiff or Anne, his then wife, or the heirs of the plaintiff. And he gave a statute of £5000 for the performance of the premises. The said Sir Anthony, in 1641, died, and the manor of Haber descended to the defendant, but charged with great debts. So the plaintiff's bill is to compel the defendant to perform the said articles according to the aforesaid covenants.

The defendant insists that the articles are voluntarily entered into on no consideration, but only to procure a reconciliation between the plaintiff and his father, and that the same was a covenant of one not in possession, not having any estate therein at that time to settle lands in case they should descend unto him, whereof, at the time of the covenant, he had no power whereby he might charge the same, but a bare possibility in case the said Sir Anthony Roper did not alien them.

This court, nevertheless, was of opinion that the consideration was good and sufficient. But, it being matter of great weight and consequence whether this court shall give relief to compel a performance of a covenant of this nature entered when the covenantor had no power over the lands to be settled, for which the defendant insists there is no precedent to be showed, this court ordered precedents to be searched for.

Divers precedents on both sides were produced and read in court, which this court took time to advise of, and then would give their resolution thereon, which having done, they declared and were of opinion that the bill being to have the performance of an agreement made by the defendant himself, which appearing to be a legal and good agreement, this court do find warranted by the precedents and constant practice of this court, where such agreements have been made, upon which the party can only recover damages at law, for this court to decree the thing in specie, wherein this court does not bind the interest of the lands, but enforces the party to perform his own agreement. And [the court] decreed the defendant to perform the said articles and convey accordingly.

British Library MS. Harley 1576, f. 234v

Roper covenanted with the father of Wiseman to settle lands upon him after the death of the uncle of Roper, to whom he was heir apparent, and the uncle died. And Wiseman exhibited a bill against Roper and his father against his [. . .] the articles that were in consideration of a past marriage and against his uncle Roper for performance notwithstanding that, at the time of the covenant, Roper had none of the [?] land but [only] a possibility of descent and even though in the name of the father to have a remedy by way of covenant and even though the consideration was a past marriage (that [was] not in the future), yet it was otherwise [?] in the time of the commissioners [to hold the great seal] decreed as before that [?] Roper perform the articles and convey the land. The other part of the decree [was] that he pay the money.

Upon this decree upon an affidavit of contempt, Roper was attached, and he denied the contempt. And now it was debated whether he should be committed. But he was excused:

First, because the affidavit, as Roper objected, was only for contempt in not conveying the land and not for the money. It was agreed [that] if it was thus, it should be an escape even though the contempt was proved by the examinations because the examinations are not the foundation and the affidavit should be the foundation of the process, which if it fails, all fails;

Second, the affidavit was 'from service of the decree' and that tender of the conveyance etc. and requires Roper to perform the decree. And it was debated whether this was sufficient without a demand for the money. But no opinion on this [was given], but

Third, because the party had served the decree, whether he required performance or payment, yet if he did not have a letter of attorney to receive [it], the party is not bound to pay, thus the affidavit and examination [were] defective, thus [there was] no ground for the contempt. And it was said that he should also [*blank*] acquittance that of this because the party is a date [?] to pay is not [*blank*] any. And it was not insisted that the defendant did not insist upon any defect of authority and it was proper for him [. . . *blank*]. As for the land, he did not tender the counterpart, and the land was to be settled upon the defendant for life [with a] remainder to the plaintiff. But the plaintiff did not greatly insist upon this part of the contempt.

It was agreed that proof of the service of the decree by one witness is sufficient and thus for process. But it was said [that], being collateral points, there should have been two.

[Orders of 16 April and 9 May 1649: Public Record Office C.33/192, ff. 510v, 695; Reg. Lib. 21 Car. I, 1645–46, ff. 268, 464.]

276

Lymbree v. Langham

(Ch. c. 1645)

In a suit in equity, the court of equity will not consider evidence tending to disprove a verdict of a jury.

British Library MS. Harley 1576, f. 229v

Lymbree received £18,000 damages against Langham for breach of a [*blank*] whereby he covenanted that the ship *Royal Merchant* was [. . .] for a voyage to the Indies. Divers suggestions were made to be relieved against the verdict of [the] customs of merchants and among others that the court directed a special verdict and notes were drawn accordingly but [it was] by the jury refused.

First [there was] a demurrer to the bill, and the said [*blank*] pleaded. The demurrer was overruled.

And the cause coming to be heard Michaelmas [term] 21 Car. [1645], the plaintiff's counsel opened the said matter, but on debate and search of [*blank*] ruled that the court would not hear that proof tending to attaint the jury in point of the verdict, but if it had been collateral matter, they might have read it. Two [*blank*] urged on Langham's part, but the court conceived them not to the point. The one was [*blank*][1]

[This case and the proceedings in the House of Lords are discussed in J. S. Hart, *Justice Upon Petition: The House of Lords* (1991), pp. 201–203.]

277

Nicholls v. Chamberlaine

(Ch. 1645 × 1648)

Where a testator appoints his debtor to be his executor, the executor's debt to the decedent's estate is assets if needed to pay legacies.

Nelson 44, 21 E.R. 785

Chamberlaine being indebted to one Ascue in £1000, the said Ascue made his will, by which he devised several legacies to persons therein named. And he made Chamberlaine, his debtor, sole executor.

The plaintiff Nicholls, who was one of the legatees, demands his legacy, which Chamberlaine denied to pay, insisting that he had not assets, for that the debt he owed to Ascue was released by his being made executor, and so [he was] not liable to pay the legacies given by his will.

But it was decreed to be assets. And, upon an appeal to the Lords in Parliament, it was referred to Baron TREVOR, Justice PHESANT, and ROLLE, who certified that it was assets in equity. And so the decree was confirmed.

278

Offley v. Jenney and Baker

(Ch. 1645 × 1648)

A party to litigation cannot be a guardian ad litem for another party in the same lawsuit.

---

[1] The rest of this case was not copied in this MS.

Nelson 44, 21 E.R. 785

The plaintiff Offley and one Jenney, the defendant's son, being an infant of five years old, were executors of Sir John Offley. And the plaintiff exhibited his bill to be relieved for a debt.

To which the defendant demurred because the infant executor was not made a party. And, the bill being amended, the defendant demurred again, for that the infant did not sue by his guardian.

And the father being not thought proper to be a guardian, he being the defendant, the eldest Six Clerk was appointed for that purpose.

279

Kinseman v. Batt

(Ch. 1646)

In this case, the purchaser of a lease who had notice of the rights of others was allowed by the court of equity to acknowledge those rights or to have his bill dismissed.

British Library MS. Harley 1576, f. 232v, pl. 2

The grandmother of the defendants, being possessed of a term of years in certain houses, devises £50 to each of the defendants, being small children, and devises the term to their father, provided that if the father did not become bound to J.S. and Heath and within three months after [her] death deliver the bond into the custody of the said J.S. and Heath, then she devised the term to the infants; the legacies were to be paid at the children's ages or marriages respectively. She died in June. In July following, it was proved that the bond was entered into, but it does not appear that the bond was, within three months, delivered into the custody of Heath. And in February following, Batt, the father, being executor to the grandmother, entered into [a] treaty with the plaintiff to purchase the term [and] affirmed the condition performed, and the plaintiff repaired unto Heath, who acknowledged the bond given and the condition performed and showed the plaintiff the bond and delivered it into his hands to take a copy thereof, which he did and redelivered [it]. This was proved, yet Heath on his oath, being a defendant, did deny it. Batt, the father of the infants, died insolvent.

And now the plaintiff sues for relief to enjoy the term against the infants; the grandmother having only provided for the father's security, which was given within the time and though not delivered within the three months (which also lay in the dark, not being proved the one way or the other), yet it was delivered into [the] custody of Heath very shortly after[wards], so the substance of the condition was performed.

Yet the court would not relieve the plaintiff unless he would secure the legacies, and then he might take his relief as the children might have done, either on the bond or against Heath for breach of the trust in embezzling the bond, as it seems he did. And a week [was] given [to] him to choose whether to secure or be dismissed.

[Orders of 20 and 27 April 1646: Public Record Office C.33/185, ff. 290, 306v.]

280

Lady Sidley's Case

(Ch. 1646)

A defendant cannot make a dilatory plea after receiving a commission to take an answer.

British Library MS. Harley 1576, f. 233, pl. 1

The lady Sidley took a commission to answer but answered not, but at the return of the commission the term following, [she] put in a plea of an outlawry, which was overruled and compared to an imparlance at law after which no dilatory plea was to be admitted, so after [a] commission. And though it was said it was like an essoin which may be cast by a stranger, yet it was not allowed. But divers precedents were shown where after [a] commission to answer, the defendant did not answer but at [the] return pleaded to the matter or demurred for the defendant could not tell what the bill was and the com[mission] be [*blank*] in his absence should not force him to answer a bad bill, but the outlawry is merely dilatory.

281

Cordell v. Limbry

(Ch. 1646)

A court of equity can grant an issue out of chancery in a suit in equity to be relieved against a verdict at common law.

British Library MS. Hargrave 99, f. 202v, pl. 348

The plaintiff brought a bill here to be relieved against a verdict at law for £18,000 in [an action of] covenant upon a charter party. Upon sight of precedents where the court takes notice that it is usual for this court in cases where the suit at law did not originally arise in this court to direct a new trial and upon very great debate in this cause, the court awarded a new trial upon the same issue first tried at law.

[Orders of 27 January, 27 March, and 7 April 1646: Public Record Office C.33/185, ff. 226v, 246, 254.]

282

Pratt v. Byard

(Ch. 1648)

Whether a conveyance of land that was mistakenly described as lying in the wrong county is valid.

British Library MS. Harley 1576, f. 234, pl. 2

Prickett and his wife, by indenture for valuable consideration, sold a house in St. Giles Cripplegate and levied a fine of a messuage in St. Giles Cripplegate, London; *revera* [that] the land lies in St. Giles Cripplegate, Middlesex; the parish extends into London and Middlesex. Former assurances and fines were in St. Giles Cripplegate, London. And Prickett and his wife took back a lease for twenty-one years at a rent, and both paid the rent, and the lease was of a [*blank*] etc. London. The heir of the wife, after the decease of the husband and wife, entered. The court delivered no opinion but referred to precedents but did settle possession in the interim; the married woman had levied a fine, which was an act, if not mistaken, sufficient to bar her.

[Orders of 3 June and 7 and 13 July 1648: Public Record Office C.33/190, ff. 860, 928, 949.]

283

Smith v. Northey

(Ch. 1648)

Witnesses cannot be examined after publication of the evidence unless an affidavit has been made that the earlier depositions have not been seen by the parties.

Lord Nottingham, *Prolegomena*, p. 318

Trinity term 24 Car. I.

Witnesses cannot be examined after publication without leave of the court and oath made that the depositions have not been seen. But, if it be done without leave and a subsequent affidavit be made to that effect, such new depositions have been allowed.

284

Bretton v. Bretton

(Ch. 1649)

The question in this case was whether specific legacies are abated along with pecuniary ones where all of the legacies cannot be paid in full.

British Library MS. Harley 1576, ff. 234, 236

[It was] decreed that where a citizen of London devised divers legacies and, among others, a lease for years and it happened [that] the legacies exceeded the value of the third part which was the legatory part so that all of the legacies could not be performed. Orders settle that each legacy in money should be abated proportionably.

But it was now a question whether any abatement will be out of the legacy in specie. And it was decreed that there should be an abatement having regard to the value of the lease and other legacies in specie as well as the legacies in money by the lords commissioners [to hold the great seal].

By direction of the court, the mayor and aldermen of London certified the custom of London in the following point, where a legacy in specie is given and [also] other legacies in money and the legatory part is not sufficient to satisfy both, there shall be no abatement of the legacy in specie in proportion unless the legatees be children unadvanced within the government of the court of orphans, but if so, then there shall be such [an] abatement. This is the effect of the certificate.

[Orders of 20 April and 1 May 1649 and 1, 3, and 4 May 1650: Public Record Office C.33/191, ff. 563v, 573, C.33/193, ff. 570v, 578, 737.]

285

Hale v. The Drapers' Company

(Ch. 1649)

A decree for land will be upheld even though the defendant conveyed the land to a good faith purchaser for value after the decree was made but before its enrollment.

British Library MS. Harley 1576, f. 234, pl. 6

[It was the] opinion of the commissioners [to hold the great seal] themselves [?] where a decree was made for Hale against Mathews for land and afterwards Mathews alienated to Mead [and] Mead to Terry for valuable consideration, the decree not being sent over to the rolls, and Terry devised it to the Company of Drapers, who exhibited an original bill to avoid the decree alleging defect of equity in the first bill and lack of proof to ground the first decree and that they claimed under purchasers and the enrollment not made of the decree (it happened [that] it was enrolled but remained in the office of the six clerks and [that] it was not removed to the rolls) in which it was [*blank*] that the purchaser could not have taken notice of it, and upon such reasons it was decreed by the Lord Coventry with the assistance of the judges, that the first decree should not be put in execution.

And *Hale* [*blank*] that this last decree was made [. . .] this bill to reverse this last decree, it will be [. . .] if such proceedings will be, and a decree should not be avoided except by a bill of review in which case the party should perform or give security [*blank*] the case is before he can have a bill of review, which advantages will be lost if the alienee can avoid the decree by such original suit. And on the other hand, it was objected that otherwise great mischief would ensue [if] this man can by connivance suffer a decree and then alienate for money and deceive the purchaser, who will be without [any] remedy if he can avoid it by such means.

The court thought [*blank*] for the plaintiff to avoid the decree, but there was a proposition to the parties for a reference for accommodation, and [to] that they consented at this time.

Afterwards, no accord being made upon the reference, the commissioners unanimously reversed the last decree upon the deed by the lord Coventry.

[Orders of 16 and 28 April and 8 May 1649: Public Record Office C.33/191, ff. 498, 546, 598.]

286

Morton v. Kinman and Poplewell

(Ch. 1649)

Where a debtor dies leaving no personal estate, his creditor can be given possession of his real estate until he has been paid his debt out of the profits of the land.

Nelson 45, 21 E.R. 785

Morton, the plaintiff's father, died intestate, leaving a very good personal estate. The widow being about to marry one Kinman, they came to an agreement by articles that he should take out administration to the goods and chattels of the said intestate Morton and should enter into a statute to pay the plaintiff, who was the son of Morton, so much yearly until he should come of age. And, accordingly, he did enter into a statute, and did administer, and, with the said personal estate, he purchased lands in fee. And, many years afterwards, he died, leaving the defendant Kinman, an infant, his son and heir. But he died without any personal estate and much indebted to the plaintiff, having neglected to pay the yearly payment according to the agreement aforesaid.

And for that the real estate could not be extended during the minority of the defendant, the court decreed against him and Poplewell and the guardian that the plaintiff should hold it until he was satisfied of his debt and arrears.

287

Hunt v. Carew

(Ch. 1649)

Where a purchaser of land is deceived as to the estate which he purchased, the court will order the tortfeasor and the seller to confirm to the purchaser the estate that he bought.

Nelson 46, 21 E.R. 786

Lords Commissioners.

The father being seised of an estate for life, remainder in tail to his son. And the plaintiff, thinking the father had the inheritance, applied himself to the son for his assistance in procuring a lease from the father, determinable upon lives, offering a £400 fine, and a small yearly rent. Whereupon, the son, informing the plaintiff that his father had a power to make such lease, procured the same of him, and the son received £300 of the money. Afterwards, the plaintiff being informed that the father had only an estate for life, desired the son to confirm the lease, which he refused.

And, thereupon, a bill was exhibited against the father and the son to compel him.

The father by his answer sets forth that his son wrote to him that he had a very urgent occasion for money to pay his Parliament Composition and earnestly desired him to consent to the making the lease. And, thereupon, he granted the same, which was brought to him engrossed before he had seen the draught, and, thereupon, he sealed the same, believing that he had the power so to do without his son. But he says that they were both circumvented in the value, for that it was worth above £200 more than was given by the plaintiff and that he had ordered his son £300 of the money.

The son, by his answer, confessed that the plaintiff came to him about the lease, which he was willing to procure of his father, because he wanted money to pay his composition, but that he treated in behalf of his father, for the plaintiff would not give the sum which he demanded. Therefore, as to that, he left him wholly to his father and that he always told him he would not join in the lease. And he denied that he ever declared that his father had the power alone to grant the lease or that it was made by his consent or that he ever saw it or a counterpart, neither did he know upon what consideration or for what term it was granted. But he confessed he sent to his father, and acquainted him that less was offered than what the lease was really worth, but he desired him to use some means to procure money for his composition. And he confessed that he had received £300 from him, not as part of the purchase money for the lease, but only as so much directed to be paid to him from his father and that the bargain was worth £200 more than was given. And the other defendant said that he was offered £150 more.

But the court ordered that, since the plaintiff was not acquainted that the father had exceeded his power and he, relying on the affirmation of the son, who had most of the money, that the lease would be good without his joining, by which he was deceived. Therefore, both should join at their own costs to make an assurance and confirm the lease to the plaintiff during the estate thereby granted.

288

Merrick v. Harvey

(Ch. 1649)

Equity will relieve against a mistake such as an erroneous dating that invalidates an instrument at common law.

British Library MS. Harley 1576, f. 235, pl. 1

Sir Job Harvey was employed by Sir Peter Wich, husband of the plaintiff, ambassador to Turkey. At his return, they made an account, and £2700 was due to Wich. Thereupon part was stricken off for diet etc. for [his] wife and child. And they agreed that the residue should be paid at the Customs [House]. Sir John Nuls and others, with whom Harvey was partner, (and accordingly £2000 was paid) and Harvey were bound to Wich for the £2000. And at the same time, it was agreed that mutual releases should be given, but it happened that the releases bore the date of 4 November and the bond 2 November, so that the bond was discharged in law. But for divers years, interest was paid after the release. No circumvention [. . .][1] was that he should pay a fifth part, because five were bound and Dawes and Crisp, two of the obligors,[2] were not solvent at this time.

[And it was ordered] by the decree [that] the releasee take no advantage of the mistake[3] [and] principal and interest [was to be paid].

Nelson 48, 21 E.R. 786

Lords Commissioners.

The plaintiff married a widow. And there being several accounts depending between her former husband and the defendant, who was much indebted to him, the account was stated. And, on the 2d of November 1639, the defendant gave a bond with sureties for the payment of the money due on the balance.

---

[1] Nul Circumvencon in on *MS*.
[2] obligees *MS*.
[3] honalty *MS*.

Two days afterwards, some things being forgotten, a farther account was adjusted between them, and, then, general releases were given to each other, which was not intended to release the bond.

And it appearing so to the court by several circumstances, it was decreed that the said release should be set aside and no advantage taken of it as to the bond.

[Orders of 14 and 18 April 1649: Public Record Office C.33/192, ff. 497v, 516. Note also British Library MS. Hargrave 174, f. 15v.]

289

Dorwell v. Dorwell

(Ch. 1649)

A bequest of money the legatee 'marrying with the consent of J.S.' is payable upon the death of the testator even though the legatee is unmarried at that time.

British Library MS. Harley 1576, f. 235, pl. 2

A man[1] devised £80 apiece to the plaintiffs in these words 'I give to Jane etc. £80 apiece, they marrying with the advice of J.S.' The plaintiffs exhibited their bill by their guardian, being young and unmarried, to have the money presently paid and laid out for their benefit in [the] present.

And it was proved by a witness that the testatrix, when she made her will by the [. . .] to this purpose but before and after the making of the will[2] said that she wished to have it put out for [the] children's benefit. It was denied by the executor of the defendant, who alleged that the money is not payable until the marriage.

The court decreed the money in the present with damages [of] four *per centum* for the time past.

[Orders of 18, 23, and 28 April 1649: Public Record Office C.33/191, ff. 510v, 519v, 667.]

290

Mouse v. Mouse

(Ch. 1649)

A court of equity will not presume without proof that a joint purchase at common law was a sole purchase in equity.

---

[1] Sic in MS.
[2] mes devant & puis le def* dl volunt *MS.*

British Library MS. Harley 1576, f. 235, pl. 3

Upon a contempt upon a decree, the case was decreed [as follows]. The father purchased lands in the name of him[self] and his son and their heirs and paid all the money and had sole possession. The said son, [a] few days before his own death, made a conveyance whereby the joint [tenancy] was severed. And [he] died leaving the plaintiff, an infant, his son and heir. And the last conveyance was in trust for him. The grandfather made his will. The grandchild had a decree for the mesne profits and damages. The point was [that] the court would not presume a trust in the case without proof and took not the possession and payment of the money for sufficient proof for to prove the grandfather [to be the] sole purchaser in equity, being a joint purchaser in [common] law. The decree was against the executor of the father.

Afterwards in the prosecution of the contempt upon the decree, which was that the executor defendant should pay if he had assets, and upon several debates, it appeared that the father was possessed of a term and he devised the term to one of the defendants, being executor and not cognizant but that the father was free of any charge to the grandchild and knowing nothing of the severing of the jointure [as] *supra* consented to the bequest of the term.[1] And [at] first it was debated whether the legatee should be charged and the defendant [should] discharge the legatee.

But afterwards in April 1650, [it was] adjudged that the executor should pay it. He was not held to assent to the legacy without security [...][2] this case whether the father and son purchased jointly as the father paid all of the money and took the profits, it will be understood *prima facie* joint without trusts for the father, so that he could not dispose of it. [...] the father answer [?] for [...] profits to the heir [...] son after [...] the son, the son having severed the jointure [...] the heir of the son being an infant.

[Orders of 20 April and 1 and 22 May 1649: Public Record Office C.33/192, ff. 511, 558, 670.]

291

Matthews v. Thomas

(Ch. 1649)

The executor of a creditor can release the debt, even though the debt was devised to a third party.

---

[1] Sic in MS.

[2] naper *MS*.

Nelson 56, 21 E.R. 788

Lords Commissioners.

A debt was owing to the testator, who, by a will, made the defendants his executors, and devised the debt to the plaintiff. The said executors proved the will, and released the debt.

And, thereupon, the plaintiff exhibited his bill against the executors and against the debtor to be relieved against their release, charging them with practice etc.

The defendants pleaded this release.

And, upon arguing it, the plea was allowed, and the bill was dismissed.

292

Underwood v. Swain

(Ch. 1649)

A court of equity can grant relief against a forfeiture of land.

Chancery Reports 161, 21 E.R. 537

The case is that Philip Swain, being seised in fee of the lands in question, by his will, devised the same to John Swain of Langston, his kinsman, and his heirs, in consideration that he should pay all his debts and legacies, by which will, the said Philip appointed his legacies to be paid within two months after the death of Sibil, his wife, who had an estate in the premises for her life and lived about twelve years after the death of the said Philip. And, in the meantime, she married the plaintiff Underwood, who having an estate in the right of his said wife for her life, purchased the reversion thereof after the death of the said John Swain of Langston, of John Swain, the son and heir of the said John Swain of Langston, the devisee of the said Philip Swain. And, afterwards, the said plaintiff Underwood paid the debts of the said Philip and all the legacies, except two £5s to two of the legatees. And for the non-payment whereof, the defendant John Swain entered on the premises as heir at law, the condition being broken. But, before the said entry, the plaintiff Underwood sold the premises to Toby Pain. And the said Toby Pain devised the premises to the now plaintiffs, Thomas and John Pain, and he died, pending this suit, which the now plaintiff revived.

This case was reduced to this short question, *viz.* whether a court of equity can control the law or give relief against an entry made by the heir for the breach of a condition.

This court, upon view of precedents in cases of like nature, was clear of opinion to give relief to the plaintiffs, notwithstanding the said forfeiture, and decreed the plaintiffs and their heirs to enjoy the premises against the defendants and their heirs.

[Reg. Lib. 1649, f. 177.]

293

King v. Chambers

(Ch. 1650)

A civil contempt is discharged by a release of the claim.

If a release of a claim is defective or inequitable, it should not be challenged by contempt proceedings but by an independent suit.

British Library MS. Harley 1576, f. 235v, pl. 1

King prosecuted Chambers, being an attorney, for breach of an injunction and for [*blank*] law until he paid the money and made a release and upon this [*blank*] was 10s. And the contempt upon the examination and proof on the part of King [was] referred. But [it was] discharged upon the argument because the release in this case discharged the contempt, and it is not the same as a contempt in which the court alone is concerned, as words or acts done against the dignity of the court. And though it was objected that here the release was gained by the contempt, there [?] will not be here [*blank*] examination [?] and proofs but upon a new bill. It is not reason[able] that the interest that depends upon it should be here in such a manner.

[Orders of 6 and 31 May 1650: Public Record Office C.33/193, ff. 590v, 703v.]

294

Clench v. Burman

(Ch. 1650)

The question in this case was whether the marriage contract in issue was enforceable.

British Library MS. Harley 1576, f. 235v, pl. 2

Upon the hearing of the cause, the case was saved by the Register[1] by the order and direction [of the court] for precedents [to be found]. Afterwards at the day when the precedents were to be debated in the court before Keble and Lisle, commissioners [to hold the great seal], the time [. . .][2] for hearing. And the plaintiff complained of divers [*blank*] of the case are [?] material in point of right but because it was not complained of before, the court would not allow nor suffer [them] to vary or not amend the case. The course [?] was to have a petition for a new hearing this is otherwise [. . .] as but amend[ment].

Other matter had upon the hearing [. . .] agreement was in writing not [?] sealed that the daughter of Burman marry the son of Clench, and Clench assured

---

[1] *I.e.* the Registrar of the court.
[2] in serve *MS*.

lands upon the son and Burman would pay money to Clench, the father. Burman declared that the marriage should not take place until the autumn past because his daughter was ill; however, afterwards upon the consent of the parents, the son and daughter married (but in the point of the consent of Burman, the fact was controverted). Afterwards the daughter [. . .] £100 as much of the portion paid. The son Clench exhibited a bill against his father for assurance of the lands. Clench, the father, exhibited a bill for the residue of the portion against Burman. Burman exhibited a bill for the £100.

The court would not [?] decree the lands until it be discussed whether Clench, the father, should have the residue of the portion because it is not [*blank*] reasonable that he assure without the portion, and the court would not [?] decree the residue of the portion because, notwithstanding that, the marriage proceeded with the consent or approbation of Burman. Therefore they respited the decree as to the lands until it be tried whether, Clench the father should recover the portion and dismissed Clench the father to sue at the common law for the portion.

[Orders of 8, 13, and 15 May 1650: Public Record Office C.33/193, ff. 589, 601, 617.]

295

Clovell v. Adler

(Ch. 1650)

The question in this case was whether the marriage contract in issue was enforceable.

British Library MS. Harley 1576, f. 236, pl. 2

Articles in writing [were made] by the parents for a marriage between the son of the one and [the] daughter of the other, the father of the one to assure lands and [the father] of the other to pay [a] £1000 portion. The children married without consent. And the father to whom the portion was to be paid, on [the] failure of payment at the day [*blank*] years after[wards], sold so much of the lands to be assured as that he had £1100 for the same. And he, being to give maintenance to the young couple, gave none, but they dwelt with him who was to pay the portion [for] divers years. The father, who was to assure to his eldest son, assured the greatest part of his lands voluntarily to his younger children and died.

The married son exhibits a bill against the younger children to have assurance from them and to avoid their assurance and [*blank*] for the ill example that else would be [for] children so to marry and the father possibly disabled to prefer his younger children by such means for want of the portion, and though he raised £1100, that shall not be recompense. He was not bound to assure unless the portion came out of the other father's purse.

[Order of 11 May 1650: Public Record Office C.33/193, f. 617v.]

296

Hungerford v. Austen

(Ch. 1650)

In this case, a contract to convey an interest in copyhold land was specifically enforced by the court of equity.

Nelson 49, 21 E.R. 786

Lords Commissioners.

The defendant was lord of a manor, and the plaintiff was a copyhold tenant thereof. And it was agreed between them that the defendant should grant a licence to the plaintiff to let the said copyhold estate for as long a time and in as large manner as had been formerly granted to his father or mother. And £300 was paid for the same to the defendant. But he denying the agreement and refusing to grant such licence, the plaintiff exhibited his bill to compel him.

And having proved the agreement and the defendant confessing that he granted a licence to the plaintiff's mother to let it for sixty years, the court did decree that he should grant the like licence now.

297

Thin v. Thin

(Ch. 1650)

A court of equity can reform a badly drafted conveyance.

1 Chancery Reports 162, 21 E.R. 538

The bill is to have lands settled according to a marriage agreement and to supply a defect in a conveyance of 15 Car. I [1639–40] made pursuant to the said agreement, the deed being since miscarried and lost, which deed contained a revocation of uses limited in former deeds, in which deed of 15 Car. [1639–40], these words, *viz.* 'shall stand and be seised' are not mentioned, for want whereof the defendant, at a trial at law in [an action of] ejectment, got a verdict.

The plaintiff insisted that, if, by the defect in the said deed, the estate intended to the plaintiff should be avoided, then the said former settlements would be wholly revoked, and the plaintiff left altogether unprovided for, contrary to his father's intentions and the agreement aforesaid.

This court, upon perusal of precedents and advising with the judges (the case, being of weight) are fully satisfied that the said deed was not voluntary or unduly obtained, but pursuant and in order to the marriage agreement, and was made on just and good considerations of marriage, although it be not so expressed in the deed, and of natural affection and settlement of an estate on his posterity, and [there was] no fraud therein.

And this court is of opinion that it cannot stand with equity or justice that the said conveyance made with an intent to advance the plaintiff's marriage should destroy the former legal settlements whereby he stood provided for and leave him totally destitute and no ways provided for through want of those words 'shall stand and be seised' in the said deed, which, if wanting, might be probably omitted by the negligence or slip of the clerk that engrossed it. And, therefore, this court is of opinion that the plaintiff ought to be relieved in equity, and [the court] decreed the plaintiff and the heirs of his body, according to the limitation of the said deed, shall, notwithstanding the omission of the aforesaid words 'shall stand and be seised' in the said deed and notwithstanding any act done by the defendant, enjoy against the defendant, his heirs, etc. as well as if the said words had been perfectly in the said deed and the said defect, not happened therein. And the said defendant, his heirs, etc. to take no advantage of the said omission.

[Reg. Lib. 1650, f. 290.]

298

Lady Ashton v. Ashton

(Ch. 1650)

A court of equity can compel the specific performance of alimony payments.

1 Chancery Report 164, 21 E.R. 538

The plaintiff's suit is to be relieved against the defendant, her husband, for alimony, which, upon several long hearings and all considerations imaginable taken in this cause, being a case of great consequence and between persons of quality, the defendant refusing to comply with the court's mediation, this court decreed the defendant to pay to the plaintiff £300 *per annum* so long as they lived apart.

[Reg. Lib. 1650, f. 534.]

299

Holmixon v. Lemman

(Ch. 1651)

Where a debtor sues to redeem two mortgages, the amount due will be computed together not separately.

A petition to reduce interest payments under the Act of 1651 cannot be made before the publication of the Act.

In a suit to redeem a mortgage, the mesne profits pendente lite are to be paid.

British Library MS. Hargrave 53, f. 47v

In the case between Holmixon against Lemman, there was a decree to relieve the plaintiff against two mortgages, the one of twenty, the other of thirty years standing. And at the hearing, the account was referred to a master, who had made his report, which was confirmed unless good cause were shown to the contrary.

And this day (being the first day of this term) Mr. *Lilliborne Longe*, of counsel with the plaintiff, moved the court (Keble and Lisle lords commissioners only being present) for a re-reference and against the confirmation of the former report. [And he] offered for cause:

First, that there were two mortgages and that the rent of one would pay the interest of the money lent and more but the rent of the other would not pay the interest of the money lent upon it and that the master had cast up the principal lent upon both mortgages together without distinguishing how much was lent upon one, how much upon the other and interest for all in one entire sum, whereas, by the course of the court, he ought to have computed them separately. But this was not allowed by the court, because then the mortgagor will redeem the good bargain and leave the bad one upon the mortgagee.

Second, that the master had cast up damages at £8 *per centum per annum* during all the time of the late troubles and by the late Act of 8 August 1651 for reducing interest of money to £6 *per centum*,[1] their lordships have power to moderate interest during the late troubles. But this was not allowed either, because the decree was made before the publication of the said Act.

Third, that the master had not computed the mesne profits since the hearing of the cause, which it was prayed he might do. And for this cause and upon this point only, a re-reference was granted.

300

Miller v. Garrett

(Ch. 1651)

A petition to reduce interest payments under the Act of 1651 cannot be made before the publication of the Act.

---

[1] C. H. Firth and R. S. Rait, edd., *Acts and Ordinances of the Interregnum* (1911), vol. 2, pp. 548–550.

British Library MS. Hargrave 53, f. 48, pl. 1

Mr. Serjeant *Greene*, of counsel with the plaintiff, moved for a re-reference, for that the master in his report made had cast up damages at £8 *per centum per annum* during all the time of the late troubles contrary to the said Act of 8 August,[1] which re-reference I, being of counsel with the defendant, opposed, for that the cause was heard before publication of the said Act, and cited their lordships' opinion and order in Holmixon and Lemman's Case[2] this very day, which was allowed, and no re-reference [was] granted.

[Order of 23 October 1651: Public Record Office C.33/198, f. 8v.]

301

Gresham v. Gresham

(Ch. 1651)

A deed of settlement can be set aside in part because of fraud while other parts are enforced.

British Library MS. Hargrave 53, f. 48, pl. 2

The plaintiff and defendant were two brothers by one father but by different mothers. The plaintiff, the elder, exhibited his bill against the younger to be relieved against a settlement by deed made by his father to his disinheritance and for the advancement of his younger brother, the defendant, upon a suggestion that the said deed was obtained and made by the contrivance and practice of the defendant's mother, who was stepmother to the plaintiff.

And after several days of hearing, the court upon Monday the 27th or Tuesday the 28th October instant (as I was informed) delivered their opinions for the plaintiff and did pronounce the said deed of settlement between the plaintiff and defendant void, because of the practice beforementioned appearing to them but, as to other settlements therein, of annuities and daughters' portions to be paid, valid. And they did decree part of the lands therein settled upon the defendant unto the plaintiff and that the defendant should pay unto the plaintiff one thousand marks.

[Orders of 3 and 21 November and 16 December 1651: Public Record Office C.33/197, ff. 73v, 115v, 263v.]

---

[1] C. H. Firth and R. S. Rait, edd., *Acts and Ordinances of the Interregnum* (1911), vol. 2, pp. 548–550.

[2] *Holmixon v. Lemman* (Ch. 1651), Case No. 299.

302

Herbert v. Herbert

(Ch. 1651)

A final decree will not be entered upon a bill of discovery even though there has been a verdict upon an issue out of chancery.

British Library MS. Hargrave 53, f. 48, pl. 3

Between Herbert and Herbert, there were cross suits upon two several bills. One bill was to be relieved against a deed with a power of revocation in it upon pretense of undue practice in the obtaining of it, which was not at all proved in the books.[1] The other bill was to be relieved against a will pretended to be made by the same person that made the deed. Both causes came to hearing together, and then a trial at law was directed, which was had at [the] Hereford assizes, and a verdict passed for the will. Afterwards a second trial was prayed, and granted, and that [one was] had at the bar in the [Court of] Upper Bench. And a verdict [was given there] for the will too.

Now this day, being Thursday 30th October instant:

First, a third trial was prayed by *Sir Thomas Widdrington* in behalf of him that exhibited the bill against the said will upon [an] offer that it should be final to him.

But [it was] denied by the court.

Second, it was prayed by Mr. Attorney General *Prideaux* that the court would decree according to the said verdicts, *i.e.* set up the will and damn the deed.

But this was opposed by Mr. *Chute*, because both bills were but bills of discovery and had no equity in them that was proved and it was not the course of that court to make any decree in such [a] case upon never so many trials at law (unless where a thing had been very litigious upon a bill of peace preferred) but to leave them to take the benefits of their verdicts at law.

And, thereupon, both bills were dismissed.

[Orders of 30 October and 28 November 1651: Public Record Office C.33/197, ff. 48v, 298.]

303

Smith v. Brounhill

(Ch. 1651)

A party to a suit in equity cannot disclaim after the cause has been heard.

---

[1] *I.e.* the written depositions of the witnesses.

British Library MS. Hargrave 53, f. 48v

Smith, Almery, and Norton were plaintiffs against Brounhill. The suit was to be relieved against a sale of a bankrupt's land made by the commissioners of bankrupts. [The suit was] by the plaintiffs, who were creditors of the bankrupt, against the defendant, who was the purchaser. And upon an offer made by the defendant to accept of his money again with damages and charges and one Pym's offer to give more, it was decreed that upon payment of a certain sum of money, part of the money which the defendant was to have, the defendant should convey to Pym, which was done accordingly. And it was referred to a master to state the defendant's account. And in the meantime, the plaintiffs were to give security to the defendant to answer him what should remain due to him.

For not giving this security, the plaintiffs Almery and Norton were prosecuted upon a contempt and committed. And it was this day prayed by Mr. Hoskins that they might be discharged, in regard [that] they did disclaim that they knew of [the] preferring [of] the bill or that they were plaintiffs.

But the court said it was now too late to disclaim, the cause having been heard; they should have done that before. If their suggestion be true, they have a remedy at [common] law against Smith, the other plaintiff who has prosecuted the cause. Yet because it did appear that Pym had the land and was made a party now by order, their commitment was suspended. And a subpoena was awarded against Pym to show cause why he should not satisfy the defendant the remainder of the purchase money.

304

Theobalds v. Nightingale

(Ch. 1651)

A person may mortgage copyhold lands and then, by a will, order his executor to redeem them and then devise them over.

British Library MS. Hargrave 53, f. 49, pl. 1

A copyholder in fee surrenders upon condition for security of money [borrowed] and afterward before redemption surrenders the same copyhold to the use of his last will. He makes his last will and by it orders his executor to pay the money and redeem (which he did) and then devises the copyhold to his grandson and three granddaughters and their heirs equally to be divided amongst them. One of the daughters dies after [the] death of the copyholder. The rest of the devisees sue the heir of the copyholder here for the said copyhold.

And [on] the 20th of November 1651 it was decreed to the plaintiffs, for the devisor did what he could to devise it well. Again that by the devise they were tenants in common and one of the granddaughters being dead, her brother was her heir, and so he was to have a moiety [and] the other two sisters a moiety.

[Orders of 23 and 27 October and 20 November 1651: Public Record Office C.33/198, ff. 2, 11, 253.]

305

Denton v. Denton

(Ch. 1651)

Where lands not liable to the debts of the decedent were conveyed for the payment of debts and for the benefit of children, the creditors must share and share alike with the children.

British Library MS. Hargrave 53, f. 49, pl. 2

Lands were conveyed for [the] payment of debts mentioned in a schedule and [for] younger children's portions. The creditors and younger children pray they may be sold according to the trust, which was decreed accordingly. The creditors pray they may be first satisfied, but the court ordered [that] the creditors and children shall have share and share alike, for these lands were not originally liable to the payment of debts and the party having charged them with debts and children's portions, his direction shall be observed.

306

Towse v. Trevilian

(Ch. 1651)

Consideration that is recited in a deed that was executed many years before the bringing of the suit need not be proved further.

British Library MS. Hargrave 53, f. 49v, pl. 1

The question was about the consideration in a mortgage deed dated about eleven years since, which was recited to be money due upon the foot of an account then made up between the plaintiff and defendant. The plaintiff pretending there was not then so much due prayed that the defendant might make it out by proof, which the court thought not fitting, because [it was] so long ago and [was] acknowledged by the plaintiff under her hand and seal in the said deed. Yet upon the plaintiff's proffer to be concluded, if the defendant would swear there was so much due at that time upon account, by [the] consent of [the] parties, the defendant this 26th November 1651 at [the] hearing of the said cause was permitted by the court to take his oath, and [he] did take it accordingly.

[Order of 25 November 1651: Public Record Office C.33/198, f. 249.]

307

Horwood v. Rolle

(Ch. 1651)

In this case, the Court of Chancery, not being able or willing to decree the validity of a long term lease, ordered the parties' counsel to settle the matter out of court.

British Library MS. Hargrave 53, f. 49v, pl. 2

Sir Henry Rolle, being seised of a great estate and having married his son and heir to the daughter and heir of one Dennis (who was likewise seised of a great estate), who had Dennis Rolle between them, settled his estate upon himself for life, the remainder to Dennis Rolle for life, the remainder to the first son of the said Dennis Rolle and the heirs male of his body etc., the remainder to divers kinsmen of his own name and the heirs male of their body etc., with a proviso, that if the said Dennis Rolle should not when he came to be twenty-one years old settle the land of the Dennis's in the same manner, that then he should enjoy none of the Rolle's land. Dennis Rolle, having none but daughters, makes a lease for two thousand years to A. and B. in trust for himself, which was concealed all his life time, and after the lease made settled Dennis's land as Rolle's was. He kept courts in all in his own name. After his death without issue male, the lease was published, and thereupon the plaintiff contracted for a lease of part of Dennis's land with one Pawlett (or Pollard), one of the defendants, who claimed under the lease for two thousand years, paid part of his fine to him and secured the rest. And because the other defendant Rolle, who claimed under the settlement made by Dennis Rolle after the said lease of two thousand years made would not let him enjoy his lease, the plaintiff exhibited his bill against them both either to have his lease confirmed or else to have his money again which he had paid in part of his fine and to be discharged of the residue, which he had secured and was sued for at law.

The cause was heard this day, and the court [was] much urged to relieve the plaintiff. But in regard [that] they could give no relief to the plaintiff but they must either damn or set up the lease for two thousand years, which it was not proper for them to do at the suit of the plaintiff, and because they thought it but reason that the plaintiff desired, they gave no opinion as to the lease for two thousand years but referred it to Mr. Attorney General [Prideaux], who was of counsel for the plaintiff, Mr. Chute, of counsel with Rolle, and Mr. Maynard, of counsel with Pollard, to mediate the business and give the plaintiff relief.

[Order of 25 November 1651: Public Record Office C.33/197 f. 209v.]

308

Hampson v. Lady Sydenham

(Ch. 1651)

When an infant debtor, by his will, orders that his debts be paid and dies under age, his executor cannot disaffirm the debt, but the debt must be paid out of the decedent's estate.

Nelson 55, 21 E.R. 788

Lords Commissioners.

The plaintiff, being guardian to an infant, lent Sir John Sydenham money, who was likewise under age. And Sir John and others entered into a bond for the repayment of the money. And, afterwards, he died under age, the money not being paid, having before his death made his will and the defendant, his lady, executrix. And, by his said will, he appointed that his executrix should, out of his personal estate, pay all his debts and, particularly, those to which he had set his hand. And he left sufficient assets to pay the same.

The executrix proved the will, and possessed herself of the said personal estate. And, refusing to pay the money due on this bond, the plaintiff exhibited his bill to discover assets and to compel the payment of the money.

The defendant, by her answer, confessed assets, but pleaded the nonage of her husband when he entered into the bond. And she insisted that she, for that reason, was not liable to pay the said debt.

But it was decreed that, though her husband was under age, yet he had a power by law to make a will of his personal estate, and, having by his said will appointed that his debts should be paid, therefore, in equity, they ought to be paid pursuant to the will, notwithstanding the minority of the obligor.

309

Orlibar v. Bromsal

(Ch. 1651)

The undevised residuum of a decedent's estate goes to the heir and not to the executor.

1 Chancery Reports 164, 21 E.R. 539

The surplusage of an estate after debts, legacies, and portions paid, was ordered by this court not to go to the executor, but to the heir.

[Reg. Lib. 1651, f. 189.]

310
Hammond v. Shaw
(Ch. 1652)

The question in this case was whether a bill lies to discover the assets of a judgment debtor before a writ of elegit is issued.

British Library MS. Hargrave 53, f. 50, pl. 1

14th January 1651[/52], in [the] Middle Temple Hall. The plaintiff had a judgment at law against the defendant [in an action] in debt and exhibited his bill here against his debtor to discover what lands the defendant had which were liable to his judgment. To this bill, the defendant demurred, because the plaintiff had not sued forth an *elegit* before the bill [was] exhibited and so made his election to have his judgment satisfied out of the defendant's lands. For though the land be charged by the judgment, yet if the plaintiff take the body of his debtor by *capias ad satisfaciendum*, the land is discharged.

But My Lord Whitelock[1] being absent, the court gave no judgment but took time to advise until the court were full.

[Order of 1 May 1652: Public Record Office C.33/197, f. 624.]

311
Clarke v. Southcott
(Ch. 1652)

The question in this case was whether a husband can sue his wife.

British Library MS. Hargrave 53, f. 50, pl. 2

The same day there [14 January 1651/52 in the Middle Temple Hall]. Dame Southcott was the relict and executrix of Popham Southcott, knight, deceased, and [she] intermarried with Clarke, the plaintiff, and afterwards removed herself and all her goods from him to the said Pettis, the other defendant. The bill now was exhibited to discover what debts the said Sir Popham Southcott did owe and what goods the defendants have which ought to pay those debts, to which the plaintiff is now liable by the intermarriage. To this bill, the said lady demurred, because a man cannot sue his own wife, for she is amenable at the pleasure of her husband.

But the court gave no judgment but would be attended with precedents.

And *Chute*, of counsel with the plaintiff put a case wherein this court had ruled that a wife might sue her husband (and not in the case of alimony) which

---

[1] Bulstrode Whitelock, one of the Lords Commissioners of the Great Seal.

was agreed [to] by the Lady Southcott's counsel and by my Lord Keble, who said that a man is not amenable at the pleasure of his wife.

But query in what case this is, for that was not expressed.

312

Fanshawe v. Darnell

(Ch. 1653)

In this case, a lease of a ward's lands was upheld even though tenure by knight's service had been abolished.

British Library MS. Hargrave 53, f. 50v, pl. 1

February 8th, Hilary [term], 1652[/53], in Chancery. A lease of a concealment of [the] lands of a ward *durante minore aetate* of the ward to the use of the lessee [was] adjudged good, notwithstanding the ordinance of Parliament for taking away the court of wards and capite and knights service tenure,[1] though the rent be pardoned by the Act of Oblivion.[2]

[Order of 8 February 1653: Public Record Office C.33/199, f. 586.]

313

Ingram v. Coply

(Ch. 1653)

In this bill of discovery for what estates the tenants had in certain lands, the answers giving only the dates, beginnings, and rents were ruled to be sufficient.

British Library MS. Hargrave 53, f. 50v, pl. 2

[On the] same day [8 February 1652/53], upon exceptions to an answer to a bill against several tenants of a manor to discover what estates they had in their tenancies and to set forth their leases, in their answer, they set forth the date, commencement, and rent reserved by their leases.

And [it was] adjudged a sufficient answer without setting forth the several covenants of the said leases, which was the point excepted to.

[Order of 8 February 1653: Public Record Office C.33/199, ff. 516, 684.]

---

[1] Ordinance of 24 February 1645/46, C. H. Firth and R. S. Rait, edd., *Acts and Ordinances of the Interregnum* (1911), vol. 1, p. 833.

[2] Act of 24 February 1651/52, C. H. Firth and R. S. Rait, edd., *Acts and Ordinances of the Interregnum* (1911), vol. 2, pp. 565–577.

314
Thomas v. Jones
(Ch. 1653)

A court of equity will decree a bill of complaint to be taken as confessed where the defendant is in prison for contempt for refusing to plead.

Nelson 50, 21 E.R. 787

Lords Commissioners.

The defendant being a prisoner in the King's Bench, refused to answer, whereupon, it was prayed that the bill might be taken *pro confesso* if he did not answer by a day.

But the court was of opinion that the bill could not be taken *pro confesso* unless the defendant was in the prison of the court. Whereupon, he was removed by [a writ of] *habeas corpus* into the Fleet [Prison].

And, having a day given him to answer and he still refusing, the bill was taken *pro confesso*, and he was ordered to be kept a close prisoner.

315
Moor v. Lady Somerset
(Ch. 1653 × 1659)

Disputes concerning land in the County Palatine of Chester should not be decided in the Court of Chancery.

Nelson 51, 21 E.R. 787

Lords Commissioners.

The plaintiff having exhibited his bill for matters arising within the County of Chester, the defendant pleaded to the jurisdiction of this court, setting forth that the County of Chester had been time out of mind a county palatine, that the privileges thereof had been established by the laws and statutes of this realm, that there was a chief officer there called the Chamberlain of Chester, who was the judge of the Exchequer Court of Chester, being a court of equity etc., that all pleas of lands and tenements and all contracts, causes, and matters arising within the said county palatine were pleadable and ought to be pleaded and determined in the said county, and not elsewhere, and that, if any such causes were pleaded and adjudged out of the said county, the said judgments were void and of no effect, except in cases of error etc. and that no inhabitant of the said county ought to be compelled by any process to appear and answer to any matter or thing, except as aforesaid. And the defendant averred that he and the plaintiff, at the exhibiting of the bill, were inhabitants of the County of Chester.

And, forasmuch as he prayed by his bill to have relief touching the possession of a moiety of a manor and certain lands therein mentioned, lying in the said county, wherein the plaintiff claimed a title with the defendant as coparceners and that all the matters in the bill concerned the title and possession of the said manor and lands, the plea was allowed, and the plaintiff's bill dismissed.

316

Wynn v. Parr

(Ch. 1654)

An order of reference to arbitrators that was entered while one party was petitioning to have it altered is nevertheless a valid order.

British Library MS. Hargrave 174, f. 72v, pl. 4

A reference [was taken] by consent. And a day after and before the order [was] entered, the defendant petitioned to alter an arbitrator.

But the plaintiff got the order entered and procured an award. And the cause was after[wards] appointed to be heard upon the certificate of the referees, and upon that hearing [it was] appointed to be heard upon the merits.

[Other copies of this report: British Library MS. Hargrave 99, f. 109, pl. 140.]

[Orders of 18 March and 6 April 1654: Public Record Office C.33/202, ff. 740v, 775.]

317

Duchess of Hamilton v. Countess of Dirlton and Lord Cranborne

(Ch. 1654)

In this case, the court enforced the terms of a gift in favor of the donee.

1 Chancery Reports 165, 21 E.R. 539

James, earl of Dirlton, being seised in fee of the manor of Wauborough and Gilford Park, mortgaged the same on the 24th of May 1649 to Finch, Prestwood, and Pratt and their heirs for £2500, redeemable on the re-payment thereof with interest, whereas the said money was never borrowed by the said earl, but the said conveyance was in trust for the said earl and to such to whom he should dispose the premises. But, in the same month of May, the said earl borrowed of the defendant Weston £2500, and, on the 7th of May 1649, he conveyed the manor of Wauborough and Ridglands and other lands unto the defendant Weston and his heirs, redeemable on the re-payment thereof with interest. And for non-payment, the premises became forfeited in the said earl of Dirlton's lifetime, who having such title, trust, and equity of redemption in the said premises, by deed 24 April 1650, granted to the countess of Dirlton the said premises for her life. And, by another deed 27 April 1650, declaring his mind touching the inheritance and trust thereof, he did grant to the plaintiff and his heirs all the manor of Wauborough, Gilford Park, and the premises from and after the death of the plaintiff's mother, the said countess of Dirlton. And, after[wards], the said earl died possessed of the said premises, leaving the plaintiff and the defendant, the Lady Cranborne, his daughters and co-heirs.

And the plaintiff, by virtue of the said grant and the declaration of the said earl, being entitled to the trust of the said premises conveyed to the said Finch, Prestwood, and Pratt after the death of the said countess of Dirlton, her mother, as aforesaid, seeks to have the same conveyed to her by the said trustees and also the said manor of Wauborough and the premises mortgaged to the said Weston, subject to the equity of redemption.

The defendants, the trustees, confess the trust aforesaid. And the defendant the Lady Cranborne insists that the said earl had no power to make the said deed, neither can the same convey the trust and equity of redemption, nor could it be so intended, the intention of the said earl appearing otherwise in a codicil of the earl's will dated the 16th of April 1650. And, if he had not made the conveyances of the premises to the defendant, but been himself legally seised of the premises when he made the said deed to the plaintiff, it would not have been good in law, and, therefore, ought not to be construed in equity to be good to pass the said trust and equity of redemption. And the said earl formerly often declared that his land should equally descend to his two daughters, which was proved by Sir John Scott.

But, on reading the deed 27 April 1650 and the declaration of the said earl at the making thereof that the plaintiff should have all the said premises as aforesaid, for that he sufficiently provided for the said defendant before, this court, being assisted with the judges, was satisfied that it was the clear intention of the said earl that the plaintiff should have all the said premises and that, by the said deed and declaration, the plaintiff is entitled unto the trust and equity of redemption aforesaid. And [the court] decreed the trustees to convey the same accordingly to the plaintiff and her heirs and that the defendant Weston and his heirs, after the mortgage be satisfied, shall convey the reversion after the countess of Dirlton's death to the plaintiff and her heirs. And [the court] decreed that the said duchess and her heirs shall enjoy all the said premises against the defendant, the Lady Cranborne, and the said trustees, paying the proportion of the said mortgage money aforesaid.

[Reg. Lib. 1654, f. 1330.]

318

Keck v. Sayers

(Ch. 1654)

A contract made to frustrate a marriage contract is a fraud upon the parties to the marriage contract, and it is unenforceable.

Lincoln's Inn MS. Hill 125, f. 20v, pl. 1

1 June 1654.

The plaintiff [was] discharged of an underhand promise made to the defendant's father against a marriage agreement between the defendant and the plaintiff's father-in-law. The father-in-law was no party to the suit.

319

Ayliffe v. Duke

(Ch. 1655)

A court of equity will grant relief against a common law judgment in order to prevent a double payment and fraud.

British Library MS. Hargrave 174, f. 21v, pl. 1

Mrs. Ayloffe tore [up] a bond of £800. [There was] a verdict against her in an action on the case for the £800, against which her bill was to be relieved.

Her equity was that the bond was but a collateral security and that, if the bond were in being, the obligee ought not in equity to be admitted to recover thereupon etc. and that, though the jury had done well in the verdict for £800 because the bond was for £800, yet she ought to have the same relief against the verdict in equity as she might have had against the bond if it were in being.

And upon this she was relieved. And in this case, the bill did not complain of or arraign the verdict but admitted the verdict and sought relief upon the original equity.

[Other copies of this report: British Library MS. Hargrave 99, f. 59v, pl. 8, 2 Freeman 152, 22 E.R. 1124.]

[Orders of 26 January, 20 and 28 February, and 2, 3, and 21 May 1655: Public Record Office C.33/203, ff. 501v, 723, 757, 871, 801v, 992.]

320

Amby v. Gower

(Ch. 1655)

Where a testator directs his executors to sell land for the payment of his debts, a court of equity can order the executors and the heirs to join in a sale.

1 Chancery Reports 168, 21 E.R. 540

The bill is, that the plaintiffs' being creditors and executors to the creditors of Robert Walker, to have lands sold according to the will of the said Robert Walker for the satisfaction of their debts, the words of the said will being:

my will and mind is and I do hereby authorize that my executors shall sell my woodlands and woods thereupon growing called Barnes to any person or persons whatsoever and their heirs and assigns forever for the best value with convenient speed as may be and, with the money, to pay all my just and due debts.

The question being whether, the executor of the said Robert Walker having not sold the said lands according to the direction of the said will, the heirs of the said Robert shall be decreed to sell the same.

This court, with the assistance of the judges and the reading of precedents, declared that they were of opinion that the plaintiffs ought to be relieved and that their said lands and woods thereon growing ought to be disposed of and sold and that the heirs of the said Robert join in the sale thereof for the payment of the debts. And [the court] decreed accordingly.

[Reg. Lib. 1655, f. 796.]

321

Smith v. Valence

(Ch. 1655)

Where a mortgagee purchases for value the mortgaged premises, the holder of the equity of redemption must pay off the debt with interest and court costs before he can challenge the mortgagee's title.

1 Chancery Reports 169, 21 E.R. 540

The defendant, being a mortgagee of the premises, afterwards, purchased the same for a valuable consideration. And the plaintiff, having the title of redemption, would before he redeem have the validity of the said mortgage tried at law. But the defendant insists that the plaintiff may pay him his principal, interest, and costs, or otherwise be at liberty to recover the premises.

And the plaintiff desiring he may not redeem until the validity of the said mortgage appear at law, which the defendants opposed, alleging the plaintiff ought then first to declare whether he will redeem or not, it being against the rules of justice for the plaintiff to have the equity of redemption from the defendant after he had endeavored to avoid his title, this court, on reading precedents on the plaintiff's part, was of opinion that, the defendant being a purchaser for a valuable consideration, the plaintiff ought now to declare he will redeem the mortgaged premises before he endeavored to avoid his title and that, if he will redeem, he ought to pay the defendant all his principal money due thereon with damages and costs. And the plaintiff refusing, this court dismissed the plaintiff's bill.

[Reg. Lib. 1655, f. 1489.]

322

Cowley v. Patron

(Ch. 1656)

The question in this case was who has the right to redeem a mortgage made by a debtor who becomes bankrupt.

British Library MS. Lansdowne 1077, f. 61, pl. 17

A. mortgaged his land for years. And then he contracted and agreed with B. to bargain and sell in fee. And part of the money was paid; then A. became bankrupt. And the commissioners sold this land. The vendee of the commissioners exhibited a bill against the mortgagee for years to redeem the mortgage against B., to whom A. had assigned. And it was resolved that B. had the equity to redeem because he had the junior equity. And [in the case] between Poole and Skipwith, it was resolved that the second purchaser should not be bound by notice of the trust or mortgage to the junior.

323

Batt v. Hughes

(Ch. 1656)

Exceptions to a referee's report must be put in in writing.

British Library MS. Hargrave 174, f. 71v, pl. 2

The matters in question were referred to Serjeant Fountaine, who made a report.
    The defendant's counsel allege that the referee had exceeded his authority.
    And the defendant was ordered to set down his exception wherein he had exceeded his authority, to which point only the court would hear counsel on the penalty of costs.

[Other copies of this report: British Library MS. Hargrave 99, f. 108, pl. 131.]

[Orders of 6 and 21 November and 16 December 1656: Public Record Office C.33/207, ff. 72, 190, 331.]

324

Cox v. Brown

(Ch. 1656)

A court of equity can give relief against a forfeiture of a lease.

1 Chancery Reports 170, 21 E.R. 540

The bill is to be relieved against the forfeiture of a lease, in which there is a covenant that, if the lessee should let the premises for any longer than three years except to the wife or children of the said lessee without licence of the lessor or his assigns first had, then the said lease to be void.

The defendants have entered upon the premises on pretence that the executors of the lessor did alien the same to the plaintiff without licence, and have ousted the plaintiff, who purchased the same.

This court on reading precedents, forasmuch as the said executors sold the lease for the payment of debts to which the same was liable and, if she had not been executrix, there had been no forfeiture, this court decreed the plaintiff to be relieved against the said forfeiture.

[Reg. Lib. 1656, f. 558.]

325

Welden v. Rallison

(Ch. 1656)

After a redemption of mortgaged lands, later judgments in favor of the creditor cannot be levied on these lands.

1 Chancery Reports 171, 21 E.R. 541

William Welden, for £600 lent, conveyed and mortgaged lands to Lewis James and his heirs in 18 Jac. [1620–21] on condition of redemption, and he acknowledged a statute of £1000 to the said James for the performance of covenants in the mortgage deed, which mortgage being forfeited, the said Welden, in 1632, exhibited his bill against the said James for redemption. And, in 1639, he obtained a decree, which is signed and enrolled, but, before the performance of the decree, James, who, since the forfeiture, had encumbered the premises. And the said Welden died, and the heirs of Welden had orders for to have the benefit of the decree against the co-heirs of the said James. And, in 1646, the heir of Welden exhibited his bill for a redemption, and had a decree to confirm the first decree, and then died. And the now plaintiff, Welden, his brother and heir, had orders to have the fruit of the said decrees, and Welden appointed the premises to be made to the plaintiff Goldston.

But the defendant Rallison, to undermine the decree, in 1649, bought of the executors of one Alexander two bonds of £200 apiece entered into by the said James in 1629 and also one bond of £100 in 1642 and three bonds entered into by the said James in 1637 for £300, which were assigned to Rallison in 1648. And he bought also a statute of £300 in 1629 and an extent for £300, which extent was not made until 1649, upon all which bonds and statutes, the said Rallison has extended the premises, which the plaintiff insists is all *pendente lite*.

The defendant Rallison insists he is a purchaser for a valuable consideration of the said encumbrances and a stranger, and not a party nor privy to the former suits, and a real creditor for £635, and, after so long a forfeiture, he ought not to be bound by the said decrees.

This court declared that the judgments recovered on the said bonds ought not to attach to the said mortgaged premises, they being after the first decree. And [the court] decreed them and the extents thereon to be set aside. And all leases made by James at rack and improved rent are to be allowed and stand good; otherwise not.

[Reg. Lib. 1656, f. 1088.]

326

Whitehorn v. Edwards

(Ch. 1656)

In this case, the court enforced the trust that was in issue.

1 Chancery Reports 173, 21 E.R. 541

The bill is to compel the defendant to perform a trust. And, to redeem the premises, the defendant denies the trust, and he insists that the premises were conveyed to him absolutely for valuable considerations and that the plaintiff has denied the same to be a trust in several answers.

This court, nevertheless, decreed the defendant to come to an account with the plaintiff touching the premises.

[Reg. Lib. 1656, f. 335.]

327

Shea v. Smith

(Ch. 1657)

In this case, the Court of Chancery ruled in favor of the defendant on the merits but sent the matter to a referee to help the parties settle the matter out of court.

Harvard Law School MS. 145, f. 1

In Michaelmas term 1657, a cause came to hearing in the court of Chancery before the lords commissioners for the custody of the great seal of England wherein Shea was plaintiff against Samuel Smith, defendant. This Shea was a beggar and long had lived upon alms, and the defendant was minister of Sandon in Essex where the beggar had lived and had been very charitable to him and his wife in their need, in recompense whereof the beggar one day, his wife being dead, and he having no child, came to the defendant and desired his secrecy in a matter he should impart to him, which being promised to him, the beggar produced a bag of money containing £100 and offered to give it to the defendant, saying it was not only his own desire but the request of his wife before she died that the defendant should have it. The defendant, much wondering at this passage refused to accept the money but being much pressed, at length told the beggar that if he would contrive some way how to receive the comfort of it during his life and give it to the defendant if he happened to survive him, he would be contented to accept it. So it was agreed between them that the defendant should allow the plaintiff £6 *per annum* for the money during the plaintiff's life and, if the plaintiff died first, the defendant should have the whole, but if the defendant died first, the plaintiff should have £80 back again. This agreement was drawn into writing, and a deed under the hand and seal of the defendant was delivered to the plaintiff. But after some short time, it being known that the beggar had some other considerable sums of money by him, a wife was found out for him that had need of a husband, for soon after their marriage, she brought him a child. And the friends of the wife, understanding that the defendant had £100 in his hands of the beggar's, upon the agreement aforesaid, it was contrived that the writing must be lost and a scandalous bill [was] exhibited against the defendant for the recovery of the money, pretending that he was only trusted with the beggar's money and intended to cozen him of it. This was so greatly to the disparagement of the minister, he refused to make a private composure of the business and suffered the bill to come to hearing.

The Lords Commissioners, upon the proof of the agreement aforesaid, declared the defendant had done nothing dishonorable and that they could not relieve the plaintiff but suspended their judgment and referred the matter by the consent of both parties to my award.

At their request, I [*Edward Turner*] did undertake the trouble of the reference, and made an award to all their contentments, in recompense whereof, the defendant presented me with these anagrams and verses upon them.[1]

[Order of 12 February 1657: Public Record Office C.33/208, f. 572.]

328

Jervis v. Maynard

(Ch. 1657)

When an infant come to full age, he can bring a new action on a case formerly adjudged against him without a charge of fraud against his former next friend.

Lincoln's Inn MS. Hill 125, f. 17, pl. 1

13 December 1657.

An infant, by *prochein ami*, exhibited a bill for a title to a copyhold descended [?], and he charged suppression of the court rolls after publication of witnesses examined as well to the title as to the suppression of the rolls. The cause, upon the hearing of it, was dismissed. The infant came to full age, and sued an action at common law. And, now, he exhibited a bill to examine witnesses in Chancery.

The defendant pleaded the former proceedings. The plaintiff replied that he was an infant at the time of the bill and dismission.

Query if, without a charge of fraud in the *prochein ami*, the court shall examine *de novo*. The plaintiff offers to go to a new trial without further examination, but pretends the defendant will not go to a new trial, that, the witnesses being dead, the plaintiff may lose the benefit of their testimony.

Aske and *Wyndham*, assistants, ordered the defendant consent [?] to go to a new trial or else the former witnesses to be examined to any matter not formerly examined to.

329

Goodwin v. Goodwin

(Ch. 1658)

Equity will not aid a volunteer.

1 Chancery Reports 173, 21 E.R. 541

The question being between two voluntary deeds, the defendant claiming by the first and executed, and the plaintiff claims by the latter.

---

[1] These have not been transcribed.

This court ordered the plaintiff to produce precedents where a former voluntary conveyance has been by this court set aside, as this case is, that a subsequent conveyance, which is also voluntary, may take place.

This court dismissed the plaintiff's bill.

[Reg. Lib. 1658, f. 922.]

330

Middleton v. Bishop

(Ch. 1658)

A consent decree must recite that it was made by the consent of the parties.

Lincoln's Inn MS. Hill 125, f. 18v, pl. 2

September 1658.

Always, in drawing up a decree by consent, the consent ought to be expressed in the decreeing clause etc., *viz.* 'it is decreed by consent of the parties' or else, if it be generally entered, it is to be intended a decree on the right, and not by consent.

331

West Ham Parishioners v. Best

(Ch. 1659)

Interest and court costs can be ordered to be paid by a person who withholds money due to a charity.

Herne & Duke 95

It was found by inquisition:

[First], that Mary Gwilliams, widow, did in her lifetime hold to her and her heirs of the then lady of the manor of West Ham [Essex][1] by copy of court roll according to the custom of that manor a messuage etc. of the yearly value of £5 and that the same were divers years in the lifetime of the said Mary held and enjoyed by Drew Best and that the said Mary, long before her death, did assign, limit, and appoint that 30s. of the rent, issues, and profits of the said tenements and premises should be yearly employed and reserved in and for the relief of the poor people for the time present and from time to time being in West Ham forever and that thirty shillings *per annum* was yearly for divers years together in the lifetime of the said Mary and by her direction and appointment paid to the

---

[1] *Victoria County Histories, Essex*, vol. 6, p. 160.

churchwardens of West Ham for the relief of the poor people there and that the said Mary, to the intent that the said yearly sum of 30s. might be the better secured to be paid to and for the relief of the poor of West Ham aforesaid, 4 August 1633, did surrender the premises to the uses in her will and did declare her will, mind, and desire to be that 30s. of the rent of the premises should yearly and every year forever then after be paid to and for the relief of the poor of West Ham and after[wards] died and that Drew Best, having notice of the said charitable devise, assignment, limitation, and appointment, did for some years enjoy the premises and pay the 30s. *per annum* to the churchwardens.

Second, that, from the death of Mary, Best and his wife enjoyed the premises by virtue, as they pretended, of a surrender made by R. Gwilliams, son and heir of Mary, and had held the same eight years and detained the 30s. from the charitable use and that £12 was [in] arrear.

Whereupon commissioners decree that Rebecca Best should pay the parishioners £12 for the arrears and £10 more for damages for detaining the money and for the costs and charges of the parishioners of West Ham expended in that commission and decree and that R.B., owners, and proprietors of the premises should yearly forever pay the 30s. *per annum* accordingly.

Rebecca Best excepted against this decree. But in [the time of] Charles II, the decree was confirmed by the then Lord Chancellor.

332

Lord Savile v. Standish

(Ch. 1659)

Possible beneficiaries of a trust may sue to protect the corpus of the trust.

Lincoln's Inn MS. Hill 125, f. 20, pl. 3

July 1659.

One exception by way of a plea to a bill of review was that the decree was not performed. The bill prayed the decree to be reversed and the subsequent orders.

The court held the non-payment of money settled by an order subsequent to the decree, but relating thereto, and was for mesne profits was barred [by] the bill of review though the decree was enrolled, not the order or report subsequent.

Second, the Lord Savile, deceased, being seised of the manors of Stapleton, Barwick, and Scoles, conveyed the same in fee in trust for the performance of his will, and, by his will, he devised them to the Lady Anne Leigh and her heirs for the payment of his debts and afterwards to the said Anne for her use and the residue of the value of the premises after her decease to her children then living. Anne obtained a conveyance of all the premises in fee and sold part, and she or the trustee paid off the debts. And, having three children, she conveyed the remainder of the lands, *viz.* the manor of Stapleton to the Lord Savile, now living.

The three children exhibited their bill in the lifetime of Anne to preserve Stapleton to such of them as should be living at the time of Anne's decease.

The Lord Savile claimed by purchase. But, at the hearing, he could not make appear the deed of purchase of any consideration paid. And having divers days given him to show the deed, he failed therein. But he insisted on two points:

First that the devise being to the children that should be living at the death of Anne, the bill was not to be brought during her lifetime, for, until her death, there was not only a contingency of the estate but of the person, and the plaintiffs have nothing while she lives and, possibly, may never have anything.

But, because it was a trust and an attempt by the alienation to break it, the plaintiffs, being the persons to whom or some of whom the trust must come in case any of them survived Anne, the court held them proper plaintiffs to complain of the attempt and to sue for a preservation use of the contingent trust.

Second, the manors or the residue of them was not devised to them who should survive, but the residue of the value thereof. And, therefore, it lay in Anne's election either to leave them the manors undisposed of or the value thereof.

But the court decreed the trust in specie as to the manor of Stapleton, as, if lands be conveyed for the payment of debts, after the debts paid, the heirs may sue to have the residue of the lands, yet the trustee might have sold all.

After this decree, Anne died, and then the now Lord Savile brought his bill of review.

But the Commissioners [To Hold the Great Seal], [WIDDRINGTON], TYRRELL, and FOUNTAINE, affirmed the decree *a fortiori* now, because the persons to whom are known and the contingent happened.

333

Anonymous

(Ch. 1659)

In this case, a gift was enforced.

Lincoln's Inn MS. Hill 125, f. 21v, pl. 1

Trinity [term] 1659.

The father conveyed lands for the payment of debts and, after, to his heirs. And he died. The son and heir conveyed to his sister voluntarily to her and her heirs, and expressed it to the same trusts as it was to him. He died. His heir, after debts paid, demands the lands.

But [it was] adjudged against him, for the benefit of the surplusage was given away though voluntary.

Nota the heir was trusted for others, not for himself [?].

334

Cooper v. Tragonwel

(Ch. 1659)

A bill of discovery lies to support an entail.

1 Chancery Reports 174, 21 E.R. 541

The bill is to have liberty to examine witnesses to support an entail in this court. The defendant pleaded. And this court would see precedents, whether the defendant should answer the plaintiff's bill so far as to enable the plaintiff to examine witnesses to the purpose aforesaid.

This court ordered the plaintiff to reply to the defendant's plea and to examine to whatsoever matter the said defendant has put in issue to his plea.

[Reg. Lib. 1659, ff. 134, 178.]

335

Earl of Carlisle v. Gobe

(Ch. 1660)

Where an heir at law of a mortgagee foreclosed the mortgagor's right of redemption and then a will was found which gave the mortgage money to an executor, the mortgagor can have a bill of interpleader against the heir and the executor.

British Library MS. Hargrave 174, f. 19, pl. 2

The plaintiff mortgaged lands to Andrews in fee for £1000 and covenanted and gave bond to pay the money and forfeited. Andrews dies leaving Gobe's wife his heir at law. Gobe and his wife exhibited a bill against the plaintiff to have the money paid [or] the plaintiff [to] be foreclosed of redemption.

It was decreed on that bill that, if the plaintiff, the earl of Carlisle, did not pay them the money by [a certain] day, that then he should be foreclosed and the land be held absolute against [him].

Afterwards the now plaintiff, discovering that Andrews, the mortgagee, made a will and an executor, which was lately proved, and had thereby given the mortgage money to his executor, did exhibit the now bill against Gobe and his wife and the executor, the time given for the payment of the money by the former decree being first passed, and did thereby set forth the matter *supra* and that the executor was no party to the decree nor was it then known that there was either [a] will or [an] executor. And so to be relieved against that decree and to be directed to pay the money and [to] have the bond [delivered] up was this bill, which was an original bill and not a bill of review.

To this bill, the heir pleaded the decree, and on that plea, it was heard.

Fountaine: It is a case of extraordinary weight, and if the executor have the right by bond, covenant, and will, [the] court cannot take it from him. And if the heir had the land, the plaintiff was liable to the executor for [the] money upon the bond and covenant and so [was liable] to a double payment, which was hard.

And the court was of opinion that in this case a bill of review would not lie, for that the executor was no[t a] party to the first bill, and was also of opinion that in this case the plaintiff could not have [this] land again, for that it was forfeited since the decree, and if the executor had the right to the mortgage money, he might by bill obtain a decree against the heir for the land or, if it were sold, for the price of it. Yet the court could not put the executor to take that course, for that he had a remedy at law upon the bond and covenant, which the court could not hinder him of. [It was] ordered that the heir should answer without prejudice to his plea.

Afterwards at another day, the plaintiff moved to be admitted to a bill of review. [It was] ordered that the heir bring the deed of mortgage into court and that the bond be also brought in and that the heir should sell the land. And the money [was ordered] to be brought in to remain here while the heir and executor interplead for the same.

[Other copies of this report: British Library MS. Hargrave 99, f. 57, pl. 3, 3 Chancery Reports 94, 21 E.R. 739.]

Nelson 52, 21 E.R. 787

Lords Commissioners Widdrington, Tyrrell, and Fountaine.

The plaintiff mortgaged his lands in fee to one Andrews to be void upon payment of £100 and interest on a certain day, and he covenanted to pay the money, and gave a bond for the performance of covenants.

The money was not paid. Andrews, the mortgagee, died. The wife, of Gober, the now defendant, was his heir at law. And she and her husband having formerly exhibited a bill against the now plaintiff to have the money paid at a certain day or the plaintiff to be foreclosed of the equity of redemption, it was thereupon decreed accordingly.

Afterwards, the now plaintiff discovering that Andrews, the mortgagee, had made a will and an executor, which will was proved and the mortgage money given to the executor, he exhibited a bill of review against the now defendants (and before the time given by the former bill for the payment of the money was lapsed) setting forth all this matter and that the executor was not party or privy to the former decree, nor was it then known that there was either a will or an executor. And so he prayed to be relieved against the decree and that the court would direct to whom the money should be paid and that the bond might be delivered up etc.

The defendants plead the former decree.

And, on arguing the plea, the court held it to be an extraordinary case and that, if the executor had the right, both by the covenant in the mortgage and by the bond and will, the court could not take it from him and that, if the heir of the mortgagee should have the mortgaged lands by virtue of the decree, the now plaintiff would be likewise liable to the executor for the money upon the bond and covenant and so to double payment, which would be very hard and that a bill of review would not lie in this case, because that must always be between the same parties to the original bill. Now, the executor was no party to that bill. And, as to the mortgaged lands, the same being forfeited since the decree, the plaintiff could not have them again. And, if the executor had any right to the money, he might obtain a decree against the heir of the mortgagee for the land or for the price of it if it was sold. Yet the court would not put the executor to take that course, because he had a remedy at law upon the bond and covenant, which the court could not hinder him to prosecute.

However, it was ordered that the heir of the mortgagee should answer without prejudice to his plea of the decree as aforesaid and that he should bring the mortgage deed and bond into court and that he should sell the land and bring the money likewise into court, there to remain whilst he and the executor interpleaded for the same.

2 Freeman 148, 22 E.R. 1121

The plaintiff mortgaged lands to Andrews in fee for £1000 and covenanted and gave a bond to pay the money, and forfeited. Andrews dies, leaving Globe his heir at law. And his wife exhibited a bill against the plaintiff to have the money or else the plaintiff to be foreclosed of his redemption.

On which bill it was decreed that, if the plaintiff the earl of Carlisle did not pay the money by a day, then he should be foreclosed. The earl paid not the money at the day. After that, it was discovered that Andrews had made a will, and had given the mortgagor's money to the executor. And, now, the plaintiff exhibited a bill, desiring that he might be admitted to pay the money to the executor, he having the right and no party to the former decree. This was by an original bill, and not a bill of review.

Curia: In this case, a bill of review would not lie, because the executor was no party to the former decree.

To this bill, Globe, the heir, pleaded the decree. It was ordered he should answer without prejudice to his plea.

Per curiam, the plaintiff is forever foreclosed, and the executor shall have a remedy against Globe, who, having the land, shall sell it, and the executor shall have the value of it, the mortgage money being given to the executor. And it was ordered that the heir shall sell accordingly and the money to be brought into court, there to remain until the heir and executor had interpleaded, and the earl to be discharged from payment thereof to the executor.

[Other reports of this case: 2 Eq. Cas. Abr. 173, 22 E.R. 148.]
[Order of 1 March 1660: Public Record Office C.33/213, f. 220v.]

336
Hatred v. Devaux
(Ch. 1660)

The question in this case was whether a court of equity will order a party not to plead the statute of limitations in an action at law where the time limit expired during the pendency of the proceedings in equity.

British Library MS. Hargrave 174, f. 19v

The plaintiff, being left to his action on the case at [common] law, moved that, inasmuch as the bill here was exhibited within the time limited by the Statute of Limitations[1] and that pending the same the time was elapsed, the defendant might be ordered not to plead the Statute at [common] law.

Maynard, for the defendant: The bill is only to examine witnesses to preserve their testimony and not to be relieved against the decree and this court cannot control any act of Parliament and the plaintiff ought to have filed his original [action at law] in time as he might.

Fountaine, [for the plaintiff]: If he had [done] so, the defendants would have brought it on by proviso before he was ready and that it was the practice of this court in like cases to enjoin the defendants from pleading the Statute and cited a case between Chambers and Abdy, which he said was soon after the Statute was made.

WIDDRINGTON: It was a doubt in *Doctor and Student*[2] whether the Chancery could relieve against statute law.

Hoskins, for the plaintiff: It was the Lord Coventry's rule that, if in like cases the defendant would not consent to waive the plea at law, he would retain the cause in this court and decree it here.

[It was] ordered [that] the court be attended with precedents herein. Reston v. Reston, 12 Car. I [1636 × 1637]; Gay v. Symcocks, both in Lord Coventry's time.[3]

[On] 11 December 12 Car. II, 1660, upon producing [those] precedents to Chancellor HYDE, [it was] ordered [for] a case to be stated, and [he said that he] would advise with the judges.

[Other copies of this report: British Library MS. Hargrave 99, f. 57v, pl. 4; 2 Freeman 149, 22 E.R. 1122; 3 Chancery Reports 97, 21 E.R. 740.

---

[1] Stat. 21 Jac. I, c. 16 (*SR*, IV, 1222–1223).
[2] *St. German's Doctor and Student* (T. F. T. Plucknett and J. L. Barton, edd., 1974), 91 Selden Soc. 158–159.
[3] Lord Coventry was Lord Keeper from 1625 to 1640.

Index of Names

[These references are to case numbers, not page numbers.]

Adney, Richard, 230
Alderbury, Salop, 230
Anville, A., 54
Ardingley, Sussex, 144
Arnold, Catherine, 121
Arnold, Elizabeth, 121
Arnold, John, 121
Arundel, Matthew, 181
Askew, James, 16
Atwell, William, 45
Atwood, Lionel, 13
Atye, Arthur, 21
Austen, Robert, 12
Axtell, Timothy, 220
Baldwin, Francis, 193
Baldwin, Richard, 239
Baldwin, Thomas, 239
Bales, John, 248
Banne, Katherine, 34
Barker, James, 80
Barnstable, Devon, 64
Barrett, Edward, 227
Barrington, Thomas, 121
Barrington, Walter, 121
Bastard, William, 120
Beddingfield, Humphrey, 270
Bennet, Simon, 240
Bennet, Thomas, 77
Bery, Humphrey, 229
Bery, Katherine, 229
Bery, Prudence, 229
Bery, Richard, 229
Best, Drew, 331
Best, Rebecca, 331
Bickley, Thomas, 21

Bishop, Alice, 31
Bishop, Thomas, 247
Blackstone, Marmaduke, 3
Blackstone, William, 3
Bland, Peter, 32
Booth, Samuel, 49
Brereton, Randall, 5
Brereton, Richard, 5
Brereton, Thomas, 5
Breton, Anne, 37
Breton, Dennis, 37
Breton, George, 37
Breton, Henry, 37
Breton, Mabel, 37
Brett, Thomas, 192
Brewin, Joan, 140
Bristol, City of, 147
Brooke, Lord, 55
Buller, Richard, 25
Butler, Thomas, 219
Calstock, Cornwall, 84
Cambridge, City of, 22
Canter, Thomas, 230
Carew, Peter, 200
Cary, John, 228
Challoner, Barbara, 144
Challoner, Thomas, 144
Chamberlaine, Rebecca, 49
Chamberlaine, Thomas, 49
Champernon, Elizabeth, 120
Champernon, Henry, 120
Champernon, John, 120
Champernon, Richard, 120
Chancey, Dorcas, 234
Chancey, Toby, 234

Chancey, William, 234
Chipping Sudbury, Glos., 62
Claydon, John, 49
Coffyn, Richard, 229
Coke, Edward, 212
Colby, John, 193
Cole, Anthony, 237
Combemantyn, Devon, 229
Compton, Cecily, 4
Compton, Henry, 4
Conock, Richard, 84
Corbet, Judith, 95
Cornwallis, Katharine, 37
Cornwallis, Thomas, 37
Cornwallis, Viscount, 37
Cotton, Edmond, 219
Cotton, Lettice, 219
Cotton, Richard, 54
Cotton, Robert, 219
Cotton, Roger, 219
Coventry, City of, 225
Curtis, Margery, 178
Cutford, G., 101
Dartford, Kent, 34
Davenport, James, 221
Dean, Richard, 257
Dean, Roger, 257
Debel, Katherine, 27
Dormer, Michael, 143
Dorset, Countess of, 4
Drury, William, 94
Edmonds, Griffith, 250
Egerton, John, 136
Egerton, Randall, 136
Egerton, Rowland, 136
Ellis, Rice, 272
Eltham, Kent, 155
Emery, Edward, 192
Emery, Thomas, 192
Erskine, Thomas, 20
Evans, Matthew, 8
Eyres, Christopher, 13
Eyres, Robert, 13
Eyres, William, 13
Farmer, Cecily, 4
Farmer, John, 4
Farmer, Richard, 4

Farnham, Surrey, 12
Felixtown, Essex, 166
Ferrers, Jane, 43
Ferrers, William, 43
Fitz-Williams, Elizabeth, 200
Ford, Charity, 184
Ford, Lionel, 184
Ford, William, 184
Forster, Robert, 144
Forster, Thomas, 144
Freeman, Alice, 42
Freeman, Richard, 42
Freeman, Robert, 52
Freeman, William, 42
Fulnethy, Robert, 80
Gallion, William, 45
Gibbens, Edward, 76
Gibbens, William, 76
Gilbie, Elizabeth, 77
Gillingham, Kent, 34
Glascock, Anne, 93
Glascock, Ignatius, 93
Glascock, Weston, 93
Glenham, Thomas, 127
Godden, Elizabeth, 205
Godden, Joan, 205
Goring, Lord, 55
Gray, Andrew, 154
Green, Michael, 143
Green, Millesent, 143
Green, William, 143
Grenville, Mary, 101
Grenville, Richard, 101
Gresham, Thomas, 241
Greville, Fulke, 55
Grills, Katherine, 45
Grills, William, 45
Grobham, Richard, 177
Gwilliams, Mary, 331
Hale, Edward, 218
Hall, Thomas, 185
Hallam, Jasper, 52
Hallam, Mary, 52
Hallam, Richard, 52
Harding, Katherine, 135
Hare, Samuel, 16
Harrison, North, 22

Index of Names

Harvey, James, 241
Harvey, Job, 288
Harvey, Sebastian, 241
Hastings, Francis, 8
Havant, Hants., 54
Havers, Robert, 38
Hawes, Alice, 11
Hays, Abraham, 239
Hayward, John, 166
Hayward, Mary, 166
Hemsworth, Yorks., 207
Henshawe, Brian, 51
Herbert, Walter, 32
Heveningham, Mary, 5
Heveningham, Walter, 5
Hicks, Baptist, 30
Hicks, Katherine, 45
Hide, Bernard, 34
Hill, Edward, 237
Hilton, John, 12
Hilton, Robert, 12
Hoe, Alice, 40
Hoe, Elizabeth, 40
Hoe, Richard, 40
Holgate, Robert, 207
Holiday, William, 16
Holmes, Nicholas, 265
Hopgood, Alice, 31
Hopton, Arthur, 270
Hopton, Thomas, 270
Horton, Kent, 103
Howard, Charles, 101
Howard, Henry, 95
Howard, William, 95
Huddlestone, Elizabeth, 76
Huddlestone, William, 76
Hynton, Anthony, 145
Ireland, Joan, 205
Ireland, John, 205
James, Lewis, 325
Jampes, Matthew, 52
Jay, John, 212
Jennings, John, 11
Jerningham, Henry, 83
Kellie, Earl of, 20
Kennedy, John, 153
Kinnaston, Margaret, 230

Kinnaston, Ralph, 230
Knoll, Kent, 103
Lambeth, Margery, 178
Lane, Francis, 229
Lasbrook, Margaret, 91
Lawson, Thomas, 11
Leicester, Earl of, 21
Leigh, Anne, 332
Leigh, Francis, 222
Leigh, Henry, 261
Leigh, Woolly, 222
Levington, James, 125
Levington, John, 125
Linsted, Sussex, 144
Lloyd, Henry, 220
London, City of
  Doctors' Commons, 50
  Durham House, 190, 228
  Fleet Prison, 50
  Gray's Inn Lane, 14
  St. Bartholomew's, 166
Lowndes, Jolliff, 32
Lowndes, Laurence, 32
Lyddal, Judith, 16
Lyddal, Richard, 16
Makerith, John, 42
Mallet, John, 55
Mansel, Anne, 77
Mantell, Jane, 103
Mantell, Matthew, 103
Mantell, William, 103
Marsh, Alice, 161
Marsh, Julius, 161
Martin, Henry, 20
Martin, Roger, 3
Martin, William, 261
Maundy, Joan, 226
Maundy, Thomas, 226
Mildmay, Henry, 227
Mills, Elizabeth, 214
Mills, James, 32
Mills, John, 214
Mills, Roger, 214
Minn, George, 145
Mitchell, John, 1
Montagu, Edward, 80
Moor, Edward, 194

Moor, Lettice, 194
Moore, George, 48
Morley, John, 103
Morpeth, Northumberland, 51
Moulton, Amy, 18
Moulton, Margaret, 18
Moulton, Mary, 18
Moulton, Mellicent, 18
Moulton, Merriel, 18
Moulton, Robert, 18
Moulton, William, 18
Mountford, Richard, 144
Newby, Westmoreland, 191
Newport, Richard, 230
Newton, Adam, 55
Newton, Grace, 181
Newton, William, 181
Noble, Walter, 205
Norton, Bonham, 58
Nuls, John, 288
Offley, John, 278
Owen, Rowland, 250
Pain, John, 292
Pain, Toby, 292
Palmer, Robert, 42
Pavior, Ellen, 230
Payne, Humphrey, 205
Peacock, Richard, 220
Pember, Francis, 231
Pennel, Roger, 95, 135
Pennington, Joseph, 69
Pennington, William, 69
Pennyman, William, 11
Pensterd, Robert, 230
Perrot, Mary, 76
Perrot, Simon, 76
Peters, William, 207
Pett, John, 194
Pett, Thomas, 194
Phillips, Thomas, 159
Pickering, Thomas, 258
Pix, Alice, 217
Pix, Elinor, 217
Pix, Richard, 217
Plunkett, Mary, 5
Pollard, Mary, 185
Powell, Edward, 153

Price, Margery, 178
Pye, Thomas, 51
Pyke, Stephen, 129
Ramsey, John, 203
Read, Richard, 220
Read, William, 241
Reade, Millesent, 143
Redbourne, Herts., 220
Robinson, Henry, 221
Robsart, Arthur, 209
Robsart, Dorothy, 209
Rolle, Dennis, 307
Rolle, Henry, 307
Roper, Anthony, 275
Rowe, Henry, 227
Rowe, Mary, 166
Rowe, Nicholas, 166
Rowlet, Robert, 11
Rowley, Ralph, 11
St. John, William, 215
St. Peters, St. Albans, Herts., 11
Sandon, Essex, 327
Sandys, Freeman, 208
Sandys, George, 208
Savage, Viscount, 37
Savil, Henry, 165
Savil, Mary, 165
Sewster, Edward, 167
Sewster, George, 167
Seymour, Edward, 156, 215
Sherborne, Edward, 144
Sherwood, John, 22
Slegge, Roger, 22
Smith, Margaret, 151
Smith, Owen, 270
Smith, Richard, 115
Smith, Thomas, 270
Smith, William, 94
Southcot, Thomas, 200
Southcot, Thomasin, 200
Southcott, Popham, 311
Sparry, John, 237
Sparry, William, 237
Spiller, Henry, 95, 103
Stadman, Seth, 220
Standon, Herts., 230
Sture, Grace, 181

Index of Names

Sture, Philip, 181
Sture, Richard, 181
Styward, Nicholas, 127
Styward, Simeon, 127
Sutton, Kent, 34
Sutton Colefield, Warw., 187
Swain, John, 292
Swain, Philip, 292
Sydbury, Devon, 81
Sydenham, John, 308
Symonds, George, 143
Tanfield, Robert, 221
Tate, Richard, 103
Thewer, Edward, 220
Thomas, Nicholas, 265
Thomas, Walter, 42
Thorpe, Co. Durham, 3
Thynn, Thomas, 228
Tottenham, Mddx., 166
Townley, Francis, 144
Townsend, John, 135
Townsend, Warren, 228
Treswell, Robert, 145
Trevannant, Salop, 230
Tucker, Charles, 164
Twyford, Hants., 156
Tyler, Margaret, 91
Vanlore, Jane, 43

Vanlore, Peter, 16, 43, 153
Verney, John, 55
Walthamstow, Essex, 47
Ward, Edmond, 188
Ward, William, 188
Warre, Roger, 120
Weldon, William, 325
West Ham, Essex, 331
Whitley, Robert, 220
Whitson, John, 147
Whitson, Rachael, 147
Whittey, Roger, 168
Wich, Peter, 288
Windsor, Thomas, 12
Winter, Bridget, 222
Wiseman, Robert, 204
Wiseman, Thomas, 275
Wiveliscombe, Somerset, 65
Wolgar, William, 54
Woodcock, Richard, 219
Woodford, Essex, 261
Worth, Arthur, 80
Worth, Sussex, 144
Wroughton, Giles, 210
Wroughton, Thomas, 210
Wyard, Elizabeth, 238
Zouch, Edward, 80

Subject Index

[These references are to case numbers, not page numbers.]

Accounts, 208, 326
Agents, 36
Alimony, 91, 234, 298
Annuities, *See* Land
Arbitration
    Amended award, 146, 168
    Awards, 323, 246
    Fraud, 15, 189
    Leases, of, 246
    Lord Keeper, by, 130
    Mortgages, 58
    Order books, 130
    Reference to, 146, 316
    Set aside, 232
    Specific performance, 246, 247
    Ultra vires, 146
    Umpires, 15
Attorneys-at-law, 48
Bankrupts
    Accounts, 303
    Mortgages, 322
    Sale of land, 303
Barrister's Fees, 48
Bequests, *See* Devises
Bishops, 100
Case, Actions of, 145
Chancery, Court of
    See also Charities, Equity
    Clerk of the Haraper, 145
    Injunctions to suits, 108
    Masters, 33
    Petty Bag Office, 128, 190
    Priority of suit, 125
    Privilege of suit, 33, 137, 138
    Warden of Fleet Prison, 175

Charities
    See also Churches, Schools, Universities
    Breaches of trust, 30, 34, 51, 155, 207
    Churchwardens, 11
    Commissioners, 47, 51, 64, 128, 139, 179, 187
    Contribution, 179
    Decrees for, 128, 179
    Devises to, 11, 147, 230
    Donees, 233
    Endowments, 19
    Enforced, 66
    Evidence of, 187
    Gifts to, 176
    Highways, 155
    Hospitals, 207, 266
    Imperfect gift to, 261
    Improper purposes, 65
    Income of, 51
    Incorporation of, 68
    Interest due to, 331
    Interest on money, 156
    Lands, 9, 207
    Litigation expenses, 62
    London Leather Sellers, 52
    Merger of estates, 261
    Ministers, 63
    Misemployed, 34
    Misnomer corrected, 233
    Money due to, 156
    Money of, 47
    Notice of, 67, 68, 220
    Paupers, for, 30, 34, 47, 147, 156, 261
    Preachers, 231
    Purposes of, 51, 65

Rents, 34, 139, 220, 261
Repairs, 155
Review, Bills of, 12
Substitute trustees, 266
Surplus money, 176, 187
Towns, 147
Trusts, 220, 230
Trustee removed, 34
Venue, 14
Vicars of churches, 268
Visitors of, 187
Chattels, *See* Personal Property
Chester, Courts in, 112, 315
Children
    Actions by, 328
    Age, evidence of, 190
    Bonds of, 170
    Copyhold, 328
    Debtors, 308
    Defendants, 110
    Devises to, 158, 305
    Estates of, 49, 199
    Gifts to, 223
    Guardians, 49, 110, 199, 289, 312, 328
    Guardians *ad litem*, 110, 278
    Lands of, 312
    'Lawful age', 184
    Litigation, 49
    Next friend, 328
    Posthumous, 161
Churches
    Advowsons, 8, 21, 24, 81
    Bishops, 100
    Bonds for expenses, 111
    Bonds to resign, 60, 81
    Gifts to, 29
    Glebes, 79
    Leases of, 181, 259
    Modus decimandi, 39, 72
    Preachers, 231
    Prebends, 89
    Profits of, 108
    Rectors, 259
    Repairs, 176
    Sequestrations of, 108
    Simony, 111
    Tithes, 26

    Vicars, 268
    Wardens, 11
    Waste, 89
Cinque Port Court, 245
Civil and Canon Law, 13
Codicils, *See* Devises
Colleges, *See* Charities, Schools, Universities
Companies, *See* Corporations
Contracts
    Annuities, 262
    Arbitrate, to, 247
    Assignable, 272
    Barristers, 48
    Bonds, for, 170
    Breach of, 31
    Collateral, 177
    Consideration, 97, 101, 103, 274, 275, 306
    Copyhold, 296
    Damages, 31
    Death of party, 53, 267
    Dower, 43, 46
    Executors, by, 204
    Fraud, 97, 186, 287, 318
    Freight, 98
    Frustrated, 53, 99
    Infants, by, 308
    Intent of, 178
    Inter-spousal, 134
    Joint purchase, 290
    Land, 53, 83
    Land, attached to, 7
    Land bought, 36
    Lease, to, 272
    Marriage, 31, 295, 297
    Marriage with(out) consent, 222
    Merchants, 274
    Mortgages, 83
    Parsonage resignations, 60
    Payments of price, 267
    Proof of, 182
    Public offices, 149
    Purchaser with(out) notice, 279
    Repairs, for, 99
    Specific performance, 23, 31, 36, 121, 247, 262, 275, 296

Subject Index

Surprise, 97
Tender, 257
Women, by, 27, 53
Contribution, 71, 84, 179, 215, 261
Conveyances
 See also Devises, Marriage Settlements, Mortgages
 Absolute, 177
 Charitable uses, 67, 261
 Chattels, 40
 Clerical mistakes, 269
 Confirmations, 103, 287
 Copyholds, 23, 198, 251, 296
 Covenants attached, 7
 Crown patents, 55
 Defective, 198, 297
 Dower, 88
 Entails, 143
 Entails barred, 248
 Equity of redemption, 192
 Executors, 204
 Executory, 222
 Fines, 102
 Fraud, 32, 228, 252, 301
 Fraudulent, 239
 Gifts, 252, 317, 329, 333
 Gifts revoked, 257
 Grantee with knowledge, 103
 Heirs, to, 7
 Imperfect, 261
 Inconsistency, 178
 Intent of, 178
 Joint tenants, 204
 Laches, 78
 Land, 23
 Manor courts, 90
 Mental capacity, 78
 Minor misdescription, 225
 Mistakes in, 282
 Parol evidence, 152
 Patents of land, 55
 Possibilities, 42
 Powers to, 157
 Purchasers *bona fide*, 285
 Purchasers for value, 23, 257
 Purchasers with(out) notice, 139, 140, 159, 187, 188, 220, 261
 Recoveries, 248
 Reformation, 269, 297
 Remainders, 178, 229
 Rents, 5
 Specific performance, 53
 Title defective, 251
 Trust beneficiaries, 95
 Witnesses to, 250
 Women, by, 53
Corporations
 Charities, 52, 68
 Devises to, 52
Creditors Rights
 See also Mortgages
 Accounts, 208, 288
 Arrearages, 87
 Assignees, 10
 Assignments, 87, 148
 Bankrupts, 148
 Bonds, 41, 70, 75, 81, 93, 136, 163, 164, 170, 172, 181, 197, 212
 Compound interest, 41
 Conditions, 8
 Confessed judgments, 197
 Contribution, 71, 84, 179, 215, 261
 Co-obligees, 127
 Co-sureties, 71, 75, 215, 263
 Debts, 1, 35
 Default of lessee, 183
 Devise as payment, 93, 235
 Discovery, 310
 Elegit, writs of, 310
 Entry for non-payment, 94
 Executions, 175
 Extents, 3, 197
 Fraud, 186, 252
 Frustration of payment, 151
 Gambling debts, 173
 Garnishment, 142
 Gift revoked, 254
 Imprisonment for debt, 50, 264
 Insolvency, 75
 Insolvent decedent, 210
 Insolvent surety, 263
 Interest, 47, 156, 199, 299, 300, 331
 Judgment debts, 142, 310
 Judgment interest, 28

Judgment liens, 3
Laches, 212
Lessor's surety, 183
Levari facias, 175
Marriage brokage bonds, 171
Pardons, 1
Payments, 35, 41, 93
Payments by devise, 235
Payments demanded, 212
Payments late, 8, 58
Payments presumed, 70, 133, 163, 164, 172, 181, 193, 194, 195, 241
Pledges, 77
Public debts, 92
Reduction of interest, 299, 300
Releases, 291, 293
Security, 77
Sequestration, 264
Statutes, 3, 41, 195, 212, 241, 252, 325
Stays, 92
Subrogation, 104, 215, 249
Sureties, 99, 104, 132, 183, 215, 249
Crown
  Awards by, 243
  Confirmations by, 103
  Debts, 92
  Fountain of justice, 243
  Grants, 103
  Pardons, 1
  Patents, 55
Customs, Local, 165
Decedents' Estates
  Accountings, 49
  Administrators, 27, 201
  Advice and guidance, 238
  Assets of, 40, 77, 277
  Bonds, 170
  Co-executors, 47
  Contribution, 84
  Creditors paid, 286
  Debts due to, 242, 277
  Debts released, 291
  Debts to be paid, 132, 270, 308
  Distributions of, 166
  Erroneous executions, 175
  Executors, 49, 84, 115, 160, 175, 204, 230, 238, 242, 277, 320
  Executors charged, 80
  Gifts, 223
  Gifts to charity, 230
  Heirs, 7, 270, 309, 320
  Insolvent, 18, 210
  Local customs, 165
  Payment of legacies, 115
  Pledged land, 77
  Probate of will, 82
  Profits of land, 286
  Residuum, 27, 309
  Sales ordered, 320
  Security for performance, 201
  Successors, 204
  Sureties, 132
  Surplusage, 309
  Will to be observed, 136
  York customs, 165
Devises
  Abated, 217, 284
  Annuities, 37
  Canon law, 13
  Charges paid by, 162
  Charities, to, 11, 47, 52, 147, 207, 230
  Chattels, 154
  Children, to, 305
  Churchwardens, 11
  Codicils, 13
  Conditional, 131
  Copyhold, 131
  Corporations, to, 52
  Construed, 166
  Debts, 291
  Debts paid by, 235
  Debts to be paid, 160, 305, 308, 320
  Dower, in lieu of, 46
  Executory, 219
  Fraud, by, 32
  General, 255
  Infants, by, 308
  Infants, to, 158
  Inofficious, 226
  Insolvent testator, 210
  Intent of, 240
  Land, 18, 35, 52, 147, 188, 265, 305, 320
  Leases, 140, 184

Local customs, 167
London widows, 38
Marriage without consent, 216, 217, 289
Misnomer, 233
Mortgages, 304, 335
Observed, to be, 136
Payments by, 93, 235
Payment of, 115
Pecuniary, 49, 284
Portions, 131, 216
Probate of, 82
Profits, 219
Refunded, 158
Remote devisees, 161
Residuum, 49
Revoked, 13, 80, 265
Specific, 284
Specific performance, 131
Successive, 217
Timber, 240
Void, 232
Wife, to, 221
Women, by, 232
Discovery
  Bills of, 302, 310, 311, 313, 334
  Breach of award, 247
  Leases, of, 10
  Penalties, of, 247
Dower, Actions of, 46, 53, 88
Duchy Chamber Court, 125
Durham
  Courts of, 108
  Lands in, 3
Ejectment, Actions of, 11, 129
Equity
  See also Chancery
  Advice and guidance, 238
  Agents, 36
  Alimony, 91
  Annuities, 37, 135
  Assignments, 101
  Boundaries, 123
  Common law order ignored, 183
  Comprises ordered, 38
  Consideration, 102
  Conveyances, 102
  Court records, 17

Discovery, bill of, 302
Donees, 102, 258, 329
Double recoveries, 319
Dower, 53
Dower lands, 124
Forfeitures, 107, 292, 324
Fraud, 32, 319
Fraudulent deeds, 239
Hardships, 38
Laches, 70, 78, 133, 163, 164, 172,
  181, 193, 194, 195, 200, 212, 237,
  241, 244, 248, 253
Legal remedy lacking, 236
Manorial fines, 74
Manorial rents, 191
Masters, 113
Mistake, 288
Modus decimandi, 39, 72
Parties to suits, 116
Payment presumed, 35, 133, 163, 164,
  172, 181, 193, 194, 195, 237, 241,
  253
Perpetuities, 247
Probate of will, 82
Quiet possession, 129
Reasonable jointures, 221
Relief against common law judgment,
  183, 319
Rents, 5
Subrogation, 104
Sureties, 99
Trustees, 4
Two-witness rule, 85
Volunteers, 102, 258, 329
Waste, 6, 211
Escape, Actions for, 50
Escheators, 190
Evidence
  Charities, of, 187
  Commissioners, 141
  Consideration, of, 306
  Court records, 17
  Credibility of, 202
  Cross-examination, 174
  Dead witness, 174
  De bene esse, 273
  Debtors in prison, 150

Deeds, of, 152
Defendants, by, 101
Depositions, 17, 96, 106, 117, 119, 174, 273, 283
Documents, of, 101
Exceptions to, 202
Legal issues, 113
Lost over time, 256
No proof made, 182
Oath of accountant, 256
Office found, 190
Parol, 152
Prisoners, by, 150
Probate of will, 82
Public records, 68
Publication of, 106, 117, 141, 206, 283
Trust breach, 14
Two-witness rule, 85
Verdict, against, 276
Witnesses, 96, 117, 202, 206
Exchequer, Court of
Accountants, 137
Extent, writs of, 197
Privilege of suit, 137, 138, 152
Receivers, 137
Fraud
Against the court, 20
Arbitration, 15, 189
Contracts, 97, 186, 287, 318
Conveyances, 32, 228, 252, 301
Generally, 32, 239, 252, 287, 301, 318, 319
Land, 21
Marriage settlements, 186, 318
Probate of will, 82
Trusts, 56
Gambling Debts, 173
Gifts, *See* Conveyances, Devises, Trusts
Good behavior certificate, 122
Guardians, 49, 110, 199, 289, 312, 328
Highways, 155
Infants, *See* Children
Jewels, 165
Justices of the Peace, 122
Laches, 70, 78, 133, 163, 164, 172, 181, 193, 194, 195, 200, 212, 237, 241, 244, 248, 253

Lancaster Palatinate Courts, 224
Land
See also Devises, Marriage Settlements, Mortgages, Trusts, Waste
Advowsons, 8, 21, 24
Annuities, 37, 73, 87, 135, 193, 200, 258, 262
Assignments, 42, 87
Boundaries, 123
Borough English, 123
Charities, of, 9, 11, 52, 63, 67, 179, 207, 220
Chester, in, 315
Co-heirs, 94
Conditional, 77
Contingencies, 219
Contracts for, 31, 36, 204
Contribution, 261
Copyhold, 23, 35, 69, 131, 159, 198, 296, 304, 328
Crops on, 35
Discovery of, 10, 313, 334
Distraint, 261
Dower, 43, 46, 53, 88, 124
Durham, in, 3
Enclosures, 79
Entails, 143, 205, 248, 334
Entry on, 94, 136
Equitable owners, 261
Forfeitures, 107, 292, 324
Gifts of, 223
Glebes, 79
Joint tenants, 204, 290
Lancaster, 224
Leases, 9, 10, 21, 54, 76, 94, 120, 140, 155, 183, 205, 214, 229, 246, 279, 324
Liens, 3
Manors, 8, 24, 54, 74, 90, 135, 143, 159, 251, 313, 315, 317, 331
Memorial customs, 251
Manorial taxes, 74
Meadows, 6
Merger of estates, 159, 261
Mills, 99, 153
Occupation of, 219
Palatine counties, 59
Partition of, 94

Subject Index

Pastures, 6, 196, 211
Perpetuities, 247
Pledged, 77
Possession, 114
Possibilities, 42
Profits, 44, 219, 286
Pur autre vie, 77
Purchasers of, 3, 8, 261, 279
Purchase price, 181
Quiet possession, 86, 129, 181
Quiet title, 21
Remainders, 161, 229
Remaindermen, 8
Rent, 5, 10, 25, 94
Rent arrearages, 34
Rent charges, 139, 220, 261
Rent of manors, 191
Rent seck, 34
Rent, seisin of, 34
Repairs, 54
School, of, 9
Sequestration of, 32
Specific performance, 36
Survivorship, 127, 214
Taxes, 74
Timber, 54, 196
Title defective, 251
Trusts, 205
Ward, of, 312
Wife, of, 204
Limitations, Statute of, 153, 208, 227, 247, 336
Local Customs, 167
London, City of
    Charity of, 233
    Customs, 167
    Debts of, 92
    Debts to, 263
    Decedent's estates, 38
    Devise to, 233
    Drapers Company, 285
    Leather Sellers Company, 52
    Orphan's Court, 199
    St. Bartholomew, 233
    St. Giles Cripplegate, 282
    Westminster liberty, 145
    Widows, 38, 43

Lord Privy Seal, 135
Lords House Cases, 12
Manor Courts 90
Marches, Court of, 44
Marriage Brokage Bonds, 171
Marriage Settlements
    After marriage, 4
    Annuities, 73, 200
    Consent afterwards, 4
    Enforced, 16, 57, 227
    Fraud upon, 186, 318
    Fraudulent, 239
    Generally, 307
    Jointures, 4, 25, 57, 101
    Laches, 200, 253
    Land, 166
    Leases, 76
    Payments of, 93
    Portions, 43
    Possibilities, 42
    Re-settlements, 25
    Specifically enforced, 76, 121, 209, 213
    Widows, 73
Mediation, 307
Merchants, 208, 274
Mills, 99, 153
Modus decimandi, 39, 72
Mortgages
    Arbitration, 58
    Bankrupts, 322
    Cancelled, 194
    Condition lacking, 177
    Consideration, 306
    Copyholds, 69, 304
    Creditors, 321
    Crown, 92
    Devised land, 265
    Enforced, 69
    Equity of redemption, 192
    Foreclosures, 45, 335
    Mesne profits, 299
    Payments of, 8
    Payments presumed, 133, 194, 237, 253
    Redemptions, 127, 299, 304, 321, 322, 325
    Survivorship, 127
    Substance of, 83

Office Found, 190
Palatine County Courts, 59
Pardons, 1
Parliament, Cases in, 12
Patents of Invention, 58
Penalties, 247
Personal Property
   See also Creditors' Rights
   Generally, 165
   Gifts of, 223
   Jewels, 40
   Life tenants of, 201
Pleading
   See also Procedure
   Answers, 280
   Demurrers, 105
   Disclaimers, 303
   Limitations, Statute of, 336
   Pardons, 1
   Specificity, 145
Prerogative, See Crown
Printers, 58
Procedure
   See also Arbitration, Evidence, Pleading
   Abatement, pleas in, 280
   Affidavits, 275, 283
   Appearances, 2, 110
   Arrests, 145, 180
   Arrests of judgment, 3, 142
   Audita querela, 3
   Auter action pendant, 137
   Compromises, 38, 55
   Confessed judgments, 197
   Consent decrees, 330
   Contempt, 2, 32, 58, 126, 141, 275, 290, 293, 314
   Court costs, 155, 331
   Day writs, 150
   Decrees, 100, 179, 285
   Default, 2, 101, 314
   Dismissals, 182
   Elegit, writs of, 310
   Enrollments, 285
   Estoppel, 250
   Exceptions, 323
   Extent, writs of, 197
   Fraud against court, 20

Guardians *ad litem*, 110, 278
Habeas Corpus, 50
Imprisonment for debt, 50
Interest, 331
Interlocutory orders, 86
Interpleader, 335
Issue out of chancery, 3, 24, 122, 142, 281
Joinder of parties, 142
Judgment interest, 28
Laches, 244, 248
Limitations, 153
Mittimus, 3
Money paid into court, 118
New trials, 302
Notice to lawyer, 47
Outlawries, 1
Parties, 66, 278, 311
Party not in privity, 227
Preliminary injunctions, 114
Priority of suit, 137
Privilege, Writs of, 33
Privilege from arrest, 180
Pro confesso, 314
Prothonotaries, 55
References, 11, 12, 13, 16, 20, 21, 113, 135, 136, 185, 200, 208, 209, 323, 327
Res judicata, 96, 108, 153, 197
Review, 12, 20, 25, 96, 135, 144, 244, 332
Scire facias, 3, 142, 175, 190
Sequestration, 2, 32, 108
Settlements, 307, 327
Status quo pendente lite, 114
Supersedeas, 175
Venire facias, 3
Venue, 126
Verdicts, 271, 281, 302
Public Offices
   Bishops, 100
   Grants of, 55
   Lord Privy Seal, 135
   Prothonotaries, 55
   Registers of bishop, 149
   Sheriffs, 50
   Successors, 100

Town clerks, 22
Wales, in, 55
Real Property, *See* Land
Schools
   See also Universities
   Endowments, 19
   Eton, 120
   Gifts to, 30
   Masters of, 61
   Morpeth, 51
   Rugby, 14
   Worcester, 9
Scriveners, 32
Settlements out of Court, 327
Sheriffs, Escapes from, 50
Ships, *See* Vessels
Simony, 111
Supplicavit, Writs of, 122
Timber, 54, 89, 155, 196, 240
Torts by Wife, 151
Trusts
   See also Charities, Land, Marriage Settlements
   Advice and guidance, 4
   Ancestors, upon, 203
   Annuities, 135
   Assets of, 95, 116
   Beneficiaries, 84, 95, 116, 332
   Breach of, 14, 30, 34, 51, 155, 207
   Charities, 14, 30, 187, 220, 266
   Chattels, 40
   Corpus, protection of, 332
   Co-Trustees, 144
   Enforced, 55, 66, 326
   Entails, 205
   Fraud, 56
   Fraudulent, 32
   Frustrated, 120, 260
   Interest, 218
   Leases, 120
   Litigation expenses, 62
   Notice of, 187
   Parties to suits, 116
   Portions, 203
   Possibilities, 42
   Profits, 144
   Prudent investments, 218

   Secret, 260
   Set aside, 254
   Specifically enforced, 214
   Substitute, 266
   Successors, 203
   Suspicious, 185
   Testamentary, 49
   Trustees, 4, 84, 144
   Trustees charged, 80
   Vicars of churches, 268
   Violation of custom, 167
   Void, 167
   Voluntary, 254
   Women, 234
Universities and Colleges
   See also Schools
   Cambridge, 169
   Emmanuel, 8
   Fraud against, 21
   Magdalen, 240
   Merton, 21
   Privilege of suit, 169
   St. John's, 85
Uses, *See* Trusts
Vessels
   Freight, 98
   Royal Merchant, 276
Wards, Court of, 200
Waste
   Forfeitures for, 271
   Meadows, 6
   Pastures, 6, 196, 211
   Prebends, 89
   Timber, 54, 89, 155, 196
Water Conduits, 65
Wills, *See* Devises
Witnesses, *See* Evidence
Women
   Administratrices, 27
   Alimony, 91, 234, 298
   Annuities, 87
   Choses in action, 234
   Contracts, 27, 53, 134
   Devises to, 221
   Dower, 43, 53, 88, 124
   Election by, 46
   Land of, 204

London widows, 38, 143
Marriage with(out) consent, 216, 217, 222, 289, 294, 295
Reasonable jointures, 221
Sued by husband, 311
Torts by, 151
Trusts, 234
Wills of, 232
Woods, *See* Timber
York Customs, 165